Get the eBook FREE!

(PDF, ePub, Kindle, and liveBook all included)

We believe that once you buy a book from us, you should be able to read it in any format we have available. To get electronic versions of this book at no additional cost to you, purchase and then register this book at the Manning website.

Go to https://www.manning.com/freebook and follow the instructions to complete your pBook registration.

That's it!
Thanks from Manning!

ASP.NET Core Razor Pages in Action

MIKE BRIND

MANNING
SHELTER ISLAND

For online information and ordering of this and other Manning books, please visit www.manning.com. The publisher offers discounts on this book when ordered in quantity. For more information, please contact

Special Sales Department
Manning Publications Co.
20 Baldwin Road
PO Box 761
Shelter Island, NY 11964
Email: orders@manning.com

Manning Publications Co.
20 Baldwin Road
PO Box 761
Shelter Island, NY 11964

Development editor: Toni Arritola
Technical development editor: Adriana Sabo
Review editor: Tanya Wilke
Production editor: Deirdre Hiam
Copy editor: Christian Berk
Proofreader: Katie Tennant
Technical proofreader: Filip Wojcieszyn
Typesetter: Gordan Salinovic
Cover designer: Marija Tudor

ISBN 9781617299988
Printed in the United States of America

contents

preface

In the beginning, there was Active Server Pages (ASP)—a page-focused web development framework from Microsoft that enabled developers to build interactive web applications that could process form submissions and communicate with databases. The development model was a simple one: each page in a website was represented by a single file, which had a name and path that shared a one-to-one mapping with the URL for the page. Each file consisted of a mixture of HTML and a scripting language that executed on the web server to generate more HTML. However, as the complexity of an individual page grew, so did its content—often resulting in difficult-to-maintain *spaghetti code.* Scripting languages lacked any type checking, which easily led to the introduction of bugs that were only discovered at run time.

Then came ASP.NET Web Forms—another page-focused web development framework. By supporting the strongly typed C# and VB.NET languages, Web Forms offered compile-time code checking, resulting in fewer bugs finding their way to the production server. It also offered a separation between the page's presentation and its behavior with the introduction of the code-behind file, reducing the amount of spaghetti code. On the downside, basic HTTP technologies were abstracted away by the Web Forms development experience, which tried to emulate that of VB6 desktop application developers. The UI was composed of *server controls,* which the developer could drag and drop onto a design surface. These controls were responsible for generating HTML, which wasn't always accessible or standards compliant, and they provided few opportunities for customizing their output.

In an attempt to appeal to Windows developers, Web Forms introduced a large number of concepts to web development totally unique to the framework. While Web Forms is undeniably a hugely powerful framework, its high learning curve makes it a difficult starting point for anyone new to web development.

ASP.NET MVC was introduced in 2008, partly to provide a more natural web development experience, and as a result, it very quickly gained traction among intermediate and experienced ASP.NET web developers as well as developers more accustomed to using competing technologies, such as Ruby on Rails and Java Spring. ASP.NET MVC was also designed to solve several other problems advanced developers have with Web Forms, including a lack of testability, a need for clearer separation of concerns, the ability to extend the framework, and so on. A notable problem MVC did not solve, however, was making learning ASP.NET any easier; if anything, the MVC framework's concept count was higher than that of Web Forms. But the traditional mapping between filenames and URLs was just one casualty. Developers also had to consider the names of controller classes and their methods when building URLs as well as the names of view templates, which had to be placed in a specific location.

Microsoft attempted to solve the high barrier to entry for beginner developers by introducing another page-focused framework: ASP.NET Web Pages. This new framework restored the easy-to-reason-about one-to-one mapping between filenames and URLs. While it undoubtedly offered a simpler learning experience, Web Pages reintroduced the same issues ASP suffered from. A heavy reliance on the `dynamic` type resulted in a loss of strong typing in key parts of the framework, and the development model encouraged mixing application logic and HTML in the same file. It should be no surprise, therefore, that only the MVC framework was retained when ASP.NET was initially rewritten from the ground up for the new cross-platform .NET Core framework.

Razor Pages was introduced as part of ASP.NET Core 2.0, with a set of specific aims. Chief among them was to make working with dynamic HTML and forms with ASP.NET Core easier by reducing the number of files and concepts required to print *Hello World* in a page or build a CRUD form. It was built on top of the existing MVC framework, and it manages to retain all the useful features that make MVC so powerful and flexible. Microsoft recommends starting with Razor Pages for all new web development that involves generating the UI on the server (see https://docs.microsoft.com/en-us/aspnet/core/tutorials/choose-web-ui).

I am all for things that make my life easier, which is why I champion the Razor Pages framework. I hope reading this book will make your life easier too.

acknowledgments

I'd like to thank my wife, Anna, for her patience and understanding (once again), while I wrote this book. I'd also like to thank a number of people at Manning, starting with Brian Sawyer for reaching out in the first place. I'd also like to thank the relay of developmental editors I worked with—in particular Toni Arritola for seeing this project across the line. Thanks also go to technical development editor Tanya Wilke, for checking code as the book was being written, and Filip Wojcieszyn, for acting as technical proofreader and sharing his subject matter expertise to make the final result better than it otherwise would have been. Thank you to all those at Manning: Deirdre Hiam, my project manager; Christian Berk, my copy editor; and Katie Tennant, my proofreader. I would also like to thank all the MEAP customers and reviewers for their invaluable contributions: Charles Lam, Chris Thomas, Foster Haines, Harry Polder, Jiří Činčura, Joe Cuevas, Karl Anderson. Karthikeyarajan Rajendran, Lakshminarayanan AS, Lee Cottrell, Luigi Zambetti, Marc Roulleau, Marek Petak, Markus Wolff, Maytham Fahmi, Michael Holmes, Mitchell Fox, Oliver Korten, Paul Brown, Richard Vaughan, Sadhana Ganapathiraju, Stephen Byrne, Tiklu Ganguly, Timo Salomäki, Tom Gueth, Wes Shaddix, Owain Williams, and Mike Baran.

about this book

ASP.NET Core Razor Pages in Action focuses on one part of the ASP.NET Core framework, Razor Pages, and how you can use it to build dynamic web applications. As you go through the book, you will build an increasingly complex application that features some of the functionality you might find in an online portal that allows users to book short vacations in cities around the world. Each chapter focuses on one of the core areas within Razor Pages, building on what has been learned in the previous chapters.

Who should read this book

This book is intended for anyone who wants to learn how to build basic or complex web applications using Microsoft technologies as simply as possible. The book focuses on the main features of the Razor Pages framework and assumes you already have some knowledge of core web technologies, such as HTML, CSS, JavaScript, and HTTP. None of these are covered in any great detail in this book, although I review one or two aspects of these fundamental technologies where appropriate. I also assume you have a familiarity with the C# language or similar. The examples in this book have been kept as simple as possible, so if you are currently learning C#, you should be able to follow along. The book also touches on the use of relational databases, so knowledge of these is also beneficial.

How this book is organized

The content of this book is spread over 14 chapters. The chapters are designed to be read sequentially, as each one builds on the teachings in the previous chapters:

- Chapter 1 introduces Razor Pages and explains what you can and can't do with the framework. It also discusses the technologies that underpin Razor Pages and where you can obtain the framework.
- Chapter 2 takes a first look at building applications with Razor Pages using prepared project templates. The chapter analyzes the generated files and explains the role of each one. Finally, the chapter provides an in-depth look at the request pipeline and how to use it to control the behavior of your application.
- Chapter 3 explores working with the page files in a Razor Pages application. It begins with an overview of the Razor templating syntax before moving on to look at how to use it to generate HTML.
- Chapter 4 explains how URLs are matched to files on disk via a process called routing. It also looks at some of the ways routing can be customized and when this might be useful.
- Chapter 5 focuses on leveraging model binding to manage form submissions in a strongly typed manner and how to validate form data.
- Chapter 6 looks at the use of tag helpers as an important part of building robust forms.
- Chapter 7 explores the dependency injection feature in Razor Pages, discussing why you need it and how you should use it.
- Chapter 8 introduces the use of Entity Framework Core for managing data in a Razor Pages application.
- Chapter 9 looks at managing authentication (knowing who your user is) within a Razor Pages application, primarily leveraging the ASP.NET Core Identity package for this task.
- Chapter 10 covers authorization within a Razor Pages application—that is, restricting what your user can do.
- Chapter 11 explores how to work with some new features aimed at simplifying some client-side technologies, such as CSS isolation, AJAX, JSON, and minimal APIs.
- Chapter 12 focuses on techniques for troubleshooting your application, including how to use logging to record and identify issues.
- Chapter 13 covers your application's security and how to protect it against a range of the most common external threats.
- Chapter 14 looks at configuring your application to run in different environments. It also covers using caching to improve performance before finally publishing your application.

About the code

This book contains many examples of source code both in numbered listings and in line with normal text. In both cases, source code is formatted in a `fixed-width font like this` to separate it from ordinary text. Sometimes code is also **`in bold`** to highlight code that has changed from previous steps in the chapter, such as when a new feature adds to an existing line of code.

In many cases, the original source code has been reformatted; we've added line breaks and reworked indentation to accommodate the available page space in the book. In some cases, even this was not enough, and listings include line-continuation markers (➥). Code annotations accompany many of the listings, highlighting important concepts.

You can get executable snippets of code from the liveBook (online) version of this book at https://livebook.manning.com/book/razor-pages-in-action/welcome/v-10/. The complete code for the examples in the book is available for download from the Manning website at https://www.manning.com/books/asp-net-core-razor-pages-in-action, and from GitHub at https://github.com/mikebrind/Razor-Pages-In-Action.

liveBook discussion forum

Purchase of *ASP.NET Core Razor Pages in Action* includes free access to liveBook, Manning's online reading platform. Using liveBook's exclusive discussion features, you can attach comments to the book globally or to specific sections or paragraphs. It's a snap to make notes for yourself, ask and answer technical questions, and receive help from the author and other users. To access the forum, go to https://livebook.manning.com/book/razor-pages-in-action/welcome/v-10/discussion. You can also learn more about Manning's forums and the rules of conduct at https://livebook.manning.com/discussion.

Manning's commitment to our readers is to provide a venue where a meaningful dialogue between individual readers and between readers and the author can take place. It is not a commitment to any specific amount of participation on the part of the author, whose contribution to the forum remains voluntary (and unpaid). We suggest you try asking him some challenging questions lest his interest stray! The forum and the archives of previous discussions will be accessible from the publisher's website as long as the book is in print.

about the author

Mike Brind has been developing web applications using Microsoft technologies since 2004, starting with classic ASP, before moving on to the Web Forms framework, and then to MVC and ASP.NET Web Pages. These days Mike works mainly with ASP.NET Core, focusing on Razor Pages. He has blogged extensively about the Razor Pages framework at https://www.mikesdotnetting.com and maintains a tutorial site dedicated to Razor Pages at https://www.learnrazorpages.com. Mike is an 11-time recipient of the Microsoft Most Valuable Professional (MVP) award for his community contributions in sharing his knowledge of ASP.NET.

about the cover illustration

The figure on the cover of *ASP.NET Core Razor Pages in Action* is “Femme de l’Isle de Nootka,” or “Woman of Nootka Island,” taken from a collection by Jacques Grasset de Saint-Sauveur, published in 1797. Each illustration is finely drawn and colored by hand.

In those days, it was easy to identify where people lived and what their trade or station in life was just by their dress. Manning celebrates the inventiveness and initiative of the computer business with book covers based on the rich diversity of regional culture centuries ago, brought back to life by pictures from collections such as this one.

1 Getting started with Razor Pages

This chapter covers
- What Razor Pages is
- Why you should use a web development framework
- What you can do with Razor Pages
- When and why you should choose Razor Pages
- The tools needed to work with Razor Pages

Thank you for picking up this copy of *Razor Pages in Action,* whether physically or virtually. By doing so, you are about to learn what Razor Pages is, what you can do with Razor Pages, and what you need to consider when deciding whether Razor Pages is a good choice for building your next web application. Spoiler alert: if you want to develop page-focused, interactive web applications, it is!

This chapter will explore Razor Pages' technologies and examine the similarities and differences between Razor Pages and other web development frameworks. By the time you have finished this chapter, you should know whether Razor Pages is a good fit for your next application and be looking forward to building your first app with Razor Pages in the following chapter.

I'm going to make some assumptions about you, if I may. I'm going to assume you already know about the core technologies of the web—HTTP, HTML, CSS, and JavaScript—and how they work together. I'm going to assume that you know that Bootstrap is not just a footwear fastening. And I'm presuming you already know C# or a similar object-oriented language or that you are capable of learning C# while also learning about Razor Pages. Finally, I'm proceeding on the premise that you understand the basics of relational databases. I mention all of this because I don't cover any of these topics in detail within this book, although I might treat you to the odd refresher where I think it helps to provide context.

Still with me? Good! Let's go!

1.1 What is Razor Pages?

Razor Pages is a server-side, cross-platform, open source web development framework from Microsoft that enables you to use your existing knowledge of HTML, CSS, and JavaScript together with the C# language to build modern, page-focused web applications. Now, that's a bit of a mouthful, so let's break it down a bit.

1.1.1 Web development frameworks

First, let's look at what a web development framework is and why you might need one. Figure 1.1 shows the home page of this book's publisher's website: Manning.com.

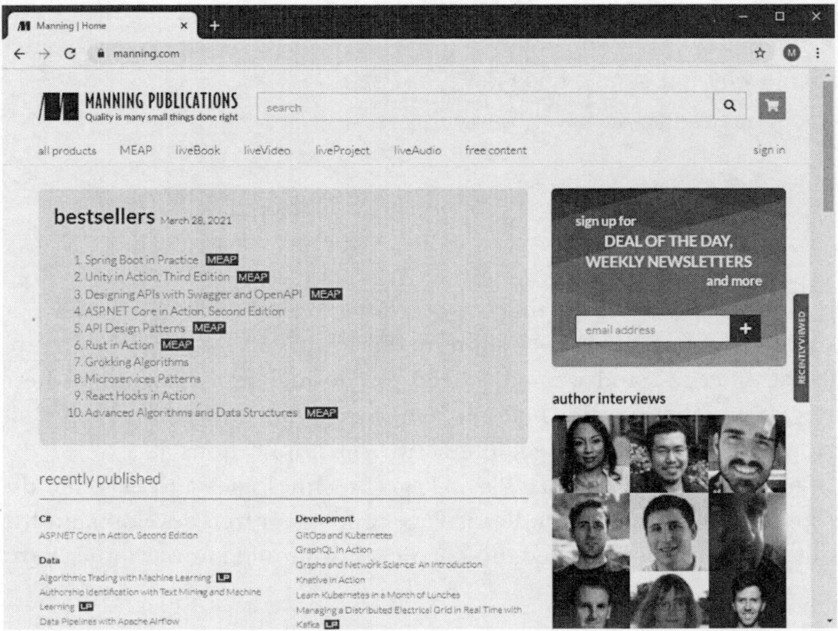

Figure 1.1 Screenshot of Manning.com

Take a look at just some of the things you can do on this site:

- You can search the site content.
- You can buy things from this site.
- You can create an account and log in.
- You can sign up for newsletters.
- You can see the latest book releases.
- You can have a look at the items you viewed on previous visits.
- You can read interviews with authors.

That's a lot of complex functionality, and with so many books and authors at Manning, there must be a huge number of pages to maintain. Think of the work required to redesign the site to give it a new look, applying changes to all those countless pages!

A web development framework makes light of these complexities by providing prebuilt solutions to common tasks, so you can get on with building your application. Take the task of displaying the details of all those books, for example. Rather than having to create a page per book, a framework—like Razor Pages—will provide you with the capability of creating a template for displaying any book. It also includes placeholders, so the details of a specific book, such as its title, author, ISBN, and number of pages, can be fetched from a central store (e.g., a database) and plugged in on demand (much like how a mail merge document works). Now you only have one page to manage for all books instead of one page per book.

How about the task of managing user information? You will need some way to store this information and match it against login details provided by the user. You also need to provide a mechanism for identifying that the current user has already successfully logged in, so they don't have to authenticate themselves again for every subsequent page they want to view. And you need to do all of this securely, employing acceptable levels of cryptography. Again, a good framework will provide these features for you. All you have to do is learn how the features work and plug them into your application, leaving the mysteries of implementing low-level specialist tasks like encryption and hashing to experts who know what they are doing.

These examples touch on a couple of features provided by web development frameworks. (figure 1.2). But the list doesn't stop there. Think of any common repetitive task that developing a web application might require of you: processing an incoming request for data, mapping URLs that don't include a file extension, communicating with databases, processing and validating form submissions, working with files, sending emails. All of these tasks are made easier when using a framework that incorporates these features. And by the time you have finished this book, you will be able to use Razor Pages to accomplish all of these tasks easily.

As well as providing solutions to functional requirements, frameworks typically offer a standard way to build and deploy applications. They might encourage you to adopt proven software design patterns when building your application to make the result easier to test and maintain.

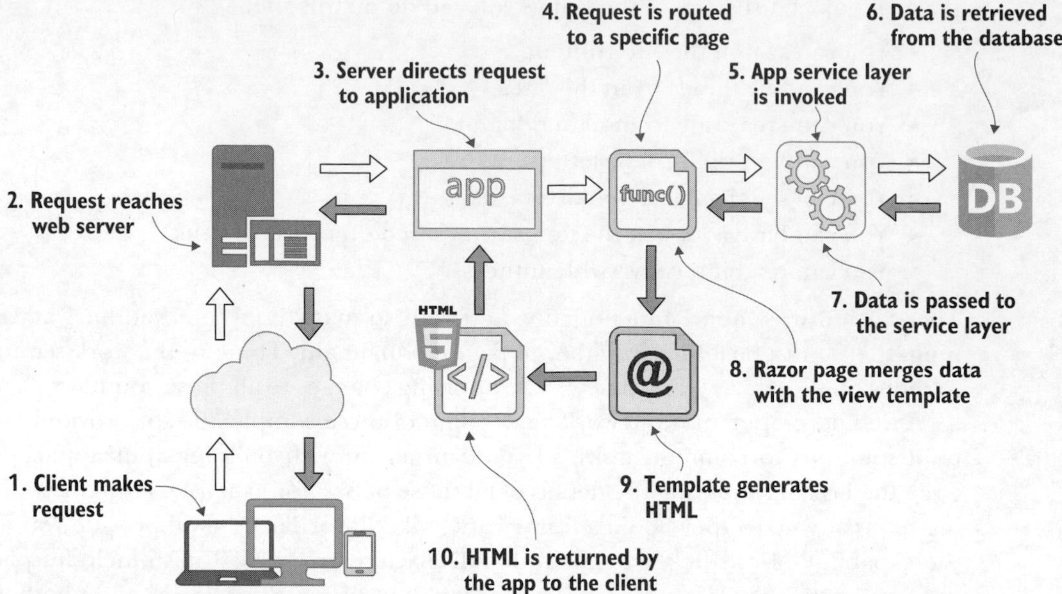

Figure 1.2 Workflow diagram showing how the process involving the use of templates works in Razor Pages. This workflow starts in the bottom left with a client requesting /book/razor-pages-in-action or similar. The white arrows show the direction of travel through the internet to the web server, which locates the correct application and then passes processing to the Razor Page (with `func()` in it). Control is then passed to the application service layer, which is responsible for retrieving the details from the database. The data is sent to the service layer (see the gray arrows) and then on to the Razor page, where it is merged with the view template (the one with the @ sign) to create HTML. The generated HTML is passed via the app out to the web server to be returned to the client.

In essence, web development frameworks can speed up the process of developing web applications by providing prebuilt and tested solutions to common repetitive tasks. They can help you produce consistent results by encouraging you to work to a set of standards.

1.1.2 Server-side frameworks

Next, we'll take a look at what it means when we say Razor Pages is a server-side framework. When developing dynamic web applications, you must decide where your HTML is generated. You can choose to generate HTML on the user's device (the client) or on the web server.

Applications that generate HTML on the client, or single-page applications (SPAs), are restricted in terms of the technologies that can be used. Up until recently, you could only really use JavaScript to create these kinds of applications. This has changed since the introduction of Blazor, which enables you to use C# as your application programming language. To learn more about this, see Chris Sainty's *Blazor in Action* (Manning, 2021). Since most of the application processing takes place on the user's device, you have to be mindful of its resources, which you have no control over. You also have to take into account differences between browser capabilities when writing your code. On the other hand, client-side applications can result in rich user experiences and even closely emulate desktop applications. Great examples of applications rendered mainly on the client include Facebook and Google Docs.

Applications that render their HTML on the server can take advantage of any framework or language supported by the server and have as much processing power available to them as the server can provide. That means the HTML generation is controllable and predictable. In addition, all application logic is deployed to the server itself, meaning it is as secure as the server. And since the output of the processing should be standards-compliant HTML, you shouldn't need to worry so much about browser quirks.

1.1.3 Cross-platform functionality

Razor Pages applications can be created and deployed on a wide variety of platforms. Windows, Linux, macOS, and Docker are all supported. If you want to create your application on your super-thin and expensive MacBook Air or Surface Pro, you can. Or if you are more at home with a reconditioned ThinkPad running Debian or Ubuntu, no problem. And you can still share your source code with colleagues who are working with different platforms. Your deployment options are equally unrestricted, which means you can take advantage of the best deals on offer from your web-hosting company.

1.1.4 Open source

Back in the day, when I was first honored as a Microsoft most valuable professional (MVP, an annual award made to people who Microsoft judges to have made significant contributions to the community through sharing their technical expertise), one of the benefits of the award was gaining direct access to the product group at Microsoft responsible for the MVP's area of expertise. In my case (which I am sure was one of mistaken identity), the area of expertise was ASP.NET, Microsoft's web development framework.

Having access to the ASP.NET product group was a privileged position. Bear in mind that in those days, Microsoft was very much a closed-source company. Microsoft MVPs learned about some of Microsoft's plans for new products in their area in advance of the rest of the community. They might even be invited to do a bit of beta testing on their new launch or contribute suggestions for improvements, although all the major design decisions had usually been made at the point you were given access.

Fast forward a few years, and Microsoft has transitioned into an open source company. The source code for their development platforms is on GitHub for all to see. More than that, everyone is encouraged to contribute to the source code by filing possible bugs and providing improvements, new features, bug fixes, or better documentation. Rather than being told what Microsoft is going to release at some point in the distant future, anyone can be a part of the conversation about the direction a framework should take. Anyone can ask questions about the framework on GitHub, often getting answers from the Microsoft developers themselves.

Microsoft wins with this approach because they get the benefit of experts outside of their company adding their technical expertise, and even time, while users of the framework benefit because they get a better product that other real users have influenced. At the time of writing, the current version of ASP.NET, ASP.NET Core, which Razor Pages is part of, has over 1,000 active contributors.

1.1.5 Using your existing knowledge

The server-side language supported by Razor Pages is C#, while the view templates are mostly composed of the languages of the web—HTML, CSS, and JavaScript. The placeholders for the dynamic content discussed earlier are C# code. You use Razor, a simple and easy-to-learn templating syntax, to embed server-side expressions and code in the view template. You don't need to learn any new languages to use Razor Pages. You don't even really need to know SQL to access a database because .NET includes frameworks that you will use to generate that for you.

1.2 What can you do with Razor Pages?

Razor Pages is a page-focused framework. Its primary purpose is to generate HTML. Therefore, it is suitable for creating *any* web application or any part of a web-based application that consists of web pages. In fact, it's probably easier to list the things you can't do with Razor Pages!

You looked at Manning's website earlier—an online catalog and e-commerce site. I'm reliably informed that it hasn't been built with Razor Pages, but it could have been. I've used Razor Pages for my blog and tutorial sites, where data is stored in databases or as Markdown files that need to be converted to HTML. I have also used Razor Pages in my day job for building magazine websites, internal web-based tools for managing business-related workflows and reporting, and even a custom content management system. Any kind of web application that includes pages as part of the requirement is a candidate for Razor Pages—from a simple blog site to the next eBay.

Razor Pages is particularly suitable for any type of forms-based application. Often referred to as CRUD applications, create, read, update, and delete represent the four basic operations related to persistent storage of a model. Tools are available for quickly scaffolding a collection of forms for managing any entity, which you will use later in the book.

1.3 The technologies that underpin Razor Pages

Razor Pages sits at the top of a stack that starts with .NET 6, a huge framework from Microsoft that supports the development of a wide array of cross-platform applications, including desktop, mobile, cloud, games, and, of course, web (figure 1.3). The base layer, also referred to as the base class library (BCL), includes the lower-level libraries common to most development types, such as those that provide data types or enable working with collections, files, data, threading exceptions, email, and so on.

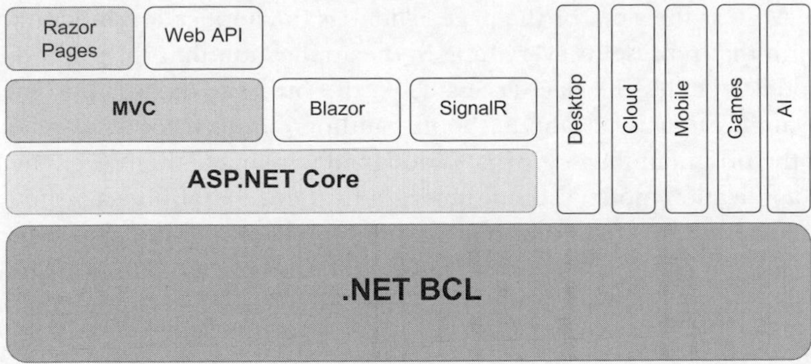

Figure 1.3 The .NET stack. Razor Pages is a feature of the MVC framework, which, in turn, is part of the ASP.NET Core framework, which represents the web development layer.

The web layer of the stack is known as ASP.NET Core. It includes libraries for working with HTTP, routing, authentication, and the classes to support the Razor syntax and HTML generation. In addition to Blazor, which I mentioned previously, ASP.NET Core also includes SignalR, a framework for pushing data from the server to connected clients. The simplest example of a use case for SignalR is a chat application.

Alongside SignalR and Blazor sits the ASP.NET Core model-view-controller (MVC) framework, with Razor Pages on top. Razor Pages is a *feature* of the MVC framework, and it supports development of web applications that adhere to the MVC design pattern. To understand what this means, it is necessary to understand the nature of the ASP.NET Core MVC framework.

1.3.1 The ASP.NET Core MVC framework

ASP.NET Core MVC was the original cross-platform web application framework from Microsoft. It is what is known as an *opinionated* framework. The framework designers have opinions about the architectural decisions, conventions, and best practices users of the framework should apply to produce the highest-quality results. Then, the framework designers produce a framework that steers users into adopting those architectural decisions, conventions, and best practices. Developers throughout Microsoft describe this process as helping customers to fall into the "pit of success."

1.3.2 Model-view-controller

The developers' main architectural decision behind the MVC framework was to support the development of web applications that implement the MVC pattern—hence, the name of the framework. This decision is because MVC is a well-known presentation design pattern in web development, with the purpose of enforcing a separation of concerns—specifically, the concerns of the application model and its presentation.

The *V* in MVC is the view, or the page. The *M* is the application model, which is a nebulous term that represents everything in the application that isn't view or controller. The model includes the data access code, the business or domain objects—the *things* your application is all about (books, authors, and customers, in Manning's case)—and the programming logic that is designed to manage them (i.e., the business logic). The application model is then subject to further separation according to other good software design practices, but that's not the business of MVC, which is purely a presentation design pattern. The main reason for enforcing a separation between the UI and the rest of the model is improving maintenance and testability. It is very difficult to test application logic if it is mixed in with HTML.

The controller part of MVC is the primary means of separation between the model and the view. Its role is to take requests and then use the information in the request to perform commands on the model. It will then take the result of that processing and pass it to the view for display.

Controllers can be implemented in different ways. You can create something like a front controller to process requests for the whole application or a subset of the application, or you can use the page controller pattern to process the requests for individual pages. The original ASP.NET MVC framework implementation leverages the front controller approach, in which a single controller is responsible for coordinating the processing for multiple endpoints related to a feature or business area within the application—`AuthorController`, `BookController`, and so on. Razor Pages implements the page controller approach, with the controller being a class that derives from `PageModel`.

Front controllers in the ASP.NET MVC framework are individually responsible for a lot more than page controllers (figure 1.4). They have to coordinate processing for all of the actions related to a specific business area—create, update, delete, get lists, get details, and so on. Over time, front controllers can grow to hundreds, if not thousands, of lines of code. The number of dependencies they take increases, which is a sure sign that the controller is doing too much. They become difficult to manage. Page controllers, on the other hand, are a lot simpler, only having to manage processing for their individual page. Some of them barely have any code in them at all.

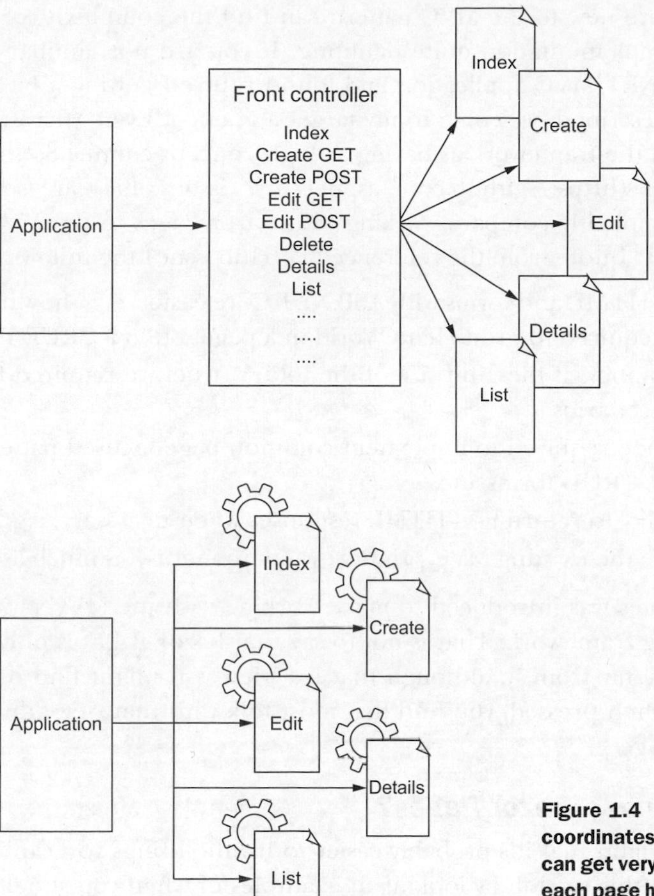

Figure 1.4 The front controller used in MVC coordinates processing for multiple views and can get very busy and complex. In Razor Pages, each page has its own controller, keeping them lean and easier to work with.

1.3.3 The design goals of Razor Pages

As you've already learned, the MVC framework is an opinionated framework. If you want to use it, you need to work with the framework authors' conventions or develop some kind of workaround. ASP.NET MVC includes a number of conventions for naming files and placing them within the application. For example, suppose your customer or boss wants you to add a new feature to an existing MVC application. Bearing in mind that front controller classes are feature-driven by convention, you would have to add a new class file representing the feature to your Models folder, a new controller class to the Controllers folder, a new folder for the feature in the Views folder, a new Razor view to that folder, and, finally, a `viewmodel` class to represent the data for your view. If you want to make any changes to the feature, you have to dip in and out of folders and files all over the code base.

Developers who are new to the MVC pattern can find the complexity of working with the ASP.NET implementation quite daunting. If you are not familiar with the structure of an ASP.NET MVC application and found yourself getting a bit lost with the workflow I just described, welcome to my target audience! Even Microsoft themselves have described the framework as having a "high concept count." So the design goals of Razor Pages (https://github.com/aspnet/mvc/issues/494) are set against that backdrop and implicitly compare working with Razor Pages to the MVC framework. They include (to quote from the referenced GitHub issue) the following:

- Make dynamic HTML and forms with ASP.NET Core easier, e.g., how many files and concepts required to print Hello World in a page, build a CRUD form, etc.
- Reduce the number of files and size of the folder structure required for page-focused MVC scenarios
- Simplify the code required to implement common page-focused patterns, e.g., dynamic pages, CRUD forms, etc.
- Enable the ability to return non-HTML responses when necessary, e.g., 404s
- Use and expose the existing MVC primitives (components) as much as possible

Ultimately, Razor Pages was introduced to make working with the MVC pattern simpler than the existing framework. That is not to say that Razor Pages is only suitable for simple scenarios—far from it, although that is a view you might find on various websites. However, when pressed, you find that most folk with that view admit to not having tried Razor Pages.

1.4 When should you use Razor Pages?

In keeping with my claim that it's probably easier to list the things you can't do with Razor Pages, I'll start this section by looking at examples of when you shouldn't consider using Razor Pages:

- *Single-page applications*—Being a server-side development framework, Razor Pages is not a suitable tool for building single-page applications, in which the application is usually written in JavaScript and executes in the browser, except where server rendering is a requirement (http://mng.bz/YGWB).
- *Static content sites*—If your site consists exclusively of static content, there is nothing to be gained by starting a Razor Pages project. You just don't need a framework with the primary purpose of generating HTML dynamically on the server.
- *Web APIs*—Razor Pages is primarily a UI-generation framework. However, Razor page handlers can return any type of content, including JSON. Nevertheless, if your application is primarily a web-based service, Razor Pages is not the correct tool to use. You should consider using MVC API controllers instead. It should be pointed out that it is perfectly possible (and easy) to mix Razor pages and API controllers in the same project, if your requirement is to generate HTML as well as to provide services over HTTP.

- *Migrating from older versions of MVC*—If you are looking to migrate an existing MVC application from previous versions of the .NET Framework to ASP.NET Core, it might make more sense to port to ASP.NET Core MVC because much of your existing code can be reused without modification. Having migrated, you can use Razor Pages for all new page-focused features within the migrated application because MVC controllers and Razor Pages happily sit together in the same application.

Razor Pages is the default project type for building page-based web applications in Visual Studio, so in all cases other than the preceding exceptions, you should use Razor Pages for page-focused applications, regardless of complexity.

ASP.NET Core has been designed with performance as a first-class feature. The framework regularly features highly, or even top, on the well-regarded TechEmpower Performance Ratings for web frameworks (https://www.techempower.com/benchmarks). So if you need a high-performance application that delivers HTML, Razor Pages has a great foundation.

ASP.NET Core applications are designed to be modular. That is, you only include the features your application needs. If you don't need a feature, it is not included. This has the benefit of keeping the published application's footprint as small as possible. If restricting the overall size of your deployed application is important to you, Razor Pages ticks that box too.

Finally, the team behind ASP.NET Core must be doing something right because ASP.NET Core is the "most loved" web development framework, according to Stack Overflow's 2020 developer survey (see http://mng.bz/GEvv).

1.5 Working with Razor Pages

At this point, you know what Razor Pages is, the basics of how it works, and what it can do for you. You should know by now whether it is the right option for your application. If it is, you need to know where to get Razor Pages from and what tools you can use to work with the framework. The next section provides answers to those questions. First, we'll cover how you can get Razor Pages; then, we'll look at the tools you need to be able to use the framework to develop your web application.

1.5.1 How do you get Razor Pages?

To begin developing Razor Pages applications, you need the .NET software development kit (SDK). This is automatically included when you first install Visual Studio, Microsoft's flagship software development environment. After that, you may need to install updated versions of the SDK manually. You will need to install the SDK manually if you use an editor that doesn't include the SDK. SDKs are available at https://dotnet.microsoft.com/download.

Versions are available for Windows, Linux, macOS, and Docker (figure 1.5). The current release is clearly marked and is recommended, as it contains the latest bug fixes and other improvements. One version will also be flagged as the long-term support

(LTS) release; this may or may not be the current release. LTS versions continue to receive critical bug fixes for an extended period. The current release, .NET 6, is an LTS release and will continue to be supported for three years from its release date, which was in November 2021. Microsoft aims to make migrating from one LTS version to the next a relatively pain-free experience.

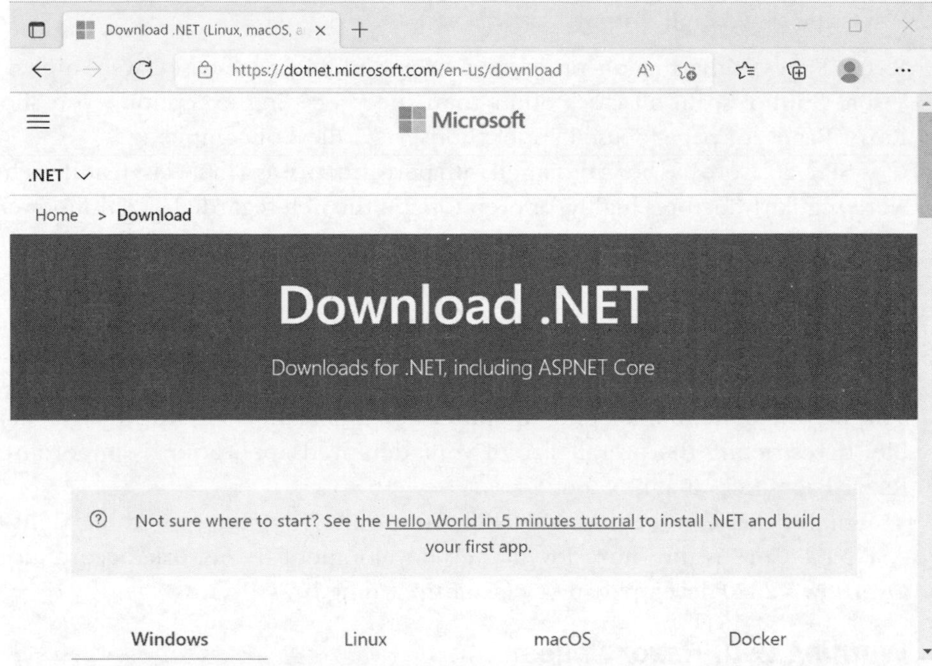

Figure 1.5 An image of the SDK download page

The download page provides access to both an SDK and a runtime for each version of .NET/.NET Core. The SDK includes the runtime and a set of tools for developing applications, including the command-line interface (CLI) for .NET. The CLI provides access to a series of commands that enable you to develop, build, run, and publish your .NET application.

The runtime includes only those components required for running .NET applications. The runtime is primarily intended for deployment on machines on which no development takes place. You can install multiple versions of the SDK and/or runtime on your machine. They happily live side by side.

1.5.2 Choosing a development environment

In theory, you could develop Razor Pages applications using nothing but the command line and, perhaps, a basic text editor like Windows Notepad, but the reality is you will want to use a tool that is designed to support .NET Core development, relieving you of much of the grunt work. The most powerful of these tools are integrated development environments (IDEs) and will include source code editors that feature syntax highlighting, code completion, static code analysis, and features for debugging, compiling, and publishing your application. IDEs usually support common workflows, such as creating applications and adding files of various types based on existing templates. They usually also include integration with databases and version control systems.

The most popular IDE for .NET development is Visual Studio from Microsoft. To enjoy .NET 6 support, you will need to use the 2022 version. It comes in three editions: Community, Professional, and Enterprise. The Community edition is a full version of Visual Studio, differing from the Professional edition only in terms of its license. The Community edition is free for individuals and small companies, as defined in the license terms (https://visualstudio.microsoft.com/vs/community/), or for academic use or contributing to open source projects. The Enterprise edition is intended for use by large teams and is priced accordingly. All editions are only available for Windows (figure 1.6).

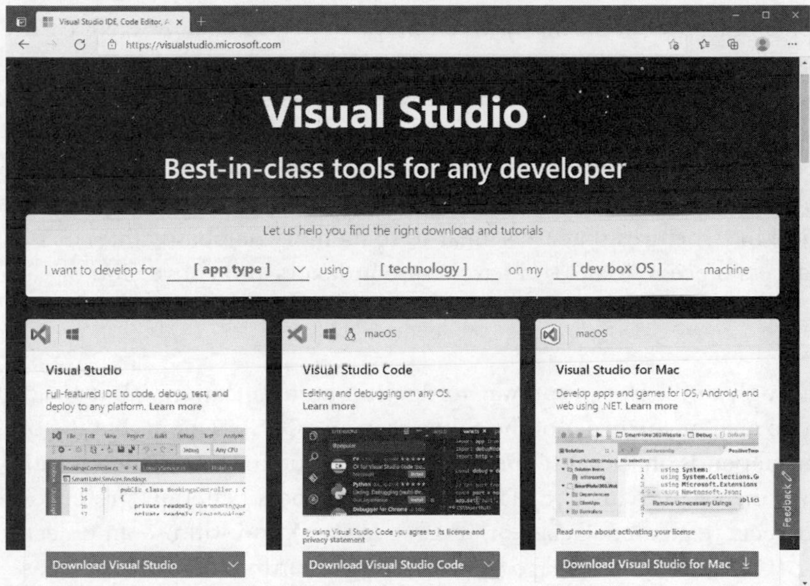

Figure 1.6 Screenshot of https://visualstudio.microsoft.com/, where readers can obtain all three IDEs mentioned so far

There is a version of Visual Studio for Mac users, but it is not a direct port of the Windows version. It is an adapted version of Xamarin Studios, which is primarily a mobile application development environment. However, it supports Razor Pages development, and there is a free Community edition available.

Visual Studio Code (VS Code) is a popular, free cross-platform code editor (as opposed to a development environment). A huge and growing number of extensions are available that make .NET Core development within VS Code quite easy, including C# language integration, debugging, and version control integration. VS Code doesn't include the same kind of tooling integration for working with Razor Pages offered by Visual Studio, but it does feature an integrated terminal, providing easy access to the .NET CLI, and the awesome OmniSharp extension provides excellent support for C# development in VS Code. How to use the VS Code terminal to execute CLI commands will be discussed throughout this book; you can download VS Code from https://code.visualstudio.com/.

If you want to develop on a Mac or Linux system, VS Code is a good option. Alternatively, Rider from JetBrains is a cross-platform .NET IDE, which offers a 30-day free trial.

Throughout this book, I will show you how to use Visual Studio Community Edition and VS Code to develop a Razor Pages application, but you can follow the examples regardless of which platform you choose to work with.

1.5.3 Choosing a database system

Web applications need a means by which they can persist data. ASP.NET Core doesn't impose any technical limits on your options. You could store data as a series of text files if you wanted, but the most commonly used data store is a relational database of some kind. You also need a means to establish connections between your application and the database, execute database commands, and access any resulting data. .NET 6 includes a low-level data access technology called ADO.NET. It exposes data to the application in structures that are similar to in-memory database tables or views. If you want to access pieces of data, you have to use indexers and conversion or casting:

```
var myInt = Convert.ToInt32(dataTable.Rows[1][4]);
```

This is an ugly and error-prone way to develop an application. All it needs to fail is someone to change the order of the columns in an SQL statement that the previous C# statement depends on, because the materialized value in the targeted location can no longer be converted to an `int`. These days, developers generally prefer to work with data as objects (e.g., a `Book` class or an `Author` class) and will use an object-relational mapping (ORM) tool to manage the communication between the database and the application. The ORM also takes care of (among other things) mapping data from a database query to a specified object or collection of objects for you.

Several ORM tools are available to .NET developers. Most of them are owned and managed by third parties. The ORM I have selected for this book is Entity Framework Core (EF Core). I will be using this ORM because it is a Microsoft technology and part of .NET. Figure 1.7 is an updated version of figure 1.3 and shows where EF Core fits within the .NET stack.

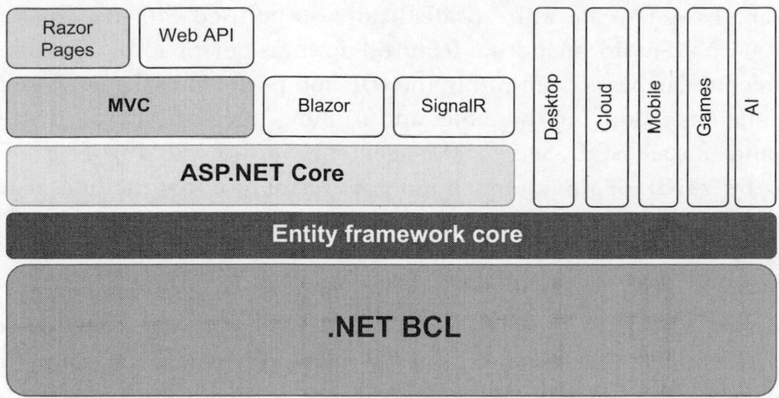

Figure 1.7 Entity Framework Core is an optional component, but it can be used to support data access in a wide variety of application types built on .NET 6, including ASP.NET, desktop, mobile, cloud, and games.

> **DEFINITION** A provider is a component that handles communication between your C# application code and the data store itself. One of the real benefits of an ORM like EF Core is that you don't need to write commands in data store–specific languages. You express your data commands in C#, which is data store–agnostic. Each individual provider is responsible for (among many other things) generating the domain-specific language (DSL) your chosen data store supports. In most cases, this DSL is SQL.

Using EF Core will improve your productivity but will also add an element of restriction to the options available to you in terms of database system, based on the availability and/or cost of a specialized provider. Having said that, EF Core supports a large number of database systems, especially the most popular ones. To check if there is a provider for your preferred database system, please refer to the official documentation: https://docs.microsoft.com/en-us/ef/core/providers/.

When you use an ORM like EF Core, the differences between database systems are more or less entirely hidden away from the application itself. The C# code you write for data storage and retrieval for one database system will work exactly the same against another system. The only real difference between one system and another is in initial configuration. I have chosen to feature two database systems in this book: a version of SQL Server, for Windows-only developers, and SQLite, for readers who want to follow along on other operating systems. I will highlight the rare differences between them as they arise.

Working in the Microsoft world, you are more likely to encounter their flagship relational database system, SQL Server, than any other option. A version of SQL Server, LocalDB, can be installed very easily when you install Visual Studio. It is not designed for production use and only includes the minimum set of files required to run an SQL Server database. For this reason, I have selected LocalDB as the edition to use for readers who want to work with Windows.

Any databases you create with LocalDB can also be used with the full version of SQL Server. Visual Studio includes a feature known as Server Explorer that enables you to connect to databases from within the IDE and perform basic database management tasks, such as modifying the tables and running queries. Alternatively, you can download and install SQL Server Management Studio (SSMS) free of charge (http://mng.bz/z47B). SSMS is a much more powerful tool that includes features for managing databases, profiling query performance, and administering SQL Server installations.

A large number of cross-platform database options are available, including the free and very popular MySQL. However, I selected the file-based SQLite database system for readers who want to develop on a non-Windows environment simply from the ease-of-use point of view. It is already installed on most versions of Linux and macOS. Having said that, there is no reason why you can't use SQLite if you are developing on Windows. It's a pretty good choice for smaller sites. It is deployed along with the rest of the application files, potentially simplifying deployment and reducing your hosting costs. In terms of managing an SQLite database, I use the free DB Browser for SQLite, which is cross-platform and available at https://sqlitebrowser.org/.

Whichever database system you choose to go with, you should now be ready to move forward with developing Razor Pages applications. You understand the role of Razor Pages in the web development diaspora and the key features that make it a great choice. It is modern and fast and doesn't get in the way of the development process. In the next chapter, you will waste no time producing your first working Razor Pages application and learning the fundamentals of building more complex applications.

Summary

- Razor Pages is a page-focused framework for developing dynamic web applications.
- Razor Pages is a Microsoft technology.
- Razor Pages is part of ASP.NET Core, which, in turn, is part of .NET 6.
- Razor Pages is cross-platform.
- Razor Pages is open source and free.
- Razor Pages builds on the best parts of ASP.NET Core MVC.
- Razor Pages is an implementation of MVC that uses the page controller pattern.
- Razor Pages is primarily concerned with generating HTML on the web server.
- You use C# to program Razor Pages applications.
- HTML is generated dynamically from templates based on the Razor syntax—a mixture of HTML and C#.
- Razor Pages works with databases.

2 Building your first application

This chapter covers

- Creating a Razor Pages application
- Adding your first page
- Exploring the project files and the roles they play
- Configuring the application pipeline with middleware

In the last chapter, you learned how the Razor Pages web development framework, as part of ASP.NET Core, fits within the overall .NET Framework. You have discovered the types of applications you can build with Razor Pages and also, importantly, when it is not the best solution to use. You have been introduced to the tools you need to be productive with Razor Pages and, hopefully, downloaded and installed Visual Studio or VS Code along with the latest version of the .NET SDK. Now that you have your development environment set up, it's time to start working with code.

In this chapter, you will create your first Razor Pages application, using both Visual Studio and the CLI, so you can follow along on the operating system of your choice. Most web development frameworks provide a starter kit or project—a simple application that forms the starting point for your own application. Razor Pages is no different. The application that forms the starter kit only has three pages, but it includes a basic configuration that you can build on to create your own more complex application.

Once you have created your application and managed to launch it in a browser, you will add a new page to the application and include some dynamic content, so you can begin to understand what a Razor page actually is. Once you have tested the page to ensure that it works, you will use the site's master template file to add the page to the site navigation.

Then, I discuss the application files generated by the tooling to understand the role each of the generated files plays within your Razor Pages application. This walk-through will help you understand the basics behind all ASP.NET Core applications.

At the end of the walk-through, we will take a closer look at the primary application configuration: the request pipeline. This is the core of your application. It defines how your application handles requests and delivers responses to clients. You will learn how it is constructed from middleware components and how you can extend it by adding your own middleware.

By the end of this chapter, you should have a good high-level understanding of how a Razor Pages application works, from receiving a request to finally sending HTML back to the client. Then you will be ready to take a deep dive into working with a Razor page and its companion, the `PageModel` class, in chapter 3.

2.1 Creating your first website

This section will cover using the available tools to generate a fully working Razor Pages application rapidly. You will use Visual Studio 2022 Community Edition on Windows 10 and the CLI for non-Windows readers. I discuss using the CLI within Visual Studio Code, although you can use any terminal application to execute CLI commands. So the following sections assume you have your environment installed and working, along with a version of the SDK that supports .NET 6 development. You can test to see whether you have a suitable version of the SDK installed on your machine by opening a command shell and executing the following command:

```
dotnet --list-sdks
```

You should see one or more versions listed, each with its own installation path. At least one of the versions should begin with *6*. At this stage, if you are a first-time user, you will also need to trust the self-signed certificate that is required for hassle-free browsing of your site over HTTPS on your local system (covered in more detail in chapter 14). To do this, execute the following command:

```
dotnet dev-certs https --trust
```

The certificate itself is installed as part of the SDK installation.

2.1.1 *Creating a website using Visual Studio*

As described in chapter 1, Visual Studio is the primary IDE for .NET developers working on Windows. It includes simple menu-driven workflows for performing the most common tasks. Razor Pages applications are created as projects within Visual Studio, so your starting point, having opened Visual Studio, is to create a new project. You can do this either by clicking the Create a New Project button on the startup splash screen or going to File > New Project… in the main menu bar.

On the next screen, you can select the type of project you want to create from a list of templates. Before you do, I recommend selecting C# from the languages selector at the top of the right-hand pane to filter out some of the noise. Choose the ASP.NET Core Web App template—the one *without* (Model-View-Controller) as part of its name, taking care also to avoid selecting the very similarly named ASP.NET Core Web API template. The correct template carries the following description: "A project template for creating an ASP.NET Core application with example, ASP.NET Razor Pages content."

Once you have chosen a suitable location for your application files and moved to the next screen, ensure that your Target Framework selection is .NET 6, leaving all other options at their defaults. Authentication Type should be set to None, Configure for HTTPS should be checked, and you should leave the Enable Docker option unchecked (figure 2.1). Once you are happy with the selections, click the Create button. At this point, Visual Studio should open, showing your new application in Solution Explorer (figure 2.2).

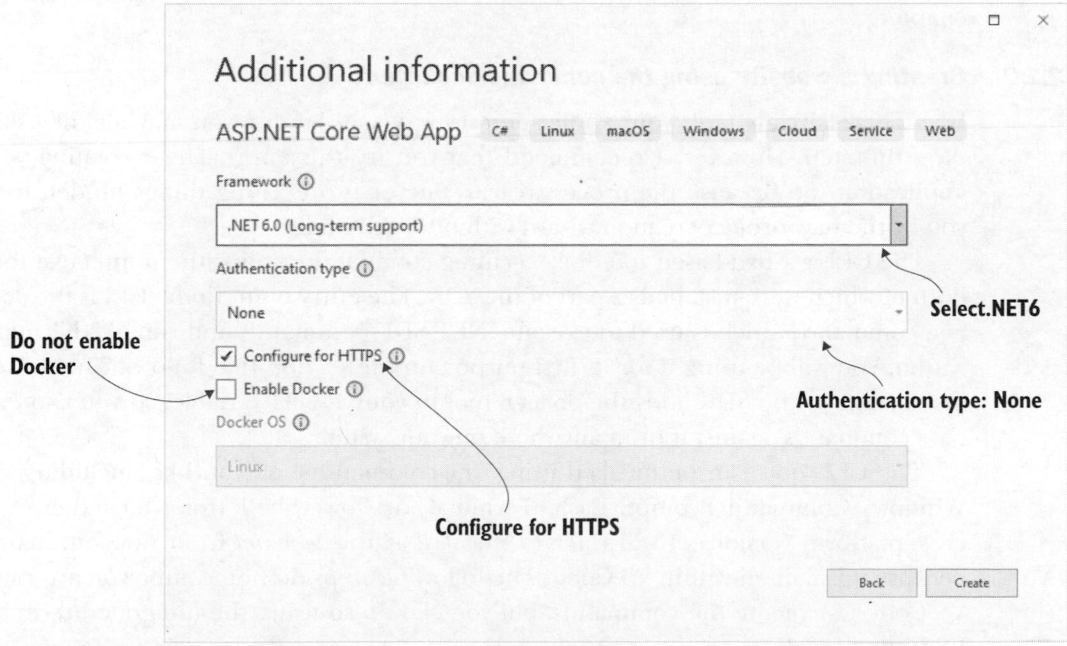

Figure 2.1 Check that you have applied these settings before clicking the Create button.

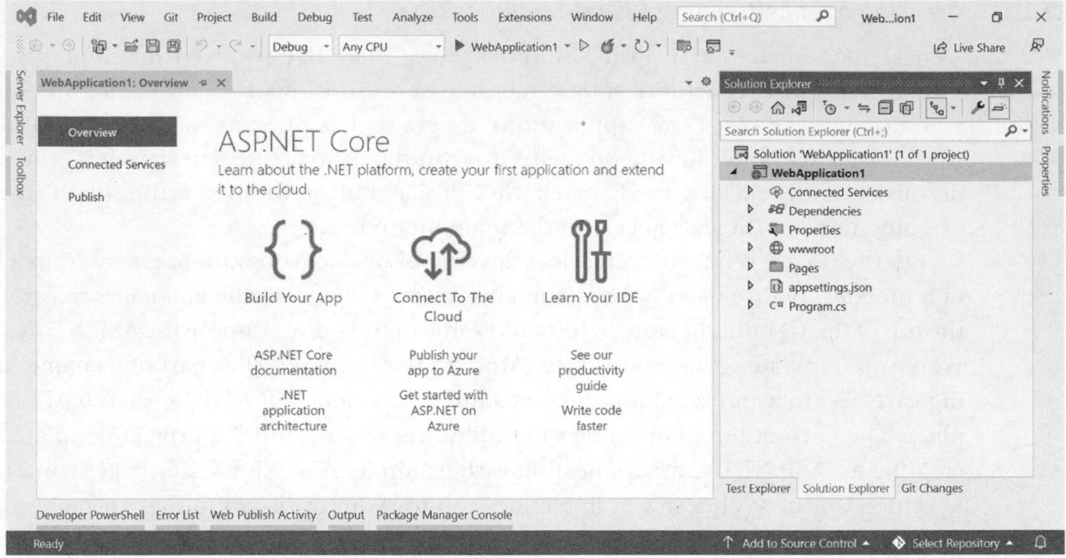

Figure 2.2 Your new application opens in Visual Studio with an overview page and the Solution Explorer window open on the right, showing the structure and contents of your WebApplication1 solution and its single project, also named WebApplication1.

Although the contents of Solution Explorer look like a file structure, not all the items that you see are actually files. We will take a closer look at these items later in the chapter.

2.1.2 Creating a website using the command-line interface

If you have already built your application using Visual Studio, you may feel like skipping this step. However, I recommend that you try this approach to creating your application too because the process reveals one or two exciting things hidden from you by the new project creation wizard within Visual Studio.

The CLI is a text-based tool for executing commands against the dotnet.exe tool, both of which were installed as part of the SDK. The entry point to the CLI is the `dotnet` command, which is used to execute .NET SDK commands and run a .NET application. You will be using it for its first purpose in the section that follows. The default installation of the SDK adds the `dotnet` tool to your PATH variable, so you can execute commands against it from anywhere on your system.

The CLI tools can be invoked using any command shell you like, including the Windows Command Prompt, Bash, Terminal, or PowerShell (for which there is a cross-platform version). I will refer to the *shell* as the *terminal* from now on, mainly because it is named within VS Code. The following steps do not assume you are using VS Code to execute the commands, but you can do so using the integrated terminal VS Code provides.

First, create a folder named WebApplication1 in a suitable location on your system, then navigate to it using the terminal, or open the folder within VS Code. If you have chosen to use VS Code, you can access the terminal by pressing Ctrl-`. At the command prompt, type the following commands, pressing the Enter key after each one.

Listing 2.1 Creating Razor Pages application using the CLI

```
dotnet new sln                                              <-- Creating a solution file
dotnet new webapp -o WebApplication1
dotnet sln add WebApplication1\WebApplication1.csproj
```

- `dotnet new sln`: Creating a solution file
- `dotnet new webapp -o WebApplication1`: Scaffolding a new Razor Pages application and placing the output into a subfolder named WebApplication1
- `dotnet sln add WebApplication1\WebApplication1.csproj`: Adding the Razor Pages application to the solution

Once you execute the last command, all of the application files should be created successfully. You should also get some feedback from the terminal related to some "post-creation actions." Your path to WebApplication1 may well differ from mine, shown in the following listing, but the rest of the feedback should be similar.

Listing 2.2 Notification of post-creation actions executed by the CLI

```
Processing post-creation actions...
Running 'dotnet restore' on WebApplication1\WebApplication1.csproj...
  Determining projects to restore...
  Restored D:\MyApps\WebApplication1\WebApplication1\WebApplication1.csproj
(in 80 ms).
Restore succeeded.
```

The CLI executed the `dotnet restore` command on your application, ensuring all packages your application depends on are obtained and up to date. If you used Visual Studio to create your application, the same command will have been executed, but the indication that it took place is not so obvious. It is shown in the status bar at the bottom of the IDE (figure 2.3).

Restored F:\MyApps\WebApplication1\WebApplication1\WebApplication1.csproj (in 3 ms).

Figure 2.3 The status bar at the bottom of Visual Studio shows that the project was restored.

2.1.3 Running the application

Now that the application has been created using whichever means you chose, you can run and view it in a browser. To run the application from Visual Studio, you simply need to press Ctrl-F5 or click on the outlined green triangle (not the solid one) in the top menu bar. This will take care of building and starting the application as well as launching it in a browser. If you are using the CLI, execute the following command:

```
dotnet run --project WebApplication1\WebApplication1.csproj
```

This command includes the `--project` switch to specify the location of the project file. If you execute the command from within the folder containing the csproj file, the `--project` switch is omitted. If you prefer to use the CLI while working in Visual Studio, press Ctrl-` to open the integrated terminal, and execute your commands from within.

You should receive feedback in the terminal that the application is being built before confirming that it is listening on two localhost ports—one of which uses HTTP and the other of which uses HTTPS. The actual port numbers vary from project to project:

```
info: Microsoft.Hosting.Lifetime[0]
      Now listening on: https://localhost:7235
info: Microsoft.Hosting.Lifetime[0]
      Now listening on: http://localhost:5235
```

Open a browser, and navigate to the URL that uses HTTPS. In the download that accompanies this example, that is https://localhost:7235. If your browser warns you that the site is not secure, you may have overlooked the command required to trust the self-signed certificate: `dotnet dev-certs https --trust`. If all goes well, you should see something similar to figure 2.4.

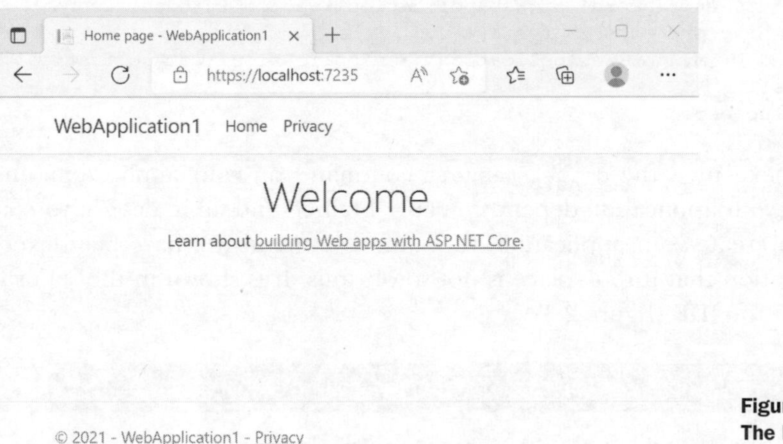

Figure 2.4
The home page

The application is elementary. The home page contains minimal styling and content. Navigate to the Privacy page, using either the navigation at the top of the page or the link in the footer. Notice that the same minimal styling has also been applied to the Privacy page (figure 2.5), and that navigation is present.

There is not much else you can do with this application at present. There aren't yet any interesting ways to interact with it, so it is time to add a page to the application.

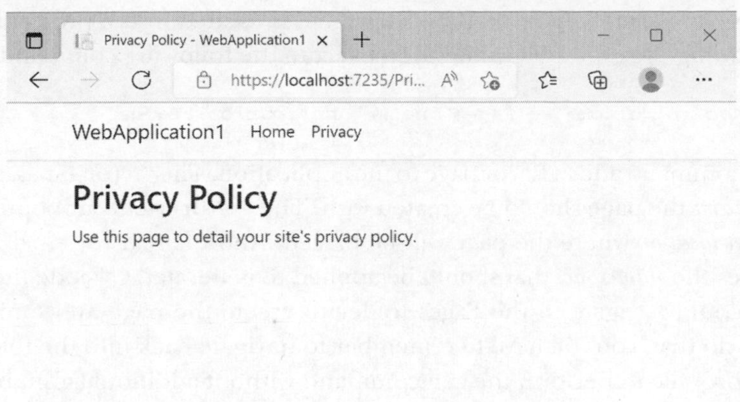

Figure 2.5 The privacy page includes the same header, footer, and styling as the home page.

2.1.4 Adding a new page

In this section, you will add a new page to the application. You will also explore a new feature that was added to .NET 6 called *hot reload.* This feature results in changes made to your code being reflected in the running application, without you having to relaunch it. This is activated automatically for Visual Studio users. VS Code users need to use a slightly different command to enable hot reload. This feature works for changes to existing files. Since you are adding a new file, you need to stop your application first. Visual Studio users can simply close the browser to stop the application. If you launched your application using the CLI command, you should press Ctrl-C in the terminal window to shut the application down.

Visual Studio users should right-click on the Pages folder in Solution Explorer and choose Add > Razor Page from the available options (figure 2.6). Name the file Welcome .cshtml.

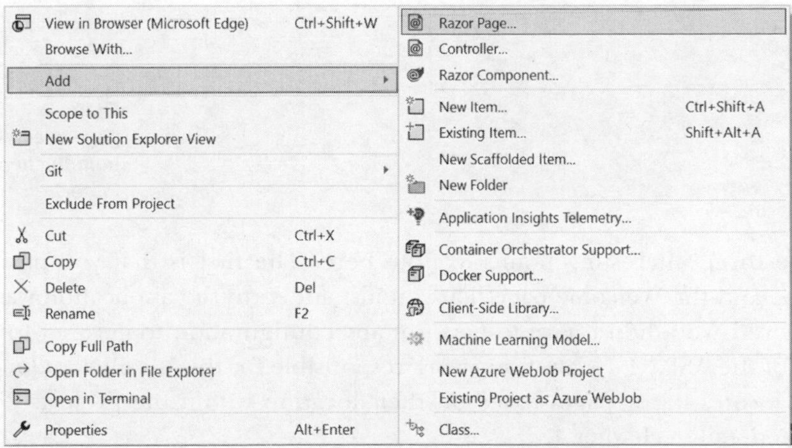

Figure 2.6 To add a new page in Visual Studio, right-click on the Pages folder, and choose Add, then Razor Page.

VS Code users should make sure that their terminal is located in the project folder—the one containing the csproj file—and then execute the following command:

```
dotnet new page -n Welcome -o Pages -na WebApplication1.Pages
```

The `new page` command adds a Razor page to the application. The `-n` (or `--name`) option specifies the *name* the page should be created with. The `-o` (or `--output`) option specifies the *output location* where the page will be placed. And the `-na` (or `--namespace`) option specifies the *namespace* that should be applied to generated C# code files. Alternatively, you could navigate to the Pages folder to create the page and omit the `-o` option. If you do that, you will have to remember to navigate back into the folder containing the csproj file to perform the `run` command without additional arguments.

Visual Studio users don't need to specify a namespace. The default namespace applied to code files created with the Visual Studio wizard is automatically generated by concatenating the project name with their location within the project.

Now run the application. Remember, it's Ctrl-F5 in Visual Studio, while CLI users (VS Code or Visual Studio) should execute `dotnet watch run` in the terminal this time (not `dotnet run`) and then open a browser and navigate to the first URL that is logged to the terminal. Navigate to /welcome. The page should appear without any content apart from the header and footer (figure 2.7).

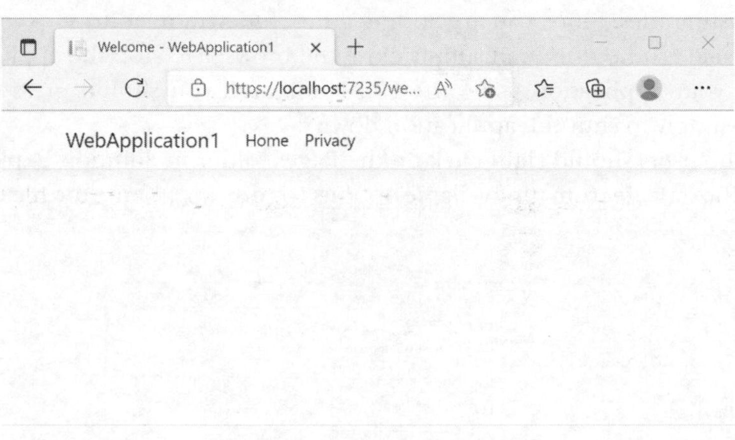

Figure 2.7 The new page is empty aside from the header and footer.

There are three interesting points to note here. The first is that you navigated to /welcome, and the Welcome page that you just added to the application was located and rendered. You didn't have to perform any configuration to get that to happen. The part of the ASP.NET Core framework responsible for this is called *routing*. It automatically locates Razor pages based on their location within the project. Routing is covered in detail in chapter 4.

The second point to note is that the new page includes the navigation, footer, and styles you saw in the home and privacy pages. Your page inherited these from a layout file, a kind of master template. Again, this happened without you having to take any specific steps to make it happen. You will learn about layout files and how to configure them in the next chapter.

The final item to note is the title of the page, as displayed in the browser tab: WebApplication1. The layout page also provides this value.

Now it's time to add some code to the page. Update the content of Welcome .cshtml, so it looks like the following.

Listing 2.3 Adding content to the Welcome page

```
@page
@model WebApplication1.Pages.WelcomeModel
@{
    ViewData["Title"] = "Welcome";
}
<h1>Welcome!</h1>
```

You don't even need to refresh the browser for the changes you applied to appear as soon as you save them. This is the hot reload feature working. You should see a level-one heading, and the title in the browser tab has changed to include the value that you applied to `ViewData["Title"]` (figure 2.8). `ViewData` is a mechanism for passing data from Razor pages to their layouts. You will see how `ViewData` works in the next chapter.

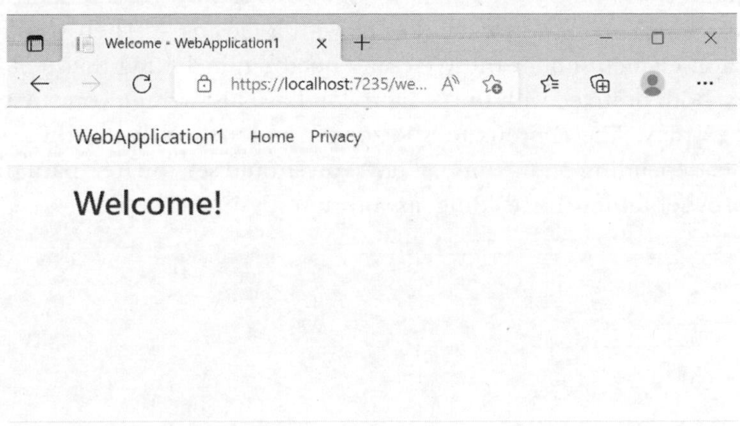

Figure 2.8 The changes that were made to the Razor page are visible without having to refresh the browser.

2.1.5 Modifying to include dynamic content

What you have added so far is static content. Every time you run this page, it will look the same. The whole point of using Razor Pages is to display dynamic content, so now it's time to add some. Let's imagine you need to include the name of the part of the day (e.g., morning, afternoon, or evening) in your output—perhaps, as part of delivery confirmation instructions (e.g., "Your package will be with you in the *morning*").

First, you need to calculate the part of the day from the time, and then you need to render it. The following listing shows how to obtain the part of the day from the current time and render that to the browser.

Listing 2.4 Adding dynamic content to the Razor page

```
@page
@model WebApplication1.Pages.WelcomeModel
@{
    ViewData["Title"] = "Welcome!";

    var partOfDay = "morning";
    if(DateTime.Now.Hour > 12){
        partOfDay= "afternoon";
    }
    if(DateTime.Now.Hour > 18){
        partOfDay= "evening";
    }
}
<h1>Welcome</h1>
<p>It is @partOfDay on @DateTime.Now.ToString("dddd, dd MMMM")</p>
```

The partOfDay variable is declared and initialized with a value of "morning".

If it is after midday, the variable is reassigned with a value of "afternoon".

If it is after 6:00 p.m., the value is updated to "evening".

The variable is rendered to the browser along with the current time of day.

The changes involve declaring a variable named `partOfDay`, which is instantiated with a value of `"morning"`. Two `if` statements subsequently change the value depending on the time of day. If it is after midday, `partOfDay` is changed to `"afternoon"`. It is changed again after 6:00 p.m. to `"evening"`. All of this is pure C# code and is placed in a code block, which starts with `@{` and ends with a closing `}`. Then you added an HTML paragraph element under the Welcome heading, including that text with two C# expressions, both prefixed with the @ sign. You have just written your first piece of Razor template syntax. The @ prefix tells Razor to render the value of the C# expressions. This time, depending on the time of day, you should see the new paragraph rendered to the browser under the heading, as shown in figure 2.9.

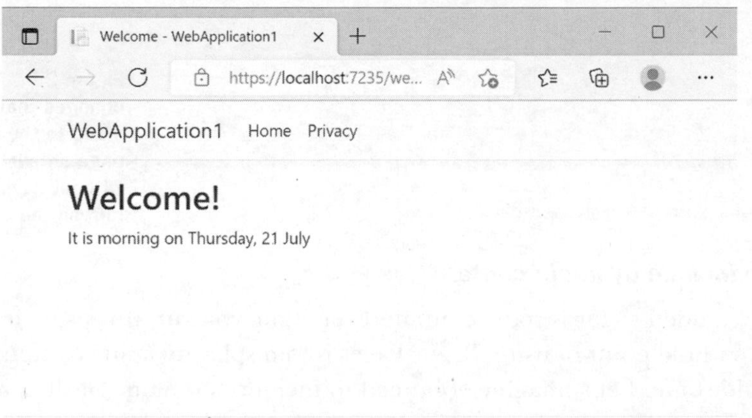

Figure 2.9 The revised Welcome page in the browser

2.1.6 Adding the page to the navigation

Next, you will add your new page to the site navigation, so you won't have to type the address in the browser to locate it. Find the _Layout.cshtml file in the Pages/Shared, folder and open it. Identify the `ul` element with a CSS class of `navbar-nav flex-grow-1`, and add the bolded lines of code in the following listing.

Listing 2.5 Adding the Welcome page to the main navigation

```
<ul class="navbar-nav flex-grow-1">
    <li class="nav-item">
      <a class="nav-link text-dark" asp-area="" asp-page="/Index">Home</a>
    </li>
    <li class="nav-item">
      <a class="nav-link text-dark" asp-area="" asp-page="/Privacy">Privacy</a>
    </li>
    <li class="nav-item">
      <a class="nav-link text-dark" asp-area="" asp-page="/Welcome">Welcome</a>
    </li>
</ul>
```

Refresh the browser again; the navigation menu at the top of every page will now include a link to the Welcome page. The change you just made has been applied to every page in the application. That is because you changed the layout file, which is used by all pages in the application. The content of the Razor page is merged with the content in the layout page to produce the final output.

You may wonder why there is no `href` attribute on the anchor element you added to the layout page to create the link. This element is called an anchor tag helper. *Tag helpers* are components that target regular HTML elements and enable server-side code to influence how they are rendered to the browser via special attributes that usually start with `asp-`. For example, the `asp-page` attribute takes a value representing the name of the page you want to generate a link to. Tag helpers are covered in more detail in the next chapter.

So you have seen some ways C# and HTML work together in the Razor page to produce HTML. Generally, the best advice is to restrict the amount of C# code you include in the Razor page to only that required to influence the presentation. Application logic, including algorithms that determine the time, should be kept out of the Razor page file. The first level of separation between the Razor page file and application logic is the `PageModel` class, which forms the focus of the next chapter, along with other view-related technology I have already touched on, including layouts, partials, and tag helpers.

2.2 Exploring the project files

Now that you have created your first Razor Pages application and experimented with a little Razor syntax, it is time to explore the contents of each folder and file that forms the web application you just created in more detail to learn about the role each plays in the application. Along the way, you will gain a clearer understanding of how ASP.NET Core applications work. You will also learn about the difference between the physical files on disk and what you see in the Solution Explorer window in Visual Studio.

2.2.1 The WebApplication1.sln file

The SLN file is known as a *solution* file. Within Visual Studio, solutions act as containers for managing related *projects*, and the solution file contains details of each project, including the paths to the project files. Visual Studio uses this information to load all related projects when you open the solution.

Larger web applications usually consist of multiple projects: a web application project responsible for the UI and multiple class library projects, each responsible for a logical layer within the application, such as the data access layer or the business logic layer. There may also be some unit test projects. Then you might see additional projects added with suffixes that denote their purpose: WebApplication1.Tests, WebApplication1.Data, and so on.

This application consists of a single project. As such, it doesn't actually need to be housed in a solution at all, but Visual Studio creates the solution file anyway. You created the solution file via the `dotnet new sln` command if you used the CLI to create your application. Then you added the WebApplication1 project to the solution explicitly via the `dotnet sln add` command. You could have skipped these steps, only creating a solution file if you needed to add additional projects to the application.

2.2.2 The WebApplication1.csproj file

The CSPROJ file is an XML-based file that contains information about the project for the build system, known as MSBuild, which is responsible for converting your source code files into a format that can be executed against the .NET runtime. To begin with, the project file contains information relating to the version of the .NET Framework the project targets and the SDK you are using. The Microsoft.NET.Sdk is the base SDK, which is used for, among other things, building console and class library projects. Web applications are built against the Microsoft.NET.Sdk.Web SDK.

The project file includes two additional properties: `Nullable` and `ImplicitUsings`. These enable you to toggle new C# features. The first sets the *nullable annotations and warnings context* for the project. In plain English, this controls the level of feedback you get from code analyzers that look for potential sources of the `NullReferenceException` in your code. This exception is the cause of more confusion and questions across .NET-focused technical communities than any other. The feature, known as *nullable reference types*, is enabled by default. You can switch it off by changing the value to `disable`.

The `ImplicitUsings` property is used to enable or disable a C# 10 feature that reduces the number of explicit `using` directives required in your code files. Instead, they are set globally within the SDK. The selection of `using` directives that have been enabled globally include the following commonly used APIs:

- System
- System.Collections.Generic
- System.Linq
- System.Threading.Tasks

In addition, the list includes a range of ASP.NET Core–specific APIs. This feature is also enabled by default. You can disable it by setting the value to `disable` or by removing the property.

Over time, the project file will contain information about packages or external libraries the project depends on. You can either add packages manually to this file or, more commonly, use a tool to add packages (a package manager), which will update the contents of the project file for you. You can edit the contents of the file to customize elements of the build.

The project file is not visible in Solution Explorer within Visual Studio. You can access it by right-clicking the project within Solution Explorer and selecting Edit Project File. If you are using VS Code, the file is visible in the file explorer, and you can access and edit it just like any other file.

2.2.3 The bin and obj folders

The bin and obj folders are used in the build process. Both folders are subdivided into two further folders—Debug and Release—which correspond to the build configuration used when the project is built. Initially, the bin and obj folders only include the Debug folder. The Release folder is not created until you build in Release mode. Unless you changed any configuration settings when you pressed Ctrl-F5 in the last section, your application has only been built in Debug mode at the moment.

The obj folder contains the artifacts used during the build process, and the bin folder contains the final output of the build. You will explore this output in more detail when you publish your application in chapter 14. If you delete either the bin or obj folder, they are recreated the next time you build your project.

Neither of these folders is visible in Solution Explorer by default. However, if you click the option to Show All Files, you can see them represented with a dotted outline. This indicator denotes that the folders are not considered part of the project itself. Once again, they are not hidden from VS Code users.

2.2.4 The Properties folder

The Properties folder contains project-specific resources and settings. The only item within the folder currently is a launchSettings.json file, which contains details of the settings to be used when you run your application.

The first group of settings is related to the IIS Express web server configuration for running your application locally. IIS Express is a lightweight version of the full IIS web server and is installed along with Visual Studio.

The second group of settings represents different launch profiles. The IIS Express profile specifies that the application should be run on IIS Express. Notice that the `applicationUrl` includes a port number. A different port number is provided to the SSL port. These are generated on a per-project basis. You are free to change the port numbers if you like.

The second profile uses the project name to identify itself. If you select this profile to launch the application, it will run purely on its internal or in-process web server. The default server implementation is known as Kestrel. You will learn more about that later in this chapter. The final profile (WSL 2) relates to running the application within Windows Subsystem for Linux. This book doesn't covering WSL, but the Microsoft documentation provides a good starting place if you would like to learn more: https://docs.microsoft.com/en-us/windows/wsl/.

2.2.5 The wwwroot folder

The wwwroot folder is a special folder within the web application. It has a globe icon in Solution Explorer. It is the web root directory and houses static files. By virtue of being the web root directory, wwwroot is configured to allow its contents to be browsed directly. It is the correct location for stylesheets, JavaScript files, images, and other content that doesn't require any processing before it is downloaded to the browser. For this reason, you should not place any files in the wwwroot folder that you don't want users to be able to access. It is possible to configure an alternative location as the web root directory, but your new location won't get the special icon in Solution Explorer.

The project scaffolder has created three folders within the wwwroot folder: css, js, and lib. The css folder houses a site.css file, containing some basic style declarations for the template site. The js folder contains a file named site.js, which has nothing aside from some comments in it. The general idea is that you will place your own JavaScript files in this folder. The lib folder contains external style and script libraries. The libraries provided by the template are Bootstrap, a popular CSS framework; jQuery, a cross-browser JavaScript utility library; and two validation libraries based on jQuery. They are used for validating form submissions.

The folder structure within wwwroot is not set in stone. You can move things around as you like.

2.2.6 The Pages folder

By convention, the Pages folder is configured as the home of your Razor page files. It is where the framework expects to find your Razor pages.

The project template starts you off with three pages. You have already seen two of them—Index, or the home page, and the Privacy page. And of course, your example includes the Welcome page you created. The third page provided by the project template is Error. Looking at the actual folder on disk, you will notice that each page comprises two files—one with a .cshtml extension (a Razor file) and another that ends with .cshtml.cs (a C# code file). This might not be immediately obvious when you look at Solution Explorer. The files are nested by default (figure 2.10). You can see them by disabling file nesting in the toolbar at the top of Solution Explorer or by clicking the expander icon next to the page, which will reveal not just the nested file but a tree showing an outline of the C# class, including properties, fields, and methods.

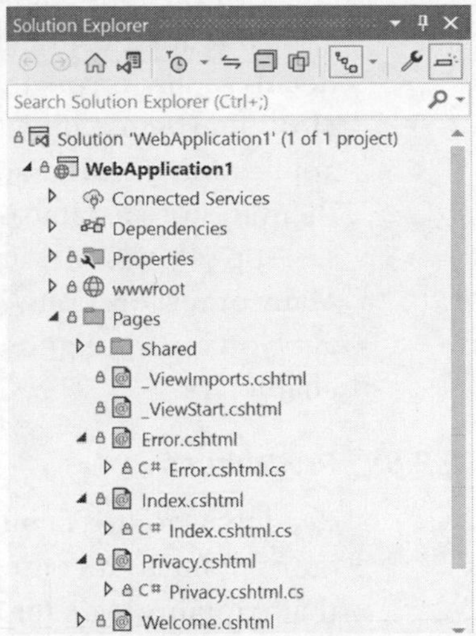

Figure 2.10 Solution Explorer automatically nests related files. You can toggle file nesting using the menu command.

The top-level file (the .cshtml file) is the Razor page file. It is also referred to as the *content* page file or the *view* file. For consistency, I'll refer to it as the Razor page (singular, with a lowercase *p* to differentiate from the Razor Pages framework) going forward. As you saw in the previous section, this file acts as the view template, containing Razor syntax, which is a mixture of C# and HTML—hence, the file extensions cs plus html. The second file is a C# code file containing a class that derives from `PageModel`. This class acts as a combined controller and view model for the Razor page. You will explore these files in detail in the next chapter.

Two other files sit in the Pages folder—one named _ViewStart.cshtml and another named _ViewImports.cshtml. Razor files named with a leading underscore are not intended to be rendered directly. These two files play an important role in the application, and they should not be renamed. The purpose of these files will be explained in the next chapter.

The Pages folder also contains a Shared folder. Within that are two further Razor files, both having leading underscores in their names. The _Layout.cshtml file acts as a master template for other files, containing common content, including the navigation you altered in the previous section. The other Razor file, _ValidationScriptsPartial .cshtml, is a partial file. *Partial files* are usually used to contain snippets of UI that you can plug into pages or layouts. They support HTML and Razor syntax. This particular partial file contains some script references to client-side validation libraries. You will work with these in chapter 5. The final file is a CSS stylesheet with an odd name: _Layout .cshtml.css. It contains style declarations that are applied to the _Layout.cshtml file. The naming convention is used by a new feature in .NET 6, called CSS Isolation. You will look at what this is and how it works in chapter 11.

2.2.7 The app-settings files

App-settings files are used as a place to store application-wide configuration settings information. The project template consists of two app-settings files: appSettings.json and appSettings.Development.json. The first, appSettings.json, is the production version that will be deployed with the published application. The other version is the one used when you are developing the application. The structure of the file contents is JSON.

Both versions contain a basic configuration for logging. The development version also contains a configuration entry named `DetailErrors` set to `true`. This enables full details of any errors that occur within the application to be rendered to the browser. Host filtering is configured in the production version. You can store pretty much any application configuration information in the app-settings files. Later, you will use them to store a database connection string and email settings.

App-settings files are not the only place you can store configuration information. Many other locations, including environment variables, are supported out of the box, and you can configure your own locations. You will learn more about configuration in chapter 14.

2.2.8 Program.cs

Readers who are familiar with C# programming know that Program.cs provides the entry point to a console application. By convention, it houses a static `Main` method that contains logic for executing the application. This file is no different, except that there is no `Main` method visible. The project template utilizes some newer C# language features, which are introduced in C# 10, one of which is *top-level statements*. This feature allows you to omit the class declaration and `Main` method in Program.cs and start writing executable code. The compiler will generate the class and `Main` method and call your executable code within the method.

The code within the Program.cs file is responsible for configuring, or *bootstrapping*, your web application and starting it. In .NET 5 and earlier, this code was split across two separate files. Much of the application configuration was delegated to a separate class named `Startup`. With the release of .NET 6, the developers behind ASP.NET have tried to reduce the amount of complexity that used to exist in basic application configuration. Rather than have code across two files, they have consolidated it into one file, taken advantage of some new C# features to further reduce the boilerplate, and then introduced what they refer to as a *minimal hosting API* to get the minimum code required to bootstrap and run a Razor Pages application down to 15 lines of code. It was nearer to 80 lines of code in the previous version, spread across the two files.

The first line of code creates a `WebApplicationBuilder`:

```
var builder = WebApplication.CreateBuilder(args);
```

Remember that this code will be executed within the compiler-generated `Main` method, so the args passed in to the `CreateBuilder` method are the standard `args` passed in to the `Main` method of any C# console application by whatever process invokes the application.

The `WebApplicationBuilder` is new in .NET 6 and forms part of the minimal hosting API together with another new type: the `WebApplication`, which you will look at shortly. The `WebApplicationBuilder` has several properties, each enabling configuration of various aspects of the application:

- `Environment`—Provides information about the web-hosting environment the application is running in
- `Services`—Represents the application's *service container* (see chapter 7)
- `Configuration`—Enables composition of the configuration providers (see chapter 14)
- `Logging`—Enables logging configuration via the `ILoggingBuilder`
- `Host`—Supports the configuration of application-host-specific services, including third-party DI containers
- `WebHost`—Enables web server configuration

The application host is responsible for bootstrapping the application, starting it up, and shutting it down. The term *bootstrapping* refers to the initial configuration of the application itself. This configuration includes the following:

- Setting the content root path, which is the absolute path to the directory that contains the application content files
- Loading configuration information from any values passed in to the args parameter, app-settings files, and environment variables
- Configuring logging providers

All .NET applications are configured in this way, whether they are web applications, services, or console applications. On top of that, a web server is configured for web applications. The web server is configured through the `WebHost` property, which represents an implementation of the `IWebHostBuilder` type. The default web server is a lightweight and extremely fast web server named Kestrel. The Kestrel server is incorporated within your application. The `IWebHostBuilder` also configures host filtering and integration with Internet Information Services (IIS), which is the Windows web server.

The `IWebHostBuilder` object exposes several extension methods that enable further configuration of the application. For example, earlier I discussed configuring an alternative to the wwwroot folder as the web root path. The `WebHost` property enables you to do that if you really have a good reason to. In the following listing, the Content folder is configured as a replacement for wwwroot.

Listing 2.6 Configuring the static files location

```
builder.WebHost.UseWebRoot("content");
```

The `Services` property provides the entry point to the dependency injection container, which is a centralized place for application services. You will explore dependency injection in more detail in chapter 7, but for the meantime, it is enough to know that the container is responsible for managing the lifetime of application services and providing instances to any part of the application, as needed. The default template includes the following line of code, which makes the essential services the Razor Pages infrastructure relies on available to the application:

```
builder.Services.AddRazorPages();
```

Those services include the Razor view engine, model binding, request validation, tag helpers, memory cache, and `ViewData`. Don't worry if these terms seem unfamiliar. You will encounter them in much more detail as you work through the book. The important thing to note is that the `Services` property provides you with a place to register and configure additional services as you need them.

Sometimes these services will be parts of the framework that you choose to enable (like the Razor Pages example), and sometimes they represent services that you install as separate packages. Often, they will be services that you write yourself that hold the application logic, like getting and saving data.

The `Build` method returns the configured application as an instance of the `WebApplication` type. This type represents a merger of three other types:

- `IApplicationBuilder`—Allows configuration of the application's request, or middleware pipeline
- `IEndpointRouteBuilder`—Enables the configuration of mapping incoming requests to specific pages
- `IHost`—Provides the means to start and stop the application

The `WebApplication` allows you to register middleware components to build and configure the application's request pipeline. For now, let's take a high-level look at the default configuration in the following listing. You will learn about the more interesting parts of the pipeline in detail later in the book.

Listing 2.7 The default request pipeline

```
if (!app.Environment.IsDevelopment())
{
    app.UseExceptionHandler("/Error");
    app.UseHsts();
}
app.UseHttpsRedirection();
app.UseStaticFiles();
app.UseRouting();
app.UseAuthorization();
app.MapRazorPages();
app.Run();
```

Each middleware is added to the pipeline via an extension method on the `IApplicationBuilder` type, which is implemented by `WebApplication`. An `IWebHostEnvironment` is accessible via the `Environment` property, which holds information about the current environment. You will learn more about environments in chapter 14, but for the time being, it will suffice to say that this property is used to determine whether the application is currently running in Development mode, and if so, the `UseExceptionHandler` method is called, which adds middleware for catching errors and displaying their details in the browser. Otherwise, the error page you saw in the Pages folder is used to display a bland message that conceals any sensitive information about the specifics of the error to the user, such as database connection strings containing user credentials or information about file paths on the server. Middleware that adds an HTTP Strict Transport Security header is also registered (`app.UseHsts()`) but only if the application is not running in Development mode. This header tells the browser to only use HTTPS when accessing the website. I cover this in more detail in chapter 13.

The `UseHttpsRedirection` method adds middleware that ensures that any HTTP requests are redirected to HTTPS. Then, after this, the static files middleware is registered. By default, an ASP.NET Core application doesn't support serving static files, such as images, stylesheets, and script files. You have to opt in for this feature, and you do so by adding the static files middleware. This middleware configures the wwwroot folder to allow static files to be requested directly and serves them to the client.

Routing middleware is responsible for selecting which *endpoint* should be executed, based on information included in the request. I discuss how routing works in Razor Pages in chapter 4. Then, authorization middleware is registered, which is responsible for determining if the current user is authorized to access the resource that is being requested. Authorization is covered in chapter 10.

Finally, the `MapRazorPages` method adds middleware to the pipeline that initially configures Razor Pages as endpoints. This middleware is also responsible thereafter for executing the request.

2.3 Understanding middleware

Wow. That was a lot of abstract terms! Endpoint, middleware, pipeline … but what do they actually mean? What do they represent? In the next section, we will explore them in more detail.

> **NOTE** ASP.NET Core middleware is quite a large topic. I will only cover the areas that are likely to be of use in the majority of Razor Pages applications. If you would like to explore more advanced middleware concepts, such as branching the pipeline, I recommend *ASP.NET Core in Action, Second Edition*, by Andrew Lock (Manning, 2021).

First, given that the purpose of a Razor Pages application is to provide responses to HTTP requests, it is appropriate to review and understand the nature of an HTTP request and how it is represented within a Razor Pages application. That will form the basis of your understanding of pipelines and endpoints.

2.3.1 An HTTP refresher

Hypertext Transfer Protocol (HTTP) is the foundation for the World Wide Web. It is a protocol for transferring information between systems in the client-server model. An HTTP transaction can be seen as consisting of two basic elements: a request and a response. The *request* is the input, and the *response* is the output. Clients initiate requests, and servers provide responses, as figure 2.11 demonstrates.

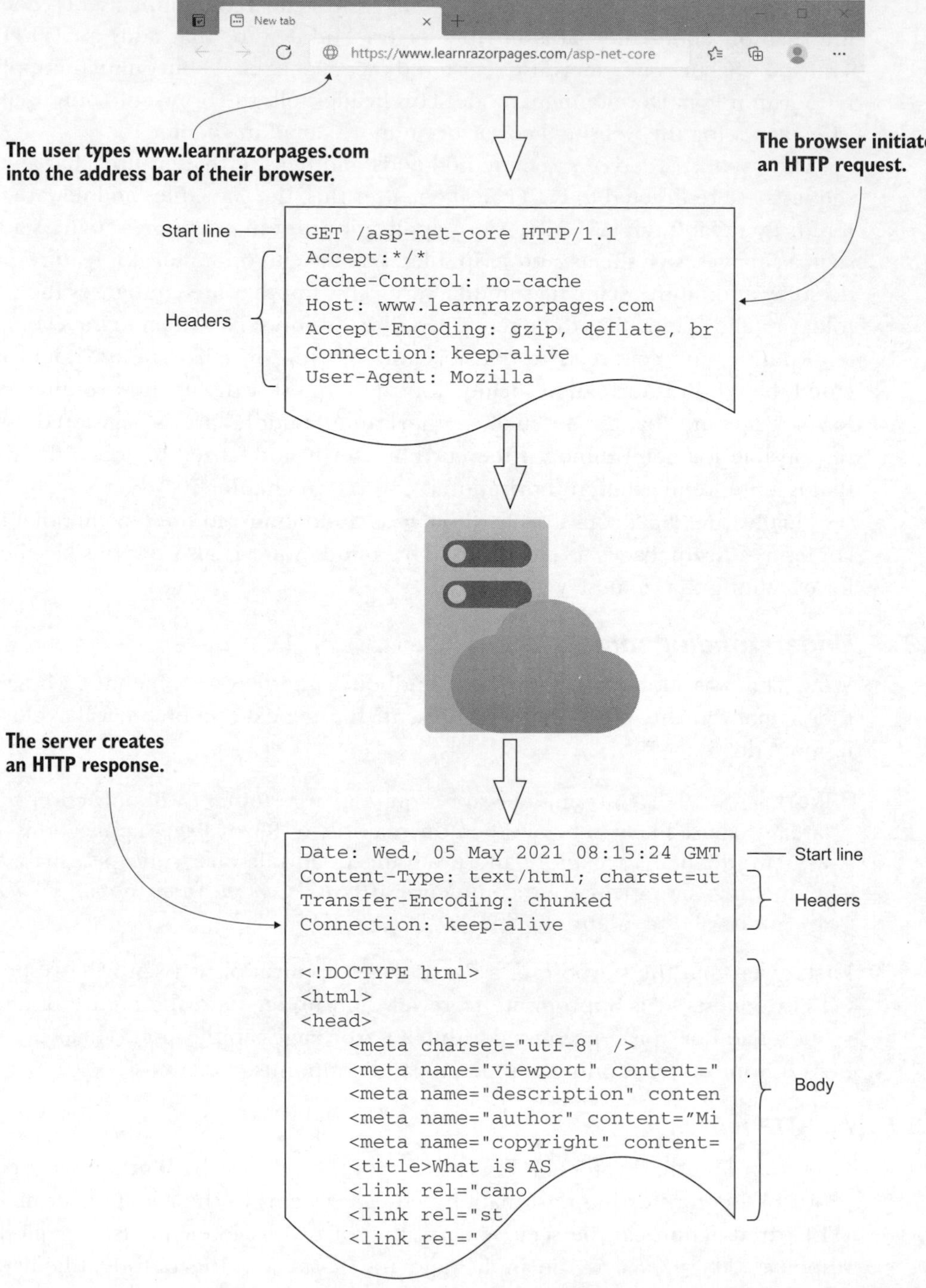

Figure 2.11 The client (browser) initiates the HTTP request, which is sent to the server. The server is responsible for routing the request to the configured application and returning an HTTP response.

An HTTP request comprises a number of pieces of data. The first line (start line) of the request message includes the following:

- The HTTP method
- The identifier of the resource
- The protocol version (e.g., HTTP/1.1)

The method is represented by a verb (e.g., `GET`, `POST`, `PUT`, `DELETE`, `TRACE`, or `CONNECT`) or a noun (e.g., `HEAD` or `OPTIONS`). The most commonly used methods for requests to websites are `GET` and `POST`, where `GET` is primarily used to request data from the server and `POST` is primarily used to transmit data to the server, although the `POST` method may also result in data being sent back to the client. These are the only two methods that will be covered in this book.

The identifier is represented by a uniform resource identifier (URI). This particular piece of data is also commonly referred to as a uniform resource locator (URL), as if they represent the same thing. Technically, they differ. For the purposes of this book, it is enough to know that all URLs are URIs, but not all URIs are URLs. Section 1.1.3 of RFC3986 explains the differences in detail: https://www.ietf.org/rfc/rfc3986.txt. The type of URI I will use in examples will be a URL in all cases.

The request also includes a collection of headers—name-value pairs that can be used to provide additional information to the server that might affect its response. For example, the `If-Modified-Since` header specifies a `datetime` value. If the requested resource has not been modified since the specified time, the server should return a 304 Not Modified status code; otherwise, it should send the modified resource. Other headers might inform the server of the preferred language for the response or the types of content the requester can handle.

The request can also include cookies—snippets of information stored by the browser that may or may not be specific to the website's user. The most common uses for cookies include the storage of the user's authentication status, once they have logged in to a site, or a token, which uniquely identifies a visitor for analytics tracking purposes.

The request can also include a body. Typically, this applies to POST requests, where the body contains the form values being submitted to the server.

The response returned by the server is structured in a similar way. It features a status line, which specifies the protocol version being used, the HTTP status code, and some text to describe the result—officially known as a *reason phrase.* An example status line might look like this:

```
HTTP/1.1 200 OK
```

The response can also include headers, which might specify the content type of the data being sent, its size, and the method used to encode the response if it has been encoded, such as gzip. The response usually includes a body containing the data that has been requested.

2.3.2 The HttpContext

All of the information in an HTTP transaction needs to be made available to your Razor Pages application. The object used to encapsulate details of the current HTTP transaction—the request and the response—is the `HttpContext` class. The in-process web server that processes the request is responsible for creating an instance of `HttpContext` using details from the actual HTTP request. It provides you, the developer, with access to request data via a formal API, rather than forcing you to parse the HTTP request for this information yourself. The `HttpContext` also encapsulates the response for this particular request. Once the web server has created the `HttpContext`, it is made available to the request pipeline. The `HttpContext` is surfaced throughout the application in various guises, so you can work with its properties as required. Table 2.1 details the main properties of the `HttpContext` and what they represent.

Table 2.1 The `HttpContext` properties

Property	Description
`Request`	Represents the current HTTP request (see table 2.2)
`Response`	Represents the current HTTP response (see table 2.3)
`Connection`	Contains information about the underlying connection for the request, including the port number and the IP address information of the client
`Session`	Provides a mechanism for storing data scoped to a user, while they browse the website
`User`	Represents the current user (see chapters 9 and 10)

The `Request` property is represented by the `HttpRequest` class. Table 2.2 details the main properties of this class and their purpose.

Table 2.2 Primary `HttpRequest` properties

Property	Description
`Body`	A `Stream` containing the request body.
`ContentLength`	The value of the content-length header detailing the size of the request, measured in bytes.
`ContentType`	The value of the content-type header detailing the media type of the request.
`Cookies`	Provides access to the cookies collection.
`Form`	Represents submitted form data. You won't work with this directly. You are more likely to use model binding to access this data (see chapter 5).
`Headers`	Provides access to all request headers.
`IsHttps`	Indicates whether the current request was made over HTTPS.
`Method`	The HTTP verb used to make the request

Table 2.2 Primary `HttpRequest` properties *(continued)*

Property	Description
`Path`	The part of the URL after the domain and port
`Query`	Provides access to query string values as key-value pairs

The `Response` property is represented by the `HttpResponse` class. Table 2.3 details the main members of this class and their purpose.

Table 2.3 Primary `HttpResponse` members

Property	Description
`ContentLength`	The size of the response in bytes, which is assigned to the content-length header.
`ContentType`	The media type of the response, which is assigned to the content-type header.
`Cookies`	The cookie collection of the outgoing response.
`HasStarted`	Indicates whether the response headers have been sent to the client. If they have, you should not attempt to alter the response. If you do, the values provided in the content-length and content-type headers may no longer be valid, leading to unpredictable results at the client.
`Headers`	Provides access to the response headers.
`StatusCode`	The HTTP status code for the response (e.g., 200, 302, 404, etc.).
`WriteAsync`	An extension method that writes text to the response body, using UTF-8 encoding.
`Redirect`	Returns a temporary (302) or permanent (301) redirect response to the client, together with the location to redirect to.

The methods and properties detailed in the previous tables are useful when you are working directly with the request and response, which you will do when creating your own middleware, for example.

2.3.3 The application request pipeline

When the web server routes a request to your application, the application must decide how to handle it. A number of considerations need to be taken into account. Where should the request be directed or routed to? Should details of the request be logged? Should the application simply return the content of a file? Should it compress the response? What should happen if an exception is encountered while the request is being processed? Is the person making the request actually allowed to access the resource they have requested? How should cookies or other request-related data be handled?

This decision-making process is known as the *request pipeline*. In an ASP.NET Core application, the request pipeline comprises a series of software components, each with its own individual responsibility. Some of these components act on the request on its way into the application, and others operate on the response returned by the application. Some might do both. The individual components that perform these functions are known as *middleware.*

Figure 2.12 illustrates this concept, showing a request coming in from the web server and then being passed through a pipeline of several middleware components before reaching the actual application itself, labeled *Razor Pages.*

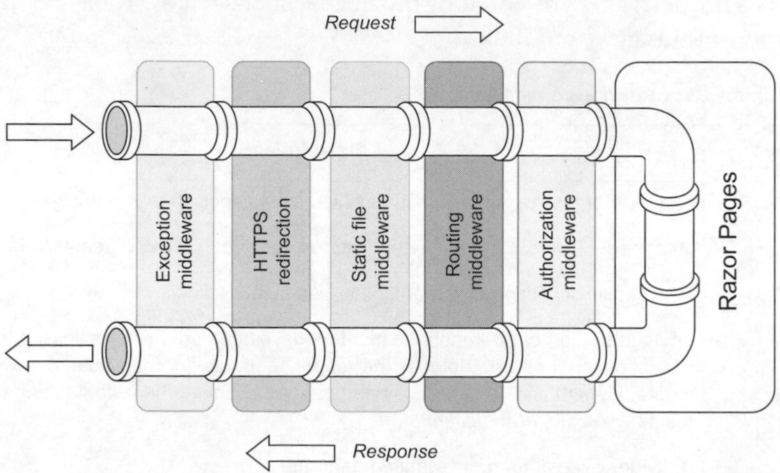

Figure 2.12 The request comes into the pipeline at the top and flows through all middlewares until it reaches Razor Pages, where it is processed and returned as a response.

This is how a request for the home page of your sample application might flow. Each middleware examines the request and determines whether it needs to do anything before passing the request on to the next middleware in the pipeline. Once the request has reached Razor Pages and has been processed, the response flows back to the server as the pipeline continues in the opposite direction. The pipeline itself begins and ends at the web server. In figure 2.13, the static file middleware makes a decision and either passes control on to the next middleware or short-circuits the process and returns a response.

The static file middleware inspects every request that reaches it to determine whether the request is for a *known file*—that is, one that resides in the wwwroot folder. If it is, the static file middleware simply returns the file, thereby short-circuiting the rest of the pipeline. Otherwise, the request is passed on to the next middleware in the pipeline.

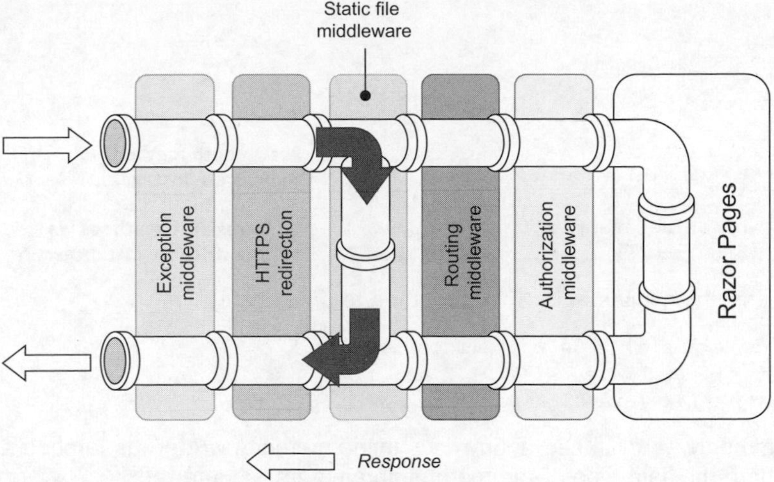

Figure 2.13 The middleware processes the request and returns the response when the request is for a known file.

2.3.4 Creating middleware

Now that you have a better understanding of the role middleware plays, you should understand how it is implemented, so you can provide your own custom functionality to the request pipeline. This section will cover creating your own middleware components and registering them with the pipeline.

Middleware components are implemented as `RequestDelegates`—that is, a .NET delegate that takes an `HttpContext` as a parameter and returns a `Task`, or, in other words, a method that represents an asynchronous operation on the `HttpContext`:

```
public delegate Task RequestDelegate(HttpContext context)
```

Delegates 101: a quick refresher

Delegates in .NET are types that represent a method signature and return type. The following example declares a delegate named `MyDelegate` that takes a `DateTime` as a parameter and returns an integer:

```
delegate int MyDelegate(DateTime dt);
```

Any method that has the same signature and return type can be assigned to an instance of `MyDelegate` and invoked, including both of the methods shown next.

Assigning methods to delegates based on matching signatures and returning types

```
int GetMonth(DateTime dt)
{
 return dt.Month;
}
int PointlessAddition(DateTime dt)
```

Both methods take a DateTime parameter and return an integer.

(continued)

```
{
    return dt.Year + dt.Month + dt.Day;
}

MyDelegate example1 = GetMonth;                    // Assign both methods
MyDelegate example2 = PointlessAddition;           // to delegate instances.
Console.WriteLine(example1(DateTime.Now));         // Invoke the methods via
Console.WriteLine(example2(DateTime.Now));         // the delegate instances.
```

You can assign an inline anonymous method to a delegate:

```
MyDelegate example3 = delegate(DateTime dt) {
➥ return dt.Now.AddYears(-100).Year; };
Console.WriteLine(example3(DateTime.Now));
```

More commonly, you will see anonymous inline methods written as lambda expressions, where the data type of the method parameters are inferred:

```
MyDelegate example4 = (dt) => { return dt.Now.AddYears(-100).Year; };
Console.WriteLine(example4(DateTime.Now));
```

So any method that takes an `HttpContext` as a parameter and returns a task can be used as middleware.

As you saw earlier, middleware is added to the pipeline via the `WebApplication`. Typically, middleware is created as separate classes that are registered via extension methods, but it is also possible to add `RequestDelegates` directly to the pipeline. Listing 2.8 shows a simple method that takes an `HttpContext` as a parameter and returns a `Task`, which means it meets the `RequestDelegate` type specification. You can add the method to Program.cs if you want to try this example out. You will also need to add a `using` directive to the `Startup` class to bring `Microsoft.AspNetCore.Http` into scope.

Listing 2.8 `RequestDelegate` takes `HttpContext` as parameter and returns `Task`

```
async Task TerminalMiddleware(HttpContext context)
{
    await context.Response.WriteAsync("That's all, folks!");
}
```

This particular middleware writes a message to the response. Control is not passed on to any other middleware components, so this type of middleware is known as *terminal middleware*. It terminates further processing within the pipeline. Terminal middleware is registered via the `WebApplication` object's `Run` method:

```
app.Run(TerminalMiddleware);
```

The `RequestDelegate` is a standard .NET delegate, so it can also be written inline as an anonymous function using a lambda expression, rather than as a named method.

Listing 2.9 Delegating bodies specified inline using a lambda expression

```
app.Run(async context =>
    await context.Response.WriteAsync("That's all, folks!")
);
```

Try registering this middleware using either approach by placing the app.Run call at the beginning of the pipeline—before the condition that checks to see if the current environment is `Development`.

Listing 2.10 Adding the middleware to the start of the pipeline

```
app.Run(async context =>
    await context.Response.WriteAsync("That's all, folks!")
);
if (app.Environment.IsDevelopment())
{
    ...
```

Then run the application. You should see the output shown in figure 2.14.

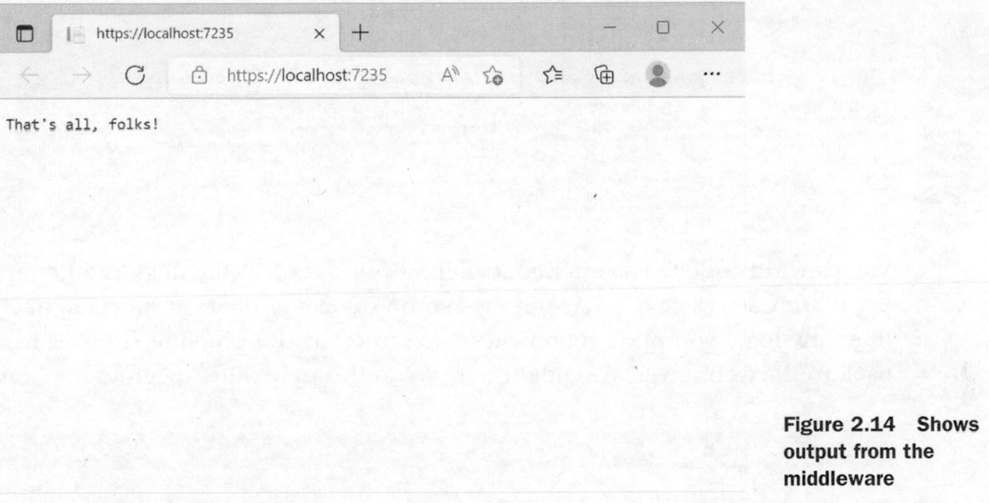

Figure 2.14 Shows output from the middleware

The next listing illustrates a middleware that conditionally passes processing on to the next middleware in the pipeline.

Listing 2.11 Middleware that conditionally passes control to the next middleware

```
async Task PassThroughMiddleware(HttpContext context, Func<Task> next)
{
    if (context.Request.Query.ContainsKey("stop"))
    {
        await context.Response.WriteAsync("Stop the world");
    }
```

```
    else
    {
        await next();
    }
}
```

This example takes the `HttpContext` as a parameter, but it also takes a `Func` that returns a `Task`, representing the next middleware in the pipeline. If the request includes a query string parameter named `stop`, the middleware short-circuits the pipeline and writes `Stop the world!` to the response. No other middleware is invoked. Otherwise, it invokes the `Func<Task>` that was passed in, passing control on to the next middleware. Middleware that passes control to the next component in the pipeline is registered with the `Use` method:

```
app.Use(PassThroughMiddleware);
```

Once again, this middleware can be written as an inline lambda.

Listing 2.12 Registering middleware inline with the `Use` method

```
app.Use(async (context, next) =>
{
    if (context.Request.Query.ContainsKey("stop"))
    {
        await context.Response.WriteAsync("Stop the world");
    }
    await next();
});
```

You can add code to run after control has been passed to the next middleware by placing it after `await next()`. Assuming that no other middleware short-circuits the pipeline, any logic you place there will be executed as the pipeline reverses its direction back to the web server. You might want to do this to include logging, for example.

Listing 2.13 Performing a function after other middleware has been invoked

```
app.Use(async (context, next) =>
{
    if (context.Request.Query.ContainsKey("stop"))
    {
        await context.Response.WriteAsync("Stop the world");
    }
    else
    {
        await next();
        logger.LogInformation("The world keeps turning");
    }
});
```

When registering middleware, the position is critical. If you were to place this middleware at the beginning of the pipeline, it would execute for every request and log the information message, unless the specified query string item is found. Suppose you were to register this middleware after the static files middleware. In that case, it would only execute and log requests for resources that are not static files, given that the static files middleware short-circuits the pipeline when returning a static file.

2.3.5 Middleware classes

All of the example middleware you have seen so far has been added as inline lambdas. This approach works for the simple middleware you have seen so far but falls short pretty quickly if your middleware involves any level of complexity, with both reusability and testability being adversely affected. At that point, you are likely to write your middleware in its own class.

There are two ways to implement middleware classes. The first option is to use a convention-based approach that has been part of ASP.NET Core since its beginning. The second option involves implementing the `IMiddleware` interface, which was introduced to ASP.NET Core 2.0 at the same time as Razor Pages.

The convention-based approach

Conventions are rules that must be applied to the design of certain components that are intended to work with a framework, so they behave in the expected manner. It might be that a class must be named in a particular way, so the framework can recognize it for what it is intended to be. This is the case, for example, with controller classes in MVC, which must have names that include `Controller` as the suffix. Or a convention might apply that specifies that a class designed for a specific use case must include a method that is named in a certain way and bears a predefined signature.

The two conventions that must be applied to a convention-based middleware class are (1) declaring a constructor that takes a `RequestDelegate` as a parameter representing the next middleware in the pipeline and (2) a method named `Invoke` or `InvokeAsync` that returns a `Task` and has at least one parameter—the first being an `HttpContext`.

To try this out, add a new class named `IpAddressMiddleware` to the application. The following example is added directly to the root of the project for simplicity. Replace the code with the next listing, which illustrates a middleware class that implements these conventions and logs the value of the visitor's IP address.

Listing 2.14 Middleware class based on the convention-based approach

```
namespace WebApplication1
{
    public class IpAddressMiddleware
    {
        private readonly RequestDelegate _next;
        public IpAddressMiddleware(RequestDelegate next) => _next =
next;
```

The constructor takes a RequestDelegate as a parameter.

```
public async Task InvokeAsync(HttpContext context,
➥ ILogger<IpAddressMiddleware> logger)
{
    var ipAddress = context.Connection.RemoteIpAddress;
    logger.LogInformation($"Visitor is from {ipAddress}");
    await _next(context);
}
    }
}
```

Performs the processing within the InvokeAsync method

The InvokeAsync method returns a task and has an HttpContext as a first parameter. Any additional services are injected into the Invoke/InvokeAsync method.

Passes control to the next middleware in the pipeline

Next, add a using directive to the top of the Program.cs file to bring the `WebApplication1` namespace into scope:

```
using WebApplication1;
var builder = WebApplication.CreateBuilder(args);
```

The middleware class is added to the pipeline via the `UseMiddleware` method on the `WebApplication`. There are two versions of this method. The first takes a type as a parameter:

```
app.UseMiddleware(typeof(IpAddressMiddleware));
```

The second version takes a generic parameter, representing the middleware class. This version is the one you are more likely to encounter:

```
app.UseMiddleware<IpAddressMiddleware>();
```

Alternatively, it is recommended that you create your own extension method on `IApplicationBuilder` to register your middleware. This example, shown in the following listing, is placed in a class named `Extensions`, which has also been added to the root of the project.

Listing 2.15 Registering middleware with an extension method

```
namespace WebApplication1
{
    public static class Extensions
    {
        public static IApplicationBuilder UseIpAddressMiddleware(this
        IApplicationBuilder app)
        {
            return app.UseMiddleware<IpAddressMiddleware>();
        }
    }
}
```

Then the extension method is used in the same way as all the other extension methods you have encountered for registering framework middleware:

```
app.UseIpAddressMiddleware();
```

In this case, you will probably want to register this middleware after the static files middleware, so it doesn't log the IP address for the same visitor for every requested file.

Middleware that follows the convention-based approach is created as a *singleton* when the application first starts up, which means there is only one instance created for the lifetime of the application. This instance is reused for every request that reaches it.

IMPLEMENTING MIDDLEWARE

The recommended approach to writing new middleware classes involves implementing the `IMiddleware` interface, which exposes one method:

```
Task InvokeAsync(HttpContext context, RequestDelegate next)
```

The next listing shows the same `IpAddressMiddleware` you created using the convention-based approach, refactored to implement `IMiddleware`.

Listing 2.16 Refactoring `IpAddressMiddleware` to implement `IMiddleware`

```
public class IpAddressMiddleware : IMiddleware     // The middleware class implements the IMiddleware interface.
{
    private ILogger<IpAddressMiddleware> _logger;
    public IpAddressMiddleware(ILogger<IpAddressMiddleware> logger)
        => _logger = logger;     // Dependencies are injected into the constructor.

   public async Task InvokeAsync(HttpContext context, RequestDelegate next)     // InvokeAsync takes an HttpContext and a RequestDelegate as parameters.
    {
        var ipAddress = context.Connection.RemoteIpAddress;
        _logger.LogInformation($"Visitor is from {ipAddress}");
        await next(context);
    }
}
```

The `InvokeAsync` is very similar to the one that was written using the conventions-based approach, except that this time the parameters are an `HttpContext` and a `RequestDelegate`. Any services the class depends on are injected via the middleware class's constructor, so fields are required to hold instances of the injected service.

This middleware is registered in exactly the same way as the convention-based example: via the `UseMiddleware` methods or an extension method. But an additional step is also required for `IMiddleware`-based components: they must also be registered with the application's service container. You will learn much more about services and dependency injection in chapter 7, but for the time being, it is enough to know that you need to add the bold line of code in the next listing to the `Program` class.

Listing 2.17 Registering `IMiddleware` as a service

```
builder.Services.AddRazorPages();
builder.Services.AddScoped<IpAddressMiddleware>();
```

So why are there two different ways to create middleware classes, and which one should you use? Well, the conventions-based approach requires that you learn the specific conventions and remember them. There is no compile-time checking to ensure your middleware implements the conventions correctly. This approach is known as *weakly typed*. Typically, the first time you discover that you forgot to name your method `Invoke` or `InvokeAsync` or that the first parameter should be an `HttpContext` will be when you try to run the application, and it falls over. If you are anything like me, you will often find that you have to refer back to the documentation to remind yourself of the convention details.

The second approach results in strongly typed middleware because you have to implement the members of the `IMiddleware` interface; otherwise, the compiler complains, and your application won't even build. So the `IMiddleware` approach is less error prone and potentially quicker to implement, although you do have to take the extra step of registering the middleware with the service container.

There is another difference between the two approaches. I mentioned earlier that convention-based middleware is instantiated as a singleton when the pipeline is first built. `IMiddleware` components are instantiated for each request by a component that implements the `IMiddlewareFactory` interface, and this difference has ramifications for services the middleware depends on, based on their lifetime. I explain service lifetimes in greater detail in chapter 7. For now, understand that services with a lifetime other than a singleton should not be injected into the constructor of a singleton. That means nonsingleton services should not be injected into the constructor of convention-based middleware. However, they can be injected into the constructor of `IMiddleware` components. Note that it is possible to inject nonsingleton services safely into the `Invoke`/`InvokeAsync` method of convention-based middleware.

I should note that the majority of framework middleware is authored using the convention-based approach. This is mainly because most of it was written before `IMiddleware` was introduced. While there is no indication that the framework designers feel any need to migrate existing components to `IMiddleware`, they recommend that you should favor `IMiddleware` for any middleware you create yourself.

We have looked in detail at how middleware is used to construct the request pipeline but haven't gone into any real detail on the middleware that has been added to the default project template. This will be covered in greater depth in forthcoming chapters. Specifically, we will look at how routing and endpoint middleware combine in chapter 4, how authorization works in chapter 10, and how to manage custom error pages in chapter 12.

Summary

- The starting point of your Razor Pages application is based on a template.
- Razor Pages applications are created as projects.
- Solutions are containers for managing projects.
- Razor syntax can be used to add dynamic content to pages.
- Razor syntax enables embedding C# code into HTML.
- Razor runtime compilation makes changes to Razor files visible by refreshing the browser.
- Layout pages act as master templates for the whole site.
- Razor Pages applications are console applications with a `Main` method as an entry point. The `Main` method is hidden from view as part of the top-level statements feature in C# 10.
- The `WebApplicationBuilder` is used to configure the application's services and request pipeline.
- The request pipeline determines the behavior of the application.
- The request pipeline is composed of middleware components.
- Middleware is implemented as a `RequestDelegate`—a function that takes an `HttpContext` as a parameter and returns a `Task`.
- Middleware is added to the pipeline via the `WebApplication` object. Middleware can terminate the pipeline or pass control on to the next middleware.
- Middleware is invoked in the order it is registered.
- Simple middleware can be added using inline lambda expressions.
- Complex middleware can be created as a separate class and registered using extension methods on the `IApplicationBuilder` type.
- Middleware classes should use conventions or implement the `IMiddleware` interface.
- Convention-based middleware is instantiated as a singleton and should take dependencies via the `Invoke/InvokeAsync` method.
- `IMiddleware` is instantiated per request and can take dependencies via its constructor.

3 Working with Razor Pages

This chapter covers

- Generating HTML with Razor templates
- Learning the Razor syntax
- Working with layouts, partials, and tag helpers
- Understanding the `PageModel` as a controller and view model
- Working with handler methods and `IActionResult`

At this point, you should have a good understanding of the working parts of a Razor Pages application—how to create one, the role of the generated files, and how to configure the application's behavior through the request pipeline. Now you are ready to take a deep dive into working with the principal actor within a Razor Pages application: the Razor page itself.

As you work through the chapter, you will learn how to use Razor syntax to generate dynamic HTML and coordinate layouts and partial files to reduce your repetition of code and improve reuse. You have already had a brief introduction to layouts and partials, but to remind you, layouts act as a kind of master template for multiple pages, and partial files consist of snippets of UI that can be plugged into a host page or layout.

You will also learn about the `PageModel` class—a fundamental feature of Razor Pages that acts as both an MVC controller and a *view model*, or a container for data specific to a particular view or page. You will explore how to use the view model aspect of the `PageModel` to expose data to the Razor page in a strongly typed manner, which will improve your efficiency as a developer. Doing this will also enable you to work effectively with *tag helpers*, or components that enable server-side code to participate in the HTML generation process. You will learn about some of the different types of tag helpers available within ASP.NET Core and how to use them.

Finally, you will see how the `PageModel` object acts as a *page controller*, handling the request for a page and deciding which model and view to use. Handler methods play a significant role in the request processing, and you will learn the important conventions behind their use and the return types, or `IActionResults`, they commonly work with.

3.1 Working with Razor syntax

All web development frameworks need to be able to generate HTML dynamically. Almost exclusively, they rely on a design pattern called *Template View*. This pattern involves using markers or placeholders consisting of server-side code embedded in HTML that resolve to calls to process and render dynamic content.

Dynamic content can take many forms. Often it will take the form of data extracted from a data store, such as a database, but as you have seen, it can also simply be the result of some computation, such as the time of day. In addition to the content itself, you will need to embed server-side code to control the presentation of the content. For example, if the dynamic content is a collection, such as a list, you will need to iterate over it in code to display each item. Or you might need to only show the data under certain conditions, such as if the user has permission to see it. So in addition to enabling you to embed instances of data into a page, the templating syntax must also enable you to include statement blocks that control processing within the page.

Many frameworks, such as older versions of ASP.NET, PHP, Ruby on Rails, and Java Server Pages, use HTML-like tags as markers to let the template processor know where the transitions are between HTML and server-side code. Razor syntax uses the `@` symbol as a transition marker and has several simple rules. The first rule is that Razor syntax is only applicable to the contents of Razor files that have a .cshtml extension. That's an amalgam of *cs* for C Sharp and *html* for Hypertext Markup Language. Further rules are covered in the following sections, which examine specific scenarios in which Razor syntax is used, starting with how to add directives and code blocks to Razor pages.

3.1.1 Directives and code blocks

Let's start by taking another look at the code you used to calculate the part of the day in the previous chapter to see how Razor syntax is used to include server side C# code within the Razor page. The example in listing 3.1 demonstrates three facets of Razor syntax: how to include directives within the page, how to include standalone blocks of

C# code, and how to include the result of C# expressions or the value of variables in the rendered HTML.

Listing 3.1 Reviewing Razor syntax in the Welcome page

```
@page
@model WebApplication1.Pages.WelcomeModel
@{
    ViewData["Title"] = "Welcome!";

    var partOfDay = "morning";
    if(DateTime.Now.Hour > 12){
        partOfDay = "afternoon";
    }
    if(DateTime.Now.Hour > 18){
        partOfDay = "evening";
    }
}
<h1>Welcome</h1>
<p>It is @partOfDay on @DateTime.Now.ToString("dddd, dd MMMM")</p>
```

Directives

A C# code block

C# inline expressions rendered as part of the output

The first instance of the `@` symbol in this example demonstrates how directives are added to a page. *Directives* are C# expressions that start with the `@` symbol followed by a reserved word (e.g., *page* or *model*) and enable functionality within the page or change how the content is parsed. Several directives are supported. The `page` directive denotes this file as representing a navigable page, and it must appear on the top line of the CSHTML file if it represents a page that is intended to be browsed. The `model` directive specifies the data type that acts as a model for this page, which, by default, is the `PageModel` class that accompanies the page. The `PageModel` is the focus of attention later in this chapter.

The next most commonly used directive is likely to be the `using` directive, which brings namespaces into scope, so their types can be referenced without using their fully qualified names. The next listing illustrates the `using static` directive being used to simplify working with the static `Path` class in `System.IO`, which would otherwise conflict with the `Path` property of the Razor page.

Listing 3.2 Adding a using directive with Razor syntax

```
@page
@model WebApplication1.Pages.WelcomeModel
@using static System.IO.Path
@{
    var extension = GetExtension("somefile.ext");
}
```

A using static directive makes the static Path class available without having to specify the class name. Notice there is no semicolon at the end of the using directive as there would be in a C# code file. The semicolon is optional in Razor files.

The static Path.GetExtension method is called without needing to include the class name.

Razor pages support many directives. Some are page-specific, such as the `page` and `model` directives, but others, including the `using` directive, can be applied to multiple pages by including them in a ViewImports file.

The *ViewImports* file, a special kind of file named _ViewImports.cshtml, provides a mechanism for centralizing directives that apply to CSHTML files, so you don't have to add them to Razor pages individually like you did with `System.IO.Path` in the preceding example. The default ViewImports file includes three directives:

- A `using` directive that references the project namespace (WebApplication1, in our example)
- A `namespace` directive that sets the namespace for all pages affected by the ViewImports (WebApplication1.Pages)
- An `addTagHelper` directive for managing tag helpers

Tag helpers are components that work with tags in markup to automate HTML generation. They are covered in more detail later in the chapter.

The directives in a ViewImports file affect all .cshtml files located in the same folder and its subfolders. There is no limit to the number of ViewImports files a Razor Pages application can support. You can place additional ViewImports files in subfolders to either add to the top-level ViewImports file's directives or override its settings. Certain directives, such as those for managing tag helpers, the `using` directive, and the `inject` directive (used for making services—covered in chapter 7—available to the page), are additive, while the other directives override each other the closer you get to the page. So, for example, the namespace specified in the ViewImports in the Pages folder will be overridden for pages in a subfolder if a different value is assigned to the `namespace` directive in a ViewImports file in that subfolder.

The second highlighted item in listing 3.1 is a code block. *Code blocks* begin with the `@` symbol, followed by an opening curly brace, then a closing curly brace:

```
@{
    … C# code goes here
}
```

Anything placed within the code block is pure C# code and must follow the rules of C# syntax. You can include multiple code blocks within a Razor page, but you should aim to keep them to the bare minimum, restricting them only to logic for managing presentation. Having too many code blocks in a Razor page is often a sign that you might have application logic within your UI, which you should avoid because it is very difficult to test when it is mixed in the HTML. For example, the logic for calculating the time of day should not be in the Razor page. It should be in the `PageModel` class, which can be tested in isolation, or if the algorithm is likely to be used in multiple places, it should be placed in its own class. You will move the algorithm to the `PageModel` class later in the chapter.

Razor also supports another type of code block: a functions block. A *functions block* is created by adding a `functions` directive followed by opening and closing curly braces:

```
@functions{
    … C# code goes here
}
```

Again, the code within the functions block is pure C#. You can refactor the algorithm that calculates the part of the day to the functions block as a method as follows.

Listing 3.3 Declaring a method in a functions block

```
@functions{
    string GetPartOfDay(DateTime dt)
    {
        var partOfDay = "morning";
        if (dt.Hour > 12)
        {
            partOfDay = "afternoon";
        }
        if (dt.Hour > 18)
        {
            partOfDay = "evening";
        }
        return partOfDay;
    }
}
<p>It is @GetPartOfDay(DateTime.Now)</p>
```

You could also add this method to a standard code block. The difference between a standard code block and a functions block is that the functions block supports the declaration of public members, whereas they are not supported within a standard code block. However, it is generally advisable to minimize the use of functions blocks for the same reason that you should minimize code blocks altogether. They encourage mixing application code with HTML, making it difficult to reuse, isolate, and test.

An appropriate use of a functions block in a Razor page file would include small routines that manage presentation logic and only apply to the page in which they are placed. They are also useful for your current purpose, which is to simplify the learning of Razor syntax without having to switch between files.

3.1.2 Rendering HTML with expressions

The main purpose of Razor is to render dynamic content as HTML. You have already seen how the value of variables or expressions can be rendered to the browser by placing them inline within the HTML where the value is to be output and prefixing them with the `@` symbol:

```
<p>It is @partOfDay on @DateTime.Now.ToString("dddd, dd MMMM")</p>
```

Expressions like this example are known as *implicit expressions.* Another type of expression you will often use within a Razor file is an *explicit expression,* where the expression itself is placed within parentheses and prefixed with the `@` symbol. You typically use explicit expressions where there is a space in the expression or where the expression includes angle brackets (i.e., < and >), such as in a generic method. If you don't place such an expression within parentheses, the angle brackets will be seen as HTML. Here's an example of an expression that involves the use of the ternary operator. The expression has spaces within it, so it must be included within the Razor file as an explicit expression:

```
<p>It is @(DateTime.Now.Hour > 12 ? "PM" : "AM")</p>
```

This example will render either `"PM"` or `"AM"` to the browser, depending on the time of day that the expression is executed.

3.1.3 Control blocks in Razor

Server-side code is mainly used in Razor files to control presentational output. Consequently, most of the Razor syntax you use will consist of *control blocks*—selection and iteration statements such as `if-else`, `foreach`, and so on in a page that apply processing logic to conditionally render output or loop through collections of items, for example. These control blocks differ from the code blocks you saw earlier in that they are embedded within the HTML content to be rendered rather than being isolated from the markup within braces.

C# selection and iteration statements are supported within Razor by prefixing the keyword that opens the block with the `@` symbol. The following listing demonstrates how this applies to an `if-else` statement.

Listing 3.4 Selection statement support in Razor

```
@if(DateTime.Now.Hour <= 12)
{
    <p>It is morning</p>
}
else if (DateTime.Now.Hour <= 18)
{
    <p>It is afternoon</p>
}
else
{
    <p>It is evening</p>
}
```

The `if-else` statement works in this example by only rendering one of the paragraphs based on the condition being tested—in this case, the time of day when the page is executed. Note that there is no need for `@` symbols prior to the `else` keywords. In fact, it will cause an error if you attempt to do so.

Listing 3.5 illustrates the use of a `switch` statement as an alternative to the `if-else` block in listing 3.4. Once again, the `@` symbol is only required before the opening `switch` keyword.

Listing 3.5 Switch statement example in Razor

```
@switch (DateTime.Now.Hour)
{
    case int _ when DateTime.Now.Hour <= 12:
        <p>It is morning</p>
        break;
    case int _ when DateTime.Now.Hour <= 18:
        <p>It is afternoon</p>
        break;
    default:
        <p>It is evening</p>
        break;
}
```

You will often find yourself needing to use iteration statements in Razor pages as you iterate collections for rendering. Let's imagine you are creating a vacation package website, and you need to render a list of possible destinations. The code in the following listing demonstrates the use of the `foreach` statement to render the members of an array of city names as an unordered list.

Listing 3.6 `foreach` statement example in Razor

```
@functions{
    public class City
    {
        public string Name { get; set; }
        public string Country { get; set; }
    }
    List<City> cities = new List<City>{
        new City { Name = "London", Country = "UK" },
        new City { Name = "Paris", Country = "France" },
        new City { Name = "Rome", Country = "Italy" } ,
        new City { Name = "Berlin", Country = "Germany" },
        new City { Name = "Washington DC", Country = "USA" }
    };
}

<ul>
    @foreach (var city in cities)
    {
        <li>@city.Name</li>
    }
</ul>
```

3.1.4 Rendering literal strings

All of the examples so far show Razor transitioning between HTML and C# code. Anything after an @ symbol is considered C# code, until an HTML tag is encountered. Sometimes you might need to render literal strings instead of HTML. There are two ways to tell Razor that a value is a literal string and not C# code. The first way is to prefix the first instance of a literal string on each line with `@:`.

Listing 3.7 Rendering literal strings in Razor

```
@foreach (var city in cities)
{
    if (city.Country == "UK")
    {
        @:Country:  @city.Country, Name: @city.Name
    }
}
```

Alternatively, you can use the `<text>` tag to surround the content. This works particularly well if you are working with multiline content, as shown in the following listing.

Listing 3.8 Using the text tag to render multiline literal strings

```
@foreach (var city in cities)
{
    if (city.Country == "UK")
    {
        <text>Country:  @city.Country<br />
        Name: @city.Name</text>
    }
}
```

The text tags are not rendered as part of the output; only their content is rendered. In addition, using text tags results in whitespace being removed from the output that appears before or after them.

3.1.5 Rendering literal HTML

The default behavior of Razor is to render any markup within the Razor page literally but to apply HTML encoding to the result of all expressions that resolve to strings. Any non-ASCII characters, as well as potentially *unsafe* characters (those that could facilitate the injection of malicious scripts into a web page), such as <, >, &, and ", are encoded to their HTML equivalents: `<`, `>`, `&`, `"`, and so on. The following listing shows some HTML being assigned to a variable that is rendered to the browser.

Listing 3.9 HTML assigned to the output variable that is rendered

```
@{
    var output = "<p>This is a paragraph.</p>";
}
@output
```

The resulting HTML that gets generated is

```
&lt;p&gt;This is a paragraph.&lt;/p&gt;
```

Figure 3.1 demonstrates how this appears in the browser.

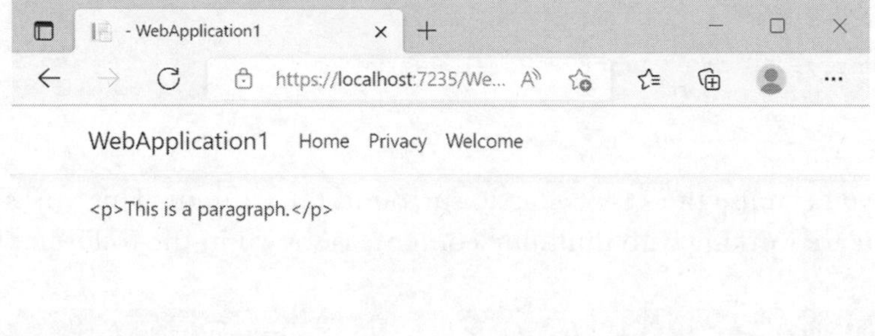

Figure 3.1 Non-ASCII and special HTML characters are encoded for output by default.

If you have an HTML string and do not want Razor to encode it, you can use the `Html.Raw` method to prevent encoding:

```
@Html.Raw("<p>This is a paragraph.</p>")
```

This is useful for scenarios in which, for example, you are storing HTML in a database for display—a typical requirement for most content management systems and the like. However, you should ensure that the HTML is sanitized prior to including it in your page. Otherwise, you could open your site up to script injection attacks. You will learn about these and other vulnerabilities in chapter 13.

The aggressive level of encoding that is applied by default may not be desirable for developers of sites that store and output content in languages that make heavy or exclusive use of non-ASCII characters. Take this snippet of German as an example (it translates to "Charges for oversized luggage"):

```
var output = "Gebühren für übergroßes Gepäck";
```

This is encoded to the following when it is embedded in the markup as `@output`:

```
Geb&#xFC;hren f&#xFC;r &#xFC;bergro&#xDF;es Gep&#xE4;ck
```

For non-Latin based languages, such as Cyrillic, Chinese, and Arabic, every character is encoded to its HTML equivalent, potentially increasing the number of characters in the generated source code significantly. While the output renders correctly, the page's resulting size and overall site performance can be affected adversely.

It is possible to arrange for a broader range of characters, so they are not encoded. You can do this in Program.cs by setting the `WebEncoderOptions`. By default, the allowed range of characters (i.e., those not encoded) is restricted to the Basic Latin character set. Listing 3.10 demonstrates how to configure the options to add the Latin-1 Supplement character set to the allowed ranges, which includes accented vowels and the German eszett character (ß).

Listing 3.10 Configuring the `WebEncoderOptions` to add the Latin-1 Supplement

```
builder.Services.Configure<WebEncoderOptions>(options =>
{
    options.TextEncoderSettings = new
     TextEncoderSettings(UnicodeRanges.BasicLatin,
     UnicodeRanges.Latin1Supplement);
});
```

Note that whatever you set here will override the default settings, which is why you need to include the `BasicLatin` range. If you are unsure which character sets you should include, you can check here: http://www.unicode.org/charts/. Alternatively, you can simply specify `UnicodeRanges.All`.

TEMPLATED RAZOR DELEGATES

The *templated Razor delegate* feature enables you to use a delegate to create Razor templates and assign them to a variable for reuse. You may remember from our discussion on middleware in the previous chapter that a delegate is a type that represents a method signature and a return type. Razor template delegates are expressed as a `Func<dynamic, object>` (a generic delegate). The body of the method contains a snippet of Razor, with the opening HTML tag prefixed with an `@` symbol. The input parameter represents data and is a `dynamic` type, so it can represent anything. The data is accessible within the template through a parameter named `item`.

In listing 3.6, we created a list of cities and then rendered it to the browser using a `foreach` statement embedded in HTML to render an unordered list. In listing 3.11, we will extract the rendering of the unordered list into a template, which forms the body of the delegate.

The `myUnorderedListTemplate` variable is defined as a `Func<dynamic, object>`, matching the definition of a templated Razor delegate. Within it, the `item` parameter is assumed to represent a collection of cities. These are iterated over and rendered as an unordered list. The following listing shows how to assign the generation of the list to a Razor template delegate.

Listing 3.11 Defining a templated Razor delegate

```
@{
    Func<dynamic, object> myUnorderedListTemplate = @<ul>
        @foreach (var city in item)
        {
            <li>@city.Name</li>
        }
    </ul>;
}
```

Once the template has been defined, you can pass the data generated in listing 3.6 into it:

```
@myUnorderedListTemplate(cities)
```

This example relies on a `dynamic` input parameter, leading to potential errors that only surface at run time if you misspelled the name of a property, for example, or tried to access members that don't exist. You can use strong typing to confine the types that your template accepts, as shown in the following listing, where the `dynamic` parameter has been replaced with a `List<City>`.

Listing 3.12 Narrowing the data item's type in a templated Razor delegate

```
@{
    Func<List<City>, object> myUnorderedListTemplate = @<ul>
        @foreach (var city in item)
        {
            <li>@city.Name</li>
        }
    </ul>;
}
```

One of the drawbacks of the templated Razor delegate is that it only accepts one argument representing the data item, although there is no restriction on the data type. It can represent a complex type, so if your template is designed to work with more than just a list of cities, you can create a wrapper type that includes everything your template needs.

There is an alternative that enables you to define a template that can take any number of parameters. To take advantage of this feature, create a method in a code or functions block that returns `void` (or `Task`, if async processing is required), and just include HTML markup in the body of the method.

Listing 3.13 Alternative way to declare a template within a Razor page

```
@{
    void MyUnorderedListTemplate(List<City> cities, string style)
    {
        <ul>
        @foreach(var city in cities)
        {
            <li class="@(city.Name == "London" ? style :
    null)">@city.Name</li>
        }
        </ul>
    }
}
@{ MyUnorderedListTemplate(cities, "active"); }
```

Markup is allowed in methods that return void or Task.

The opening tag is not prefixed with the @ symbol.

Since the method returns void or Task, it must be called within a code block.

Notice that, unlike the template delegate, the method can specify any number of parameters, and the leading HTML tag is not prefixed with the `@` symbol. This method takes two parameters—the second one representing the name of a CSS class that should be applied conditionally to the list items. If you wanted to be able to achieve something similar with a template delegate, you would need to create a new type that wrapped the `List<City>` and the `string`.

Whether you use this approach or the template delegate, these helpers are only intended for reuse within the same Razor page. If you want to reuse snippets of HTML in multiple pages, there are much more flexible alternatives, including partial pages, tag helpers, and view components. We will look at partial pages and tag helpers in more detail later in this chapter. View components are covered in chapter 14.

COMMENTS IN RAZOR

Razor page files support standard HTML comments within the markup area of the page and C# comments within code blocks. They also support Razor comments, which begin with `@*` and end with `*@`. Anything between Razor comments is not rendered to the browser, unlike the content within HTML comments. The code in listing 3.14 shows a C# `foreach` statement within HTML comments. When the page is rendered, the Razor code is processed, and the resulting list of items appears as a comment in the source code.

Listing 3.14 HTML comments resulting in the content being rendered

```
<!--<ul>
    @foreach(var city in cities)
    {
        <li>@city.Name</li>
    }
</ul>-->
```

The following listing features the same `foreach` statement within Razor comments. None of the contents are included in the source code.

Listing 3.15 Excluding content within Razor comments from source code

```
@*<ul>
    @foreach(var city in cities)
    {
        <li>@city.Name</li>
    }
</ul>*@
```

That completes your look at the Razor syntax, which demonstrates how to embed server-side code within HTML to form a template for a single page. In the following sections, you will find out how to use layout pages and partials to create code templates that are reused across multiple pages.

3.2 Layout pages

It is a rare website that doesn't share common content across multiple pages. Later in the book, you will build a web application that offers vacation packages. An outline sketch of this type of site might well look something like figure 3.2.

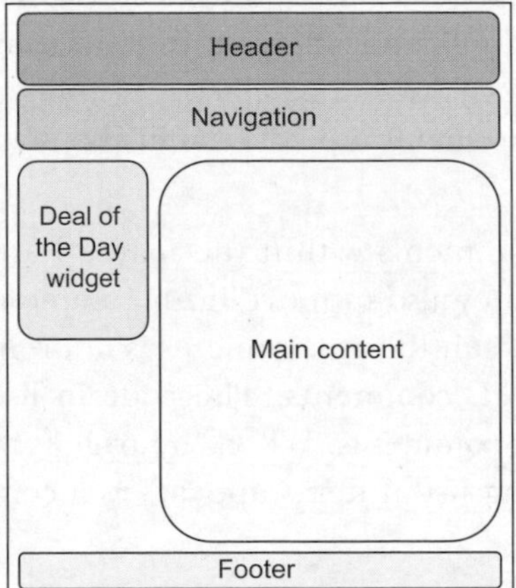

Figure 3.2 The header, navigation, Deal of the Day widget, and footer in this example are intended to appear on all pages. The main content area represents the content specific to each page.

In the sample sketch, the header, navigation, Deal of the Day widget, and footer are intended to appear on all pages in the site. The actual content of some of those elements might vary from page to page, but the basic structure will apply to all pages. The main content area represents the page-specific content, which might be a contact form and a postal address on a Contact Us page, or it might be details of breaks on offer in a specific location. The following listing shows how the image might be translated to HTML, using basic Bootstrap styles.

Listing 3.16 A basic outline of a web page containing content that will be repeated

```
<!DOCTYPE html>
<html>
<head>
    <title></title>
    <link rel="stylesheet" href="~/lib/bootstrap/dist/css/bootstrap.min.css"
    ➥ />
</head>
<body>
    <div class="container">
        <header class="card alert-success border-5 p-3 mt-3">Header</header>
        <nav class="card alert-primary border-5 p-3 mt-2">Navigation</nav>
        <div class="row mt-2">
            <div class="col-3">
                <div class="card alert-warning p-5 border-5">
                    Deal Of The Day Widget 1
                </div>
            </div>
            <div class="col-9 card border-5">
                Main Content
            </div>
        </div>
        <footer class="card border-5 p-3 mt-2">Footer</footer>
    </div>
</body>
</html>
```

If you created multiple pages that included this common content in each page separately, the burden of maintaining it would likely become intolerable. Every time you added a new page to the site, you would have to update the navigation in all the existing pages. Ideally, you want to centralize these pieces of repeating content in one location to be easy to maintain. This approach is known as *DRY* (don't repeat yourself). DRY is one of the essential principles in software development.

Layout pages enable a DRY approach to managing common page content. They act as a parent or master template for all content pages that reference it. You have already looked briefly at the layout page in the sample application when you added your new page to the site navigation. A layout is a regular Razor file with a .cshtml extension, but what makes it act as a layout is that it contains a call to the `RenderBody` method, where the page-specific content is rendered, as shown in the following listing.

Listing 3.17 A Razor layout page including a call to `RenderBody`

```
<!DOCTYPE html>
<html>
<head>
    <title></title>
    <link rel="stylesheet" href="~/lib/bootstrap/dist/css/bootstrap.min.css"
    ➥ />
</head>
<body>
    <div class="container">
```

```
        <header class="card alert-success border-5 p-3 mt-3">Header</header>
        <nav class="card alert-primary border-5 p-3 mt-2">Navigation</nav>
        <div class="row mt-2">
            <div class="col-3">
                <div class="card alert-warning p-5 border-5">
                    Deal Of The Day Widget 1
                </div>
            </div>
            <div class="col-9 card border-5">
                @RenderBody()
            </div>
        </div>
        <footer class="card border-5 p-3 mt-2">Footer</footer>
    </div>
</body>
</html>
```

This is the point at which the output from the content page is injected into the layout.

The RenderBody method call is the only requirement for a layout page. Everything else within the layout page is included in all content pages that reference it, which makes managing it very easy. Any changes you make to the layout are immediately applied to all pages that reference it.

3.2.1 Assigning the Layout property

The layout for a specific page is assigned programmatically via the page's Layout property. The value that you pass to the Layout property is a string, representing either the name of the layout file without its extension or the path to the layout file. Either of the approaches in the following listing will work.

Listing 3.18 Setting the layout page via the Layout property

```
@{
    Layout = "_Layout";
    Layout = "/Pages/Shared/_Layout.cshtml";
}
```

When you use the first approach to set the layout by name, the framework searches a number of predefined locations for a file with the matching name and a preconfigured extension, which is .cshtml by default. The folder containing the calling page is searched first, and if applicable, all folders in the hierarchy up to the root Pages folder will be searched. Finally, two further locations are searched: \Pages\Shared and \Views\Shared. The latter of these is a legacy of applications built using the MVC framework itself. If you placed the calling page in \Pages\Admin\DestinationsOrders, for example, the search locations will be as follows:

- \Pages\Admin\DestinationsOrders_Layout.cshtml
- \Pages\Admin_Layout.cshtml
- \Pages_Layout.cshtml
- \Pages\Shared_Layout.cshtml
- \Views\Shared_Layout.cshtml

Setting the layout on a page-by-page basis is not a very efficient approach if you want to assign the same layout to multiple pages for the same reason that you use a layout in the first place: updating it in multiple locations becomes a chore. To solve this problem, you can use a ViewStart file. This is a special Razor file named _ViewStart.cshtml, which you will find an example of located in the Pages folder. This file usually consists of a code block only, although it can contain markup too. The code within the ViewStart file is executed before any page that it affects, which is any Razor page in the same folder and all subfolders. Figure 3.3 shows the order of execution as a request comes in. First is the ViewStart file, then the content page, followed by any code in the layout file.

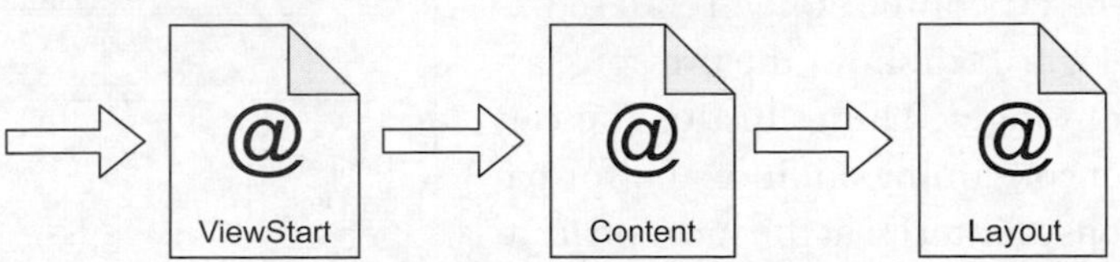

Figure 3.3 Order of execution of Razor files: ViewStart, followed by the content page, then the layout page

ViewStart is executed before any pages it affects, making it the ideal way to set the layout for all those pages. If you take a look at the contents of the existing ViewStart file, you will see that is exactly what it does:

```
@{
    Layout = "_Layout";
}
```

I mentioned that the ViewStart code is executed before the code in the page, enabling you to alter the global setting on a page-by-page basis if you need to. Any layout assignment that takes place in an individual page will override the ViewStart. Equally, if you place additional ViewStart files lower down the Pages folder hierarchy, layout assignments in those will override any assignments in ViewStart files higher up the hierarchy.

One final note about layouts: it is possible to nest layout files, so one layout references another. To achieve this, you need to explicitly assign a layout in a child layout. Figure 3.4 shows the relationship between a page, a nested (child) layout, and the main layout. The Index content is injected into the nested layout wherever `RenderBody` is placed. The merged content is injected into the layout file.

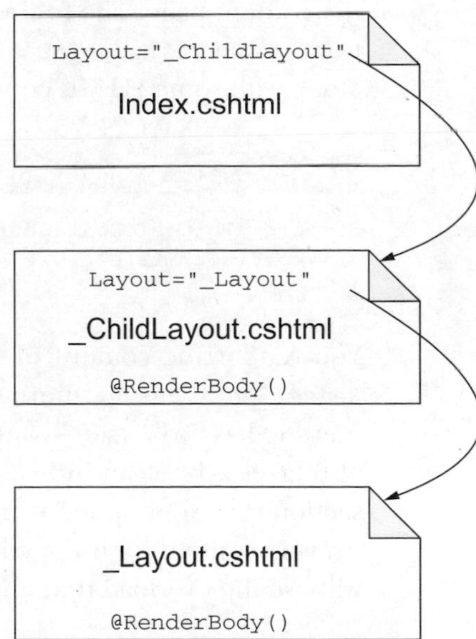

Figure 3.4 The Index page references the _ChildLayout file, which, in turn, references the main _Layout file.

You can't rely on the ViewStart file for setting the parent layout file in a child layout. The ViewStart file has no effect over layouts within its folder or subfolders. Nested layouts can enable some valuable scenarios in which you have additional content you want to display for a subset of pages, for example, which you would apply to the child layout.

3.2.2 *Injecting optional content with sections*

There will likely be occasions when you want some of your content pages to be able to optionally provide additional HTML-based content to be rendered as part of the layout. Figure 3.5 shows the previous layout with a different widget: Things to Do. You can imagine this widget containing additional information about attractions of interest at the vacation location you are currently viewing—for example, visiting the Eiffel Tower if you chose Paris as a destination. This widget is included in the layout area, which is common to all pages, but it will only appear when a destination has been selected, and its content will depend on the selected destination.

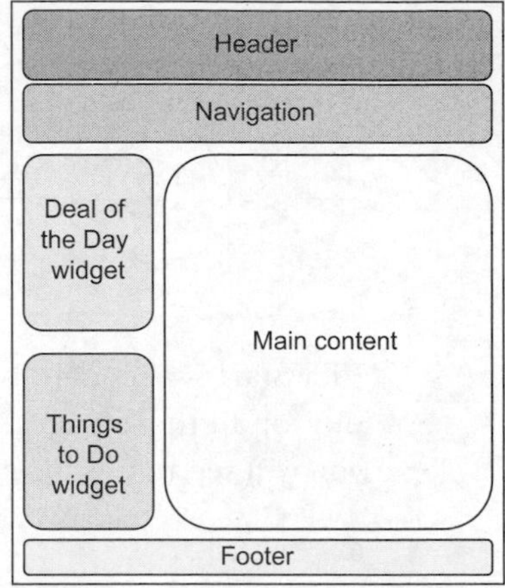

Figure 3.5 The Things to Do widget represents page-specific content that is positioned within the layout.

Razor includes sections that enable this scenario, defined using the `@section` directive within the content page. The following listing shows a section named `ThingsToDoWidget` being defined along with some HTML content.

Listing 3.19 Defining a Razor section with the `@section` directive

```
@section ThingsToDoWidget{
    <p>Visit Eiffel Tower</p>
}
```

You render the content of a section within the layout page by placing a call to the `RenderSectionAsync` method at the location you want the content to appear. The method has two versions: one that takes the section's name as a string and another that also takes a Boolean indicating whether all content pages are required to define the section (`true`) or optional (`false`). In the next example, only the destination page will provide content for the section, so it is optional for all other pages. Consequently, you will use the overload that enables you to pass `false` to the second parameter:

```
@await RenderSectionAsync("ThingsToDoWidget", false)
```

As it happens, there is already a call to the RenderSectionAsync method that refers to the scripts section in the default project layout file, located just before the closing body element:

```
    <script src="~/lib/jquery/dist/jquery.min.js"></script>
    <script src="~/lib/bootstrap/dist/js/bootstrap.bundle.min.js"></script>
    <script src="~/js/site.js" asp-append-version="true"></script>

    @await RenderSectionAsync("Scripts", required: false)
</body>
```

The purpose of this section is including page-specific JavaScript files within the layout, so they appear after global script files. That way page-specific files can make use of the content of the global files.

The IsSectionDefined method can be used in the layout page to determine whether the content page has defined a specific section. This method can be useful, for example, if you want to display some default content if the calling page doesn't define the section.

Listing 3.20 Using IsSectionDefined to determine if the calling page defined a section

```
<div class="card alert-danger p-5 border-5 mt-2">
@if (IsSectionDefined("ThingsToDoWidget"))
{
    @await RenderSectionAsync("ThingsToDoWidget")
}
else
{
    <p>Things To Do Widget default content</p>
}
</div>
```

If a content page defines a section, it must be handled within the layout page, usually with a call to RenderSectionAsync. However, you might have conditions when you don't want to render the content of a section. In those cases, you can use the IgnoreSection method to prevent rendering.

Listing 3.21 Using IgnoreSection to prevent the rendering of section content

```
@if(!IsAdmin)
{
    IgnoreSection("admin");
}
else
{
    @await RenderSectionAsync("admin")
}
```

Note that the `IgnoreSection` method returns `void`, so it is not prefixed with the `@` symbol and must be terminated with a semicolon.

3.3 Reusable HTML with partial views, tag helpers, and view components

Layouts are one way of achieving reusable HTML. You define the site layout in one place, and it is used by all pages referencing the layout. ASP.NET Core provides other Razor-based mechanisms for working with reusable HTML: partial views, tag helpers, and view components. In this section, I introduce all three features and explain how they are used.

3.3.1 Partial views

A partial view is a Razor (.cshtml) file that contains a chunk of HTML and, optionally, some Razor syntax. It differs from a standard Razor page in that a partial view does not include an `@page` directive because it is not intended to be browsed directly. Partial views can be used

- To break up a complex UI into more manageable pieces
- To avoid repetition of code
- To generate HTML for asynchronous partial page updates in AJAX scenarios

Strangely, there is no partial view template in Visual Studio. You can use any of the options that generate a single Razor file. I usually use the Razor View > Empty template and then remove the default content. VS Code users can just add a new file with a .cshtml suffix or use the CLI to generate a new ViewStart or ViewImports file, then change the filename and remove the default content:

```
dotnet new viewimports
dotnet new viewstart
```

Conventionally, partial views are named with a leading underscore in the filename—_myPartial.cshtml, for example. This convention is not required, but it might help differentiate partials from other files. You can place a partial view anywhere within the Pages folder. The discovery process for partials is the same as for layouts: the folder containing the current page and all parents followed by the Pages\Shared and Views\Shared folders.

The layout file in the application we built so far is very simple, but it could grow to become more complex. Separate sections of the UI are all candidates for partial views. Take the navigation, for example. The code for this area can be separated out into another file, which is then referenced from within the layout file.

To test out creating a partial view, you can cut the `nav` element from the example layout file in listing 3.16 and paste it into a new Razor file named _NavigationPartial.cshtml, which you should place in the Pages\Shared folder. Now that you have a hole in your layout, you need to reference the partial view. The recommended mechanism for including partial views is the partial tag helper. We will cover tag helpers in more detail shortly, but for now, it is enough to know that the following will render the contents of a partial view in a calling page:

```
<partial name="_NavigationPartial" />
```

The tag helper must be placed in the location you want to output from the partial view to be rendered. In the default template, it goes under the header element within the layout.

Listing 3.22 The partial tag helper used to include the content of a partial view

```
<body>
    <div class="container">
        <header class="card alert-success border-5 p-3 mt-3">Header</header>
        <partial name="_NavigationPartial" />
        <div class="row mt-2">
            <div class="col-3">
                <div class="card alert-warning p-5 border-5">
                    Deal Of The Day Widget 1
                </div>
```

Figure 3.6 provides an illustration of the process where the contents of the partial file (_NavigationPartial.cshtml) are inserted into the calling page at the point where the partial tag helper is placed. In this example, the navigation goes under the header, rather than inside it, as in the default project template (figure 3.6).

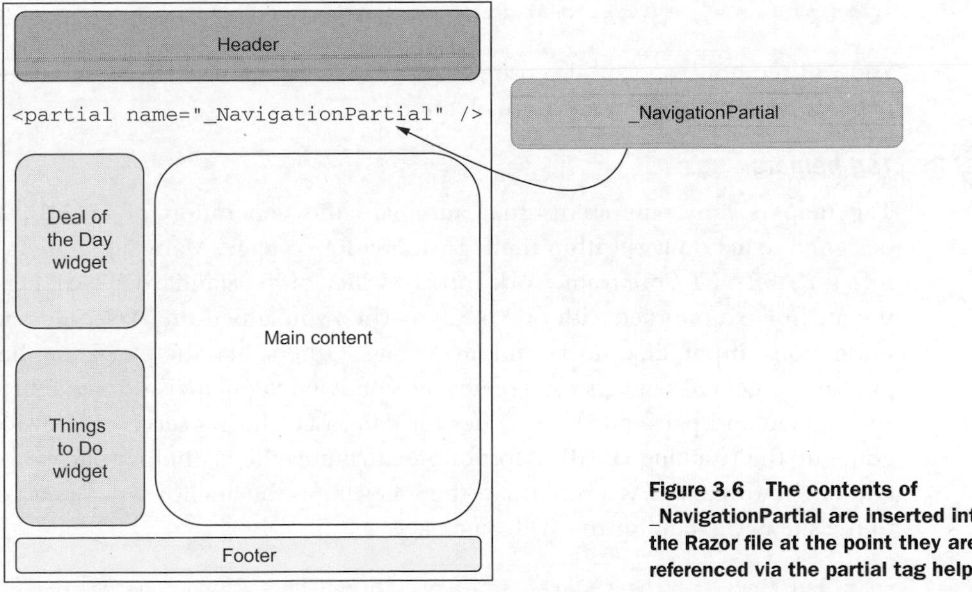

Figure 3.6 The contents of _NavigationPartial are inserted into the Razor file at the point they are referenced via the partial tag helper.

Partial views can also be used to avoid repetition of code. The standard project template includes a partial file in the Pages\Shared folder named _ValidationScriptsPartial.cshtml. It contains two script elements that reference scripts for validating form values. You will use this partial in chapter 5 when you look at form validation.

The partial in the example and the validation scripts partial consist of static content. Partials can also work with dynamic content. The nature of the dynamic content is specified using the `@model` directive at the top of the partial file. For example, imagine that the data for your navigation menu is generated by the parent page and consists of a `Dictionary<string, string>`, where the keys represent the name of the page to link to, and the values represent the text for the link, perhaps. This is how the first line of the _NavigationPartial.cshtml file will look:

```
@model Dictionary<string,string>
```

The data itself will be generated by the page that references the partial and included in its own model as a property. You will see how this is done a bit later when you explore the `PageModel`. For the time being, you can assume that the data for this partial is represented by a property of the host page named `Nav`. You will pass this data to the partial tag helper's `model` attribute:

```
<partial name="_NavigationPartial" model="Model.Nav" />
```

Alternatively, you can use the `for` attribute to specify the data for the partial. This time, the `Model` is implicit:

```
<partial name="_NavigationPartial" for="Nav" />
```

You will see how you can also use partial views to generate HTML for use in partial page updates in AJAX scenarios in chapter 11.

3.3.2 Tag helpers

Tag helpers are components that automate the generation of HTML. They are designed to act on tags within the HTML of a Razor page. Many tag helpers are built into the ASP.NET Core framework, most of which target standard HTML tags, such as the anchor (you worked with one of these when you added the Welcome page to the navigation), input, link, form, and image tags. Others, like the partial tag helper you just saw, target custom tags you create yourself. Each tag helper is designed to act on a specific tag and parse attribute values for data used during server-side processing to generate the resulting HTML. Most of the attributes the tag helper parses are custom and begin with `asp-`. As a reminder, the following is the anchor tag helper you added to the site navigation for the Welcome page:

```
<a class="nav-link text-dark" asp-area="" asp-page="/Welcome">Welcome</a>
```

The asp-area and asp-page attributes are custom attributes. Their role is to provide information to the anchor tag helper about the area and page the tag helper should use to generate a URL. You will look at areas in the next chapter, when you explore routing and URLs. When the anchor tag helper has finished processing and the tag is rendered as HTML, the generated URL will appear as a standard href attribute. The custom attributes are not rendered.

ENABLING TAG HELPERS

Tag helpers are an opt-in feature. They are not enabled by default; although, if you start with the standard project template, they are enabled globally within the _ViewImports .cshtml file located in the Pages folder by the following line of code:

```
@addTagHelper *, Microsoft.AspNetCore.Mvc.TagHelpers
```

The addTagHelper directive takes two arguments: the tag helpers to enable and the name of the assembly containing the tag helpers to enable. The wildcard character (*) specifies that all tag helpers in the specified assembly should be enabled. The framework tag helpers are located in Microsoft.AspNetCore.Mvc.TagHelpers, which is why you see the name of this assembly added by default. You can create your own custom tag helpers. This book won't cover that, but if your custom tag helper belonged to the WebApplication1 project, you would enable it as follows:

```
@addTagHelper *, WebApplication1
```

Guidance on building your own custom tag helper can be found in the official documentation (http://mng.bz/06jN) or Andrew Lock's *ASP.NET Core In Action, Second Edition* (Manning, 2021).

The addTagHelper directive has a twin, removeTagHelper, that enables you to selectively opt certain tags out of processing. The following line of code opts out of anchor tag helper processing:

```
@removeTagHelper "Microsoft.AspNetCore.Mvc.TagHelpers.AnchorTagHelper,
➥ Microsoft.AspNetCore.Mvc.TagHelpers"
```

You can opt individual tags out of processing by placing the ! prefix just prior to the tag name. For instance, you might want to do this if the specific element is only to be used by client-side code. Then there is no need to waste cycles having it processed on the server. The following example illustrates how that is applied to an anchor tag to prevent it from being processed unnecessarily:

```
<!a href="https://www.learnrazorpages.com">Learn Razor Pages</!a>
```

The prefix is placed in both the start and end tags. Any tag without the ! prefix will be processed by an associated tag helper. The alternative is to opt specific tags *into* processing at parse time. You achieve this by registering a custom prefix with the

`@tagHelperPrefix` directive and then applying your chosen prefix to tags you want to take part in the processing. You can register your prefix in the ViewImports file where you initially enabled tag helper processing:

```
@tagHelperPrefix x
```

You can use pretty much any string you like as a prefix. Then you apply it to both the start and end tags, just like the `!` prefix:

```
<xa asp-page="/Index">Home</xa>
```

Only those tags that feature the prefix will be processed. For the sake of clarity, most developers are likely to use punctuation to separate the prefix from the tag name—for example:

```
@tagHelperPrefix x:
<x:a asp-page="/Index">Home</x:a>
```

This should reduce any visual confusion, especially for designers when they look at the HTML content.

3.3.3 View components

View components are a more advanced solution for generating reusable HTML. They are similar to partial views in that they can be used to help break up and simplify complex layouts, or they can represent part of a UI that can be used in multiple pages. View components are recommended instead of partial pages whenever any type of server-side logic is required to obtain or process data for inclusion in the resulting HTML snippet (specifically, calls to an external resource, such as a file, database, or web service). Typical scenarios in which view components work well include database-driven menus, tag clouds, and shopping carts—widgets that usually appear in a layout page and rely on their own source of data. View components also lend themselves to unit testing.

Since view components rely on advanced concepts that have not been covered so far, further discussion on the topic will have to wait if it is to make any sense. But rest assured, you will build a view component in chapter 14.

3.4 The PageModel

You have now been introduced to the primary mechanisms for generating HTML within a Razor Pages application—the Razor page and the Razor syntax that enables dynamic content generation by mixing HTML with server-side C# code. You have also learned about some of the components that aid UI code reuse, including layouts, partial views, tag helpers, and view components. Now it is time to learn about the partner to the Razor page: the `PageModel` class.

In this section, you will learn about the two primary roles of a `PageModel`: *controller* and *view model*. Recall from the discussion in chapter 1 about the controller in MVC. You will remember that its role is to take requests, use the information in the bid to perform commands on the model, and then take the result of that processing and pass it to the view for display. Figure 3.7 shows the relevant part of the process.

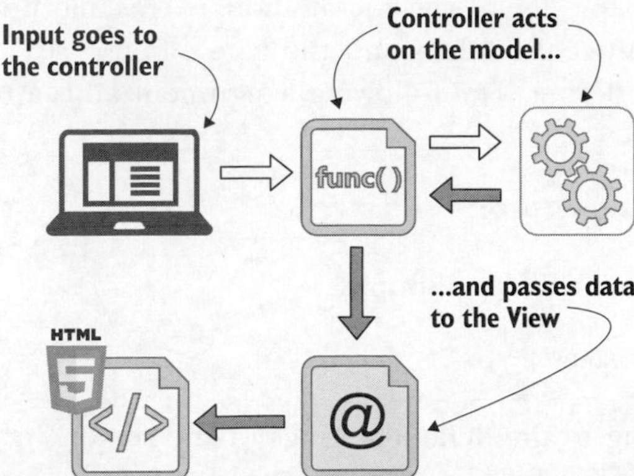

Figure 3.7 The controller takes the input, acts on the model, and passes the resulting data to the view.

As part of request processing, the controller has to prepare the view's data and make that available to the view in a form the view can work with. This form is referred to as a *view model* and is the focus of the first part of this section. Before that, I discuss `ViewData`, which also provides a way to pass data to view pages.

The `PageModel` class is generated automatically when you add a new Razor page to your application. It is named after the page, with the word *Model*, so the `PageModel` class for your Welcome page is `WelcomeModel`. `PageModel` classes are derived from the `PageModel` type, which has a lot of properties and methods related to working with HTTP requests within the `PageModel` class itself. Public `PageModel` properties are exposed to the Razor page through the inclusion of an `@model` directive that references the `PageModel` type.

3.4.1 Passing data to pages

You have many options for passing data to pages. The recommended approach is working with data in a strongly typed manner as a view model. There is another option which, while it is weakly typed, is also of use sometimes. You have already used this approach to pass the Welcome page's title to the layout in the previous chapter. It is called `ViewData`.

`ViewData` is a dictionary-based feature. Items are stored within the `ViewDataDictionary` as key-value pairs and accessed by referencing the case-insensitive string key of the `ViewData` property within the page. The following is how you used `ViewData` to assign the Welcome page's title:

```
ViewData["Title"] = "Welcome!";
```

This value is accessed in the layout page as follows:

```
<title>@ViewData["Title"] - WebApplication1</title>
```

The values within the `ViewDataDictionary` are `object` types, which means you can store anything you like there. Non-string types need to be cast to their correct types if you want to work with them (e.g., to call type-specific methods). This may not be necessary if all you want to do is render the values and the type's `ToString()` method results in a suitable value for rendering. The following assignment adds a `DateTime` type to `ViewData`:

```
ViewData["SaleEnds"] = new DateTime(DateTime.Now.Year, 6, 30, 20, 0, 0);
```

If you want to render that value, you can do so simply:

```
<p>Sale ends at @ViewData["SaleEnds"]</p>
```

The output is rendered according to the default settings of the server. In my case, that's English (United Kingdom), which results in `Sale Ends at: 30/06/2021 20:00:00` being rendered. If I want to use date and time formatting strings to control the rendering, I need to cast to a `DateTime`:

```
Sale Ends at: @(((DateTime)ViewData["SaleEnds"]).ToString("h tt, MMMM dd"))
```

Now I get the output I want: `Sale Ends at: 8 PM, June 30.`

You can set the value of `ViewData` items in the `PageModel` class. The next listing shows the title of the page being assigned to `ViewData` in a handler method called `OnGet`; you will learn about handler methods shortly.

Listing 3.23 Assigning the `ViewData` value in `OnGet` in a `PageModel` class

```
public class WelcomeModel : PageModel
{
    public void OnGet()
    {
        ViewData["Title"] = "Welcome!";
    }
}
```

For this assignment to take effect in the Razor page, you must ensure that the Razor page includes an `@model` directive referencing the `WelcomeModel` type:

```
@model WelcomeModel
```

You should also be aware that assignments made within the `PageModel` will be overridden if it is also set in the Razor page itself.

Another way to access `ViewData` values is via a property called `ViewBag`. This property is a wrapper around `ViewData` that enables you to treat it as a dynamic object. Consequently, you access items through property names that match their key. Because the values are dynamic, there is no need to explicitly cast when working with non-string types:

```
@ViewBag.SaleEnds.ToString("h tt, MMMM dd")
```

`ViewBag` is only available in Razor files. It is not available in the `PageModel` class, although it is available in MVC controllers, where it was carried over from an old framework called ASP.NET Web Pages. The ASP.NET Core team decided not to implement `ViewBag` in Razor Pages `PageModel` classes because, being dynamic, it produced a measurable performance impact on views and pages that used it. For that reason, use of `ViewBag` is not recommended at all.

`ViewData` is weakly typed, so you get no compile-time checking or IntelliSense support. It relies on referencing items using a string-based key—an approach that is sometimes referred to as *working with magic strings*. Consequently, working with `ViewData` can cause errors because it is so easy to mistype a string or rename it in one place and forget to update other references. If you try to render an item that doesn't exist, nothing is rendered. If you attempt to call a method on a `ViewData` entry that doesn't exist, a `NullReferenceException` will be raised. If you attempt to cast a `ViewData` entry to the wrong type, you will generate an `InvalidCastException`. These exceptions will occur at run time.

`ViewData` itself should only be used sparingly. It is useful for passing small pieces of simple data to layout pages, such as the page's title. For all other scenarios in which you need to pass data from a `PageModel` class to a Razor page, you should use public `PageModel` properties, which we will look at next.

3.4.2 The PageModel as a view model

If there is one thing that consistently seems to confuse developers who are new to any form of MVC with ASP.NET, it is the concept of a view model—what it is, its purpose, and how to create one. In essence, a view model is an extremely simple thing. It is a class that encapsulates the data required for a particular view or page. Conceptually, it performs the same function as a static database view. A view model contains a subset of data from one or, usually, more objects.

Think about an order summary page on a website, for example. It usually contains a subset of the details related to the product or service that you are ordering—perhaps, just its identifier, name, and price. It might also include your name, billing address, and a check box to indicate that you also want to ship to that address. Those pieces of information will come from the Products table and the Customers table in the website's database. However, none of the rest of the information in those database tables is required by the order summary view. The order summary page doesn't display the customer's password or the date they created their account, for example. Nor does it show in-house details of the product that might be stored in the Products table, such as the supplier's details or the reorder level.

Figure 3.8 provides an indication of how little of the total information held by the Products and Customers tables is required for the view. This subset of data forms the basis of your `OrderSummaryViewModel`—the model for the order summary view, which might look like the content of listing 3.24.

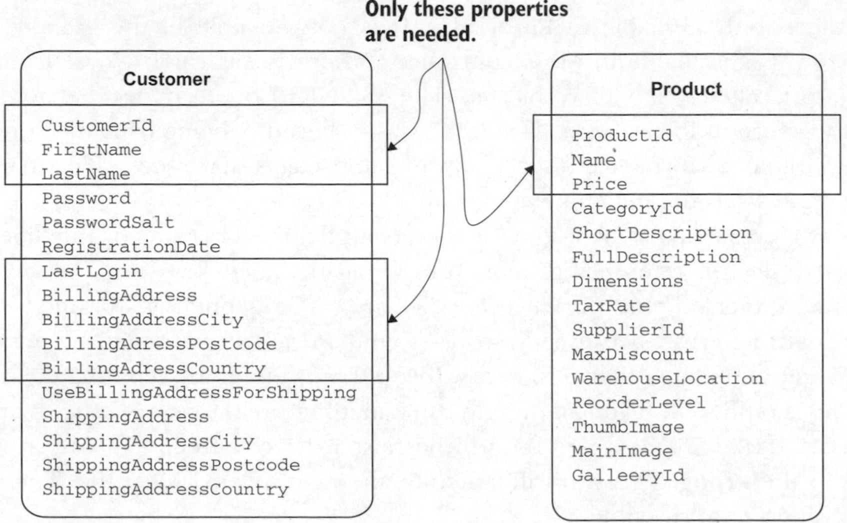

Figure 3.8 Only the outlined columns or properties are required by the order summary view

Listing 3.24 An example view model class

```
public class OrderSummaryViewModel
{
    public int CustomerId { get; set; }
    public string CustomerName { get; set; }
    public string BillingAddress { get; set; }
    public bool UseBillingForShipping { get; set; }
    public int ProductId
    public string Name { get; set; }
    public decimal Price { get; set; }
}
```

And there you have it: a view model—a container for only the data required for a view. View models are used extensively by developers who work with the MVC framework. Their views typically include an `@model` directive that references the `ViewModel` class designed for the specific view:

```
@model OrderSummaryViewModel
```

You have already seen the `@model` directive in your Razor page files. It references the `PageModel` class that accompanies the Razor page. So the `PageModel` in Razor Pages is a view model in the MVC sense. Any public properties added to the `PageModel` will be accessible to the Razor page that references the `PageModel` via a special `Model` property within the page.

Listing 3.25 shows the `WelcomeModel`, the `PageModel` class for the Welcome page you created in the last chapter. This version has a public property named `SaleEnds`, which is the equivalent of the `ViewData` value you saw earlier.

Listing 3.25 Public properties in a `PageModel`

```
public class WelcomeModel : PageModel
{
    public DateTime SaleEnds { get; set; } = new DateTime(DateTime.Now.Year,
    ➥ 6, 30);
    public void OnGet()
    {
    }
}
```

Listing 3.26 shows the Welcome Razor page, which includes the `@model` directive referencing the `WelcomeModel` type and the `SaleEnds` value being accessed via the page's `Model` property.

Listing 3.26 `PageModel` properties being exposed via the page's `Model` property

```
@page
@model WebApplication1.Pages.WelcomeModel      <-- The PageModel type is referenced by the @model directive.
@{
}
<p>Sale ends at @Model.SaleEnds.ToString("h tt, MMMM dd")</p>
```

The SaleEnds property of the PageModel is accessible via the special Model property of the Razor page.

Unlike `ViewData`, which is weakly typed, you get IntelliSense support for `PageModel` properties, as you can see in figure 3.9, which shows IntelliSense kicking into life in VS Code to help with code completion.

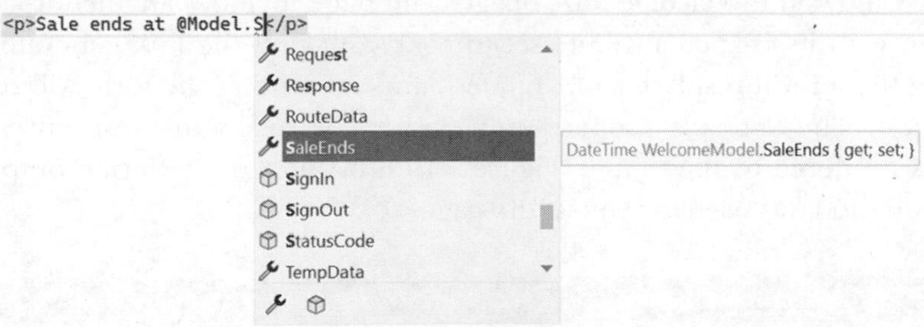

Figure 3.9 `PageModel` properties are supported by IntelliSense.

This is the primary reason PageModel properties are recommended over ViewData as a mechanism for passing data to pages. Tooling support in both Visual Studio and VS Code makes you more productive and minimizes the chances of errors creeping into your code.

3.4.3 The PageModel as a controller

The primary role of a controller is to process requests. Request processing in a PageModel is performed within *handler methods*. For readers familiar with MVC frameworks that support them, PageModel handler methods are analogous to controller actions. By convention, handler method selection is based on matching the name of the HTTP method that was used for the request with the name of the handler method using the On[method] pattern with Async appended optionally to denote that the method is intended to run asynchronously. The OnGet or OnGetAsync method is selected for GET requests, and the OnPost or OnPostAsync method is selected for POST requests.

Listing 3.27 shows the WelcomeModel class with a simple string property, Message, added to it, along with both OnGet and OnPost handler methods. Each handler sets the value of the Message property to report which handler was executed.

Listing 3.27 Different handler methods assigning different values to the Message property

```
public class WelcomeModel : PageModel
{
    public string Message { get; set; }

    public void OnGet()
    {
        Message = "OnGet executed";
    }

    public void OnPost()
    {
        Message = "OnPost executed";
    }
}
```

- The public property is added, which will be accessible in the Razor page via the Model property.
- If the OnGet handler is executed, the message includes "OnGet".
- If the OnPost handler is executed, the message includes "OnPost".

Listing 3.28 shows the Welcome Razor page. The page includes an anchor tag helper and a form with its method attribute set to post. Clicking the link generated by the anchor tag helper will result in a GET request, and submitting the form will result in a POST request. The Message property value, which is set in the respective handler method, is rendered to the output. Figure 3.10 illustrates the differing output based on which method was used to request the page.

Listing 3.28 Welcome page including mechanisms for generating GET and POST

```
@page
@model WebApplication1.Pages.WelcomeModel
```

- The WelcomeModel is referenced via the @model directive.

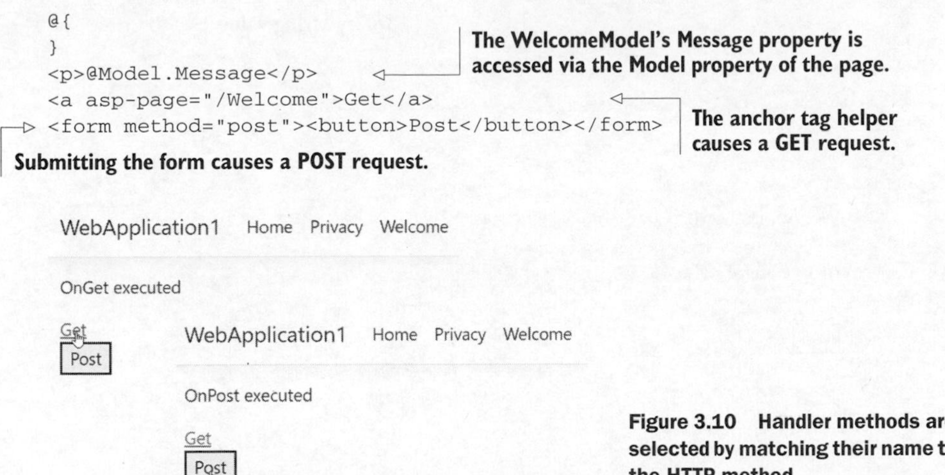

Figure 3.10 Handler methods are selected by matching their name to the HTTP method.

HANDLER METHOD PARAMETERS

Handler methods can take parameters. Data passed in the URL will be bound to handler method parameters based on a match between the parameter's name and the name associated with the URL data item. To understand how this works, take a look at the next listing, where the `OnGet` method has been altered to accept a parameter named `id`, and the `Message` property incorporates the value that is bound to the `id` parameter.

Listing 3.29 Adding a parameter to the `OnGet` handler method

```
public void OnGet(int id)
{
    Message = $"OnGet executed with id = {id}";
}
```

A numeric parameter named id is added to the OnGet method.

The value of the parameter is incorporated into the value assigned to the Message property.

The anchor tag in the Razor page is updated to include an `asp-route-id` attribute with a value of `5`, as shown in listing 3.30. The `asp-route-*` attribute is used to pass data in the URL. By default, the data is passed in the query string, with the name of the query string item taken from the part of the attribute represented by the asterisk.

Listing 3.30 Using the asp-route-* attribute on the anchor tag helper to pass a value

```
<a asp-page="/Welcome" asp-route-id="5">Get</a>
```

There is no query string value when you first run the page, so the handler parameter is set to its default value of `0`. The generated value for the anchor tag's `href` attribute is `/Welcome?id=5`. When you click the link, the message is updated to include the parameter value, as shown in figure 3.11.

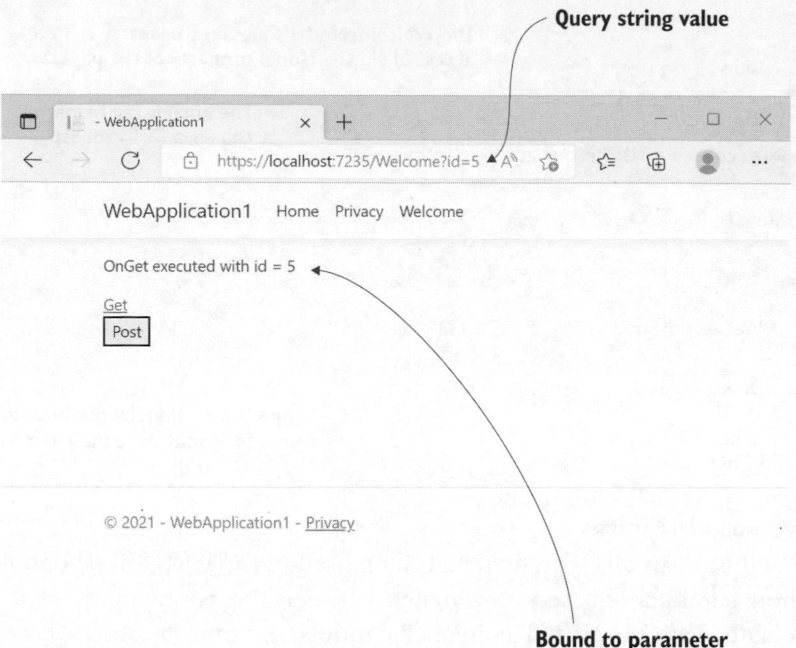

Figure 3.11 The query string value is bound to the parameter based on matching their names.

The magic that is responsible for matching incoming data to parameters is called *model binding*. I go into detail on model binding in chapter 5 when we look at working with forms.

NAMED HANDLER METHODS

C# allows you to create overloads of methods by varying the number and type of parameters they accept. While it is possible to create multiple versions of the `OnGet` or `OnPost` methods that vary by parameters in a single `PageModel` class and have them compile successfully, the Razor Pages framework does not allow it. You can only have one `OnGet` or one `OnPost` method in a `PageModel`. In fact, you can't even have an `OnGet` and an `OnGetAsync` method in the same `PageModel` class. Razor Pages ignores the `Async` suffix when it matches a handler to an HTTP method name. If more than one handler matches a given request, you will get an `AmbiguousActionException` at run time.

There may be times you want different code to execute for the same HTTP method. For example, you might have a page with multiple forms in it. The Manning home page features both a search form and a registration form. One takes a search term, and the other one takes an email address. Assuming they both post back to the same page, how will you know which one the user submitted? You could add some logic in the `OnPost` handler to try to identify whether the user was attempting to register for a newsletter or searching for an author by their email address—or you can use *named handler* methods.

Named handler methods start with the same convention as standard handler methods: `On` followed by the HTTP method name. This is followed by the *name* of the handler method and is used to disambiguate it from standard handler methods and other named handler methods. For example, you might want to create a method named `OnPostSearch` to process a search form submission and another named `OnPostRegister` to process the registration form submission. The following listing shows how you would implement these in the `WelcomeModel` of your sample application.

Listing 3.31 Showing two named handler methods

```
public class WelcomeModel : PageModel
{
    public string Message { get; set; }
    public void OnPostSearch(string searchTerm)
    {
        Message = $"You searched for {searchTerm}";
    }

    public void OnPostRegister(string email)
    {
        Message = $"You registered {email} for newsletters";
    }
}
```

- The Message property is added.
- The OnPostSearch method takes a string named searchTerm.
- The message incorporates the searchTerm parameter value.
- The OnPostRegister method processes a registration, with a parameter named email.
- The message incorporates the email parameter value.

Two handler methods are created: one is named `OnPostSearch`, and the other `OnPostRegister`. *Search* and *Register* represent the *name* part of the named handler methods. Both methods take a string parameter, but they each set the `Message` property to a different value based on which method was invoked.

Listing 3.32 shows two simple forms in the Index page—one for searching and the other for registering. The form tag is one of those that a tag helper targets, so custom attributes are made available. The `page-handler` attribute accepts the name of a page handler method to be used to process the request when the form is submitted.

Listing 3.32 The `page-handler` attribute enables targeting of different handler methods

```
@page
@model WelcomeModel
@{
}

<div class="col">
    <form method="post" asp-page-handler="Search">
        <p>Search</p>
        <input name="searchTerm" />
        <button>Search</button>
    </form>

    <form method="post" asp-page-handler="Register">
        <p>Register</p>
```

- The name part of handler methods is assigned to the page-handler attribute of the form tag helper.
- The input name attribute matches the parameter name on the targeted handler method.

```
        <input name="email" />
        <button>Register</button>
    </form>
    <p>@Model.Message</p>      <—— The value of Message is rendered to the browser.
</div>
```

Figure 3.12 shows what happens when the page is rendered and the user searches for *Razor Pages*. The form tag helper appends the name of the handler to the query string using the key `handler`:

```
?handler=Search
```

Based on the successful match between the handler query string value and the name of a handler method, Razor Pages selected the `OnPostSearch` handler to process the request, and the resulting output is generated accordingly.

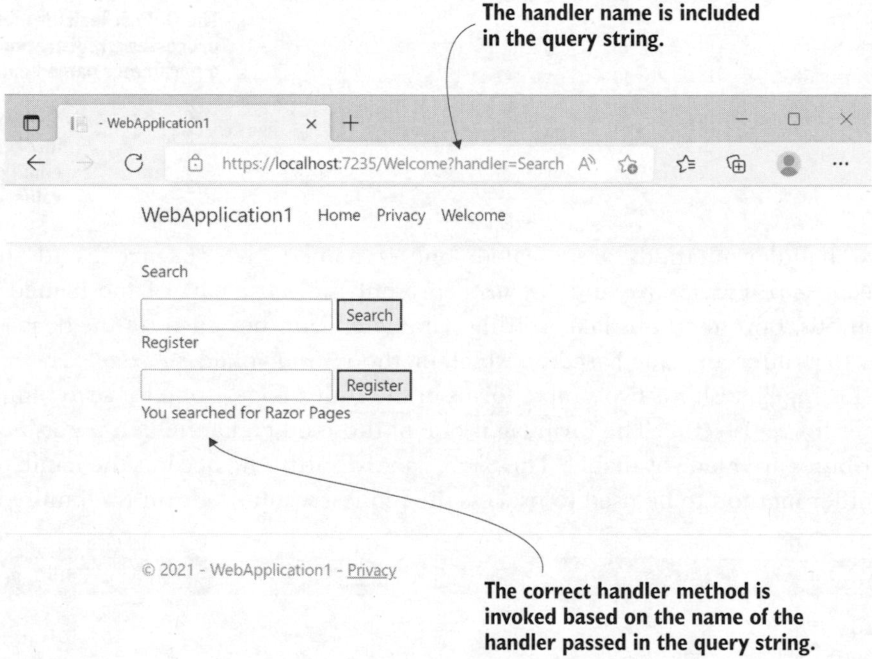

Figure 3.12 Named handler method selection in action

HANDLER METHOD RETURN TYPES

All the examples of handler methods you have seen so far have a return type of `void`. The other supported return types are `Task` and any type that implements the `IActionResult` interface, known as action results, which have the role of generating the response. A variety of action results are available for different types of response. For example, instead of rendering a Razor page, you might want to return a file. Or you might want to return an empty response with a specific HTTP status code. Or you might want to redirect the user to a different location.

At this point, you might be wondering how your pages have generated responses when your handler methods haven't returned `IActionResult` types. This is because handler methods that have a return type of `void` or `Task` implicitly return a `PageResult`, an action result that renders the associated Razor page. The following listing shows the `OnPostSearch` handler updated to include an explicit return type of `PageResult`.

Listing 3.33 A handler method explicitly returning an action result

```
public PageResult OnPostSearch(string searchTerm)
{
    Message = $"You searched for {searchTerm}";
    return new PageResult();
}
```

The OnPostSearch method has been altered to return PageResult.

A new PageResult instance is created and returned.

The `PageModel` class includes a number of helper methods that provide a shorthand way of creating action results to save you from using the `new` operator. The next listing shows the use of the `Page()` helper method, which is a wrapper around the expression `new PageResult()`.

Listing 3.34 `Page()` method shorthand for new `PageResult()`

```
public PageResult OnPostSearch(string searchTerm)
{
    Message = $"You searched for {searchTerm}";
    return Page();
}
```

The OnPostSearch method has been altered to return PageResult.

The Page() method acts as a wrapper around a call to new PageResult().

Generally, if your handler only ever results in the current page being processed and rendered, there is no need to explicitly return a `PageResult`. Table 3.1 shows the action result types you are most likely to work with in a Razor Pages application, along with their helper methods.

Table 3.1 Action results in Razor Pages

Action result class name	Helper method	Description
`PageResult`	`Page`	Renders the current Razor page.
`FileContentResult`	`File`	Returns a file from a byte array, stream, or virtual path.
`NotFoundResult`	`NotFound`	Returns an HTTP 404 status code indicating that the resource was not found.
`PartialResult`	`Partial`	Renders a partial view or page.

Table 3.1 Action results in Razor Pages *(continued)*

Action result class name	Helper method	Description
`RedirectToPageResult`	`RedirectToPage`, `RedirectToPagePermanent`	Redirects the user to the specified page. The `RedirectToPage` method returns an HTTP 302 status code, indicating that the redirect is temporary.
`StatusCodeResult`	`StatusCode`	Returns an HTTP response with the specified status code.

You should be as specific as possible when specifying the return type of your handler methods. There will be occasions when you need to return one of two or more action result types, based on application logic. For example, you might use the parameter value to look up an entry in a database, and if that entry doesn't exist, you will want to return a `NotFoundResult`. Otherwise, you will return a `PageResult`. In that case, you should specify `IActionResult` as the return type for the handler method.

Listing 3.35 Returing `IActionResult` to represent any `ActionResult` type

```
public IActionResult OnGet(int id)
{
    var data = database.Find(id);
    if (data == null)
    {
        return NotFound();
    }
    else
    {
        return Page();
    }
}
```

- The method returns an IActionResult.
- An attempt to locate data matching the parameter value is made.
- The NotFound helper method is used to create a NotFoundActionResult if no matching data is returned from the database.
- The page is rendered if data was obtained.

At the beginning of this chapter, I mentioned that the @page directive denotes a Razor file representing a navigable page that is intended to be browsed. In the next chapter, we will look at the process known as *routing*, which is responsible for ensuring that URLs are mapped to Razor files that include this directive.

Summary

- Razor is templating syntax that enables you to embed server-side code within HTML markup.
- Razor syntax is placed in Razor files, which have a .cshtml extension.
- C# code blocks are enclosed in `@{ ... }`.
- Variables and expressions are rendered to the output when they are prefixed with `@`.

- Control blocks can be embedded within the markup section of a Razor file by prefixing them with `@`.
- Razor HTML encodes all output it renders for security reasons.
- You can use `Html.Raw` to disable HTML encoding.
- Layout pages are used to eliminate duplication of common content across multiple pages.
- Tag helpers target specific tags and automate the generation of HTML.
- The `PageModel` is a combined view model and controller.
- The `@model` directive makes the `PageModel` available to the Razor page.
- The `Model` property of the Razor page provides access to `PageModel` properties.
- Handler methods within `PageModels` are responsible for processing requests. They target specific HTTP methods and can return `void`, `Task`, or an `IActionResult`.
- Handler method parameters can get their values from query strings parameters that have the same name.
- Named handler methods allow you to specify multiple handlers for the same HTTP method.

4 Matching URLs to Razor Pages with routing

This chapter covers

- Evaluating how URLs are matched to Razor pages
- Examining the use of route templates to control the matching process
- Working with data passed in URLs
- Overriding conventional routes
- Generating outbound URLs

In the last chapter, we looked at how to influence which handler method is invoked for a particular request by incorporating an HTTP method name into the name of a handler method—for example, `OnGet`, `OnPost`, and so on. Before the handler selection process can take place, the correct page must be selected. This chapter focuses on *routing*, which is the process that maps the incoming request to a specific page, or *endpoint* (incoming URLs), and generates URLs that map to those endpoints (outgoing URLs).

Many web application frameworks map URLs to a web page's file path on disk based on matching the URL segments to a folder structure. Continuing the theme of a web application that provides vacation packages from the last chapter, table 4.1 provides some examples of this one-to-one match between some imagined segmented URLs and their file paths in a web application.

Table 4.1 It is common to find a one-to-one mapping between incoming URLs and page file paths.

Incoming URL	Maps to
https://domain.com/city/london	c:\website\city\london.cshtml
https://domain.com/booking/checkout	c:\website\booking\checkout.cshtml
https://domain.com/login	c:\website\login.cshtml

This chapter will explore how Razor Pages uses *page-based routing*—mapping between URLs and file paths as the basis for routing within an application. It will also explore how you can use configuration to customize how URLs map to endpoints when a direct relationship between the URL and the location on disk is insufficient for your needs.

The one-to-one correspondence between the URL and the file path is easy to reason about, but it is very limiting on its own. The first example in table 4.1 hints at a page that provides information about London as a vacation destination. If you also wanted to provide information about Paris (https://domain.com/city/paris), you would have to add another page to the city folder named paris.cshtml. As discussed in previous chapters, this is not a sustainable way to build an application. In the last chapter, we looked at passing data in the URL as a query string value. This chapter will explore passing data as part of the URL itself and getting a single page to respond differently based on that data.

URLs are considered part of your web application's UI. So you need to be able to exercise as much control over them as you have over the generation of HTML within your application. The routing system controls how the framework generates URLs to endpoints, but there are customization options available. You will see how to use them to ensure your URLs are descriptive and human readable.

In the last chapter, we looked at some examples of using Razor syntax to iterate over a list of cities. To demonstrate the concepts in this chapter and in subsequent chapters, we will continue with this scenario and start building an application that offers vacation packages in cities worldwide (we call them *city breaks* in the UK). If you would like to try the code samples featured in this and the following chapters, you should create a new Razor Pages application based on the instructions from chapter 2 and name it CityBreaks.

4.1 Routing basics

Routing is not part of the Razor Pages framework. It comes as separate components and, as such, is plugged into your application as middleware. The two key components that control routing in a Razor Pages application are the `EndpointRouting` middleware and the `Endpoint` middleware, illustrated in figure 4.1. They are added to the application pipeline via the `UseRouting` and `MapRazorPages` methods, respectively. Listing 4.1 shows the relevant lines of code in the `Program` class as a reminder.

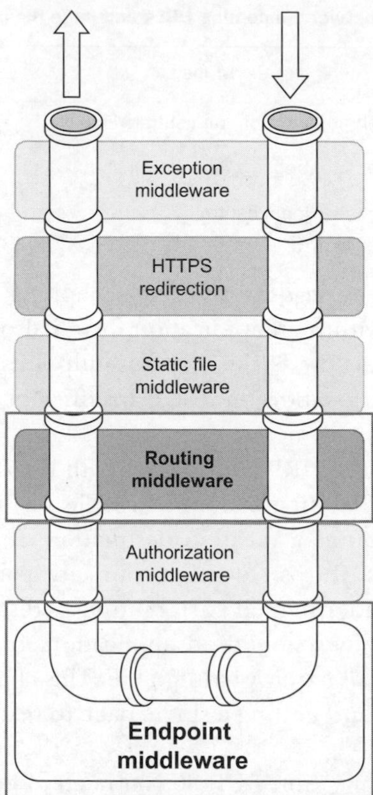

Figure 4.1 Routing middleware is registered after static file middleware. Endpoint middleware is registered at the end of the pipeline.

Listing 4.1 Calling `UseRouting` before `UseEndpoints`

```
app.UseStaticFiles();
app.UseRouting();
app.UseAuthorization();
app.MapRazorPages();
```

- `app.UseStaticFiles();` — Static files middleware is registered before routing.
- `app.UseRouting();` — EndpointRouting middleware is registered in the UseRouting method.
- `app.MapRazorPages();` — Endpoint middleware is registered at the end of the pipeline and registers endpoints based on Razor Pages conventions.

The role of `EndpointRouting` middleware is to match incoming URLs to endpoints. In the case of a Razor Pages application, an endpoint is generally a Razor page. If a match is made, information about the matched endpoint is added to the `HttpContext`, which is passed along the pipeline. Figure 4.2 illustrates this process. Once the endpoint has been added to the `HttpContext`, it can be accessed via the `GetEndpoint` method of the `HttpContext`.

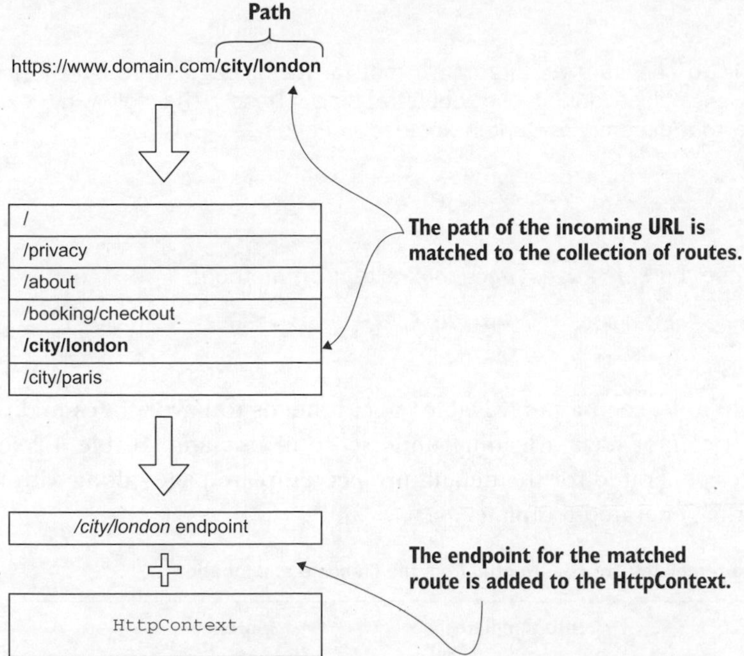

Figure 4.2 The path of the incoming URL is matched to a collection of routes. The endpoint related to the matched route is added to the `HttpContext`.

The `Endpoint` middleware is responsible for executing the selected endpoint. If no matching endpoint is found, the last middleware, which is registered in the pipeline by the framework, returns a 404 Not Found HTTP status code.

Middleware that does not rely on routing, such as the static file middleware, should be placed prior to the call to `UseRouting`. Any middleware that needs to know about the selected endpoint is placed between `UseRouting` and `UseEndpoints`. Authorization middleware needs to know about the selected endpoint, for example, to determine whether the current user is authorized to access it.

4.1.1 Route templates

The `EndpointRouting` middleware attempts to match URLs to endpoints by comparing the *path* of the URL (the part after the domain) to route templates. A *route template* is a string representation of a route pattern. The call creates route templates to `MapRazorPages` in the `Endpoint` middleware registration, which instructs the framework to create endpoints based on Razor Pages conventions. Specifically, a collection of `RouteEndpoint` objects is created. A `RouteEndpoint` is a type of endpoint that can be used in URL matching and generation.

Route templates for Razor pages are created from the file path and name of Razor files found in the default root directory: the Pages folder.

Note

It is possible to configure an alternative root for Razor pages through the `RazorPagesOptions` object during the bootstrapping phase. The following example changes the root directory to Content instead of Pages:

```
builder.Services.AddRazorPages().AddRazorPagesOptions(options => {
    options.RootDirectory = "/Content";
});
```

Or you can use the `WithRazorPagesRoot` extension method:

```
builder.Services.AddRazorPages().WithRazorPagesRoot("/Content");
```

For a Razor file to be seen as a navigable page, it needs to have an `@page` directive at the top, and it cannot have a leading underscore in its name. Table 4.2 shows the route templates generated for the default project template pages along with the URL that matches the generated template.

Table 4.2 Route templates are constructed from the filename and location

Page	Route template	Matches
\Pages\Index.cshtml	`"Index"`	https://domain.com/index
\Pages\Index.cshtml	`""`	https://domain.com/
\Pages\Privacy.cshtml	`"Privacy"`	https://domain.com/privacy
\Pages\Error.cshtml	`"Error"`	https://domain.com/error

The Index.cshtml file is a special case. Two route templates are generated for it—one that includes the filename and another consisting of an empty string instead of Index. This happens because Index is seen as the default document. Therefore, it can be reached just by matching the folder name in the URL. If you are not careful, this can cause problems resulting from ambiguous routes. For example, if you add a folder named Privacy with an Index file in it, the route templates in table 4.3 will be generated.

Table 4.3 Ambiguous routes might be generated.

Page	Route template
\Pages\Privacy\Index.cshtml	`"Privacy/Index"`
\Pages\Privacy\Index.cshtml	`"Privacy"`
\Pages\Privacy.cshtml	`"Privacy"`

The last two route templates in table 4.3 are identical. There is no way for the endpoint selection process to distinguish which endpoint (page) should match, so the framework throws an `AmbiguousMatchException` when you attempt to navigate to http://domain.com/privacy. Sometimes this type of file configuration is unavoidable, so you will need to know how to resolve ambiguous routes, which is covered in this chapter.

4.2 Customizing route templates

The route template patterns you have seen so far consist of literal text. They require an exact match between characters in the URL and the route template if endpoint matching is to succeed. It would be rather pointless if the routing system was restricted to generating templates that matched existing file paths exactly. As you would expect from any real-world web application framework, Razor Pages provides plenty of scope to customize the route template generation process.

The principal entry point to route template customization is the `@page` directive in the Razor page itself. The only other thing permitted on the first line of a Razor page file, after the `@page` directive, is a string that is used to customize the route template for the page:

```
@page "route-template"
```

As well as literal text, route templates can include two other types of elements: parameters and separators, as shown in figure 4.3. Parameters are placeholders for dynamic values, like parameters for C# methods, and separators represent the boundary between segments in a URL. The difference between a literal and a parameter is that the latter is enclosed in curly braces. Parameters are an extremely powerful tool in terms of URL-to-endpoint matching. You will learn a lot more about working with parameters in routes soon, but before that, we will take a look at using literal text to override the default route template for a page.

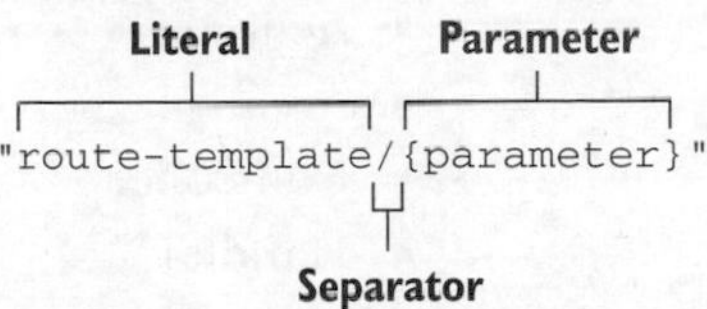

Figure 4.3 Demonstrates a literal within a route template, a separator character, and a placeholder for a parameter value within curly braces

4.2.1 Overriding routes

Suppose you find yourself in the kind of pickle illustrated in table 4.3, where two pages generate the same route template. In that case, you might want to override the template generated by one of them to prevent exceptions from being thrown at run time. You can do this by providing an alternative literal text value to the `@page` directive that starts with the separator character (`/`). For example, you can add `"/privacy-policy"` after the `@page` directive in the \Pages\Privacy.cshtml file like this:

```
@page "/privacy-policy"
```

This will replace the default route template. The routes that get generated as a result of this change are shown in table 4.4.

Table 4.4 Using literal text in a route template to override default route generation

Page	Route template
\Pages\Privacy\Index.cshtml	`"Privacy\Index"`
\Pages\Privacy\Index.cshtml	`"Privacy"`
\Pages\Privacy.cshtml	`"privacy-policy"`

You can consider route templates as behaving the same way as URLs, in that those that do not begin with the path separator are relative to the current page, whereas those that start with the path separator are absolute and not appended to the current page's route.

4.2.2 Route parameters

We saw at how the URL https://domain.com/city/london might map to a single file named london.cshtml located within a folder named City. Instead of representing a filename, *london* could represent data. In Razor Pages, data passed in the URL is known as *route data* and is represented in route templates by *route parameters.* The city is no longer a folder; it is a page that processes the incoming data. Parameters are added to route templates by specifying their name in curly braces { }. The name itself can be more or less anything, except the following reserved words:

- Action
- Area
- Controller
- Handler
- Page

If you would like to follow along, add a new Razor page to the Pages folder named City. The following line of code shows a parameter named `cityName` being added to the route template for the City page:

```
@page "{cityName}"
```

The resulting route template that gets created for the page will be

```
City/{cityName}
```

Any value passed in to the `name` parameter is added to a `RouteValueDictionary` object (literally a dictionary of route values), which is added to a `RouteData` object. Then, within the page, the value can be retrieved using `RouteData.Values`. Listing 4.2 shows how the product route parameter is defined and how the value of the parameter is retrieved in code within the City page.

Listing 4.2 Adding a route parameter to the page and retrieving its value for display

```
@page "{cityName}"
@model CityBreaks.Pages.CityModel

<h2>@RouteData.Values["cityName"] Details</h2>
```

The route template is added with a parameter in curly braces named "name".

The value of the name parameter is obtained from RouteData.Values and displayed in the page.

Now if you navigate to /City, the first thing you notice is that you get a 404 Not Found error.

Figure 4.4 The application returns a 404 HTTP error code if no value is provided for a required route parameter.

The reason for this is that, by default, a value for the `name` parameter is required. The URL /City doesn't match any existing route template on its own (figure 4.4). Navigate to /City/London instead, and the parameter value is retrieved and displayed (figure 4.5).

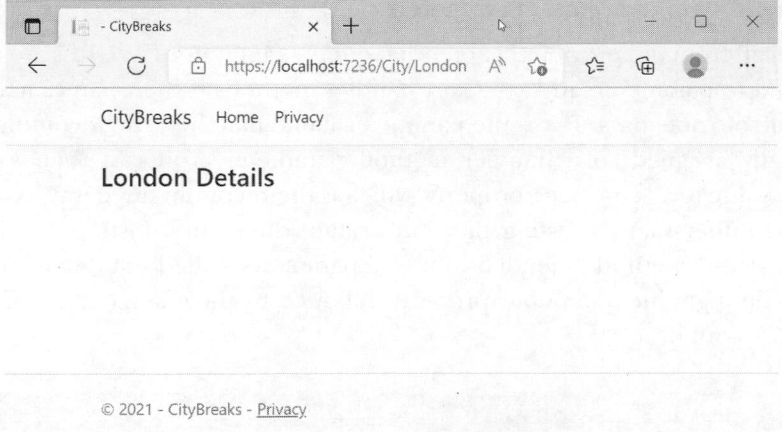

Figure 4.5 The parameter value is retrieved and displayed.

Parameters can be made optional by placing a question mark after the parameter name—for example, {cityName?}. Once the parameter has been made optional, you can navigate to the page without having to provide a value. Optional parameters can only be used as the last parameter in a route template. All other parameters must either be required or have a default value assigned to them.

Default values are assigned to route parameters in the same way they are assigned to normal C# method parameters, albeit without the quotes around string values:

```
"{cityName=Paris}"
```

Now if you navigate to /City, the default value is displayed (figure 4.6).

Figure 4.6 Default values can be assigned to route parameters.

4.2.3 Binding route data to handler parameters

You will recall from the previous chapter that query string values in URLs are automatically bound to parameters in `PageModel` handler methods if their names match. The same is true of route data. If a route parameter name matches, the incoming value is automatically assigned to a handler method parameter. You can then assign the parameter value to a `PageModel` property, which is the recommended way to work with route data, rather than accessing the route values dictionary. Listing 4.3 shows the `CityModel` `OnGet` method amended to take a parameter called `cityName` and assigning the incoming value to a public property, followed by the change in the City Razor page to work with it.

Listing 4.3 Binding route data to `PageModel` handler parameters

```
[City.cshtml.cs]
public class CityModel : PageModel
```

```
{
    public string CityName { get; set; }
    public void OnGet(string cityName)
    {
        CityName = cityName;
    }
```

A public property is added to the PageModel.

A parameter is added to the OnGet, which is named the same as the route parameter and is the same data type.

The parameter value is assigned to the PageModel property.

```
[City.cshtml]
@page "{cityName=Paris}"
@model CityBreaks.Pages.CityModel
@{
}
<h3>@Model.CityName Details</h3>
```

The PageModel property is referenced in the page instead of RouteData.Values.

You can specify multiple parameters in a route template. Often, each parameter will occupy its own segment in a URL. Listing 4.4 shows the City page and its `PageModel` updated to handle an additional optional parameter in a new URL segment that might enable the user to specify the minimum acceptable rating of potential venues within the specified city.

Listing 4.4 Multiple parameters in separate URL segments

```
[City.cshtml.cs]
public class CityModel : PageModel
{
    public string CityName { get; set; }
    public int? Rating { get; set; }
    public void OnGet(string cityName, int? rating)
    {
        CityName = cityName;
        Rating = rating;
    }
}

[City.cshtml]
@page "{cityName}/{rating?}"
@model CityBreaks.Pages.CityModel
@{
}
<h3>@Model.CityName Details</h3>
<p>Minimum Rating: @Model.Rating.GetValueOrDefault()</p>
```

Multiple parameters within the same segment are also permitted. Each parameter must be separated by literal text that doesn't feature in the parameter value. Suppose your City page accepts a value representing the desired arrival date instead of a rating value being passed in. Since the hyphen doesn't appear in the date parts, the route template can be constructed like this:

```
"{cityName}/{arrivalYear}-{arrivalMonth}-{arrivalDay}"
```

This will match /City/London/2022-4-18, for example, but not /City/London/2022/4/18.

4.2.4 Catchall parameters

So far, the route parameters you have seen are used to match specific segments within the URL. There may be occasions when you don't know how many segments the URL will consist of. For example, you may build a content management system that allows users to construct their own arbitrary URLs that don't map to file paths. They map to database entries instead. You will need a route template that matches anything, so the endpoint that is selected can take care of looking up the URL in the database and displaying the related content. The routing system provides a *catchall parameter* to cater to this scenario.

A catchall parameter is declared by prefixing the name with one or two asterisks—for example, `{*cityName}` or `{**cityName}`. Catchall parameters match everything from the parameter position in the URL to the end, so it doesn't make sense to include other parameters after a catchall parameter. The matching process is identical, regardless of whether you use one asterisk or two. The difference between using one or two asterisks is apparent when you use the route template to generate URLs (which you will see later in this chapter). If you use one asterisk, path separators within the generated URL will be URL-encoded—that is, they will be rendered as `%2F`. So for example, the URL /City/London/2022/4/18 will be rendered as /City%2FLondon%2F2022%2F4%2F18. When you use two asterisks, the encoding is decoded, or *round-tripped*, and the generated URL will include literal path separators: /City/London/2022/4/18.

4.2.5 Route constraints

As you should have gathered by now, route parameters are analogous to the method parameters you encounter in most programming languages. They are placeholders for variable data provided to parts of the application at run time. Therefore, it is inevitable that you will want to be able to perform some kind of processing on these inputs more often than not. You may want to construct a .NET `DateTime` object with the route values passed in to the arrival date example, so you can work with it in .NET code:

```
public DateTime Date { get; set; }
public void OnGet(string cityName, int arrivalYear, int arrivalMonth, int
     arrivalDay)
{
    Date = new DateTime(arrivalYear, arrivalMonth, arrivalDay);
}
```

A potential problem arises because there is no type of checking being performed against the incoming values. As far as routing is concerned, all URL data is a string type. Consequently, a request for /City/London/foo-bar-baz will match the route and result in an exception being raised when .NET attempts to construct a valid date in the year `foo`. Route constraints provide a solution to this problem. They enable you to specify the data type and range of acceptable values a route data item must comply with for it to be considered a match against the route template.

Route constraints are applied by separating them from the parameter name with a colon. The following example shows how to constrain each of the date parts to integer types:

```
"{cityName}/{arrivalYear:int}-{arrivalMonth:int}-{arrivalDay:int}"
```

The URL City/London/foo-bar-baz no longer matches this template, but /City/London/2022-4-18 does. However, the user can still fiddle with the URL and provide values that result in an invalid date being created, such as /City/London/2022-4004-18. To protect against this, you could use the `range` constraint to constrain the range of valid values. The `range` constraint accepts minimum and maximum acceptable values and can be applied to the month parameter as follows:

```
"{cityName}/{arrivalYear:int}-{arrivalMonth:range(1-12)}-{arrivalDay:int}"
```

More likely, however, you would change the template altogether and constrain the incoming value to a `datetime` type:

```
"{cityName}/{arrivalDate:datetime}"
```

A wide range of constraints is available that restrict matching to specific data types and ranges. The most commonly used constraints are listed in table 4.5. The full range of constraints is available at http://mng.bz/gwME.

Table 4.5 Constraints available in routing templates

Constraint	Description	Example
`alpha`	Matches uppercase or lowercase Latin alphabet characters (a–z or A–Z)	`{title:alpha}`
`bool`	Matches a Boolean value	`{isActive:bool}`
`int`	Matches a 32-bit integer value	`{id:int}`
`datetime`	Matches a `DateTime` value	`{startdate:datetime}`
`decimal`	Matches a decimal value	`{cost:decimal}`
`double`	Matches a 64-bit floating-point value	`{latitude:double}`

Table 4.5 Constraints available in routing templates *(continued)*

Constraint	Description	Example
`float`	Matches a 32-bit floating-point value	`{x:float}`
`long`	Matches a 64-bit integer value	`{x:long}`
`guid`	Matches a GUID value	`{id:guid}`
`length`	Matches a string with the specified length or within a specified range of lengths	`{key:length(8)} {postcode:length(6,8)}`
`min`	Matches an integer with a minimum value	`{age:min(18)}`
`max`	Matches an integer with a maximum value	`{height:max(10)}`
`minlength`	Matches a string with a minimum length	`{title:minlength(2)}`
`maxlength`	Matches a string with a maximum length	`{postcode:maxlength(8)}`
`range`	Matches an integer within a range of values	`{month:range(1,12)}`
`regex`	Matches a regular expression	`{postcode:regex(^[A-Z]{2}\d\s?\d[A-Z]{2}$)}`

Earlier in the chapter, you saw how ambiguous routes were created when an Index file was added to a Privacy folder. The same situation will arise if you add a City folder and place an Index file there. Last time, I provided an entirely new route template to one of the pages to prevent duplicate route templates being generated. Constraints can also be used to ensure each page is seen as different. A template of `"{cityName:alpha}"` requires parameters to consist only of letters (a–z or A–Z), while a template `"{id:int}"` will only match numbers.

It is possible to apply multiple constraints to a parameter. For example, you might want to specify that a value must be composed only of letters of the alphabet and must not exceed nine characters in length. This is achieved by appending additional constraints using the colon separator:

```
"{cityName:alpha:maxlength(9)}"
```

CUSTOM ROUTE CONSTRAINTS

As table 4.5 demonstrates, an extensive range of route constraints that should meet most of your needs is available to you. It is also possible to create your own custom route constraint and register that with the routing service for application-specific needs.

Eventually, your City page is likely to take the value passed in to the `cityName` parameter and use that to perform a lookup against a database to obtain more details for the specified location. This works fine, but you soon begin to realize that sometimes the database query doesn't return a result. When you review your logs, you see that the value being passed to the database query is not what you expect to see in your URLs. It might be part of a city name, it might have some extra characters added, or, indeed, it might bear no resemblance to anything in your database at all. There are countless ways links to your site can get broken when shared or stored by a poorly written bot. Or savvy users might hack your URLs and add the name of a city that does not exist in your database.

It may be savvy to prevent the wasted processing these database lookups for nonexistent values incur and inform the requester that the page they are looking for doesn't exist. In this case, you want to return a 404 Not Found status code.

The following steps show you how to create your own route constraint that checks the value for the `cityName` parameter against a predetermined collection of cities. If the route data item is not in the list, the match fails, and the application returns a 404 Not Found status code. The collection in this example is a simple array. In a real-world application, the data will reside in a database, but you would perform the lookup against a cached version of the cities to prevent the need to make a database call. In chapter 14, you will explore the use of the caching features offered by ASP.NET Core to query a collection stored in memory on the web server.

Route constraints are classes that implement the `IRouteConstraint` interface. So the first step is to create a C# class named `CityRouteConstraint`. This should be placed in a folder named RouteConstraints, so you don't have miscellaneous code files cluttering up the root folder of your project. The code for the `CityRouteConstraint` class is detailed in the following listing.

Listing 4.5 The custom `CityRouteConstraint` class

```
using Microsoft.AspNetCore.Http;
using Microsoft.AspNetCore.Routing;
using System;
using System.Linq;

namespace CityBreaks.RouteContraints
{
    public class CityRouteConstraint : IRouteConstraint
    {
        public bool Match(HttpContext httpContext, IRouter route,
        ➥ string routeKey, RouteValueDictionary values, RouteDirection
        ➥ routeDirection)
        {
            var cities = new[] { "amsterdam", "barcelona", "berlin",
                                ➥ "copenhagen", "dubrovnik", "edinburgh",
                                ➥ "london", "madrid", "paris", "rome",
                                ➥ "venice" };
```

The constraint must implement IRouteConstraint.

The IRouteConstraint specifies a Match method that returns a Boolean.

The array of valid values

```
            return cities.Contains(values[routeKey]?.ToString()
            ➥ .ToLowerInvariant());          ◁── The code that determines
        }                                          if the match is valid.
    }
}
```

The IRouteConstraint interface has one member—a method named Match that returns a Boolean. It takes a number of items as parameters, not all of which will be needed in order to perform the match in every case. In this example, only the RouteValuesDictionary and the routeKey are needed. The routeKey value is the name of the parameter to be checked. If there is a match between the incoming parameter value and an item in the cities array, the Match method returns true.

> **NOTE** The Match method in IRouteConstraint is a synchronous method, which makes IRouteConstraint unsuitable for any requirement that should involve asynchronous processing. If you want to constrain incoming routes in a real-world application asynchronously, alternative mechanisms that support this include middleware (see chapter 2) and IEndPointSelectorPolicy (http://mng.bz/5Q5B), which is not covered in this book.

Custom route constraints must be registered. This is done in the Program class. The constraint is added to the ConstraintMap collection, as illustrated in the following listing, by passing in a name for the constraint and the matching type that should be used.

Listing 4.6 Custom route constraints registered using RouteOptions

```
builder.Services.AddRazorPages();
builder.Services.Configure<RouteOptions>(options =>
{
    options.ConstraintMap.Add("city", typeof(CityRouteConstraint));   ◁── The constraint is registered with the name "city".
});
```

Once the constraint has been registered, it can be used just like any other by placing the name of the constraint after the parameter name:

```
@page "{cityName:city}"
```

4.2.6 Creating additional routes

When you customize the route template through the @page directive, you affect the routing system's resulting template. In addition to replacing the default route template, you can specify additional templates a page can match. The most direct way to do this is to use the AddPageRoute method when configuring RazorPagesOptions (which is similar to specifying an alternative root folder for pages), as shown in listing 4.7, where the Index page has an additional route applied to it, so it can be found at the URL /FindMe as well as the routes the system generates.

Listing 4.7 Adding additional route templates via configuration

```
builder.Services
    .AddRazorPages()
    .AddRazorPagesOptions(options =>
    {
        options.Conventions.AddPageRoute("/Index", "FindMe");
    });
```

There is no limit to the number of additional routes you can define for a particular page using this approach, which takes the name of the page to be mapped and a route template that matches the page. This particular example shows a route template with the literal value `"FindMe"`, but the template applied to the `AddPageRoute` method can include parameters and constraints just like the ones you have been working with so far.

4.2.7 Working with PageRouteModel conventions directly

In the previous section, you declared an additional route template for a page through the `AddPageRoute` method. This method offers a convenient way to add new routing conventions to the application, albeit to one page at a time. But what if you wanted to apply a new routing convention to multiple pages, or even all the pages in the application? The `AddPageRoute` approach doesn't scale very well. You could potentially end up with hundreds of lines of code in your `ConfigureServices` method, and you would have to remember to add a new registration for every new page.

When you use the `AddPageRoute` method, the framework creates a new `PageRouteModelConvention` and adds it to the `PageConventionCollection` represented by the `RazorPagesOptions Conventions` property. The convention is represented by the `IPageRouteModelConvention` interface, which you can work with directly to apply new conventions to multiple pages. To illustrate how this works, imagine that your budding application needs to support displaying content in multiple languages.

> **NOTE** The process of providing support for content to be displayed in multiple languages is known as *localization*, which is a specialized topic and won't be covered in any detail in this book beyond this example. If you would like to know more about localization in Razor Pages, check out my series of blog articles here: http://mng.bz/6X6o.

To present a localized (translated) version of the content, the application needs to know which *culture*, or language, the user prefers. Often, this is determined by asking the user to select from a number of options and then tracking that selection in some way. One of the common ways to store the selection and pass it from page to page is in the URL as data. A typical example of a URL that includes the preferred culture might be https://domain.com/en/Welcome, where the /en/ segment specifies English as the culture, or https://domain.com/fr/Welcome for the French version.

As already established, you pass data in URLs as parameter values, and route templates that incorporate parameters need to be declared explicitly. If you want to support adding a route template to multiple pages, you can create a PageRouteModelConvention that can be applied to any number of pages.

PageRouteModelConventions implement the IPageRouteModelConvention interface, which specifies a single method that must be implemented—the Apply method, which takes a PageRouteModel as a parameter:

```
public interface IPageRouteModelConvention : IPageConvention
{
    void Apply(PageRouteModel model);
}
```

Notice that the IPageRouteModelConvention interface, in turn, implements the IPageConvention interface. This is a *marker interface*. It has no methods and is used as part of the route discovery process to denote the implementing class as one that contains route model conventions that should be applied to the application.

The PageRouteModel parameter provides a gateway for applying new conventions to generate routes for a Razor page. It is through this object that you can apply your custom convention. The PageRouteModel has a Selectors property, which represents a collection of SelectorModel objects. Each one of these has an AttributeRouteModel property, which, in turn, has a Template property representing a route template that enables mapping a URL to this particular page. The following is how this structure looks for the current Index page in our application:

```
PageRouteModel
    RelativePath: "/Pages/Index.cshtml"
    Selectors: [Count = 3]
        SelectorModel[0]:
            AttributeRouteModel:
                Template: "Index"
        SelectorModel[1]:
            AttributeRouteModel:
                Template: ""
        SelectorModel[2]:
            AttributeRouteModel:
                Template: "FindMe"
```

This is a massively simplified representation, focusing only on those properties that are of immediate interest. The PageRouteModel class and the classes that make up its properties are a lot more complex than this. Notice that there are three SelectorModel objects in this representation of the Index page. The final SelectorModel contains the FindMe route template, which was added in the previous section through the AddPageRoute method.

Within the Apply method, you can access the existing SelectorModel objects and amend the value of the Template property to change the existing templates, or you can add SelectorModel objects to the Selectors collection to add additional route templates. The following listing shows a PageRouteModelConvention that copies the existing route templates, inserts an optional route parameter called culture as the first segment, and then adds the copy to a new `SelectorModel` for every page that is discovered in the application.

Listing 4.8 Creating a `PageRouteModelConvention` to add a custom route convention

```
using Microsoft.AspNetCore.Mvc.ApplicationModels;

namespace CityBreaks.PageRouteModelConventions
{
    public class CultureTemplatePageRouteModelConvention :
    ➥ IPageRouteModelConvention
    {
        public void Apply(PageRouteModel model)
        {
            var selectorCount = model.Selectors.Count;

            for (var i = 0; i < selectorCount; i++)
            {
                var selector = model.Selectors[i];

                model.Selectors.Add(new SelectorModel
                {
                    AttributeRouteModel = new AttributeRouteModel
                    {
                        Order = 100,
                        Template =
                    ➥ AttributeRouteModel.CombineTemplates("{culture?}",
                    ➥ selector.AttributeRouteModel.Template)
                    }
                });
            }
        }
    }
}
```

A using directive is required for the Microsoft.AspNetCore.Mvc.ApplicationModels namespace.

You are calling this class CultureTemplatePageRouteModelConvention and implementing the IPageRouteModelConvention interface.

The class implements the Apply method.

The PageRouteModel's collection of SelectorModels is iterated over to obtain information about its route template.

A new SelectorModel is added to the collection by combining a new parameter named culture with a copy of the existing selector.

The order is set to a high number for the new template, so it doesn't interfere with existing routes.

You register the `CultureTemplatePageRouteModelConvention` by adding it to the `RazorPagesOptions Conventions` collection similarly to how you called the `AddPageRoute` method previously:

```
builder.Services.AddRazorPages().AddRazorPagesOptions(options => {
    options.Conventions.AddPageRoute("/Index", "FindMe");
    options.Conventions.Add(new CultureTemplatePageRouteModelConvention());
});
```

Once the convention has been registered, it is invoked, and its `Apply` method is executed for every Razor page in the application at startup. The end result is that the total number of route templates within the application is doubled. For example, the total number of `SelectorModels` for the Index page is now six with the following route templates:

```
"Index"
""
"FindMe"
"{culture?}/Index"
"{culture?}"
"{culture?}/FindMe"
```

Now you can reach the home page with or without a culture included in the URL. If you wanted to make a culture mandatory, you would have updated the existing template instead:

```
foreach (var selector in model.Selectors)
{
    selector.AttributeRouteModel.Template =
     AttributeRouteModel.CombineTemplates("{culture}",
                selector.AttributeRouteModel.Template);
}
```

That completes our exploration into how URLs are mapped to individual Razor pages and how you can use a variety of ways to customize the process when necessary. The next section looks at the tools available for generating URLs based on the application's route information.

4.3 Generating URLs

Anyone with a modicum of HTML knowledge knows you create links in your application just by adding anchor elements to a page with the destination URL applied to the `href` attribute as a hardcoded string, so why has this book devoted a section to the topic of generating URLs? If the URL you want to create links to is external to your site, a plain anchor element and a hardcoded `href` value are exactly what you will use. You could also use hardcoded URLs for internal links too, but as you have just been reading, you can alter how URLs map to pages very easily. If you need to adjust how a specific page or group of pages is found, you need to update the URLs that link to those pages in all the locations within the application. Now, that could present a maintenance headache—and the developers of the Razor Pages framework don't like maintenance headaches, so they provided solutions to this issue.

Razor Pages includes some tools that generate URLs based on the application's routing configuration. So if you change the routing, the links they generate are automatically updated. The main tools are the anchor tag helper, which we have looked at briefly before, and the `LinkGenerator` service. Those are what we will look at next.

4.3.1 The anchor tag helper

As established in the last chapter, tag helpers are components that automate the generation of HTML. The anchor tag helper is responsible for generating an anchor element that links to pages within the application. The `href` attribute's value is the essential part of the anchor element. The anchor tag helper is responsible for generating this based on the routing configuration for the application. If you change the routing system configuration by adjusting a route template for a page or adding a new convention, the output from the tag helper is automatically adjusted accordingly. You don't need to go through your Razor pages to update links all over the application.

As a reminder, following is the anchor tag helper for the Welcome page you added to the navigation in chapter 2:

```
<a class="nav-link text-dark" asp-area="" asp-page="/Welcome">Welcome</a>
```

This particular anchor tag helper includes two custom attributes, both prefixed with `asp-`. Notice that there is no `href` attribute. You cannot include an `href` attribute in an anchor tag helper. If you try to, your application will throw an `InvalidOperationException` at run time. The custom attributes supported by the anchor tag of most interests to Razor Pages applications are as follows:

- `page`
- `page-handler`
- `route-*`
- `all-route-data`
- `host`
- `protocol`
- `area`

The `page`, `page-handler`, and `route-*` attributes are the ones you will work with most often. The `page` attribute is the most important; it takes the name of the page (the path without the extension, rooted in the Pages folder) you want to generate a link to, preceded by a forward slash (e.g., /Welcome). You must pass in a valid page name, including path separators if the page is in a subfolder. So if the page you want to generate a link to is located at \Pages\Admin\Index.cshtml, the value you pass to the `page` attribute will be `/Admin/Index`. If the routing system cannot find a matching page, it will generate an `href` attribute with an empty string. Therefore, if you find that the rendered output of an anchor tag helper unexpectedly takes you to the home page of your application, you should double-check the value you assigned to the `page` attribute.

Some pages have multiple route templates. Where this is the case, the last template will be used to generate the `href` value (see figure 4.7). The default convention for files named Index.cshtml is to generate two route templates; the first is `Index`, and the last is an empty string, as you saw earlier. When you pass `/Index` or `/Admin/Index` to the `asp-page` attribute, the resulting output is `href="/"` or `href="/Admin/"`. You added a third route template for the Index page earlier—`"FindMe"`—via the `AddPageRoute` method in Startup, which will generate the `href` value. Consequently, the rendered HTML for `<a asp-page="/Index">Home</a>` will be `<a href="/FindMe">Home</a>`.

```
PageRouteModel
    RelativePath: "/Pages/Index.cshtml"
    Selectors: [Count=3]
        SelectorModel[0]:
            AtributeRouteModel:
                Template: "Index"
        SelectorModel[1]:
            AtributeRouteModel:
                Template: ""
        SelectorModel[2]:
            AtributeRouteModel:
                Template: "FindMe"
```

The template belonging to the last `SelectorModel` is used for generating URLs.

Figure 4.7 The template belonging to the last `SelectorModel` is used for generating URLs.

The `page-handler` attribute is used to specify the name of the named handler method that should be executed. This works in the same way it did in the form tag helper you saw in the last chapter when I discussed named handlers with the use of a `Search` handler and a `Register` handler. By default, the value passed to the `page-handler` attribute is applied to the query string with a key named `"handler"`:

```
?handler=Search
```

You can change this behavior so that the name of the handler becomes part of the URL by altering the page's route template to include a parameter named `"handler"`. This is usually added as an optional parameter, so the regular `OnGet` and `OnPost` handlers can also be reached:

```
@page "{handler?}"
```

The `route-*` attribute caters to route parameter values, where the `*` represents the name of the parameter. Following is a tag helper that generates a link to the city page for Rome using the `cityName` parameter you specified in the route template:

```
<a asp-page="/City" asp-route-cityName="Rome">Rome</a>
```

If the parameter is not part of the route template, the name and value passed to the `route-*` attribute is applied to the URL query string. So if you replace the `route` attribute in the previous example with `asp-route-foo="bah"`, the resulting URL will be `/City?foo=bah`.

The `all-route-data` parameter takes a `Dictionary<string, string>` as a value, which is used to wrap multiple route parameter values. It is provided as a convenience that relieves you from having to add multiple `route-*` attributes:

```
var d = new Dictionary<string, string> { { "cityName", "Madrid" },{ "rating",
➥ "5" } };
<a asp-page="/City" asp-all-route-data="d">Click</a>
```

The default behavior of the anchor tag helper is to generate a relative URL based on the location of the target page. Suppose you choose to specify the protocol (e.g., HTTPS) using the `protocol` attribute or the hostname (domain) using the `host` attribute. In this case, the anchor tag helper will generate an absolute URL using the value(s) specified.

The final attribute in the list is the `area` attribute, which is used to specify the *area* the target page is in. The name of the `area` is included as the first segment of the generated URL.

> **Areas in Razor Pages**
>
> The `areas` feature in Razor Pages is a strange one in that the most important thing to know about it is that you should generally avoid using it. I wouldn't bother mentioning `areas` in this book at all, except that the default template includes anchor tag helpers that feature the `area` attribute (albeit, they have an empty string assigned to them) and areas are used within the Identity framework, which you will work within chapter 9.
>
> Areas originate from the MVC framework. One of the problems with the MVC framework is the convention placing your controller classes in a folder named Controllers and the view files in a folder named Views—a convention that is enforced by the automated code scaffolding system. In a large application, you can end up with huge numbers of controller class files in this folder. The `areas` feature was devised to help break up large applications into separate subapplications. Each area in an MVC project has its own Controllers, Views, and Models folders. The contents of an area are reached by placing the name of the area as the first segment in the URL, so the area also implements a hierarchy for the purposes of routing. You can achieve exactly the same hierarchical routing effect in Razor Pages by adding a new subfolder to the Pages folder, which is generally why `areas` are not recommended within Razor Pages. They add significant complexity to a more easily resolved problem.
>
> The primary reason for enabling `areas` in Razor Pages is that they facilitate Razor class libraries—another feature that will not be covered in detail in this book. If you are interested in learning more about Razor class libraries, you can refer to the official documentation (http://mng.bz/o2zd). The Identity framework includes a sample UI, which is implemented as a Razor class library. So while you won't add any areas of your own, you may well find yourself having to work with `areas` if you want to customize the Identity UI.

4.3.2 Using the IUrlHelper to generate URLs

The anchor tag helper is used to generate URLs for internal links, but sometimes, you need to generate URLs that will be used for other purposes. You might need to generate a URL that will be included in an email—like the one that you are often required to click to validate your registration on a website, for example. Or you might need to generate a URL in an `img` tag on a Razor page. The `IUrlHelper` service can be used for this. It is made available to you in Razor Pages through the `Url` property of the `PageModel` class and the Razor page itself.

The `Url` property has a number of methods, two of which are of particular interest within a Razor Pages application: the `Page` method and the `PageLink` method. The `Page` method offers a number of versions or overloads that generate relative URLs as strings from the name of the page passed in to it, along with the name of a page handler method and route values. Other overloads can be used to generate absolute URLs. The `PageLink` method generates absolute URLs based on the current request. The following example shows how to use the `Page` method to generate a relative URL that includes route data, which is passed in to the `Page` method as an anonymous type, where the property names match route parameter names.

Listing 4.9 Generating a relative URL with the `IUrlHelper`

```
public class IndexModel : PageModel
{
    public void OnGet()
    {
        var target = Url.Page("City", new { cityName = "Berlin", rating = 4 });
    }
}
```

The value of the `target` variable, based on the `"{cityName}/{rating?}"` template from listing 4.4, is `"/City/Berlin/4"`. Any properties within the anonymous type that don't have names matching parameter names will be added to the URL query string.

The next listing demonstrates the use of the `PageLink` method to generate an absolute URL. The output, based on the same route template, is `"https://localhost:5001/City/Berlin/4"`.

Listing 4.10 Generating an absolute URL with the `IUrlHelper`

```
public class IndexModel : PageModel
{
    public void OnGet()
    {
        var target = Url.PageLink("City", values: new { cityName = "Berlin",
        ➥ rating = 4 });
    }
}
```

4.3.3 Generating redirect URLs from ActionResults

At the end of the last chapter, we looked at different `ActionResult` types that can be used as a return type for handler methods and the helper methods for creating instances of the `ActionResult` class. Two of those helper methods generate URLs that are included in the location header as part of the response: `RedirectToPage` and `RedirectToPagePermanent`. Both of these methods are used to instruct the browser to redirect to the generated URL. The `RedirectToPage` method also generates an HTTP 302 status code, which indicates that the location change is temporary. In contrast, the

RedirectToPagePermanent method generates a 301 HTTP status code, indicating that the redirection should be viewed as representing a permanent change. You would typically use the latter method when you want to inform search engines that a resource has been moved to a new URL. The following listing shows how to use the RedirectToPage method to generate a RedirectToPageResult that sends the user to a specific city page.

Listing 4.11 Generating an absolute URL with the IUrlHelper

```
public class IndexModel : PageModel
{
    public RedirectToPageResult OnGet()
    {
        return RedirectToPage("City", new { cityName = "Berlin", rating = 4 });
    }
}
```

It is good practice to set the handler return type as specifically as possible—in this case, RedirectToPageResult.

The user will be directed to /City/Berlin/4.

If you want to redirect the user to a page within an area, you must pass the name of the area as a route parameter:

```
return RedirectToPage("/Account/Login", new { area = "Identity" });
```

4.3.4 Customizing URL generation

At the beginning of this chapter, I stated that URLs should be considered to be part of your web application's UI. On that basis, you need to be able to exercise as much control over their generation as possible. You ideally want your URLs to be readable and memorable. The conventions used to generate URLs might not suit your purposes. For example, it is common to use Pascal casing (where the first letter of each word in a compound word is capitalized) for Razor page names. Page routes use the same case as the name of the page by default. If, like me, you prefer lowercase URLs in your application, you can use the RouteOptions object to configure this in the Program class. It is the same RouteOptions object you used to add your custom constraint earlier. It has a Boolean property named LowercaseUrls, which, when set to true, results in the path part of outbound URLs being generated in lowercase.

Listing 4.12 Configuring outbound URL paths to use lowercase

```
builder.Services.Configure<RouteOptions>(options =>
{
    options.LowercaseUrls = true;
    options.ConstraintMap.Add("city", typeof(CityConstraint));
});
```

Setting lowercase as the default for the path part of generated URLs.

The RouteOptions object enables you to apply the same case preference for your query strings through its LowercaseQueryStrings property, which is also a Boolean:

```
options.LowercaseQueryStrings = true;
```

Going forward, the application you will build while reading this book will have lowercase URLs set to `true`. You won't apply lowercasing to query string values because that will break security tokens, which you will work with in chapter 9 as part of user management.

Some people prefer their URLs to end with a forward slash (`/`). Technically, there is no benefit to doing so, but if you do choose to implement this pattern, you have to be consistent because search engines see *City/London* and *City/London/* as two different URLs. The `RouteOptions` object includes a property named `AppendTrailingSlash`, which will always result in the slash being appended when set to `true`:

```
options.AppendTrailingSlash = true;
```

4.3.5 Using parameter transformers to customize route and parameter value generation

You now have your URLs generated in lowercase, but there are still some aspects of URL generation you might want to customize. Let's say you have a page named CityReview.cshtml. The generated URL for this page will be /cityreview, whereas you might prefer each word in the compound word *CityReview* to be separated with a hyphen: `city-review`. This is known as *kebab case* (think of skewers). You could achieve this by naming the page City-Review.cshtml, which will result in a `PageModel` named `City_ReviewModel`. You could change the name of the `PageModel` class if you don't like the underscore in the name, but you might also be under some global naming constraints that prevent you from including the hyphen in the page name in the first place. Another possible solution is to use the `AddPageRoute` method to apply an additional route template, which will be used for URL generation, but you will need to remember to do that for all other pages that might have compound words in their names. So ideally, you want a global solution that affects all pages in the application. Parameter transformers provide a global solution.

Parameter transformers are classes that implement the `IOutboundParameterTransformer` interface that specifies one method: `TransformOutbound`. The method takes an object as a parameter and returns a string. Despite its name, a parameter transformer can be used to transform the generated page route as well as the parameter values, depending on how it is registered with the application. The transformation logic is placed in the `TransformOutbound` method.

The following listing shows a parameter transformer that inserts hyphens prior to the first letter of the second and subsequent words in a Pascal case compound word, so *CityReview* becomes *City-Review*, for example.

Listing 4.13 A parameter transformer that acts on a page route

```
using Microsoft.AspNetCore.Routing;
using System.Text.RegularExpressions;
```

IOutboundParameterTransformer is in the Microsoft.AspNetCore.Routing namespace.

You are using a regular expression in the method body, so you need to add a using directive for the appropriate namespace.

```
public class KebabPageRouteParameterTransformer :
➥ IOutboundParameterTransformer
{
    public string TransformOutbound(object value)
    {
        if (value == null)
        {
            return null;
        }
        return Regex.Replace(value.ToString(), "([a-z])([A-Z])", "$1-$2");
    }
}
```

The class implements the IOutboundParameter-Transformer interface and its TransformOutbound method.

A null check is needed, just in case the page name passed in is incorrect.

A simple (if there is such a thing) regular expression to identify locations in a string where an uppercase letter follows a lowercase letter and insert a hyphen where they are found

This particular transformer is designed to work on the route of the page, not the parameter values, so it must be registered as a `PageRouteTransformerConvention`. Registration takes place in the `Program` class, like the `CultureTemplatePageRouteModelConvention` from earlier in the chapter:

```
builder.Services.AddRazorPages().AddRazorPagesOptions(options => {
    options.Conventions.AddPageRoute("/Index", "FindMe");
    options.Conventions.Add(new CultureTemplatePageRouteModelConvention());
    options.Conventions.Add(new PageRouteTransformerConvention(
        new KebabPageRouteParameterTransformer()));
});
```

The `PageRouteTransformerConvention` type implements the `IPageRouteModelConvention` interface. You were introduced to that interface and its `Apply` method earlier as part of the `CultureTemplatePageRouteModelConvention`. When the application starts up, your new parameter transformer is assigned to the `PageRouteModel`'s `RouteParameterTransformer` property within the `Apply` method of the `PageRouteTransformerConvention`. From there, its logic is applied whenever an outbound route is required.

TRANSFORMING ROUTE PARAMETER VALUES

The final part of our look at managing URLs generation focuses on customizing route parameter values. Imagine you have a list of cities, and you want to generate links for each one as the route parameter value for the City page. Putting into practice what you have learned over the last couple of chapters, you might come up with some code that looks like the following listing in your `PageModel` class.

Listing 4.14 Generating an array of cities in the `PageModel`

```
public class IndexModel : PageModel
{
    public string[] Cities { get; set; }
    public void OnGet()
```

An array of string is declared as a public property on the PageModel.

```
    {
        Cities = new[] { "London", "Berlin", "Paris", "Rome" };
    }
}
```

It is assigned the values of a number of cities.

You will iterate over the array within the Razor page and use the anchor tag helper to render links for each city.

Listing 4.15 Generating a list of links to each city

```
<ul>
@foreach (var city in Model.Cities)
{
    <li><a asp-page="/City" asp-route-cityName="@city">@city</a></li>
}
</ul>
```

Remember, you have `LowercaseUrls` set to `true`, so the generated HTML looks like figure 4.8.

```
<ul>
    <li><a href="/city/london">London</a></li>
    <li><a href="/city/berlin">Berlin</a></li>
    <li><a href="/city/paris">Paris</a></li>
    <li><a href="/city/rome">Rome</a></li>
</ul>
```

Figure 4.8 The links rendered by the anchor tag from the data

This is just what you want, but what happens if you include New York in the collection? Well, the space between the two words is URL encoded to `%20` when the anchor tag is rendered (figure 4.9).

```
<ul>
    <li><a href="/city/london">London</a></li>
    <li><a href="/city/berlin">Berlin</a></li>
    <li><a href="/city/paris">Paris</a></li>
    <li><a href="/city/rome">Rome</a></li>
    <li><a href="/city/new%20york">New York</a></li>
</ul>
```

Figure 4.9 Spaces in URLs are encoded to %20 by default.

This isn't such a great look, especially if your links start appearing in search engine results with lots of what can best be described by the average visitor as *gobbledygook* in them. You really want to render these route values using the same kebab case as routes to make them more readable, this time replacing spaces in the parameter values with hyphens. You often see this type of thing when a URL includes content like a blog post headline or the name of a book—take, for example, the URL for this book: www.manning.com/books/**asp-net-core-razor-pages-in-action**. The bold part of the URL is often referred to as a *slug*.

You will now transform the parameter value using another parameter transformer. The code for this is shown in the following listing.

Listing 4.16 Transforming spaces into hyphens within a route parameter value

```
public class SlugParameterTransformer :
➥ IOutboundParameterTransformer
{
    public string TransformOutbound(object value)
    {
        return value?.ToString().Replace(" ", "-");
    }
}
```

The class implements IOutboundParameterTransformer and its TransformOutbound method.

The processing logic simply replaces spaces with hyphens.

This particular implementation is very naive. For instance, it doesn't take account of any existing hyphens in the value being transformed or any double spaces, but it is sufficient to serve as an example. The registration process for parameter transformers that act on route parameter values is very similar to the one used to register your custom route constraint earlier. The parameter transformer is added to the `ConstraintMap` property of the `RouteOptions` object, and it is assigned to the target route parameter in the same way as a route constraint. The next listing shows how the `SlugParameterTransformer` is registered as part of `RouteOptions`.

Listing 4.17 Registering a parameter transformer like a constraint

```
builder.Services.Configure<RouteOptions>(options =>
{
    options.LowercaseUrls = true;
    options.ConstraintMap.Add("city", typeof(CityConstraint));
    options.ConstraintMap.Add("slug", typeof(SlugParameterTransformer));
});
```

Having registered the parameter transformer, you apply it to selected route parameters in the same way as a route constraint with the name that was specified at registration:

```
@page "{name:slug}/{rating?}"
```

> **NOTE** Despite the fact that you registered and applied the parameter transformer in a way similar to a route constraint, the parameter transformer does not act in the same way as a constraint. It plays no part in mapping URLs to route templates.

Now when you rerun the application, the link to the New York page looks a lot better (figure 4.10).

```
<ul>
    <li><a href="/city/london">London</a></li>
    <li><a href="/city/berlin">Berlin</a></li>
    <li><a href="/city/paris">Paris</a></li>
    <li><a href="/city/rome">Rome</a></li>
    <li><a href="/city/new-york">New York</a></li>
</ul>
```

Figure 4.10 The parameter transformer works on outbound routes.

That ends our exploration of the routing system within Razor Pages. You have learned about the default behavior of mapping URLs to route templates, which are generated from the location of the Razor page within an application. You have also learned how to customize this behavior on an individual page basis and a global basis as well as how to pass data in URLs using route parameters.

You have seen how to use the anchor tag helper to generate URLs for links and use the `IUrlHelper` via the Razor page and the `PageModel`'s `Url` property to generate URLs for potential use for other purposes. Finally, you looked at customizing the generated URLs using `RouteOptions` and parameter transformers. The next chapter focuses on using forms within a Razor Pages application to capture and process data.

Summary

- Routing is the process that maps incoming URLs to endpoints and generates outgoing URLs.
- Routing is added as middleware with the `UseRouting` and `UseEndpoints` methods.
- Route templates represent the endpoint to be matched. They consist of literals, separators, and parameters, which represent data in URLs.
- Routes are generated from the location of the Razor page on the disk.
- You can customize individual page routes by providing a new template to the `@page` directive.
- You can use route constraints to disambiguate between similar route patterns.
- You can add additional routes to a page using `AddPageRoute`.
- Alternatively, you can create your own `PageRouteModelConvention` to customize routing for multiple pages.
- The anchor tag helper generates outgoing URLs based on the routing system, as does the `IUrlHelper`.
- The `RouteOptions` object provides some ways to customize the URL generation process.
- You can use parameter transformers to take full control over the URL generation process.

Working with forms: Model binding

This chapter covers

- Model binding in Razor Pages
- Binding complex objects easily
- Protecting your application by validating user input
- Leveraging data annotation attributes to manage validation

At the beginning of this book, I congratulated you for choosing *ASP.NET Core Razor Pages in Action* if you wanted to learn how to build "page-focused interactive web applications." I didn't really expand on the meaning of "interactive" at the time; essentially, an interactive web application is one in which users can provide input and affect the behavior of the application. In the last chapter, you saw how a user can alter a URL to interact with the application, causing the City page to display different content based on the value of a route parameter. In this chapter, you will begin to understand and work with the primary interaction mechanism in a web application: the form.

Forms come in all shapes and sizes. At the beginning of this book, you looked at the Manning website home page, which features a couple of forms that have a single input each. Other forms—insurance quote forms spring to my mind—can span multiple pages. If you want to build interactive web applications, you are going to have to work with forms at some stage, whether it is just a simple contact form or a large, CRUD-based system that drives critical business goals. You will need to create the forms and process the data they are designed to capture. You will also need to validate the data to ensure its integrity and provide informative and timely feedback to users when the data they submit fails to meet your business rules.

One of the design goals behind the Razor Pages framework, as stated in the GitHub issue quoted in chapter 1, is to "simplify the code required to implement common page-focused patterns, e.g., dynamic pages, *CRUD forms.*"

Razor Pages includes great features for minimizing the amount of code needed to create robust forms, process their data, and validate it. They are

- Form control tag helpers
- Model binding
- A validation framework

These topics leave us with a lot of ground to cover, so I focus on model binding and validation in this chapter and focus on tag helpers in the next chapter.

In chapter 3, you saw that query string values can be bound to handler method parameters through a feature called *model binding*. This feature also plays a key part in simplifying the processing of posted form values by automating the capture of data sent in an HTTP request and assigning it to C# code. You will explore model binding in detail in this chapter when you see how it works with `PageModel` properties and route data as well as handler parameters.

You will also see how to protect your application from bad data by validating user input both on the client and, crucially, on the server. Validation tag helpers and model binding combine to reduce the amount of code you need to write to protect your data integrity and inform users of errors in their submission.

Data annotation attributes provide a way for you to add additional information, or *metadata*, to types in .NET, including specific rules the data should honor, such as business requirements related to presence, data type, and range. The validation framework is one area among many in the .NET Framework that is responsive to the hints provided by data annotations. You will explore how to take advantage of this capability to further eliminate boilerplate code when building your forms and easily validate your data against your business rules.

The examples in this chapter build on the CityBreaks application that was started in the last chapter. We'll assume you have configured the application to use the lowercase options for URLs and implemented both parameter transformers, so routes and parameters use kebab casing. The downloads for this chapter include a version that has these settings applied if you require a starting point.

5.1 Forms basics

Forms consist of an HTML form tag that encloses a number of controls for gathering user input and, usually, a control of some description that enables the user to submit the content of the input controls to the server for processing. The form submission itself results in an HTTP request. The request will use whichever HTTP method is specified by the form element's method attribute, with GET being the default if no method is specified. When the GET method is used, the form values are appended to the URL as key-value pairs in a query string (see figure 5.1). The key is generated from the name attribute of the form control, and the value is obtained from the control. When the POST method is used, the content of the form is included in the body of the request as key-value pairs constructed using the same pattern as the GET method.

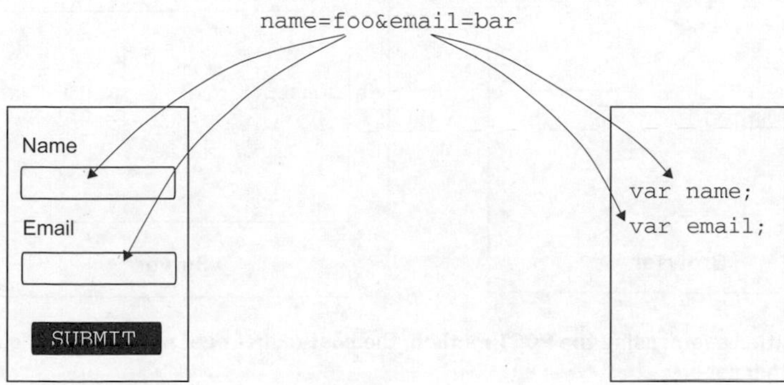

Figure 5.1 Form values are transferred to the server as key-value pairs.

Although it is the default, the GET method is not generally used with forms. You would only normally use the GET method for forms designed to capture query criteria, such as search engines, where the ability to bookmark the URL with the query criteria embedded in the query string enables you to effectively execute the form submission again. Most of the time, you will use the POST method, especially for form submissions that change the state of the application—for example, those that execute operations, resulting in adding new content or updating existing content. The POST method also provides some benefits. It adds a level of security in that the submitted data is not visible in the query string. You wouldn't want your username and password to be visible in the browser address bar for anyone to see, for example.

5.1.1 Using the post-redirect-get pattern

With respect to forms submitted using the POST method, after the form contents have been processed successfully on the server, the user is usually redirected to another URL. This procedure is known as the *post-redirect-get* (PRG) pattern and is useful as a mechanism for preventing the user from refreshing the page containing the form, thereby accidentally resubmitting it, which would result in the processing operation being executed again.

It is particularly important to implement this pattern when processing any form that is designed to add items to the application's data store. The last thing you want is

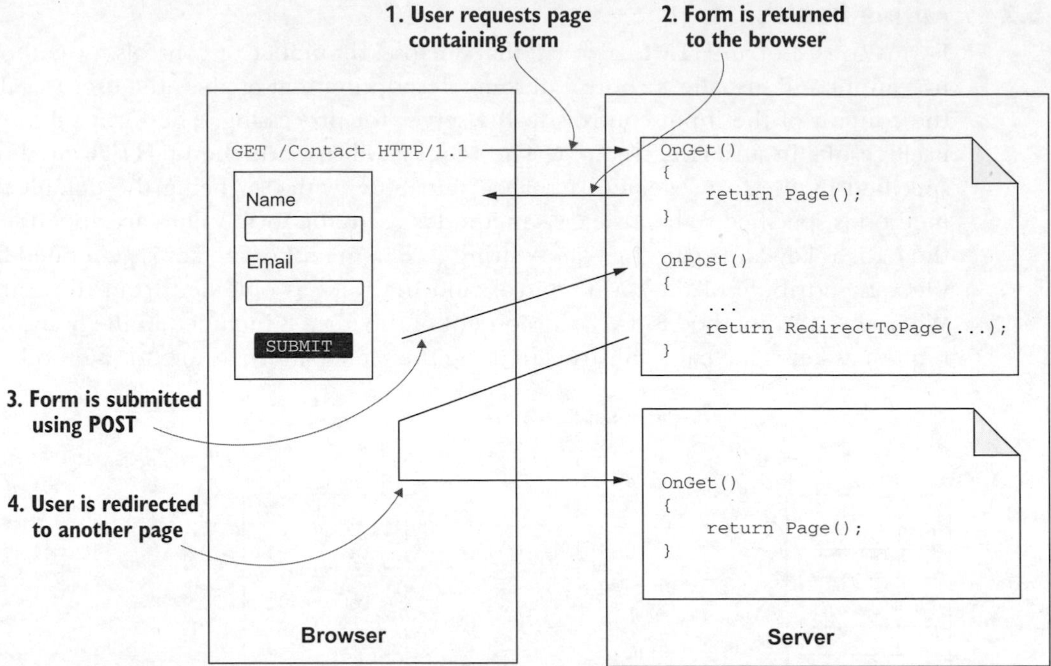

Figure 5.2 Having submitted a form using the POST method, the post-redirect-get pattern specifies that the user is redirected to another page.

duplicate data or your customer to complain that they only ordered one item, yet two have been charged for! Having said that, you won't implement the PRG pattern during the early examples that follow, while you learn how to access the values from the form submission.

Maintaining state during postbacks

As a reminder, `OnGet` handlers execute for `GET` requests, and `OnPost` handlers execute for `POST` requests. As part of form management, you will often need to initialize data in the `OnGet` handler, such as preparing options for select lists and so on. Once the framework has used that data as part of the HTML generation process and the response has been sent to the browser (step 2 in figure 5.2), any data that was generated on the server is lost. This is because, by default, Razor Pages is stateless. That is, it doesn't maintain that data anywhere. This makes sense because HTTP is a stateless protocol.

If you want to work with the same data in the `OnPost` handler, you must re-initialize it within the `OnPost` handler. Failure to do so may result in runtime exceptions as you try to reference data that doesn't exist because you haven't created it! This most often tends to happen when the form submission fails validation checks and needs to be presented again. It can be easy to overlook the fact that select lists, in particular, often rely on data generated on the server, which needs to be generated each time you display the form.

Clearly, a vital part of form processing is being able to access the submitted values, so you can validate and process them. In this section, I show how they are assigned to the `Request` object, which, as you will remember, is a property of the `HttpContext`, along with the various options available to you for retrieval of these values for `POST` and `GET` requests. While you will access the `Request` object directly in the following examples, this is not the recommended approach when working with form data in a Razor page. However, once you understand the limitations of this approach, the role of model binding—the approach you should use as your default—and the benefits it brings will make a lot more sense.

5.1.2 Accessing values from Request.Form

When a form is submitted using the `POST` method, the form values are processed by the underlying ASP.NET Core framework and assigned, with their form control names, as key-value pairs to the `Request.Form` collection. In ASP.NET Core, each item can be accessed using a string-based index (e.g., `Request.Form["password"]`), where the value of the index is the name of the original form control. The return type is a `StringValues` object, which differs from previous versions of ASP.NET, where the return type was a simple string.

To see this in action, you will create a very simple form that enables a user to type the name of a city into a form, and then submit that information to the server for processing. Your server-side code will extract the name of the submitted city from the HTTP request and display it back to the user.

First, create a new folder in the Pages folder, and name it CityManager. Then add a new Razor page named Create.cshtml to the CityManager folder. Replace the code in Create.cshtml with the following.

Listing 5.1 The Create page with a form

```
@page
@model CityBreaks.Pages.CityManager.CreateModel
@{
   ViewData["Title"] = "Create City";
}
<div class="col-4">
    <form method="post">     ◁── The form method is set to post.
        <div class="mb-3">
            <label for="name">Enter city name</label>
            <input class="form-control" type="text" name="cityName" />  ◁── The name attribute of the text input is set to "cityName".
        </div>
        <button class="btn btn-primary">Submit</button>
    </form>
    <p>@Model.Message</p>    ◁── A PageModel property called Message is rendered here.
</div>
```

This is standard HTML for a form that is styled with Bootstrap classes. It includes an input with the `name` attribute set to `"cityName"`. The `name` attribute is the most important one on any form control because this is used as the key of the key-value pairs sent to the server when the form is submitted. This often surprises ASP.NET Web Forms developers, who are conditioned to see the `id` property of a server control as the means for identifying the source of incoming form values and tend to confuse this with the `id` attribute on an HTML element.

The incoming collection of key-value pairs is assigned to the `Form` property of the `Request` object. Both the `PageModel` class and the Razor page provide direct access to the `Request` object via a property conveniently named `Request`, which bypasses the need to access it via the `HttpContext` property. The next step is to change the `PageModel` class file content, so it looks like the content of the following listing.

Listing 5.2 Processing the form values using `Request.Form`

```
using Microsoft.AspNetCore.Mvc.RazorPages;
using Microsoft.Extensions.Primitives;

namespace CityBreaks.Pages.CityManager
{
    public class CreateModel : PageModel
    {
        public string Message { get; set; }
        public void OnPost()
        {
            if(!StringValues.IsNullOrEmpty(Request.Form["cityName"]))
            {
                Message = $"You submitted {Request.Form["cityName"]}";
            }
        }
    }
}
```

- Include a using directive for Microsoft.Extensions.Primitives, so you can reference the StringValues type without having to use its fully qualified name.
- Add a public string property named Message.
- Add an OnPost handler to process POST requests.
- Check the Request.Form collection to see if an item with the key of "cityName" has a value.
- If it does, include it as part of the value assigned to the Message property.

Run the application, navigate to /city-manager/create (remember the routing customizations you have already applied), and enter a value into the input. The value is included in the rendered message (figure 5.3).

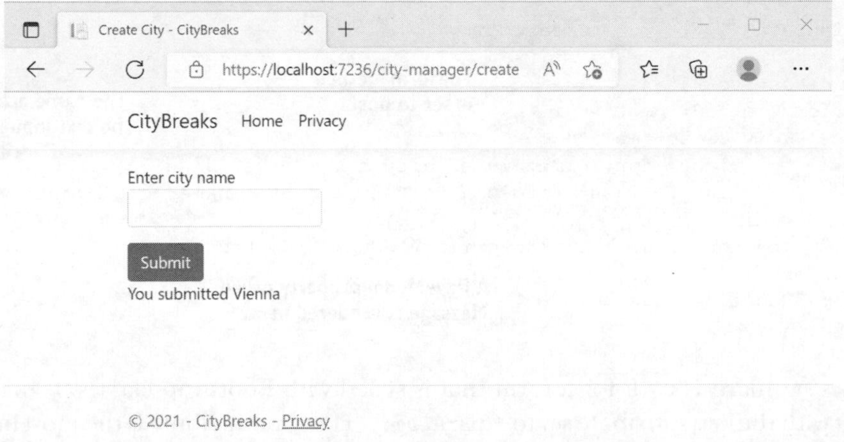

Figure 5.3 The posted value is successfully rendered to the browser.

The example in listing 5.2 demonstrates how to use the value assigned to the `name` attribute of the input (`"cityName"`) as a string-based index to access items within the `Request.Form` collection. This type of approach is common in many web frameworks and should be familiar to classic ASP and PHP developers as well as developers who dabbled with the ASP.NET Web Pages framework. You use `StringValues.IsNullOrEmpty` to determine whether a value exists for the specified key. It will return `false` if no value has been provided or if the specified key doesn't exist in the form collection.

The reason for StringValues

The `StringValues` type was introduced to streamline the handling of values that may be empty, single strings, or multiple strings. It is perfectly possible to assign the same name to multiple controls in a form. You might do this if you want to allow the user to make multiple selections using a series of check boxes, for example. Suppose you want to provide the user with the ability to select multiple cities, and you provide multiple check boxes—each with their name attribute set to `city`. When a selection has been made and the form has been submitted, the selection might look like this as part of the request body:

```
city=London&city=Paris&city=Berlin
```

In previous versions of ASP.NET, `Request.Form` would return multiple values based on the same key as a single comma-separated string, so `Request.Form["city"]` would return `"London,Paris,Berlin"`. It would be your responsibility to convert this string—perhaps using the `string.Split` method to generate an array from it—so the posted values could be iterated and processed individually.

The `StringValues` object represents zero (null), one, or more strings and supports an implicit conversion to `string[]`, which means you can use iteration statements directly in an item in the `Request.Form` (and `Request.Query`) collection without having to manually convert it to a collection of some kind:

```
foreach(var city in Request.Form["city"])
{
    ...
}
```

It also has an implicit conversion to string, so if only one value is expected, you can treat it as a string. If there are multiple values, the first one is returned.

5.1.3 Accessing values from Request.Query

As I mentioned earlier, most forms will use the `POST` method, but there will be occasions when the `GET` method is preferred, especially for features like searching with which you might want to be able to store, share, and reuse the search result URL. In this section, you will make two small modifications to the existing code to retrieve the values submitted in a form using the `GET` method.

The only change required to the code presented in listing 5.1 is of the method attribute on the form to specify "get":

```
<form method="get">
```

The PageModel code requires two changes, shown in listing 5.3. The handler method should be changed to OnGet, and the references to Request.Form should be changed to Request.Query.

Listing 5.3 Accessing the submitted values from Request.Query

```
public class CreateModel : PageModel
{
    public void OnGet()    <-- The handler method is changed to OnGet.
    {
        if (!StringValues.IsNullOrEmpty(Request.Query["cityName"]))
        {
            Message = $"You submitted {Request.Query["cityName"]}";
        }
    }
}
```

Request.Form is replaced with Request.Query.

Run the page, and submit a value. Take a look at the browser address bar. You should notice that the submitted value appears in the URL as a query string value (figure 5.4).

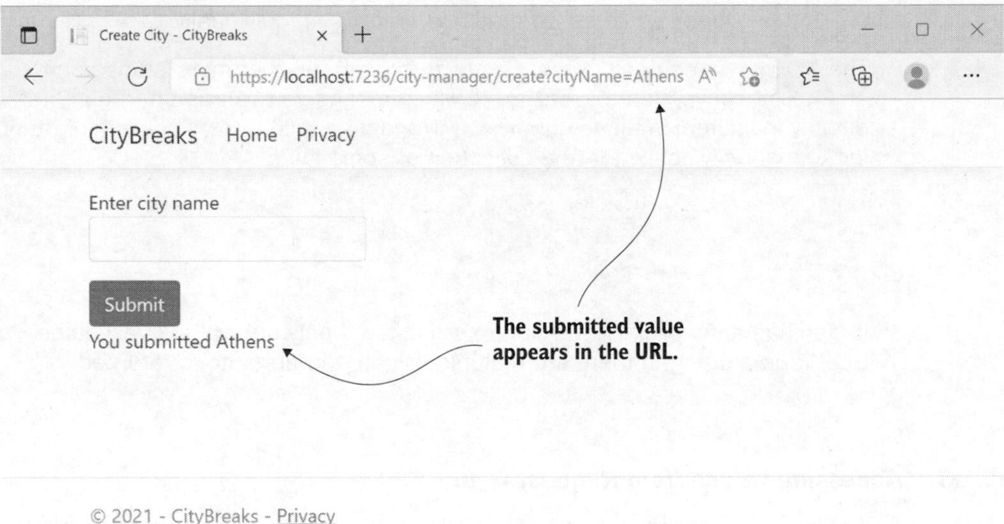

Figure 5.4 When using the GET method to submit a form, the form values are included in the URL as a query string.

If you copy the URL, including the query string, and browse to it, the application behaves as if the form was submitted again and processes the value from the query string into the `Message` property.

NOTE You may not see the query string in some browsers (e.g., Opera and Safari). Click the address bar to see the complete URL.

As I mentioned earlier, accessing form values directly from the `Request.Form` or `Request.Query` collections is not recommended within a Razor page. It is all too easy to misspell the index value, so it no longer references a valid form control, or change the name attribute of the control, resulting in the same issue. But there are use cases in which being able to access these collections directly is useful. You saw one such case in chapter 2 when you created the `PassThroughMiddleware` example.

You might also want to access these collections when logging activity within the application, which I cover in more detail in chapter 12. The one thing that is certain about the users of your application is that they will find ingenious ways to use it, well outside of your expectations or imagination. Since you can't stand over their shoulders and watch them all, you need some way to record users' activity, so you can stand some chance of replicating the steps they took in the event they encounter problems. As part of that, you need to gather as much information about the request they made as possible, including the contents of any form submissions. The following listing iterates the form collection and outputs the name of all the keys and their values.

Listing 5.4 Iterating the `Request.Form` collection and outputting the contents

```
<ul>
@if (Request.HasFormContentType)
{
    foreach (var item in Request.Form)
    {
        <li>@item.Key: @Request.Form[item.Key]</li>
    }
}
</ul>
```

- You must check the content type of the request prior to accessing Request.Form to prevent an InvalidOperationException being raised. (annotates `@if (Request.HasFormContentType)`)
- Render the name of the collection keys and their associated values. (annotates the `<li>` line)

If you include this code in your existing page, after you have changed the form's method back to `post`, you should see that an item with the key `__RequestVerificationToken` is also included in the output. It is included as part of a security measure to combat cross-site request forgery attacks. I discuss this in greater detail in chapter 13.

The code that iterates `Request.Form` is wrapped in a check to establish the content type of the request. Specifically, the `HasFormContentType` property of the `Request` object is referenced. This returns `true` if the request was performed using the `POST` method. If you don't perform this check outside of an `OnPost` handler, the framework raises an `InvalidOperationException` with the following message: `Incorrect Content-Type`.

5.2 Model binding

Rather than delving into the depths of the form or query collections, the recommended way to work with user input within a PageModel class is leveraging the model-binding framework built into ASP.NET Core. Model binding is the process that takes user input from various parts of an HTTP request (the source) and attempts to bind it to C# code (the target). The model-binding framework considers one or more of the following ways users can interact with the application as a source:

- Forms
- Route data
- Query strings
- Request body (useful for accessing data posted as JSON, as you will see in chapter 10)

The binding targets supported in Razor Pages are handler parameters and public PageModel properties that have been explicitly opted in to model binding.

You already encountered binding to handler parameters in chapter 3, when we looked at working with named handlers. In the next section, we will look at this process in more detail, and after that, we will explore binding to PageModel properties in depth.

5.2.1 Using model binding with handler parameters

In this section, you will alter the OnPost handler slightly, so you don't access the Request object directly. This time, you will rely on model binding to bind the incoming form value to a handler parameter as the binding target. Alter the existing OnPost method, so it takes a string parameter named cityName and uses that to build the value of the Message property.

Listing 5.5 Adding a parameter to the OnPost method

```
public class CreateModel : PageModel
{
    public string Message { get; set; }
    public void OnPost(string cityName)    <-- Add the cityName parameter to the OnPost handler method.
    {
        Message = $"You submitted {cityName}";    <-- Include the parameter value in the value assigned to Message.
    }
}
```

When you run this page again, you should see no difference in the output. The value you entered into the form should be incorporated into the rendered Message.

Once the OnPost handler method has been selected by the routing system, the model-binding system does the following (depicted in figure 5.5):

1 Examines the names of the handler method parameters
2 Searches the binding sources in the incoming request for a value with a matching key
3 If a match is found, it attempts any type conversion required from the raw string data presented by the request
4 Assigns the resulting value to the parameter if the conversion is successful

```
public class CreateModel : PageModel
{
    public string Message { get; set; }

    public void OnPost(string cityName)
    {
        Message = $"You submitted {cityName}";
    }
}
```

▾ Form Data view source
cityName: Prague

Figure 5.5 Handler parameters are matched to incoming HTTP values based on their names.

5.2.2 Using model binding with public properties

In this section, you will look at public properties on the `PageModel` class as a binding target. This is the recommended way to work with the model binder in Razor Pages when the binding source is form data. This approach is recommended because public properties are accessible within the Razor page, where they work with form control tag helpers and can take part in validating user input. You will look at both of those features in detail soon enough, but for now, you will alter the existing `PageModel` class, so it no longer works with handler parameters. You will add a new property to represent the city name while removing both the existing `Message` property and the `OnPost` handler. The new property will be decorated with an attribute named `BindProperty`, which designates the property as a binding target.

Listing 5.6 Binding to a public property

```
public class CreateModel : PageModel
{
    [BindProperty]
    public string CityName { get; set; }
}
```

CityName is declared as a public property and has the BindProperty attribute applied to it.

Now that the `Message` property has been removed, you need to work directly with the `CityName` property in the Create page instead. The changes are shown in bold in the following listing.

Listing 5.7 Update the Create page to work with the `CityName` property

```
<div class="col-4">
    <form method="post">
        <div class="mb-3">
            <label for="name">Enter city name</label>
            <input class="form-control" type="text" name="cityName" />
```

```
        </div>
        <button class="btn btn-primary">Submit</button>
    </form>
    @if(Request.HasFormContentType &&
    ➥ !string.IsNullOrWhiteSpace(Model.CityName))
    {
        <p>You submitted @Model.CityName</p>
    }
</div>
```

As before, if you run the page it should produce the same output when the form is submitted.

The handler parameter has been replaced with a public property with the same name. The `CityName` property differs from the removed `Message` property in that it is decorated with the `BindProperty` attribute, which specifies that the property is a binding target. Without this attribute, the property will not take part in model binding.

By default, the `BindProperty` attribute only opts properties in to model binding for `POST` requests. If you want to bind values to public properties during `GET` requests (e.g., from route data or the query string), an extra step is required to opt in. The `BindProperty` attribute has a property named `SupportsGet`, which you must set to `true`:

```
[BindProperty(SupportsGet=true)]
public int Id  { get; set; }
```

In addition to the `SupportsGet` property, the `BindProperty` attribute has a `Name` property, which enables you to bind a public `PageModel` property to an arbitrarily named form field. For example, you might need to bind from a form control that has a `name` attribute set to `"e-mail"`. That's not a valid C# identifier, so you use the `Name` property to map the incoming form value to a property C# will tolerate:

```
[BindProperty(Name="e-mail")]
public string Email { get; set; }
```

If you have a large number of `PageModel` properties you want to include in model binding, you can decorate the `PageModel` class with a `BindProperties` (plural) attribute:

```
[BindProperties]
public class IndexModel : PageModel
```

This approach must be used with care. It will result in *all* public properties in the `PageModel` class being included in model binding, which could expose your application to an overposting attack.

> **Overposting attacks**
>
> *Overposting*, also referred to as mass assignment, is a vulnerability that happens when the user is able to modify items of data they should not have access to. Imagine you are creating a checkout page where the user confirms details of their purchase. Clearly you don't want them to be able to modify the price of the item, so there is no form field for this piece of data. However, let's assume you have included the `Price` as a public property on the `PageModel`, where the `PageModel` class is decorated with the `BindProperties` attribute, thereby opting in all public properties, including the `Price` property, as binding targets.
>
> It is perfectly possible for a web-savvy user to craft their own HTTP request using basic development tools, such as Postman or even the browser developer tools (which we will look at in chapter 11), and include a form item for the price. Because the `Price` property is exposed to the model binder, the user is able to modify the value. Before you know it, those $300 headphones on your site are being sold for $3.

5.2.3 Binding complex objects

Up to this point, you have been using model binding to populate simple properties from incoming form values. As the number of form fields grows, the `PageModel` class will start to creak with either a long list of properties, all decorated with the `BindProperty` attribute, or a large number of parameters applied to a handler method. Fortunately, model binding also works with complex objects, so the properties to be bound can be encapsulated in an object that can be exposed as a property of the `PageModel` or a parameter for the handler method. Some developers refer to the object as an *input model* when it is used in this manner, and it provides an excellent way to limit the scope of the binding target. To see how this works, you will start expanding the functionality of the CityBreaks application.

Each of your cities belongs to a country. You will produce a form that enables you to capture country data using an input model. It will be a very simple input model, but it will do for the sake of example.

Create a folder named Models in the root of the CityBreaks application, and add a C# class named Country.cs to it. Amend the code, so it is the same as the following listing.

Listing 5.8 The `Country` class

```
public class Country
{
    public string CountryName { get; set; }
    public string CountryCode { get; set; }
}
```

The `CountryName` property represents the name of the country, and the `CountryCode` property represents the two-character ISO 3166-1 alpha-2 code for each country. For example, the United States is `us`, and the United Kingdom is `gb`. You can find a full list of these codes from Wikipedia: https://en.wikipedia.org/wiki/ISO_3166-1_alpha-2. You are going to use these codes to display flag icons for each country, so you also need to download a free set of flag icons that have been named after the alpha-2 codes. You can get a free set from Flagpedia at https://flagpedia.net/download/icons (I selected the 40-px-wide original versions), or you can copy them from the download for this chapter that covers binding complex objects (http://mng.bz/yvOB). Create a folder named Images in the wwwroot folder, and within that, create another called Flags. If you choose to download the flag, extract the image files into the Flags folder. Open the layout file, and amend the footer to include attribution shown in bold in the next listing.

Listing 5.9 Updating the footer to include attribution

```
<footer class="border-top footer text-muted">
    <div class="container">
        &copy; 2021 - CityBreaks | Flag icons from
        ➥ <a href="https://flagpedia.net">flagpedia.net</a>
    </div>
</footer>
```

Now add a new folder to the Pages folder, and name it CountryManager. Within that, add a new Razor page named Create. Change the `CreateModel` class content to the following.

Listing 5.10 Using an input model to encapsulate the binding target

```
using CityBreaks.Models;                     // Add a using directive to bring in
using Microsoft.AspNetCore.Mvc;              // the CityBreak.Models namespace.
using Microsoft.AspNetCore.Mvc.RazorPages;

namespace CityBreaks.Pages.CountryManager
{
    public class CreateModel : PageModel
    {
        [BindProperty]
        public InputModel Input { get; set; }    // Add the input model and a property, and make it a binding target by adding the BindProperty attribute.
        public Country Country { get; set; }     // Add a Country property to the PageModel.

        public void OnPost()
        {
            Country = new Country
            {
                CountryName = Input.CountryName,   // Instantiate the Country property from
                CountryCode = Input.CountryCode    // the properties of the InputModel.
            };
        }

        public class InputModel    // Declare a class that encapsulates the fields for the country entry form. This is the input model.
        {
            public string CountryName { get; set; }
```

```
            public string CountryCode { get; set; }
        }
    }
}
```

The `InputModel` class is declared *within* the `PageModel` class, so it is a *nested* class. This limits its scope to the current `PageModel`, thereby allowing you to use the same name (`InputModel`) for classes that act as binding targets on other pages.

The key to binding complex objects is to ensure that the `name` attribute of the input is in the form `<property>.<property>`, where the first `property` is the name of the complex `PageModel` property (the input model) that has the `BindProperty` attribute applied, and the second `property` is the name of the property in the input model class, as shown in figure 5.6.

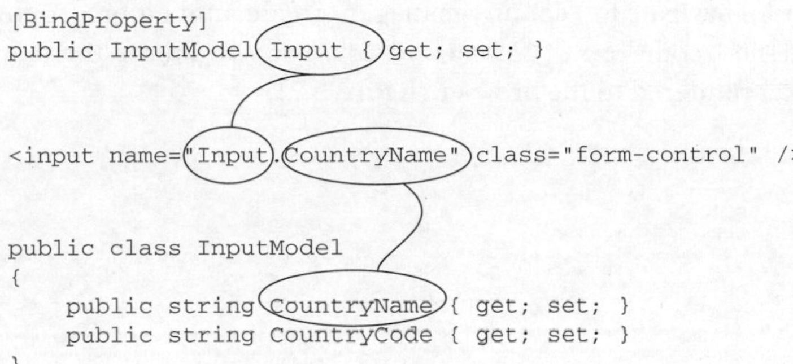

Figure 5.6 Using dot notation to ensure binding works with complex objects

To put this into practice, amend the Create.cshtml file to accommodate the following code.

Listing 5.11 The Create Country form

```
@page
@model CityBreaks.Pages.CountryManager.CreateModel
@{
}

<h4>Create Country</h4>

<div class="row">
    <div class="col-md-4">
        <form method="post">
            <div class="form-group">
                <label for="Input.CountryName"
                ➥ class="control-label">Name</label>
                <input name="Input.CountryName"
                ➥ class="form-control" />
            </div>
            <div class="form-group">
```

The pattern `<property>.<property>` has been used for the for and name attributes of the label and input elements.

```
                <label for="Input.CountryCode"
                ➥ class="control-label">ISO-3166-1 Code</label>
                <input name="Input.CountryCode"
                ➥ class="form-control" />
            </div>
            <div class="form-group">
                <input type="submit" value="Create" class="btn btn-primary" />
            </div>
        </form>
    </div>
</div>
@if(Model.Country != null){
    <p>You submitted @Model.Country.CountryName
    <img src="/images/flags/@(Model.Country.CountryCode).png" /></p>
}
```

The pattern <property>.<property> has been used for the for and name attributes of the label and input elements.

Run the application, navigate to /country-manager/create, and enter a country name and a valid ISO-3166-1 code (e.g., `Ireland` and `ie`). You should see the name of the country and its flag rendered to the browser (figure 5.7).

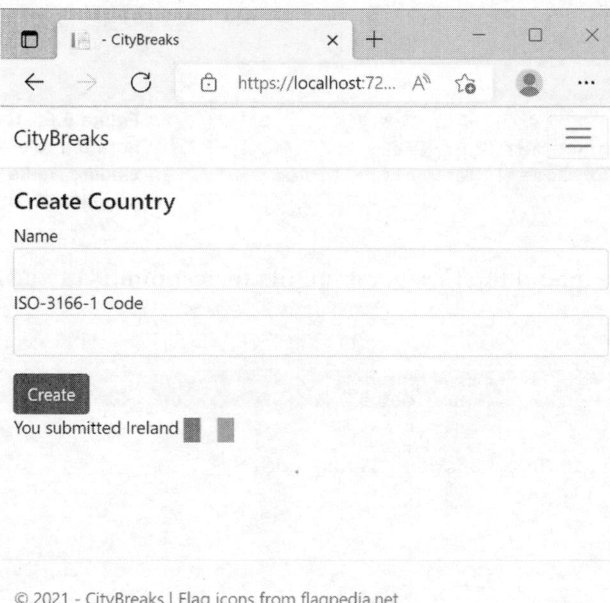

Figure 5.7 You use dot notation to construct form control names to ensure values are bound to complex objects.

You may be wondering why the input model is necessary when it is identical to the `Country` class in the Models folder. It is true at the moment that they are the same, but later in the book, the `Country` class will acquire new properties you don't want to expose to the model binder when a new instance is being created.

You might also start to wonder about the mapping code in the `OnPost` method that takes the values from one object and assigns them to identically named properties on another object. You might think that looks like it could get quite laborious for objects that have many properties. And you would be absolutely right. The good news is there are at least two solutions to speed up the mapping. The first is a very popular open source library called AutoMapper that does this for you. I won't be covering how to use it in this book, but the documentation at the project's site is very good: https://automapper.org/. The second solution may be one you have already noticed if you are using Visual Studio 2022. The ever-improving AI-assisted IntelliCode feature seems to be able to guess the assignments you want to make and often provides the full line of code as a suggestion; you just need to press Tab twice to accept it (figure 5.8).

```
0 references
public void OnPost()
{
    Country = new Country
    {
        CountryName = Input.CountryName,
        CountryCode = Input.CountryCode,   Tab Tab  to accept
    };    CountryCode  string Country.CountryCode { get; set; }
}
```

Figure 5.8 IntelliCode speeds up simple mapping between objects.

The following example shows the `InputModel` class as a public property of the `PageModel`, but it is also possible to apply complex objects as parameters to the `OnPost` handler:

```
public void OnPost(InputModel model)
```

Most often, you will use the public property approach because it works best with form tag helpers, which you will learn about in greater detail in the next chapter. One key point to mention now is that when you use tag helpers in conjunction with public `PageModel` properties, you don't need to worry about constructing the value of the `name` attribute on the input element because the tag helper generates it for you.

Binding to complex objects during a `GET` request works with complex objects decorated with the `BindProperty` attribute as long as the `SupportsGet` parameter is set to `true`—just as with simple types. Binding also works directly to complex objects that act as a handler parameter.

Listing 5.12 Complex object as a handler parameter

```
public void OnGet(InputModel input)
{
    if (input.CountryName != null)
    {
        Country = new Country
        {
            CountryName = input.CountryName,
            CountryCode = input.CountryCode
        };
    }
}
```

5.2.4 Binding simple collections

So far you have looked at binding single instances of simple or complex types. The model binder also supports binding to collections. This is useful for cases where you might want to enable the user to make multiple selections, for example, or provide them with a form for entering multiple rows of data.

HTML provides two options for making multiple selections: a `select` element with the `multiple` attribute applied to it (aka a *list box* control) and a series of inputs with their `type` attribute set to `checkbox`. They must all share exactly the same name attribute; you can use whichever you prefer. The choice between them depends on your UI preference.

The next code example features a form where the user can select more than one option using check boxes. In this case, the user is invited to select from a number of cities. The selection will be bound to a `List<int>`, where each element represents one of the values that was selected. You need to add another class to the Models folder that will represent a city and have two properties.

Listing 5.13 The `City` class

```
public class City
{
    public int Id { get; set; }
    public string Name { get; set; }
}
```

Next, change the `CityModel` in City.cshtml.cs to include a `List` of `int` as a binding target and some code to generate a `List` of cities.

Listing 5.14 The `CityModel` class

```
public class CityModel : PageModel
{
    [BindProperty]
    public List<int> SelectedCities { get; set; } = new List<int>();
    public List<City> Cities = new List<City>
    {
        new City{ Id = 1, Name = "London"},
        new City{ Id = 2, Name = "Paris" },
        new City{ Id = 3, Name = "New York" },
        new City{ Id = 4, Name = "Rome" },
        new City{ Id = 5, Name = "Dublin" }
    };
}
```

Add a public List<int> property, and make it a binding target. Instantiate it, so you don't need to check for null.

Declare a List<City>, and instantiate it.

Finally, change the City.cshtml file content to include a `foreach` loop that iterates over the list of cities and renders a check box and the name of the city for each entry in the collection (listing 5.15). Each check box will have the city's `Id` applied to its `value` attribute. You will also add some code that will execute if any cities are selected by the user. Their `Id` values will be bound to the `SelectedCities` property, so you will loop through any values there and extract the matching city from the collection you just generated in the `PageModel` code. You will render the total number that was selected along with the selection as a list.

Listing 5.15 Multiple selection with checkboxes

```
@page
@model CityBreaks.Pages.CityModel
<h4>Select Cities</h4>
<div class="row">
    <div class="col-md-4">
        <form method="post">
            <div class="form-group">
                @foreach(var city in Model.Cities)
                {
                    <div><input type="checkbox"
                    ➥ name="SelectedCities"value="@city.Id"/>
                    ➥ @city.Name</div>
                }
            </div>
            <div class="form-group">
                <input type="submit" value="Select" class="btn btn-primary" />
            </div>
        </form>
    </div>
</div>
@if(Model.SelectedCities.Any())
{
    <p>Number of cities selected: @Model.SelectedCities.Count()</p>
    <ul>
    @foreach(var city in Model.Cities.Where(
    ➥ c => Model.SelectedCities.Contains(c.Id)))
    {
        <li>@city.Name</li>
    }
    </ul>
}
```

Loop through the collection of cities, and render a check box for each one.

Check to see if there are any selected cities.

Render the total number of elements in the collection.

Render the name of each element.

When you run the page and select some cities, you should see the kind of output in figure 5.9.

The key to getting this example working is ensuring all the check boxes share the same name attribute (`SelectedCities`) and the value assigned to the name attribute is assigned to the binding target in the `PageModel` class. Another point to note: if you are going to refer to a collection in the Razor page, it is useful to initialize it as part of its declaration. That way, you don't have to check for null. You only need to check whether it is an empty collection, using the `Any` extension method.

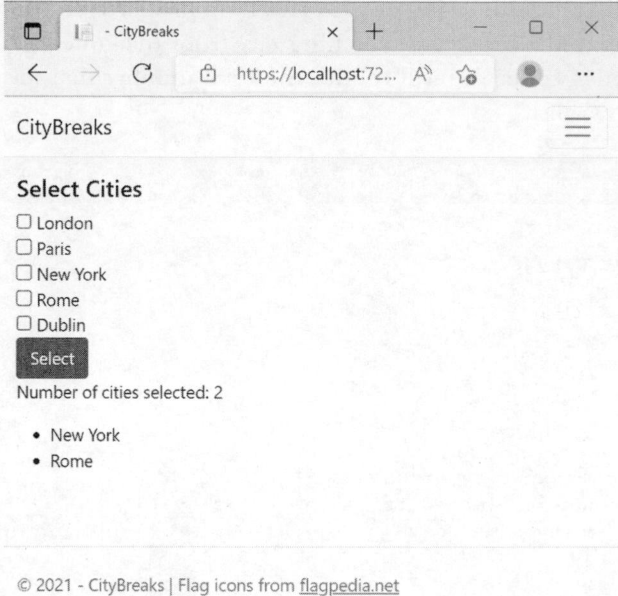

Figure 5.9 Binding multiple selections to a collection

5.2.5 Binding complex collections

The model binder also supports binding to collections of complex objects. When you work with collections of complex objects, you incorporate an index value to identify each element in the collection when you construct the form controls' name attributes. The index can be one of two kinds:

- *Sequential index*—A numeric index that starts at zero and increases by an increment of one each time with no gaps
- *Explicit index*—An index made up of arbitrary but unique values of any type

THE SEQUENTIAL INDEX APPROACH

The following example illustrates the use of a sequential index. You will modify the Create page in the CountryManager folder for this. You will continue to use the `InputModel` class from the previous examples, but you will change the properties in the `PageModel` class to represent collections as well as alter assignment code in the `OnPost` handler accordingly.

Listing 5.16 The `CreateModel` class in the country manager

```
public class CreateModel : PageModel
{
    [BindProperty]
    public List<InputModel> Inputs { get; set; }
    public List<Country> Countries { get; set; } = new List<Country>();

    public void OnPost()
```

```
    {
        Countries = Inputs
            .Where(x => !string.IsNullOrWhiteSpace(x.CountryCode))
            .Select(x => new Country {
            CountryCode = x.CountryCode,
            CountryName = x.CountryName
        }).ToList();
    }
}
```

Next, you need to change the data entry form to accept multiple countries instead of just one at a time. You will render five rows in a table, each containing inputs for the country name and its ISO-3166-1 code. You need to ensure that the format of the `name` attribute's value on each of the input controls adopts the following pattern:

```
<property>[index].<property>
```

This is the same pattern as for a single complex object. The only change is the incorporation of the indexer. So the rendered HTML for the inputs should end up looking like the following listing (removing the extraneous markup).

Listing 5.17 Rendered markup for multiple inputs using a sequential index

```
<input name="Inputs[0].CountryName" /><input name="Inputs[0].CountryCode" />
<input name="Inputs[1].CountryName" /><input name="Inputs[1].CountryCode" />
<input name="Inputs[2].CountryName" /><input name="Inputs[2].CountryCode" />
<input name="Inputs[3].CountryName" /><input name="Inputs[3].CountryCode" />
<input name="Inputs[4].CountryName" /><input name="Inputs[4].CountryCode" />
```

The following listing shows the code that generates those inputs, using a simple `for` loop that starts with zero.

Listing 5.18 Using a sequential index to enable multiple data entry

```
@page
@model CityBreaks.Pages.CountryManager.CreateModel
<h4>Create Countries</h4>

<div class="row">
    <div class="col-md-8">
        <form method="post">
            <table class="table table-borderless">
                <tr>
                    <th>Name</th>
                    <th>ISO-3166-1 Code</th>
                </tr>
            @for (var i = 0; i < 5; i++)
            {
                <tr>
                    <td class="w-75">
```

```
                    <input name="Inputs[@i].CountryName"
                    ➥ class="form-control" />
                </td>
                    <td class="w-25">
                    <input name="Inputs[@i].CountryCode"
                    ➥ class="form-control" />
                </td>
                </tr>
            }
            </table>
            <div class="form-group">
                <input type="submit" value="Create" class="btn btn-primary" />
            </div>
        </form>
    </div>
</div>
@if (Model.Countries.Any())
{
    <p>You submitted the following</p>
    <ul>
    @foreach (var country in Model.Countries)
    {
        <li>
            <img src="/images/flags/@(country.CountryCode).png" />
            @country.CountryName
        </li>
    }
    </ul>
}
```

Increment the variable `i` by 1 on each iteration, and use its value to generate the index value on the form controls.

When the form is submitted, a collection of five `InputModel` objects is instantiated by the model binder and populated with the posted values. If the user only provides values for the first three countries, the final two will have their properties set to the default for the type—`null` for strings. So you only map those that have non-null values to the `Countries` collection in the `PageModel`. Then they are rendered along with their flag icon (if you entered valid ISO codes).

USING AN EXPLICIT INDEX

The approach that relies on an explicit index is more suited to forms designed for editing existing values, where a unique identifier, such as a database primary key of each item, is often used as the index value. In addition to incorporating an index value in the name of the form controls, this approach requires an additional hidden field for each item, named `<property>.Index`, which has a value set to the unique identifier. This is used by the model binder to group related controls together.

To see this working, you are going to simulate editing countries in bulk. First you need to modify the `Country` class to include an integer property named `Id`, which will be used to store the country's unique identifier. This is shown in bold in the next listing.

Listing 5.19 Adding a unique identifier property to the Country class

```
public class Country
{
    public int Id { get; set; }
    public string CountryName { get; set; }
    public string CountryCode { get; set; }
}
```

Next, add a new Razor page to the CountryManager folder named Edit. You are going to use an input model to represent the editable properties of countries, and then instantiate a collection of them in the `OnGet` handler. The properties will be presented in a form as editable values. When the form is submitted, the updated values will be assigned to a collection of countries, just as in the last example, and rendered to the browser.

Listing 5.20 The EditModel for working with explicit indexes

```
public class EditModel : PageModel
{
    [BindProperty]
    public List<InputModel> Inputs { get; set; }
    public List<Country> Countries { get; set; } = new List<Country>();
    public void OnGet()
    {
        Inputs = new List<InputModel> {
            new InputModel{ Id = 840, CountryCode = "us",
            ➥ CountryName ="United States" },
            new InputModel{ Id = 826, CountryCode = "en",
            ➥ CountryName = "Great Britain" },
            new InputModel{ Id = 250, CountryCode = "fr",
            ➥ CountryName = "France" }
        };
    }

    public void OnPost()
    {
        Countries = Inputs
            .Where(x => !string.IsNullOrWhiteSpace(x.CountryCode))
            .Select(x => new Country
            {
                Id = x.Id,
                CountryCode = x.CountryCode,
                CountryName = x.CountryName
            }).ToList();
    }

    public class InputModel
    {
        public int Id { get; set; }
        public string CountryName { get; set; }
        public string CountryCode { get; set; }
    }
}
```

A collection of InputModels is created. The unique identifier is in fact the country's ISO 3166-1 numeric code. This will be used as the index value.

In this example, the data for the item with the `Id` of `826` is incorrect. The country should be named `United Kingdom`, and the alpha code should be `gb`. You will get a chance to edit that and see the result after you have created the form and submitted it. The following listing shows the code for the Razor page.

Listing 5.21 The edit form using an explicit index

```
<h4>Edit Countries</h4>

<div class="row">
    <div class="col-md-8">
        <form method="post">
            <table class="table table-borderless">
                <tr>
                    <th>Name</th>
                    <th>ISO-3166-1 Code</th>
                </tr>
                @foreach (var country in Model.Inputs)
                {
                    <input type="hidden" name="Inputs.Index"
                    ➥ value="@country.Id" />
                    <tr>
                        <td class="w-75">
                        <input name="Inputs[@country.Id].
                        ➥ CountryName"
                            value="@country.CountryName"
                            class="form-control" />
                    </td>
                        <td class="w-25">
                        <input name="Inputs[@country.Id].
                        ➥ CountryCode"
                            value="@country.CountryCode"
                            class="form-control" />
                    </td>
                    </tr>
                }
            </table>
            <div class="form-group">
                <input type="submit" value="Update" class="btn btn-primary" />
            </div>
        </form>
    </div>
</div>
@if (Model.Countries.Any())
{
    <p>You submitted the following</p>
    <ul>
    @foreach (var country in Model.Countries)
    {
        <li>
            <img src="/images/flags/@(country.CountryCode).png" />
            @country.CountryName
        </li>
```

- The collection of input models is iterated.
- The hidden field is created to hold the explicit index value for each item. The Id property value is assigned to it.
- CountryName and CountryCode inputs are created, with their index value also set to the Id property of the current element. Their current values are assigned to the value attribute on the respective input control.

```
    }
    </ul>
}
```

Run the application, and navigate to /country-manager/edit. You should see the data rendered within the form fields (figure 5.10).

Figure 5.10 The bound values are rendered to the input controls.

Make the modifications to the second entry, and press Update. Not only have the revised values been rendered with their flags in a list, but they have been retained in the form controls (figure 5.11).

Figure 5.11 The updated values are rendered to the browser.

By now you should have a clear idea of how model binding works with handler parameters and public properties of a `PageModel` or an input model for simple values and complex objects. So how should you choose between binding to handler parameters and `PageModel` properties?

There is no single correct answer to this question. It will very much depend on individual circumstances. As a brief summary of what the text has covered so far, table 5.1 provides a comparison of handler parameters and `PageModel` properties as binding targets, so you can make an informed choice that works in your specific scenario.

Table 5.1 Comparing handler parameters and `PageModel` properties

	Handler parameter	`PageModel` property
HTTP method	Supports binding during both `GET` and `POST` requests by default	Requires opt-in using the `BindProperty` attribute and additional opt-in for GET request binding
Scope	Only accessible within the handler they belong to	Accessible throughout the `PageModel` class and in the associated Razor page via its `Model` property
Validation	Cannot participate in client-side validation	Participates in both client-side and server-side validation

The last entry in the preceding table touches on a topic we have yet to explore: input validation. That is what we will look at next.

5.3 Validating user input in Razor Pages

When you allow users to provide values that you then process, you need to ensure the incoming values are of the expected data type, they are within the permitted range, and required values are present. This process is known as *input validation.*

The term *user input* covers any value the user has control over. Values provided via forms constitute the bulk of user input, but user input also comes in the form of values provided in URLs and cookies. The default position should be that all user input is to be considered untrusted and should be validated against business rules. In this section, you will concentrate on validating form values.

You can perform validation on form data in two places in a web application: in the browser, using either client-side script or the browser's in-built data type validation, and on the server, using C# code. However, you should only ever view client-side validation as a courtesy to the user because it is easily circumnavigated by anyone who knows how to use the browser's developer tools, for example. Server-side validation should be seen as essential.

The MVC framework, on which Razor Pages is built, includes a robust validation framework that works against inbound model properties on the client side and the server. This framework massively reduces the developer burden of writing validation code and maintaining it in two places.

The key players in the input validation framework are

- `DataAnnotation` attributes
- jQuery Unobtrusive Validation
- Tag helpers
- `ModelState`

5.3.1 DataAnnotation attributes

The primary building block of the validation framework is a set of attributes that inherit from `ValidationAttribute`. Most of these attributes reside in the `System.ComponentModel.DataAnnotations` namespace. Each attribute is designed to perform a specific type of validation—be it for presence, data type, or range. Some also enable you to test the incoming value against an expected pattern. Table 5.2 lists the validation attributes you are most likely to use and the type of validation they provide along with example usage.

Table 5.2 Validation attributes for use in Razor Pages

Attribute	Description
`Compare`	Used to specify another property that the value should be compared to for equality. `[Compare(nameof(Password2))]`
`MaxLength`	Sets the maximum number of characters/bytes/items that can be accepted. `[MaxLength(20)]`
`MinLength`	Sets the minimum number of characters/bytes/items that can be accepted. `[MinLength(2)]`
`PageRemote`	Enables client-side validation against a server-side resource, such as a database check to see if a username is already in use.
`Range`	Sets the minimum and maximum values of a range. `[Range(5,8)], Range(typeof(DateTime),"2021-1-1", "2021-12-31")]`
`RegularExpression`	Checks the value against the specified regular expression. `[RegularExpression(@"[a-zA-Z]+")]`
`Required`	Specifies that a value must be provided for this property. Non-nullable value types, such as `DateTime` and numeric values, are treated as required by default and do not need this attribute applied to them. `[Required]`
`StringLength`	Sets the maximum and, optionally, the minimum number of string characters allowed. `[StringLength(2)], [StringLength(10, MinimumLength=2)]`

In addition, there are some data type validation attributes, including `Phone`, `EmailAddress`, `Url`, and `CreditCard`. These validate incoming values against predetermined formats to ensure that they are "well formed." Documentation on what the attribute authors consider to be well formed is sparse, but you can always resort to looking at the source code to see the logic used to test the incoming value to ensure the implementation covers your business rules. The .NET Source Browser is a great tool for this purpose (https://source.dot.net/). Using that, or going directly to the source code for the `EmailAddressAttribute` (http://mng.bz/44ww), for example, will show you that the "validation" consists of little more than checking the presence of the `@` character in the input. The check ensures there is only one instance of the character, and it is not at the beginning or end of the input. So `a@b` will pass this validation.

Aside from the `PageRemote` attribute, all the other attributes cause validation to occur on both the client and the server. The `PageRemote` attribute uses client-side code to validate against the server. See http://mng.bz/QvBG for more details on usage.

Attributes are applied to `PageModel` properties or properties of an input model. They can also be applied to handler method parameters, but you lose out on automatic client-side validation if you bind to handler parameters rather than `PageModel` properties. We will only look at applying validation attributes to properties. Server-side validation is enabled by default. Client-side validation must be specifically enabled.

5.3.2 Client-side validation

Client-side validation should only ever be viewed as a courtesy to users, in that it provides immediate feedback to the user in the event that they have not provided satisfactory input. Your application must not rely solely on client-side validation because it is very easy to circumvent by anyone who has a small amount of HTML or JavaScript knowledge. Client-side validation support is currently provided by the jQuery Unobtrusive Validation library, developed by Microsoft, which builds on the popular and well-tested jQuery Validation library.

The future of jQuery-based validation

There is an open work item in the ASP.NET Core Github repo (https://github.com/dotnet/aspnetcore/issues/8573) that discusses the potential future removal of jQuery as a dependency in the project templates. Clearly this would impact future client-side validation approaches. It appears to be a major undertaking if it is to happen, but it is worth keeping an eye on to see how the issue unfolds. Obviously, if jQuery is removed from future templates, that will have no impact on applications that have been developed prior to that point.

You must include jQuery Unobtrusive Validation scripts within the page containing the form for client-side validation to work. This is most easily accomplished by the inclusion of the _ValidationScriptsPartial.cshtml file (located in the Shared folder) within the page, using the partial tag helper you saw in chapter 3:

```
@section scripts{
  <partial name="_ValidationScriptsPartial" />
}
```

You must also ensure jQuery is available to the page. It is included in the default layout page, so as long as your form is in a page that references the layout, there is nothing else you need to do.

Client-side validation depends on custom HTML5 `data-val-*` attributes emitted by tag helpers. To see how that works, in listing 5.22, you revert the Create page in the

CountryManager back to inserting one country at a time, with one difference: the addition of validation attributes on the `InputModel` properties.

Listing 5.22 Adding validation attributes to the input model properties

```
public class CreateModel : PageModel
{
    [BindProperty]
    public InputModel Input { get; set; }
    public Country Country { get; set; }

    public void OnPost()
    {
        Country = new Country{
            CountryCode = Input.CountryCode,
            CountryName = Input.CountryName
        };
    }

    public class InputModel
    {
        [Required]
        public string CountryName { get; set; }
        [Required, StringLength(2, MinimumLength = 2)]
        public string CountryCode { get; set; }
    }
}
```

Both properties are marked as required. The CountryCode must be 2 characters in length.

The attributes have been applied to the properties. Both properties have the `Required` attribute, which means the user has to provide a value. In addition, you are validating the `CountryCode` value for length. The value provided by the user must be two characters long. You have used the `StringLength` attribute for this, setting both the maximum and minimum values to 2. You can apply multiple attributes in one set of square brackets, separated by commas, or you can apply them individually if you prefer.

The revised form uses input tag helpers along with validation tag helpers. The validation tag helpers target the `span` element and are responsible for rendering validation error messages for the property specified by its `validation-for` attribute.

Listing 5.23 Using validation tag helpers to emit validation error messages

```
<form method""pos"">
    <div class""form-grou"">
        <label for""Input.CountryNam"" class""control-labe"">Name</label>
        <input asp-for""Input.CountryNam"" class="form-control" />
        <span asp-validation-for="Input.CountryName"
        ➥ class="text-danger"></span>
    </div>
    <div class="form-group">
        <label for="Input.CountryCode" class="control-label">ISO-3166-1
        ➥ Code</label>
```

Input tag helpers and validation tag helpers are added to the form for both properties.

```
        <input asp-for="Input.CountryCode" class="form-control" />
        <span asp-validation-for="Input.CountryCode"
        ➥ class="text-danger"></span>
    </div>
    <div class="form-group">
        <input type="submit" value="Create" class="btn btn-primary" />
    </div>
</form>
```

Input tag helpers and validation tag helpers are added to the form for both properties.

In addition, to activate client-side validation, you must reference the validation scripts, so add the following to the bottom of the Razor page.

Listing 5.24 Adding `ValidationScriptsPartial` for client-side validation

```
@section scripts{
    <partial name="_ValidationScriptsPartial"/>
}
```

Run the application, and navigate to /country-manager/create. If you try to submit the form without entering any data, you will see error messages. If you try to submit a single character in the `CountryCode` input, a different error message will appear. Notice that you cannot enter more than two characters into that control. Take a look at the HTML that was generated for the `CountryCode` input.

Listing 5.25 The rendered HTML for the `CountryCode` property input

```
<input
    class="form-control"
    type="text"
    data-val="true"
    data-val-length="The field CountryCode must be a string
    ➥ with a minimum length of 2 and a maximum length of 2."
    data-val-length-max="2"
    data-val-length-min="2"
    data-val-required="The CountryCode field
    ➥ is required."
    id="Input_CountryCode"
    maxlength="2"
    name="Input.CountryCode"
    value=""
/>
```

This is the default error message generated by the inclusion of the Required attribute.

These attributes were generated because the StringLength attribute was applied to the property.

I've broken it over multiple lines for readability, but you can see a number of `data-val` attributes have been added to the rendered input. These attributes relate to the various types of validation you want to subject the value to. They include the default error messages that will be displayed along with the parameters that valid values must fall within. Following is the content of the span tag helper generated by the client-side validation library when the user attempts to submit a value that is less than the `data-val-length-min` value.

Listing 5.26 The generated source for the validation tag helper when an error occurs

```
<span class="text-danger field-validation-error"
    data-valmsg-for="Input.CountryCode"
    data-valmsg-replace="true">
    <span id="Input_CountryCode-error" class="">
        The field CountryCode must be a string with a minimum length
            of 2 and a maximum length of 2.
    </span>
</span>
```

The span automatically has a CSS class of `field-validation-error` applied to it when an error occurs. You could use this class to apply styles to the rendered error message, but you have already used the Bootstrap `text-danger` class to apply a red color to the output.

All validation attributes have an `ErrorMessage` property that enables you to set your own custom error message instead of relying on the default error messages set by the attribute authors. The following listing illustrates how you could change the error message for the country code field.

Listing 5.27 Setting a custom error message through the `ErrorMessage` property

```
[Required, StringLength(2, MinimumLength = 2,
    ErrorMessage = "You must provide a valid two character ISO 3166-1 code")]
public string CountryCode { get; set; }
```

You can opt a property out of validation by adding the `ValidationNever` attribute to it. This attribute belongs to a different namespace, so you will need to add a using statement:

```
@using Microsoft.AspNetCore.Mvc.ModelBinding.Validation
```

The `data-val` validation attributes are not rendered by a tag helper with a property that has this attribute applied to it.

The validation tag helper is responsible for outputting validation error messages for individual properties. You may also want to present the user with a summary of validation errors or a general validation error message, which you can use the validation summary tag for. It targets a `div` element and allows you to control the level of detail included in the message by passing a value to the `validation-summary` attribute. Acceptable values are `None`, `ModelOnly`, and `All`:

```
<div asp-validation-summary="All" class="text-danger">There are errors</div>
```

When you pass `None`, only the content of the div is rendered. Effectively, the tag helper does nothing. The `ModelOnly` option results in `ModelState` errors that apply to named form fields (property-level errors) being included in the message as an unordered list of error messages. When you specify `All`, model-level errors (i.e., those that don't apply to a particular form field) are included along with the property-level errors you have been generating through the validation attributes. You will look at adding a model-level entry when you examine `ModelState` in more detail later.

The content of the validation summary tag helper is visible by default, so if you want to include a default error message, you should ensure it is hidden. You can use the `validation-summary-valid` CSS class applied to the rendered div element to manage that:

```
.validation-summary-valid{ display: none };
```

If there are validation errors, that class is removed from the element and replaced with `validation-summary-errors`.

5.3.3 Server-side validation

Because it is so easy to circumvent client-side validation, server-side validation is included as part of the ASP.NET Core validation framework. Once property values have been bound on the server by the model binder, the framework looks for all validation attributes on those properties and executes them. Any failures result in an entry being added to a `ModelStateDictionary`—a dictionary-like structure where validation errors are stored. This is made available in the `PageModel` class via `ModelState`. It has a property named `IsValid` that returns `false` if there are any entries. The recommended practice for handling form submissions on the server is to test `ModelState.IsValid`, process the form submission if there are no validation errors, and then redirect the user to another page using the post-redirect-get (PRG) pattern you have already looked at. If there are errors, you redisplay the current page with the form.

To test this out, you should first remove the `ValidationScriptsPartial` tag helper from the Country Create page, so client-side validation is disabled for the form. Then make the following changes to the `PageModel` class.

Listing 5.28 Changing the `OnPost` handler to use the PRG pattern

```
[TempData]
public string CountryCode { get; set; }
[TempData]
public string CountryName { get; set; }

public IActionResult OnPost()
{
    if (ModelState.IsValid)
    {
        CountryCode = Input.CountryCode;
        CountryName = Input.CountryName;
        return RedirectToPage("/CountryManager/Success");
    }
    return Page();
}
```

- Add two string properties, decorated with the TempData attribute.
- Check ModelState.
- If all is OK, assign the form values to the TempData properties and redirect to another page.
- Or redisplay the form.

You have introduced a new item here: `TempData`. This is another dictionary that is designed to hold values for the duration of the next request. Its most common use is to retain state during a redirect, such as is used in this example. If you apply the `TempData` attribute to a simple property (e.g., a string), it is automatically added to the dictionary.

The `OnPost` handler has been altered to test `ModelState.IsValid`. If it is valid, the incoming values are assigned to the string properties, and the user is redirected to a page called Success. If not, the user is shown the form again. So you need a new page named Success.cshtml. This should be added to the CountryManager folder, and the Razor page should be altered to look like the following listing.

Listing 5.29 The Success page content

```
@page
@model CityBreaks.Pages.CountryManager.SuccessModel
<h1>Success!</h1>
<p>Your form submission was completed. You submitted:</p>
<p>
    @TempData["CountryName"]
   <img src="/images/flags/@(TempData["CountryCode"]).png" />
</p>
```

Run the application, and navigate to country-manager/create. If you try to submit an invalid form, you will see the error messages, as previously. The difference is that these error messages were generated by the server, not the browser. Despite that, any values you entered into the form are retained, which are repopulated from the `ModelState` dictionary. When you submit valid values, you are redirected to the Success page, and details of your submission are shown (figure 5.12).

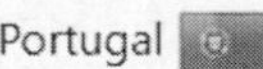

Figure 5.12 Values retained in `TempData` during a redirect

5.3.4 Managing more complex validation with ModelState

Validation attributes work for the vast majority of simple validation needs, but they are relatively limited in that the validation scenarios they handle are binary. A value either passes the test, or it doesn't. Also, they only operate on one value. There will be occasions when your validation scenarios are complex. Perhaps some values will only be required under certain circumstances, for example, or the range that you want to apply could be variable. And that variability could apply from time to time or from one user to another, perhaps.

The most direct way to apply this type of validation is to use C# code in your `OnPost` handler. You write code to validate values, and if validation fails, you add an entry into the `ModelState` object using its `AddModelError` method. Let us say, for instance, you have a validation rule stating that the first letter of the country name and its code must match. The following code shows the OnPost method in the country's CreateModel adapted to apply this validation test.

Listing 5.30 Adding an error to ModelState

```
public IActionResult OnPost()
{
    if(!string.IsNullOrWhiteSpace(Input.CountryName) &&
       !string.IsNullOrWhiteSpace(Input.CountryCode) &&
       Input.CountryName.ToLower().First() !=
       Input.CountryCode.ToLower().First())      <-- The validation test is applied.
    {
        ModelState.AddModelError("Input.CountryName",
            "The first letters of the name and code must match");   <--
    }
    if (ModelState.IsValid)
    {
        CountryCode = Input.CountryCode;
        CountryName = Input.CountryName;
        return RedirectToPage("/CountryManager/Success");
    }
    return Page();
}
```

If the test returns false, an error is logged with ModelState as a property-level entry.

The version of the AddModelError method you are most likely to use takes two strings: the name of the property that the error applies to and the error message you want to show the user. If the name of the property matches one passed in to a validation tag helper, that tag helper will display the error message.

Since this error message applies to two form fields, you may decide you don't want it to appear against one without the other. To prevent this issue, you can add another error message relating to the other property:

```
ModelState.AddModelError("Input.CountryName",
    "The first letter must match the first letter of the ISO 3166-1 code");
ModelState.AddModelError("Input.CountryCode",
    "The first letter must match the first letter of the country name");
```

Alternatively, you can pass an empty string to the property name, making this a model-level entry, which will be displayed by the validation summary tag helper whether it is set to ModelOnly or All:

```
ModelState.AddModelError(string.Empty,
    "The first letters of the name and code must match");
```

5.3.5 *Custom validation attributes*

There is one problem with writing validation code in a handler method: it is not reusable. You have established that the country name and code must start with the same letter, and you have ensured that when countries are created, that rule is enforced.

However, you also need to enforce the rule when countries are updated for whatever reason. You could copy and paste the code from the Create page's `OnPost` handler, but then you introduce a maintenance problem. If changes are required to the validation logic, they have to be applied in multiple places. Instead, you can centralize the logic in a custom validation attribute, which you can reuse throughout the application.

Custom validation attributes derive from `ValidationAttribute`. The validation logic is placed within an overridden `IsValid` method that returns a `ValidationResult` object. An overload of the `IsValid` method provides us access to the `ValidationContext`, which holds information about aspects of the validation operation, including the rest of the model being validated. This is the version you need to use, so you can get a reference to other properties. Create a folder within the project named ValidationAttributes, and within that, add a C# class named `CompareFirstLetterAttribute` with the following code.

Listing 5.31 Custom validation attribute

```
public class CompareFirstLetterAttribute : ValidationAttribute
{
    public string OtherProperty { get; set; }

    protected override ValidationResult IsValid(object value,
    ➥ ValidationContext validationContext)
    {
        var otherPropertyInfo =
        ➥ validationContext.ObjectType.GetRuntime
        ➥ Property(OtherProperty);
        if (otherPropertyInfo == null)
        {
            return new ValidationResult(
            ➥ "You must specify another property to compare to");
        }
        var otherValue =
        ➥ otherPropertyInfo.GetValue(validationContext.
        ➥ ObjectInstance, null);
        if (!string.IsNullOrWhiteSpace
        ➥ (value?.ToString()) &&
        ➥ !string.IsNullOrWhiteSpace(otherValue?.ToString()) &&

        ➥ value.ToString().ToLower().First() !=
        ➥ otherValue.ToString().ToLower().First())
        {
            return new ValidationResult(ErrorMessage
            ?? $"The first letters of
            ➥ {validationContext.DisplayName}
            ➥ and {otherPropertyInfo.Name} must match");
        }
        return ValidationResult.Success;
    }
}
```

Derive the class from ValidationAttribute, and override the IsValid method.

Add a public property representing the name of the form property to compare to.

Use the ValidationContext to get a reference to the other property.

Implement the validation logic.

Return a ValidationResult in the event of failure or ValidationResult.Success if validation succeeded.

The validation logic within this custom attribute is virtually identical to the page handler. You use the `ValidationContext` to access the other property's value to compare to. Its `ObjectType` property represents the object being validated, which is the `InputModel` in this case. If the other property cannot be found, you return a `ValidationResult` with an error message, which is stored in `ModelState`. If it is found, the first letters of each property are compared. Then you either return a `ValidationResult` with a different error message if the validation fails, or you return `ValidationResult.Success`.

Now that the attribute has been created, you can remove the original check in the `OnPost` method—the lines of code before checking `ModelState.IsValid` in listing 5.29. Then you apply the attribute to the target property, which is the `CountryName` property of the `InputModel`:

```
[Required, CompareFirstLetter(OtherProperty = nameof(CountryCode))]
public string CountryName { get; set; }
```

The custom attribute is executed along with framework attributes after model binding.

In addition to writing your own validation logic, whether inline within handlers or as a custom attribute, you can also consider using `IValidatableObject` (http://mng.bz/XZRv) for more complex validation requirements. Alternatively, you can explore some third-party validation libraries. One particularly popular open source library is Fluent Validation (https://fluentvalidation.net/). It offers much more flexibility than the validation attributes provided by various parts of .NET.

This has been an in-depth chapter, but we are only halfway through working with forms in a Razor Pages application. We have touched on using some form-related tag helpers so far, but we have barely scratched the surface. In the next chapter, you continue your journey by taking a deeper dive into more tag helpers that ease the burden of working with forms in Razor Pages.

Summary

- Forms can be submitted using both `POST` and `GET` methods.
- Values submitted using `GET` are included in the URL as query string values.
- Values submitted using `POST` are included in the request body.
- Model binding takes values from HTTP requests (sources) and assigns them to handler method parameters and public `PageModel` properties decorated with the `BindProperty` attribute (targets).
- The name attribute in the form control must match the name of the binding target, whether it is a parameter or property.
- Model binding supports binding to collections.
- Include an index within the control's name attribute to identify individual elements within a collection.
- The indexer can be sequential or explicit.
- Explicit indices are more useful when updating existing items.

- Validation can be performed on the client but must be performed on the server.
- Validation attributes work on both the client and the server.
- You must opt in to client validation by including the required scripts in the page.
- You can write your own validation attributes to handle more complex validation scenarios.

6 Working with forms: Tag helpers

This chapter covers

- Building forms with tag helpers
- Controlling input types with data annotations
- Populating select lists with server-side code
- Working with check boxes and radio buttons in forms
- Uploading files to the server

The last chapter covered how model binding takes form input and binds it to handler parameters and public properties in Razor Pages. You learned that the key to ensuring successful binding is ensuring that the name of the binding source matches that of the binding target. Up to now, you have generated the name of your form controls manually. This potentially error-prone approach doesn't move you much beyond fishing around in the `Request.Form` collection for your posted values.

In Razor Pages applications, forms are where tag helpers shine. You have already seen their role in client- and server-side validation with the validation tag helpers. This chapter will explore how to generate forms to collect data from users and work with the model-binding system. You will see how they can be used to ensure control names work smoothly with binding target names. The following tag helpers are available for form building:

- Form
- Form action
- Label
- Input
- Select
- Option
- Textarea

Each tag helper targets the HTML element it is named after, except the form action tag helper, which targets buttons and input elements that have their `type` attribute set to `submit` or `image`.

This chapter starts by covering the form tag helper to help you understand its role and configure it. We will look extensively at the input tag helper and learn how to control the type of input it renders based on the binding target data type as well as how to use data annotation attributes to fine-tune things when needed.

Select lists, check boxes, and radio buttons seem to raise most form-related questions on technical community support sites and forums, so we will look at how to work with their tag helpers in detail. Finally, we will look at using forms to upload files.

6.1 The form and form action tag helpers

The form tag helper targets the HTML `form` element and has two primary responsibilities. It ensures that a request verification token is included in a hidden field within every form that has its method set to `post`. It also generates the URL for the form's `action` attribute from the values you supply to its custom attributes.

The form action tag helper targets buttons and inputs with their `type` attribute set to `submit` or `image`. Its role is to set the URL for the `formaction` attribute on those elements, which specifies the location the form should be submitted to. As such, it overrides the form's `action` attribute.

Going forward, when I refer to a tag helper's custom attributes in text, I will omit the `asp-` prefix. Just remember that all framework attributes are prefixed with `asp-`. The custom attributes for generating URLs available on both the form tag helper and the form action tag helper are identical to those on the anchor tag helper I covered in detail in chapter 4, and they work in the same way to construct values based on the application's routing configuration:

- `page`
- `page-handler`
- `route-*`
- `all-route-data`

- host
- protocol
- area

If you include an action attribute in a form element and any of these custom routing attributes, the framework will raise an error. The form tag helper uses the values passed to these custom attributes to generate an action attribute, similar to how the anchor tag helper generates an href attribute from the same custom routing attributes. You can either explicitly set the URL via the action attribute yourself or use tag helper attributes to configure it. But you cannot do both. If you don't include the action attribute or any custom routing attributes, the form will submit to the current page's URL. For the vast majority of CRUD situations, that is most likely what you will do, and you will process the submission in the OnPost handler of the same page that generated the form. You will often use the tag helper attributes to set the form's action when the processing page is a different page or the form is processed within a named handler. You already saw, for example, where you might want to set the page handler name when we covered named handlers in chapter 3:

```
<form method="post" asp-page-handler="Search">
```

The form tag helper supports one additional custom attribute: antiforgery. This takes a Boolean value to control whether the request verification token is rendered or not, so it provides a way for you to disable request verification on a form-by-form basis selectively. If the attribute is omitted, the value defaults to true. Thinking back to the example where we covered named handlers in chapter 3, the search form in listing 3.32 could have been written to use a form action tag helper instead of setting the submission URL via the form tag helper. The following listing demonstrates how to use the page-handler attribute to generate a formaction attribute in the rendered button.

Listing 6.1 The form action tag helper

```
<form method="post">
    <p>Search</p>
    <input name="searchTerm" />
    <button asp-page-handler="Search">Search</button>
</form>
```

The page-handler attribute is applied to the button, resulting in a formaction attribute being rendered to the browser.

6.2 Input and label tag helpers

In the last chapter, you progressed from the potentially error-prone practice of mapping the names of form field controls to keys in the Form and Query collections to binding to public properties that are explicitly marked as binding targets due to having the BindProperty attribute applied to them. But you still have room for error because the value of the control's name attribute must match the target PageModel property's name. Recall the HTML for the form in the city's Create page, where you assign the string "cityName" to the name attribute:

```
<input class="form-control" type="text" name="cityName" />
```

As discussed previously, you cannot rely on strings matching. A change to one or the other will only result in errors at run time. Since the properties are accessible within the Razor page, it is possible to use the `nameof` expression directly in your Razor code to ensure the generated value for the form control's name attribute matches the property name:

```
<input name="@nameof(Model.CityName)" type="text" />
```

However, using an input tag helper achieves something similar with less ceremony and offers more bang for your buck. It has a `for` attribute that takes the name of the `PageModel` property and effectively binds that property to the tag helper, generating both a `name` and an `id` attribute in the rendered HTML for the form control. The input tag helper will also render the `type` attribute, setting its value to a suitable one based on the data type of the bound property, so you don't need to include that in your markup either. And the tag helper also renders a `value` attribute, which is set to the value assigned to the property. The following simple code is all that is required to generate a fully wired-up input element:

```
<input asp-for="CityName" />
```

The rendered output from the line above is

```
<input type="text" id="CityName" name="CityName" value="" />
```

In this way, you achieve a kind of two-way binding between the form control and the public `PageModel` property, or the binding source and its target (figure 6.1).

```
[BindProperty]
public string CityName { get; set; }

<input asp-for="CityName" />
```

Figure 6.1 Using tag helpers achieves a two-way binding between binding sources and their targets.

The existing label element in your Create City page can be replaced with a tag helper. The current HTML `for` attribute needs to be prefixed with `asp-` to activate the tag helper. Just like the input tag helper, the value passed in to the `for` attribute should be the name of the model property:

```
<label asp-for="CityName"></label>
```

In this example, the label tag helper is empty. It has no content. When used like this, the property name is rendered within the label:

```
<label for="CityName">CityName</label>
```

You can override this by adding your text to the label's content or by using a data annotation attribute, which we will look at shortly.

So to summarize, the benefit of using tag helpers in forms is that you establish a two-way binding relationship between the property in your server code and the form control rendered to the browser. If the value is updated in the form, that update is applied automatically on the server when submitted. Equally, if you change the value on the server, the rendered form control will reflect those changes automatically.

6.2.1 Understanding the input types

Now that you understand the benefits of using tag helpers in forms, it's time to look at ways to ensure the correct type of input is rendered. First, we will look at the default mapping between .NET and HTML types. HTML 5 added support for a collection of new input types for different kinds of data—`number`, `datetime-local`, `week`, and `range`—on top of the existing options that include `checkbox`, `radio`, `file`, and so on. Some of the HTML 5 input types only enjoy limited support across browsers, but where you can, you should make use of them before reaching for third-party libraries (e.g., date pickers) that provide similar features.

You can often rely on Razor Pages generating the correct type based purely on the property's data type that is bound to the tag helper. Table 6.1 provides details on which value is generated for the HTML `type` attribute by the input tag helper for the specified .NET data types.

Table 6.1 Mapping between .NET data types and the type attribute generated by the input tag helper

.NET type	HTML input type
`string`	`text`
`bool`	`checkbox`
`int, byte, short, long`	`number`
`decimal, double, float`	`text`
`DateTime`	`datetime-local`
`IFormFile`	`file`

To test this out, add a new folder to the Pages folder named PropertyManager. This will house pages for managing details of rental properties available on the website. Then add a new Razor page named Create.cshtml. Add the following public properties to the `PageModel` representing information about a rental property that allows users to work with a range of .NET types.

Listing 6.2 The `CreateModel` for the Property Manager

```
public class CreateModel : PageModel
{
```

```
    [BindProperty]
    public string Name { get; set; }
    [BindProperty]
    public int MaxNumberOfGuests { get; set; }
    [BindProperty]
    public decimal DayRate { get; set; }
    [BindProperty]
    public bool SmokingPermitted { get; set; }
    [BindProperty]
    public DateTime AvailableFrom { get; set; }
}
```

Next you change the Create.cshtml file to include a form, using tag helpers for each of the `PageModel` properties, so the code looks like the following.

Listing 6.3 The form for the Create Property page, using tag helpers

```
@page
@model CityBreaks.Pages.PropertyManager.CreateModel
@{
    ViewData["Title"] = "Create Property";
}

<form method="post">
    <div class="mb-3">
        <label class="form-label" asp-for="Name"></label>
        <input class="form-control" asp-for="Name" />
    </div>
    <div class="mb-3">
        <label class="form-label" asp-for="MaxNumberOfGuests"></label>
        <input class="form-control" asp-for="MaxNumberOfGuests" />
    </div>
    <div class="mb-3">
        <label class="form-label" asp-for="DayRate"></label>
        <input class="form-control" asp-for="DayRate" />
    </div>
    <div class="mb-3">
        <label class="form-label" asp-for="AvailableFrom"></label>
        <input class="form-control" asp-for="AvailableFrom" />
    </div>
    <div class="mb-3">
        <label asp-for="SmokingPermitted"></label>
        <input asp-for="SmokingPermitted" />
    </div>
    <div class="mb-3">
        <button class="btn btn-primary">Submit</button>
    </div>
</form>
```

Aside from the Bootstrap classes used for presentation, the form consists of a series of label and input tag helpers representing each property in the `PageModel`. When you navigate to /property-manager/create, you should see something similar to figure 6.2.

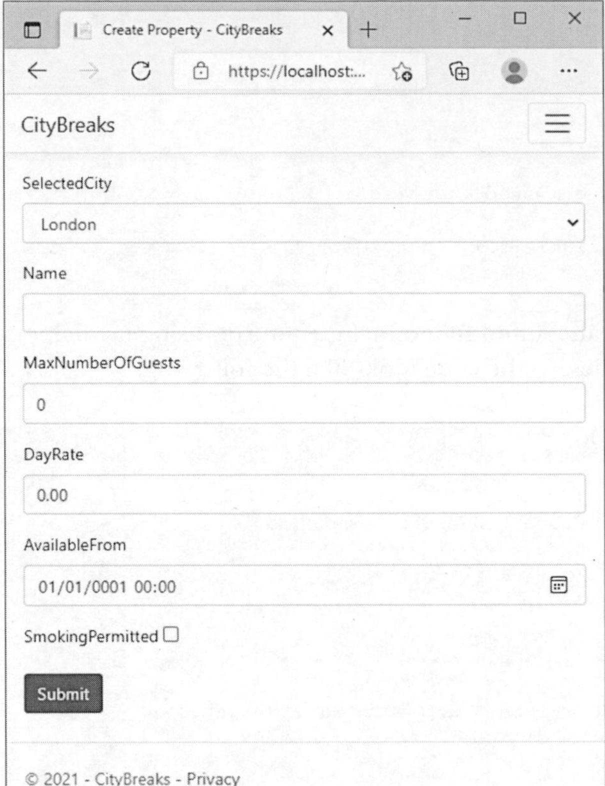

Figure 6.2 The rendered form for the Create Property page

The label tag helpers have rendered the name of the property, and this value has also been assigned to the rendered label's `for` attribute. Some of these label values are not particularly user friendly. We'll look at ways you can manage that a bit later.

The inputs have been generated according to the data type of the associated property, as described in the table 6.1. Notice that several inputs already have a value assigned even though you haven't set one. The associated properties are not nullable, so they are considered to be required, and their default value has already been assigned to them. Now let's take a look at the rendered source code for the form.

Listing 6.4 The rendered source for the form

```
<form method="post">
    <div class="mb-3">
        <label class="form-label" for="Name">Name</label>
        <input class="form-control" type="text" id="Name"
        ➥ name="Name" value="" />
    </div>
    <div class="mb-3">
        <label class="form-label"
        ➥ for="MaxNumberOfGuests">MaxNumberOfGuests</label>
        <input class="form-control" type="number" data-val="true"
```

```
data-val-required="The MaxNumberOfGuests field is required."
id="MaxNumberOfGuests" name="MaxNumberOfGuests" value="0" />
    </div>
    <div class="mb-3">
        <label class="form-label" for="DayRate">DayRate</label>
        <input class="form-control" type="text" data-val="true"
data-val-number="The field DayRate must be a number."
➥ data-val-required="The DayRate field is required."
➥ id="DayRate" name="DayRate" value="0.00" />
    </div>
    <div class="mb-3">
        <label class="form-label" for="AvailableFrom">AvailableFrom</label>
        <input class="form-control" type="datetime-local" data-val="true"
        ➥ data-val-required="The AvailableFrom field is required."
        ➥ id="AvailableFrom"
 name="AvailableFrom" value="0001-01-01T00:00:00.000" />
    </div>
    <div class="mb-3">
        <label for="SmokingPermitted">SmokingPermitted</label>
        <input type="checkbox" data-val="true"
        ➥ data-val-required="The SmokingPermitted field is required."
        ➥ id="SmokingPermitted" name="SmokingPermitted" value="true" />
    </div>
    <div class="mb-3">
        <button class="btn btn-primary">Submit</button>
    </div>
<input name="__RequestVerificationToken" type="hidden" value="CfDJ...F4" />
<input name="SmokingPermitted" type="hidden" value="false" />
</form>
```

All of the non-nullable properties include the additional client-side validation attributes you met in the last chapter: `data-val` and `data-val-required`. The `data-val` attribute is set to `true` for each property. The `data-val-required` attribute has an error message assigned to it customized to the associated property.

Ignoring the request verification token, which I cover in chapter 13, one other point of interest is that two inputs have been generated for the `SmokingPermitted` property. The first is the check box you would expect to see rendered for a Boolean value, based on the mapping described in table 6.1. The second is a hidden input included just before the closing form tag:

```
<input name="SmokingPermitted" type="hidden" value="false" />
```

Normally, no value is passed to the server for the associated property when the form is submitted if a check box is not checked. The hidden field will ensure that a name-value pair will be included in the form submission, regardless of whether the check box is checked or not. If the check box is checked, the posted value will be `true,false`. Otherwise, it will be `false`. Based on this, the model binder will be able to infer the correct value to assign to the `PageModel` property. This behavior is really a feature of MVC, where a selection of which particular action to execute on a controller can come down to the parameters the action method takes as determined from the collection of posted values.

If you don't want a hidden field to be rendered, the workaround is to avoid using the tag helper to render your check box for Boolean properties. In these cases, use plain HTML instead.

6.2.2 Using data annotation attributes to control presentation

Residing in the `System.ComponentModel.DataAnnotations` namespace, data annotation attributes provide a way for you to add extra information, or *metadata*, to a type. Various component frameworks within .NET can use this additional information to influence their behavior. Data annotation attributes are widely used with forms in Razor Pages to influence validation, as you have already seen, and presentation. This section looks at how attributes can be used to influence the HTML generated as part of a form. Two attributes are of particular interest in respect to managing the UI: the `DataTypeAttribute` and the `DisplayAttribute`.

USING THE DATATYPEATTRIBUTE TO INFLUENCE THE RENDERED INPUT TYPE

The `DataTypeAttribute` enables you to specify the name of a more specific type than the .NET type system provides for and associate that type with a property. Input tag helpers will use the metadata you specify to override the value generated for the input tag helper's `type` attribute, resulting in UI behavior that is unique to the specified type. For example, there is no `Password` type in .NET, but you can specify that a string should be considered a password type through data annotation attributes. Most of the framework ignores this metadata, but the input tag helper will respond to it by setting the `type` attribute on the rendered control to `password`. A browser will render an input that has its type set to the password as a form control that obscures the characters being entered by default as a security measure.

The `DataType` attribute has two constructors. One takes a `DataType` enumeration value, and the other takes a string. A wide range of enumeration values are available, but only a subset influences the generated type on an HTML input. They are detailed in table 6.2.

Table 6.2 Mapping between `DataType` enumeration and input type

`DataType` enumeration	Input element's type attribute
`Date`	`date`
`EmailAddress`	`email`
`Password`	`password`
`PhoneNumber`	`tel`
`Time`	`time`
`Url`	`url`

When you apply multiple attributes to a property (e.g., the `BindProperty` attribute and a `DataType`) you can apply them individually within their own set of square brackets or use one set of brackets and separate each attribute with a comma. Both of the examples in listing 6.5 are valid.

Listing 6.5 Different options for applying multiple attributes to a single property

```
[BindProperty]
[DataType(DataType.Time)]
public  DateTime ArrivalTime { get; set; }

[BindProperty, DataType(DataType.Time)]
public  DateTime DepartureTime { get; set; }
```

Most leading browsers support the `week` and `month` inputs that enable the user to specify a week of the year or a month. These input types don't have matching `DataType` enumeration values. Instead, you can use the `DataType` attribute's constructor that takes a string to set input types to these options and any others that aren't covered in table 6.2:

```
[DataType("week")]
public  DateTime ArrivalWeek { get; set; }
```

In addition to the `DataType` enumerations, there are similarly named standalone attributes:

- `EmailAddress`
- `Phone`
- `Url`

While these also influence the value assigned to the rendered `type` attribute, they inherit from `ValidationAttribute` and take part in validation, as you saw in the last chapter. `System.ComponentModel.DataAnnotations` is not the only place these types of attributes can be found. `HiddenInput` is another standalone attribute that belongs to the MVC framework; it can be found under the `Microsoft.AspNetCore.Mvc` namespace. When applied to a `PageModel` property, the associated input will be rendered with its `type` attribute set to `hidden`.

6.2.3 Formatting the rendered date or time value

When reviewing the form you just created for adding new properties, you might have noticed that the HTML 5 `datetime-local` input type, generated for a `DateTime` `PageModel` property, supports setting values to the millisecond (figure 6.3). However, it rarely makes sense to expose this capability to users.

By default, if a value is assigned to the bound `DateTime` property, its millisecond portion is exposed to the browser control, activating the capability to set this part of the value. You can control this by applying a format string to the `DateTime` value. The

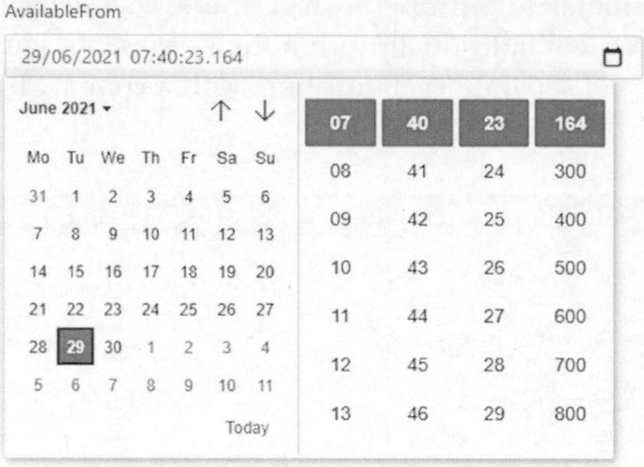

Figure 6.3 The default binding of a `DateTime` value activates the capability to set milliseconds in the `datetime-local` control.

`DisplayFormat` attribute enables you to apply the format string to the property. The format is applied wherever the property is used (assuming that the location is one where the framework recognizes and applies data annotation hints). The format string is specified via the attribute's `DataFormatString` property, and another property, `ApplyFormatInEditMode`, must be set to `true` for the format string to be applied in an editable setting, such as a form input:

```
[BindProperty, DisplayFormat(DataFormatString = "{0:yyyy-MM-ddTHH:mm}",
ApplyFormatInEditMode = true)]
public DateTime AvailableFrom { get; set; } = DateTime.Now;
```

Alternatively, you can use the input tag helper's `format` attribute to control the format on individual input controls:

```
<input asp-for="AvailableFrom" asp-format="{0:yyyy-MM-ddTHH:mm}" />
```

Having applied the format string shown in these examples, only the hour and minute elements of the time are available to be set in the browser (figure 6.4).

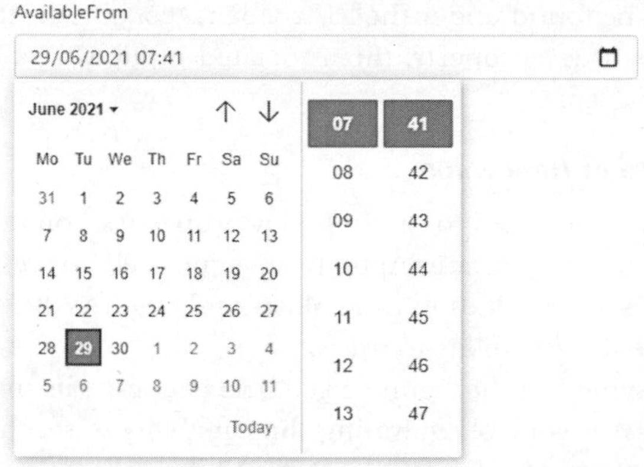

Figure 6.4 The seconds and milliseconds part of the time are no longer available to be set.

Supported date and time formats

The date- and time-based input types mostly support values formatted according to the rules specified within RFC 3339 (https://datatracker.ietf.org/doc/html/rfc3339). In brief, they require the year to be expressed as four digits and the date and time components to be ordered from the least specific (i.e., the year) to the most specific. The time portion should be separated from the date by an uppercase T. Within .NET, the following format string represents this:

```
yyyy-MM-ddTHH:mm:ss.fff
```

The seconds (`ss`) and milliseconds (`fff`) are optional for most browsers if you include the time element.

The week input type is used to select a week of the year, based on the ISO 8601 week number. The format supported by the week input is `yyyy-Www`, where `-W` is literal and `ww` represents the week of the year. The default model binder doesn't include support for this format because .NET doesn't support this as a valid date/time format string. If you need to work with the week input type, you must generate a value in the correct format yourself. Then you can either parse the value from `Request.Form` yourself, or you can implement your custom model binder. That is an advanced topic that won't be covered in this book, but you can refer to my blog post that provides an example specific to working with the week input type: http://mng.bz/M5eW.

6.2.4 Using the DisplayAttribute to control labels

Earlier, I noted that many of the rendered label values in the form (figure 6.1) lacked user friendliness. The label tag helper simply took the name of the C# property and rendered it as is—Pascal casing included. This is what happens if you leave the content of the label tag helper empty, as we did in this example form. One way to override this behavior is providing your content within each instance of the label tag:

```
<label asp-for="DayRate">Day Rate</label>
```

Alternatively, you can apply the `DisplayAttribute` to the property to control the output by assigning your preferred label text to its `Name` property:

```
[BindProperty]
[Display(Name="Day Rate")]
public decimal DayRate { get; set; }
```

The primary benefit of this approach is that you centralize the configuration, so you don't have to hunt around in the Razor page to make changes. The following listing shows the revised `PageModel` properties for the Create Property page with data type and display attributes applied. Figure 6.5 illustrates how the framework applies the attribute values to the rendered labels.

Listing 6.6 Public `PageModel` properties decorated with suitable attributes

```
[BindProperty]
public string Name { get; set; }
[BindProperty]
[Display(Name = "Maximum Number Of Guests")]
public int MaxNumberOfGuests { get; set; }
[BindProperty]
[Display(Name ="Day Rate")]
public decimal DayRate { get; set; }
[BindProperty]
[Display(Name = "Smoking Permitted")]
public bool SmokingPermitted { get; set; }
[BindProperty]
[DataType(DataType.Date)]
[Display(Name ="Available From")]
public DateTime AvailableFrom { get; set; }
```

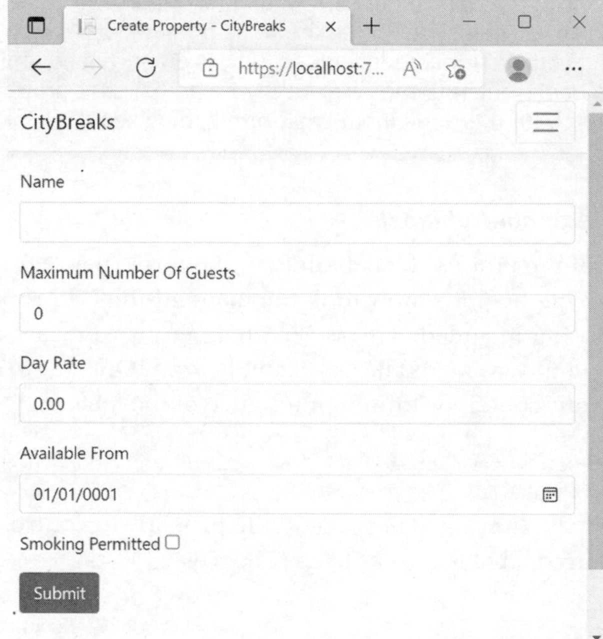

Figure 6.5 Data annotation attributes are used to manage the label and input presentation.

This completes our look at basic input and label tag helpers. In the next sections, we will focus on the select tag helper used to present a range of fixed options to the user, before moving on to the special nature of the check box and radio input types.

6.3 The select tag helper

In our application, each property must be located in a particular city, so when the user adds a new property, they should be able to specify the city in which the property is located. You could provide a text input for this, but the problem with allowing users to enter whatever they want is that you are likely to get typos and variations. For example, do they enter *New York* or *New York City*? The solution provides a predetermined set of options the user can select from. The most economical and usable way to do this from a UI perspective is to present the options in an HTML select element for a list that could grow quite a bit.

The select tag helper targets the HTML select element. It has two custom attributes: the now-familiar `for` attribute, which is used to bind a `PageModel` property representing the selected value to the select element, and an `items` attribute, by which you assign the options. Options are populated from a collection of `SelectListItem` objects, a `SelectList` object, or an enumeration. Options can also be set individually via the option tag helper.

6.3.1 Creating options

The HTML option element represents a single option in a select element. At the very least, it consists of text displayed in the browser. The simplest way to create options for a select tag helper is to pass a collection of some kind, like the array of cities you worked with in the last chapter, to the constructor of a `SelectList`. To see how this works, you will add a new element to the property creation form that enables the user to specify the city where the property is located. Adjust the `CreateModel` class in the PropertyManager folder to include the two additional highlighted properties, ensuring the `SelectedCity` property is decorated with the `BindProperty` attribute.

Listing 6.7 Adding properties to represent options and the selected value

```
public class CreateModel : PageModel
{
    [BindProperty]
    public string Name { get; set; }
    [BindProperty]
    public int MaxNumberOfGuests { get; set; }
    [BindProperty]
    public decimal DayRate { get; set; }
    [BindProperty]
    public bool SmokingPermitted { get; set; }
    [BindProperty]
    public DateTime AvailableFrom { get; set; }
      [BindProperty]
    [Display(Name="City")]
    public string SelectedCity { get; set; }
    public SelectList Cities { get; set; }

    public void OnGet()
    {
        var cities = new[] { "London", "Berlin", "Paris",
                            "Rome", "New York" };
        Cities = new SelectList(cities);
    }
}
```

The SelectedCity property represents the selected value.

The Cities property represents the options that the user can select from.

An OnGet handler containing code that creates an array of city names and passes to the SelectList constructor is added.

You should also add a using directive to include the Microsoft.AspNetCore.Mvc.Rendering namespace, which is where the SelectList type resides. Now make the changes detailed in the next listing to the markup part of the Create.cshtml.cs file located in the PropertyManager folder. The changes will include a select tag helper that presents a range of cities for the user to choose from, and when the form is submitted, the name of the selected city will be rendered to the page.

Listing 6.8 Amending the form to include a select tag helper

```
@if (Request.HasFormContentType)
{
    <p>You selected @Model.SelectedCity</p>
}
<form method="post">
    <div class="mb-3">
        <label class="form-label" asp-for="SelectedCity"></label>
        <select class="form-control" asp-for="SelectedCity"
            asp-items="Model.Cities"></select>
    </div>
    <div class="mb-3">
        <label class="form-label" asp-for="Name"></label>
        <input class="form-control" asp-for="Name" />
    </div>
    <div class="mb-3">
        <label class="form-label" asp-for="MaxNumberOfGuests"></label>
        <input class="form-control" asp-for="MaxNumberOfGuests" />
    </div>
    <div class="mb-3">
        <label class="form-label" asp-for="DayRate"></label>
        <input class="form-control" asp-for="DayRate" />
    </div>
    <div class="mb-3">
        <label class="form-label" asp-for="AvailableFrom"></label>
        <input class="form-control" asp-for="AvailableFrom" />
    </div>
    <div class="mb-3">
        <label asp-for="SmokingPermitted"></label>
        <input asp-for="SmokingPermitted" />
    </div>
    <button class="btn btn-primary">Submit</button>
</form>
```

Add this code block to render the selected city if the form has been submitted.

Add a label and the select tag helper for managing city selection.

Navigate to /property-manager/create. You should see London appear in the select control (figure 6.6).

Feel free to leave the selection as London, or choose another city from the options, and then submit the form. You should notice two things: the first is that the selected city is rendered to the browser, and the second is that the list of options is empty (figure 6.7).

So where did the options go? The options are currently generated in the OnGet handler. When the form is submitted to the server using the POST method, the OnGet

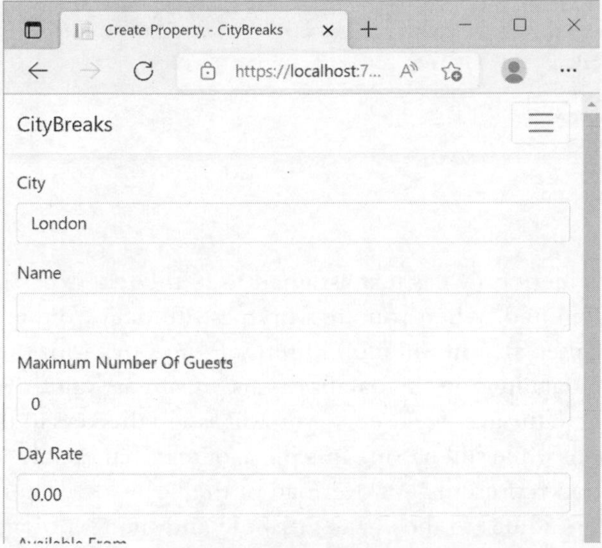

Figure 6.6 London is the default option in the select control.

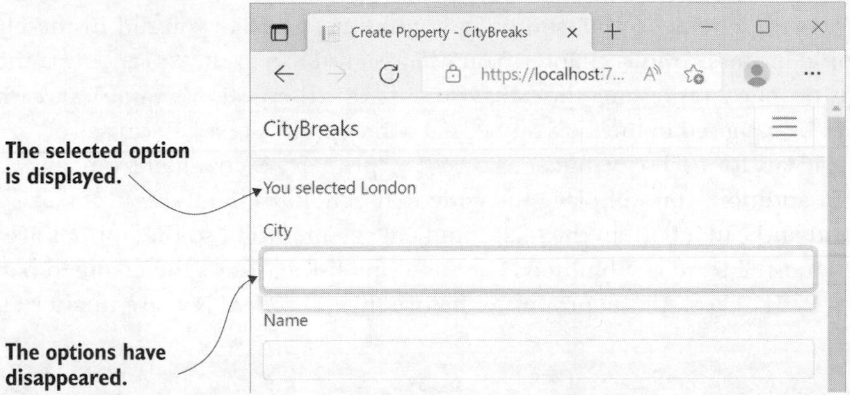

Figure 6.7 The selected option is displayed, but the list of options has disappeared.

handler is not executed. Since there is nothing in the `OnPost` handler to restore the city options, no options are generated for a `POST` request. We will look at a simple strategy for correcting this in the next example when you pass more complex objects to the `SelectList`.

SETTING THE VALUE OF OPTIONS

So far, you have passed a simple array of strings into the `SelectList`. The `SelectList` assigned each element of the array to an option's text, resulting in the following HTML for the select element.

Listing 6.9 The generated HTML for the select city element

```
<select class="form-control" id="SelectedCity" name="SelectedCity">
    <option>London</option>
    <option>Berlin</option>
    <option>Paris</option>
    <option>Rome</option>
    <option>New York</option>
</select>
```

When an HTML option element only has text assigned to it, the text is passed as the value when the form is submitted. When you are working with data from a database (as you will, starting in chapter 8), you will more often want to work with the unique identifier associated with a data item in the database—its *primary key* value. These key values don't mean anything to the average user, so you will assign the keys to the `value` attribute of the select options while still passing in a piece of text that enables a user to understand what each option represents. An overload of the `SelectList` constructor enables you to map different values to the `value` attribute and the text of an option. The next example shows how to use this overload to mimic the process of mapping a numeric identifier for each city to the option value, while still presenting the name of the city to the user.

You will generate a collection of `City` objects, just like you did in the check box example in the previous chapter. You will assign these to the `SelectList` and specify which property represents the `DataValueField` (the option's value) and which one should be assigned to the `DataTextField` (the option's text). Because you are using a numeric key for each city, the `SelectedCity` property is changed from a `string` to an `int`. In addition, you will place the code that generates the `SelectList` in a separate method and call it both in the `OnGet` and `OnPost` methods, so the options are repopulated after the form is submitted. The following listing shows the changed parts of the `CreateModel` class. All the properties before the `SelectedCity` are unaltered.

Listing 6.10 The amended `CreateModel` for the property manager

```
[BindProperty]
[Display(Name = "City")]
public int SelectedCity { get; set; }
public SelectList Cities { get; set; }
public string Message { get; set; }
public void OnGet()
{
    Cities = GetCityOptions();
}

public void OnPost()
{
    Cities = GetCityOptions();
    if (ModelState.IsValid)
    {
```

Change the SelectedCity from a string to an int.

Add a string property named Message.

Assign the Cities from a new private GetCityOptions method.

```
        var city = GetCityOptions().First(o => o.Value ==
        ➥ SelectedCity.ToString());
        Message = $"You selected {city.Text} with value of {SelectedCity}";
    }
}

private SelectList GetCityOptions()
{
    var cities = new List<City>
    {
        new City{ Id = 1, Name = "London"},
        new City{ Id = 2, Name = "Paris" },
        new City{ Id = 3, Name = "New York" },
        new City{ Id = 4, Name = "Rome" },
        new City{ Id = 5, Name = "Dublin" }
    };
    return new SelectList(cities, nameof(City.Id), nameof(City.Name));
}
```

Get details of the selected city from data generated by the GetCityOptions method.

Add a private method for generating the cities, so the logic is centralized in one place.

The only change required to the Razor page is including the `Message` property, so you can see confirmation of which city was selected. I place this at the top of the page, before the opening `form` element:

```
<p>@Model.Message</p>
```

Run the page and select a city. Once you submit the form, you will notice the details of the chosen city are rendered to the browser (figure 6.8).

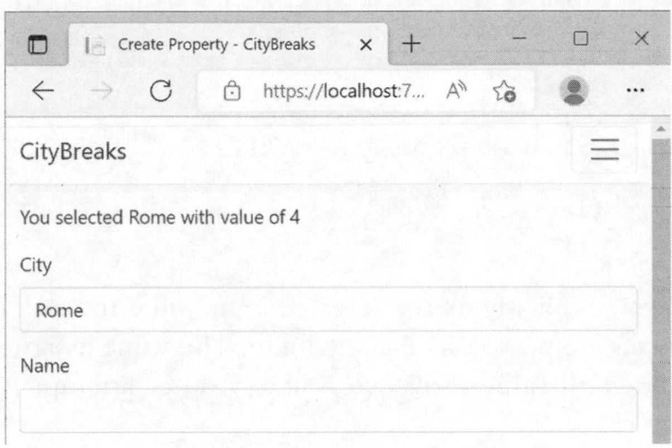

Figure 6.8 Details of the selected city are rendered to the browser.

When you view the source of the page, you will see the option you selected has the selected attribute applied to it too (figure 6.9).

You should be able to deduce from this behavior that you can set the selected item in a select tag helper by assigning its value to the property that is bound to its `for` attribute. You didn't assign the value to the `SelectedCity` property yourself, of course; the model binder did it for you.

```
    <p>You selected Rome with value of 4</p>
<form method="post">
    <div class="mb-3">
        <label class="form-label" for="SelectedCity">City</label>
        <select class="form-control" data-val="true" data-val-req
<option value="2">Paris</option>
<option value="3">New York</option>
<option selected="selected" value="4">Rome</option>
<option value="5">Dublin</option>
</select>
    </div>
```

Figure 6.9 The selected option has the selected attribute applied to it.

SETTING THE SELECTED VALUE

In addition to assigning a value to the bound property, you can set the selected value by passing in an additional parameter value to the `SelectList` constructor representing the value of the selected option:

```
var cities = new SelectList(cities, nameof(City.Id), nameof(City.Name), 3);
```

Or you can explicitly construct a collection of `SelectListItems` and set the `Selected` property on one of the elements to `true`.

Listing 6.11 Constructing a collection of `SelectListItems`

```
private SelectList GetCityOptions()
{
    var cities =  new List<SelectListItem>
    {
        new SelectListItem{ Value = "1", Text = "London"},
        new SelectListItem{ Value = "2", Text = "Paris" },
        new SelectListItem{ Value = "3", Text = "New York", Selected =
        ➥ true },
        new SelectListItem{ Value = "4", Text = "Rome" },
        new SelectListItem{ Value = "5", Text = "Dublin" }
    };
    return new SelectList(cities);
}
```

Methods like these, where you explicitly set the selected item, will only work if you do not bind a property to the tag helper via its `for` attribute. The value assigned to the bound property—even its default value—will override any other attempt to set the selected item.

6.3.2 *Binding multiple values*

So far you have used the select tag helper to enable the user to select one of a range of available options. In some cases, you might want to allow them to select more than one option. When you are working with HTML, you enable this by simply adding a `multiple` attribute to the select element:

```
<select name="cities" multiple>
```

When this attribute is present, the browser responds by rendering what is commonly called a list box—a box that lists all the options and may have a scroll bar if the contents exceed the height of the control (figure 6.10). The user can select multiple options by holding down the `Ctrl` key while selecting in most browsers.

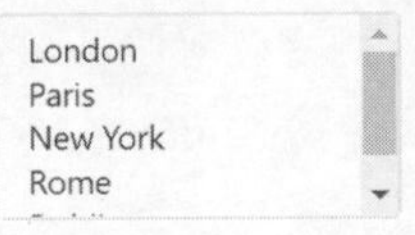

Figure 6.10 Select with `multiple` attribute applied

The select tag helper automatically renders the Boolean `multiple` attribute if the property is bound to be a collection. To be accurate, it renders `multiple="multiple"`, but the mere presence of the `multiple` attribute is all that is required to enable multiple selection. Most browsers ignore any values passed to the `multiple` attribute.

When a user arrives on the website, they may not have decided which city to visit yet. They might want to view various options. You can provide them with a way to easily select multiple options by binding a collection property to a select tag helper. Let's explore this by adding a selection form for the user on the site's home page. Open the Index.cshtml.cs file in the Pages folder, and add the following public properties to the `IndexModel`, representing the binding for the select tag helper (`int[] SelectedCities`), and the options with a message.

Listing 6.12 The `PageModel` properties for the multiple select list

```
[BindProperty]
[Display(Name = "Cities")]
public int[] SelectedCities { get; set; }
public SelectList Cities { get; set; }
public string Message { get; set; }
```

Now copy the same private `GetCityOptions` method from the Create Property page you have been working with to generate the `SelectList`, and add it to the `IndexModel`.

Listing 6.13 Copying the `GetCityOptions` method and adding it to the `IndexModel`

```
private SelectList GetCityOptions()
{
    var cities = new List<City>
    {
        new City{ Id = 1, Name = "London"},
        new City{ Id = 2, Name = "Paris" },
        new City{ Id = 3, Name = "New York" },
        new City{ Id = 4, Name = "Rome" },
        new City{ Id = 5, Name = "Dublin" }
    };
    return new SelectList(cities, nameof(City.Id), nameof(City.Name));
}
```

Finally, assign the `Cities` in the `OnGet` method. Then add an `OnPost` method that works with the bound values in the `SelectedCities` property and uses them as a filter on the `Cities` collection to extract details of the selected cities.

Listing 6.14 Adding the handler methods to the IndexModel to set the city options

```
public void OnGet()
{
    Cities = GetCityOptions();
}
public void OnPost()
{
    Cities = GetCityOptions();
    if (ModelState.IsValid)
    {
        var cityIds = SelectedCities.Select(x => x.ToString());
        var cities = GetCityOptions().Where(o =>
    cityIds.Contains(o.Value)).Select(o=>o.Text);
        Message = $"You selected {string.Join(", ", cities)}";
    }
}
```

Convert the collection of ints to strings.

Filter the city options to select only those that have been selected.

Use the string.Join method to construct the message from the resulting collection.

Now replace the existing content in Index.cshtml with the simple form shown in the next listing, which contains just the select tag helper and a button.

Listing 6.15 Adding the form to the home page

```
<div class="col-4">
    <form method="post">
        <div class="mb-3">
            <label class="form-label" asp-for="SelectedCities"></label>
            <select class="form-control" asp-for="SelectedCities"
            ➥ asp-items="Model.Cities"></select>
        </div>

        <div class="mb-3">
            <button class="btn btn-primary">Submit</button>
        </div>
    </form>
</div>
<p>@Model.Message</p>
```

When you run the application, it is immediately apparent that the output of the `select` tag helper is different from previous examples because you should see the list box appear. Select a couple of options while holding down the Ctrl key, and submit the form. Confirm that your selections have been included in the `Message` output and that they remain selected in the list box (figure 6.11).

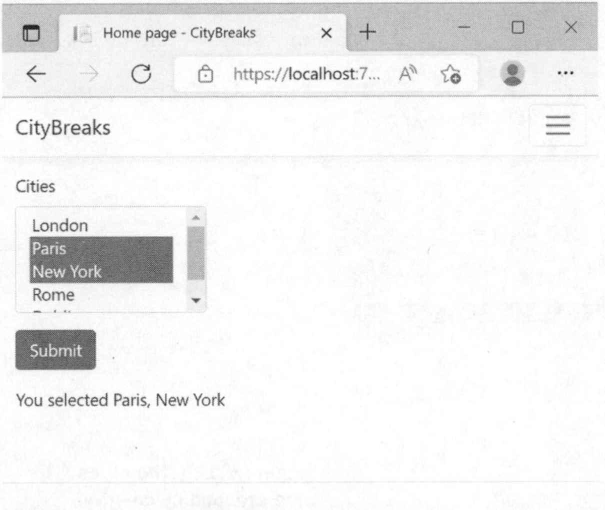

Figure 6.11 The selected options remain selected and are included in the rendered message.

6.3.3 Working with OptGroups

The `SelectList` class includes another constructor that enables you to specify the name of a property that should be used to represent an HTML `optgroup` element, the `DataGroupField`, which is used to group related options together within the list of options displayed to the user.

Each city belongs to a country. It seems reasonable to use option groups to group city options by country within the select element. When the user is creating a new property in the application, they can find the city where the property is located more easily. So let's add a new public property to the `City` class to represent the country name:

```
public string CountryName { get; set; }
```

Now you'll change the `GetCityOptions` method in the Pages\PropertyManager\Create .cshtml.cs file to assign a country name to a selection of cities and then pass in `nameof(City.CountryName)` to represent the `DataGroupField`.

Listing 6.16 Adding an option group to the city options

```
private SelectList GetCityOptions()
{
    var cities = new List<City>
    {
        new City{ Id = 1, Name = "Barcelona" , CountryName = "Spain" },
        new City{ Id = 2, Name = "Cadiz" , CountryName = "Spain" },
        new City{ Id = 3, Name = "London", CountryName = "United Kingdom" },
        new City{ Id = 4, Name = "Madrid" , CountryName = "Spain" },
        new City{ Id = 5, Name = "Rome", CountryName = "Italy" },
```

```
        new City{ Id = 6, Name = "Venice", CountryName = "Italy" },
        new City{ Id = 7, Name = "York" , CountryName = "United Kingdom" },
    };
    return new SelectList(cities, nameof(City.Id), nameof(City.Name),
    ➥ null, nameof(City.CountryName));
}
```

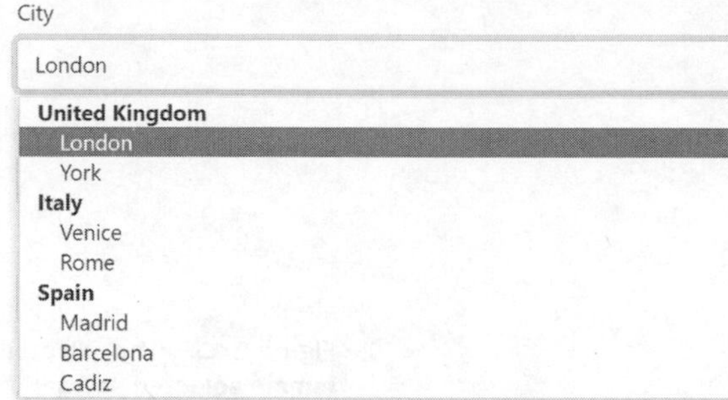

Figure 6.12 The cities are grouped by country.

When you run the page, you should see the data grouped by country, with the country name set as the grouping label (figure 6.12). Most often, you will work in an object-oriented way with your data. You already have a `Country` class, so you can use composition to represent the relationship between cities and countries by adding a `Country` property to the `City` class (bolded in the following listing).

Listing 6.17 Replacing the `CountryName` property with a `Country` property

```
public class City
{
    public int Id { get; set; }
    public string Name { get; set; }
    public Country Country { get; set; }    <-- Replace the string property with a Country property.
}
```

The next listing shows a revised version of the `GetCityOptions` method, where the country name is set through the `Country` property.

Listing 6.18 Using composition to set the country for each city

```
private SelectList GetCityOptions()
{
    var cities = new List<City>
    {
        new City{ Id = 1, Name = "London", Country = new Country{
            ➥ CountryName = "United Kingdom"} },
        new City{ Id = 2, Name = "York" , Country = new Country{
            ➥ CountryName = "United Kingdom"} },
        new City{ Id = 3, Name = "Venice", Country = new Country{
            ➥ CountryName = "Italy"} },
        new City{ Id = 4, Name = "Rome", Country = new Country{
```

```
        ➥ CountryName = "Italy" } },
    new City{ Id = 5, Name = "Madrid" , Country = new Country{
        ➥ CountryName = "Spain" } },
    new City{ Id = 5, Name = "Barcelona" , Country = new Country{
        ➥ CountryName = "Spain" } },
    new City{ Id = 5, Name = "Cadiz" , Country = new Country{
        ➥ CountryName = "Spain" } }
};
return new SelectList(cities, nameof(City.Id), nameof(City.Name),
            ➥ null, "Country.CountryName");
}
```

You use a literal string to represent the DataGroupField when working with complex objects.

This time you cannot use the `nameof` operator to represent the `DataGroupField` name. You must pass in the full property name as a string; otherwise, it will not be found, resulting in a `NullReferenceException` at run time.

6.3.4 Binding enumerations

In most real-life applications, the options you populate your select lists with will come from a database, especially if they are likely to change. When the range of options is naturally limited, you might decide that an enumeration can handle them instead. For example, there are a limited number of ways to reasonably describe their work status: employed full-time, employed part-time, self-employed, seeking work, retired, or in education. So you might create an enumeration named `WorkStatus` that has members representing all possible options.

In your application, the rating that is applied to a property that one can stay in is a good candidate for an enumeration. Ratings range from one star to five, and you also have to handle properties that have not been rated. So you will create an enumeration with members that will cover all options. Add a new C# class file to the Models folder named Rating.cs, and change the class to an `enum`.

Listing 6.19 The `Rating` enumeration

```
public enum Rating
{
    Unrated, OneStar, TwoStar, ThreeStar, FourStar, FiveStar
}
```

The next step is to add a property to the `CreateModel` in the PropertyManager folder:

```
[BindProperty]
public Rating Rating { get; set; }
```

You want to be able to reference this type in the Razor page, so you need to make the `CityBreaks.Models` namespace available to it. If you cast your mind back to chapter 3, you will recall you can achieve this globally by adding a suitable `using` directive to a

ViewImports file, so open the one in the Pages folder, and do just that by adding the bold code in the following listing.

Listing 6.20 Adding a using directive to `ViewImports`

```
@using CityBreaks
@using CityBreaks.Models
@namespace CityBreaks.Pages
@addTagHelper *, Microsoft.AspNetCore.Mvc.TagHelpers
```

The `Html.GetEnumSelectList` method is provided, so you can easily bind an enumeration as the data source for a select list. You are going to use that method in the `asp-items` attribute on a select tag helper you will add to the Create Property form. Add the following block of code just after the select city list.

Listing 6.21 Using the `Html.GetEnumSelectList` method to bind enumerations

```
<div class="mb-3">
    <label asp-for="Rating"></label>
    <select class="form-control" asp-for="Rating" asp-
      items="Html.GetEnumSelectList<Rating>()"></select>
</div>
```

Run the page. The enumeration values should appear in the select list (figure 6.13).

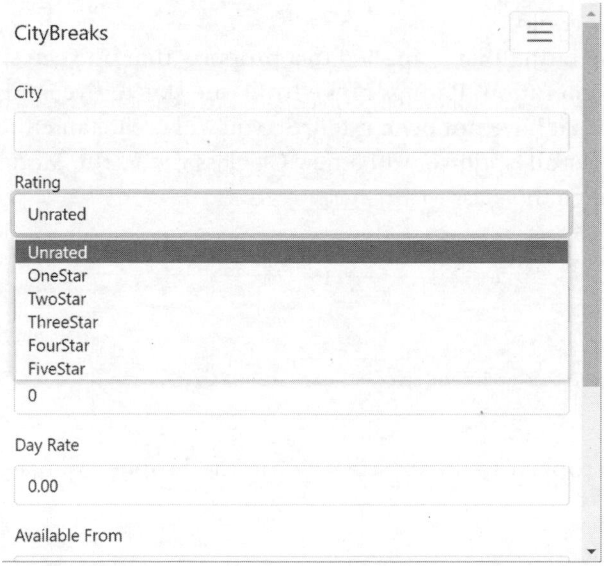

Figure 6.13 Enumeration bound to select list by the `Html.GetEnumSelectList` method

In this example, the Unrated option is selected. You can check the source code for the page to confirm that fact. This is because its option value (zero) is the default for

Rating. If you don't want the value to be preselected, you can make the PageModel property nullable:

```
[BindProperty]
public Rating? Rating { get; set; }
```

Recall from the previous chapter that you will need to add a Required attribute if you make the property nullable, but you still want to make the associated form control a mandatory field.

The actual values presented to the user could do with a little tidying up. If you have worked with enumerations before, you might be tempted to apply the Description attribute to each member that you want to be more user friendly. However, that will not affect the select tag helper. Just like other form-related tag helpers, the select tag helper responds to the DisplayAttribute. The following listing demonstrates how to apply that to each member for which you want something other than the raw property name to be presented to the user.

Listing 6.22 Using the DisplayAttribute to change the value presented

```
public enum Rating
{
    Unrated,
    [Display(Name="1 Star")]
    OneStar,
    [Display(Name = "2 Star")]
    TwoStar,
    [Display(Name = "3 Star")]
    ThreeStar,
    [Display(Name = "4 Star")]
    FourStar,
    [Display(Name = "5 Star")]
    FiveStar
}
```

The rendered result is shown in figure 6.14.

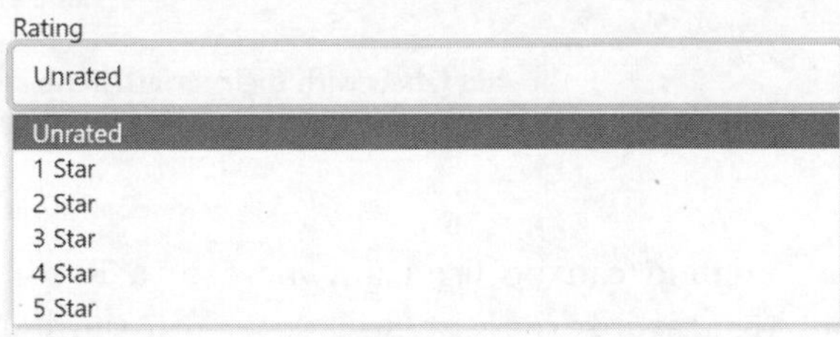

Figure 6.14 The Display names are automatically applied to the option text.

Now that we have covered the most common issues that arise when working with select lists, we can move on to look at check boxes and radio controls. While the input tag helper targets them, aspects of their behavior are unique and warrant attention.

6.4 Check boxes and radio controls

We have already covered some aspects of working with check boxes in Razor Pages forms, but it is worth reprising that knowledge, while we explore working with a similar control: the radio button. Check boxes are designed to enable users to make zero or more selections from predefined options—like select lists. Check boxes can stand alone to represent a Boolean choice, and when this is the requirement, you should bind a `PageModel` property to them that is either a Boolean or a string with a value that can be converted to a Boolean (e.g., "true"/"false"). Check boxes can also be grouped together by sharing the same name to enable the user to make multiple choices—like the list box you just worked with. You did this when looking at model binding to simple collections in the previous chapter. Whether you choose to use a list box or a group of check boxes to facilitate multiple selections is a presentation design decision as much as anything.

Radio controls represent mutually exclusive options. They are primarily used to allow the user to select one, and only one, from a number of options. As such, they are nearly always grouped together. All others are deselected automatically when one radio in a group is selected. You cannot deselect a single radio, which is why they can't really be used on their own. The only way to deselect one radio is to select another in the same group. It might make sense to use one radio control in a form in which selection is mandatory, such as indicating your agreement to terms and conditions before proceeding.

In the next example, you will use radio buttons instead of a select element for selecting one of the property rating enumeration values. The only change required is in the form itself. Replace the `select` element with the code in the next listing.

Listing 6.23 Replacing a select element with a group of radio controls

```
<p>Rating</p>
<ul class="list-group border-0">
@foreach(var option in Html.GetEnumSelectList<Rating>())
{
    <li class="list-group-item p-0 border-0">
        <input asp-for="Rating" type="radio"
          ➥ id="rating-@option.Value" value="@option.Value">
        <label for="rating-@option.Value">
          ➥ @option.Text</label>
    </li>
}
</ul>
```

- Use the Html.GetEnumSelectList method to convert the enumerations to an IEnumerable<SelectListItem>, and loop through them.
- Bind the radio to the Rating property, but set the type, id, and value explicitly.
- Add labels with their for attribute set to the id of the corresponding radio control.

The `Html.GetEnumSelectList` method can be used anywhere in a Razor page to convert an enumeration to an `IEnumerable<SelectListItem>`. You can iterate over these and render an input for each one. You can use the input tag helpers' `for` attributes to bind the radio control group to the `Rating` property, but you must set the `type` explicitly with this input tag helper. There is no mapping from a .NET type to the radio control. When you explicitly set HTML attributes on a tag helper, the tag helper honors your assignment. You have done the same thing with the `id` attribute, which the tag helper normally generates. You will need to set the value yourself. Otherwise, all inputs will have the same autogenerated ID of `"Rating"`, and you cannot have multiple elements in the same document with the same ID value. So you have constructed unique values by concatenating the rating's numerical value to `"rating-"`, resulting in `"rating-0"`, `"rating-1"`, and so on. Figure 6.15 shows the final rendered collection of radio buttons.

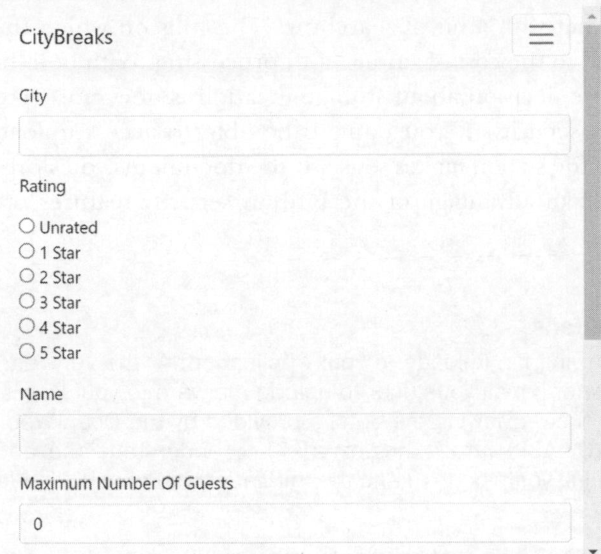

Figure 6.15 The rendered radios based on an enumeration

I've used the `Html.GetEnumSelectList` here to generate a collection of suitable types to work within the Razor page because the return type—`IEnumerable<SelectListItem>`—makes it easier to bind enumeration values to the radios. The data can be represented by any type that exposes properties that can be mapped to the value on the input and a descriptive label of some kind.

6.5 Uploading files

For the most part, you will use forms to capture data from the user as simple strings, although on the server, they might be converted to numeric, `DateTime`, or Boolean values. Forms can also be used to send binary data to the server, which enables the uploading of files. To combine model binding with successful file uploading, you have to meet three basic requirements:

1. The form must use the `POST` method.
2. The form must have an `enctype` attribute set to `multipart/form-data`.
3. The uploaded file must map to an instance of the `IFormFile` type or a collection of them, if you want to enable multiple file uploading.

The `IFormFile` interface lives in the `Microsoft.AspNetCore.Http` namespace and represents a file sent over HTTP. As well as some properties that provide access to information about the file—its `FileName`, `Length`, `ContentType`, and so on—the `IFormFile` interface specifies a couple of methods for copying the content to a `Stream`, so you can save it.

In a Razor Pages application, you can save the file locally to a database in binary form, or you can save it to the file system. Religious wars have broken out in the past over which approach is better! You can find remnants of these historical battlegrounds all over the internet with a bit of searching. The hills on which the battles tended to rage were related to the cost of storage and processing. With both being relatively cheap these days, the decision about storage location is now more likely to be based on accessibility and security. If you want to be able to access uploaded files quickly for any reason, the file system makes sense. If the documents you store are sensitive, you might want to take advantage of the built-in security features offered by your database system.

The dangers of file uploads

There are dangers in allowing file uploads to your application. At the very least, file uploads provide a means for a malicious user to upload malware to your web server. You should spend some time reviewing the details provided by the Open Web Application Security Project (OWASP; http://mng.bz/aJx7) to understand the potential issues you could be opening yourself up to and the mitigations you should implement to protect yourself.

Previous versions of the ASP.NET runtime limited the maximum size of an HTTP request to 4 MB by default to help prevent denial of service (DOS) attacks caused by overwhelming the web server with too much data to process in memory. In ASP.NET Core, the Kestrel web server's request length limit is imposed at 30 MB. You can implement a lower limit by applying the `RequestSizeLimit` attribute to your `PageMode` class, providing a value in bytes that represents the maximum permitted size of the request. For example, the following will enforce a limit of 1 MB for the total request:

```
[RequestSizeLimit(1048576)]
public class CreateModel : PageModel
```

If the total size exceeds that value, the framework returns a 400 Bad Request status code.

In the final example for this chapter, you will upload a file and save it to the file system. You will introduce a page for creating cities, and the form will include a file upload control to store an iconic image for each city. This will give you an opportunity to review other knowledge from these two chapters on forms. You will apply validation to ensure that each city has a name and an image as well as validate the upload file extension to ensure that only JPG files are accepted and processed. You will author your custom validator for this purpose because you might want to reuse the validation logic. There is an extensions validator available, but it validates against strings, not file uploads.

When the file is uploaded, you will rename it to the city's name. That way, you can ensure each city's image is uniquely named, and you don't accidentally overwrite another city's image should there be a naming clash. It also mitigates against overwriting a critical file on the server, should the uploaded file contain a malicious filename. Once the upload has been processed successfully, you will use the PRG (post-redirect-get) pattern to redirect to another page where the image will be displayed, having used `TempData` to store the city name and the image name.

Let's start with the custom validator. Add a C# class file to the existing ValidationAttributes folder, and name it UploadFileExtensionsAttribute.cs. Following is the full code for the validator, including the using directives.

Listing 6.24 The `UploadFileExtensions` custom validator

```
using System.ComponentModel.DataAnnotations;

namespace CityBreaks.ValidationAttributes
{
    public class UploadFileExtensionsAttribute : ValidationAttribute
    {
        private IEnumerable<string> allowedExtensions;
        public string Extensions { get; set;  }
        protected override ValidationResult IsValid
        ➥ (object value, ValidationContext validationContext)
        {
            allowedExtensions = Extensions?
                .Split(new char[] { ',' },
                    ➥ StringSplitOptions.RemoveEmptyEntries)
                .Select(x => x.ToLowerInvariant());
            if (value is IFormFile file &&
                ➥ allowedExtensions.Any())
            {
                var extension =
                ➥ Path.GetExtension(file.FileName.ToLowerInvariant());
                if (!allowedExtensions.Contains(extension))
                {
                    return new ValidationResult(ErrorMessage
                        ?? $"The file extension must be
                        ➥ {Extensions}");
                }
            }
            return ValidationResult.Success;
        }
    }
}
```

Create a private field to house the allowed extensions.

Create a public property, so the user of the attribute can set the allowed extensions.

Assign the user-supplied extensions to the private field, converting them from a comma-separated string to a collection of lowercase values.

You use pattern matching to ensure the property this attribute has been applied to is an IFormFile. If it is, and the user has provided extensions, you check to see if the filename matches any of them. If not, you return an error message.

In all other cases, validation succeeds.

This is not a production-ready validator. It doesn't, for example, take into account users not knowing whether to include the leading dot in the list of allowed extensions.

However, it will suffice for demonstration. It is very similar to the previous validator in that it provides a public property enabling the user to pass in a list of accepted file extensions. Suppose the property the attribute has been applied to is an `IFormFile` type. In that case, the validation logic is executed, and if the file extension has not been provided, the validation fails.

Now you need to add a page for creating cities. Add a new folder to the Pages folder named CityManager, and within that, add a new Razor page named Create. Open the Create.cshtml.cs file, and change the `using` directives to the following.

Listing 6.25 Using directives for the city's `CreateModel` class

```
using CityBreaks.ValidationAttributes;
using Microsoft.AspNetCore.Mvc;
using Microsoft.AspNetCore.Mvc.RazorPages;
using System.ComponentModel.DataAnnotations;
```

Then change the content of the `CreateModel` class itself.

Listing 6.26 City `CreateModel` class

```
public class CreateModel : PageModel
{
    private readonly IWebHostEnvironment _environment;
    public CreateModel(IWebHostEnvironment environment)
    {
        _environment = environment;
    }

    [BindProperty]
    [Required]
    public string Name { get; set; }
    [BindProperty]
    [Required]
    [UploadFileExtensions(Extensions = ".jpg")]
    public IFormFile Upload { get; set; }
    [TempData]
    public string Photo { get; set; }

    public async Task<IActionResult> OnPostAsync()
    {
        if (ModelState.IsValid)
        {
            TempData["Name"] = Name;
            Photo = $"{Name.ToLower().Replace(" ", "-")}
            ➥ {Path.GetExtension(Upload.FileName)}";
            var filePath = Path.Combine(
            ➥ _environment.WebRootPath, "images", "cities", Photo);
            using var stream = System.IO.File.
            ➥ Create(filePath);
            await Upload.CopyToAsync(stream);
```

Inject the IWebHostEnvironment service into the CreateModel, so you can use it to locate the wwwroot folder.

Add binding targets for the city name and image upload.

Add a TempData property to represent the image filename.

Assign the submitted city name to TempData.

Rename the uploaded file, and save it to a folder named cities in the image folder.

```
            return RedirectToPage(
            ➥ "/CityManager/Index");          Redirect the user.
        }
        return Page();
    }
}
```

The `IWebHostEnvironment` service provides information about the web hosting environment an application is running in. You inject it into the `CreateModel` to use its `WebRootPath` property to locate the wwwroot folder, then you add binding targets for the city name and the file upload. Both are made mandatory—being decorated with the `Required` attribute—and the `Upload` property is also decorated with your new validation attribute. You have chosen only to accept JPG files. You have also added another property that is decorated with the `TempData` attribute. You will use this to store the filename of the uploaded image, so it is available when you redirect the user.

If validation succeeds, you will take the submitted city name and add it to `TempData`:

```
TempData["Name"] = Name;
```

But why didn't you just add a `TempData` attribute to the existing `Name` property, as you did with the `Photo` property? Well, the `TempData` attribute enables you to both set *and* get values from `TempData`. Model binding and `TempData` conflict with each other because they both provide a mechanism to populate page properties with values from an HTTP request. One must execute after the other, and the default behavior is that `TempData` population takes place *after* model binding. So any value assigned to the property by model binding will be overwritten by whatever is in `TempData`, which is usually nothing. Consequently, you will make the assignment manually.

Your fairly simple renaming logic removes spaces and hyphens from the city name and then uses the lowercase version as a filename. Then the file is saved in the cities folder, located in wwwroot\images, alongside the Flags folder you created in the last chapter. You will need to create that folder manually before saving files to it. After the file is saved, you redirect the user to a page that doesn't exist yet.

Before you create that page, you need to add the form to the Create.cshtml file. Listing 6.27 shows the code for the upload form. You should be familiar with most of this by now. The only point of real note is the addition of the `enctype` attribute on the form tag helper, specifying how the form's data should be encoded. This is set to `multipart/form-data`, which is one of the three requirements for successful form uploading. If you omit this, the encoding will default to `application/x-www-form-urlencoded`, resulting in only the filename being posted to the server. You have applied an `accept` attribute to the file input. Its value is set to the file extension the upload should be restricted to. User agents that support this attribute will apply a filter to the available files the user can select from to prevent the wrong type being uploaded. This could be considered an additional means of client validation, but you should not rely on it.

Listing 6.27 Create City form

```
@page
@model CityBreaks.Pages.CityManager.CreateModel
@{
}

<h4>Create City</h4>

<div class="row">
    <div class="col-md-4">
        <form method="post" enctype="multipart/form-data">
            <div class="form-group">
                <label asp-for="Name" class="control-label"></label>
                <input asp-for="Name" class="form-control" />
                <span asp-validation-for="Name" class="text-danger"></span>
            </div>
            <div class="form-group">
                <label asp-for="Upload" class="control-label"></label><br />
                <input asp-for="Upload" accept=".jpg" />
                <span asp-validation-for="Upload" class="text-danger"></span>
            </div>
            <div class="form-group">
                <input type="submit" value="Create" class="btn btn-primary"
    />
            </div>
        </form>
    </div>
</div>
@section scripts{
    <partial name="_ValidationScriptsPartial"/>
}
```

Now you will add the page that a successful form submission redirects to. Add a new Razor page to the CityManager folder named Index.cshtml, and change the page content to the following.

Listing 6.28 Confirmation of the image upload

```
@page
@model CityBreaks.Pages.CityManager.IndexModel
@{
}
@if(TempData["Name"] != null){
    <div class="col-6">
        <h3>@TempData["Name"]</h3>
        <img src="/images/cities/@TempData["Photo"]" class="img-fluid"
    alt="@TempData["Name"]"/>
    </div>
}
```

Again, there is nothing new here. You check that `TempData` contains something and then render the values to the browser. You then assign the image filename to part of the `src` of an `img` element, and you use the Bootstrap `img-fluid` CSS class to make the image responsive to fit its container.

Run the application, navigate to /city-manager/create, and enter a city name. Find an image for that city (I used Unsplash—https://unsplash.com/—for images that are free for commercial and noncommercial use), and upload that too. If all is correct, you should see the city's name and image rendered to the browser as well as the image saved to the Images\cities folder (figure 6.16).

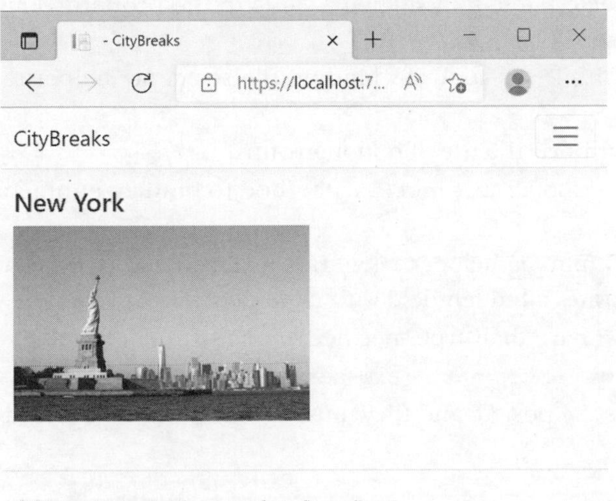

Figure 6.16 The uploaded image file rendered to the browser

You've done a lot of work with forms over the last couple of chapters, which will stand you in good stead when you create your own applications. Previously, you looked at how to use the Razor syntax to generate dynamic content and how to surface your pages through routing. So you have covered a lot in terms of your application's presentation layer.

In the following few chapters, you will start to look at the logical components of your application: its services. The next chapter looks at what a service is and how services are managed in an ASP.NET Core application. Beyond that, you will start looking at the services provided by ASP.NET Core for managing data and users.

Summary

- The form and form action tag helpers generate URLs for form submission.
- The form tag helper generates a hidden input containing the request verification token.
- Input tag helpers generate different `type` attributes in response to the data type of the model property bound to them. They also generate `data-val` attributes for client-side validation.

- You can use the `DataType` attribute on model properties to generate more specific `type` attributes.
- The label tag helper renders the raw property name by default. You can use the `Display` attribute to render something more user friendly.
- The select tag helper targets the HTML select element. It renders the options bound to it via its `items` attribute.
- Options can be provided as a collection of `SelectListItems` or as a `SelectList`.
- You can set the selected item by assigning a value to the property bound to the `for` attribute on a select tag helper.
- You can enable multiple selections by binding the select tag helper to a collection property.
- The `SelectList` supports the use of option groups.
- You can use the `Html.GetEnumSelectList` method to bind an enumeration to a select tag helper.
- When you use the input tag helper to generate a check box, binding a Boolean property to it generates a hidden field with its value set to `false`.
- Radio controls must have their type specified explicitly.
- File uploading requires `multipart/form-data` encoding to work.
- Uploaded files must be posted, and they must be bound to an `IFormFile` type.

7 Using dependency injection to manage services

This chapter covers

- Understanding the role of dependency injection
- Examining dependency injection in ASP.NET Core
- Creating and using your own services
- Managing service lifetime

Dependency injection (DI) is a software engineering technique included as a feature in many web frameworks these days. Its *raison d'être* is enabling *loose coupling* between software components, resulting in code that is less brittle, more adaptable to change, easier to maintain, and easier to test. If you have worked with dependency injection before, all of this will feel familiar to you. In case dependency injection is a new concept to you, this chapter will help by explaining what it is and why you should care.

DI is at the heart of ASP.NET Core. The entire framework uses the built-in DI feature to manage its own dependencies, or *services*. Services are globally registered within a container when the application starts up and then provided by the container when needed by consumers. You encountered the main entry point to the service container when you looked at Program.cs in chapter 2. It is accessed via the `Services` property of the `WebApplicationBuilder`. You will recall that services that comprise the Razor Pages framework are registered with the container via the `AddRazorPages` method:

```
var builder = WebApplication.CreateBuilder(args);
// Add services to the container.
builder.Services.AddRazorPages();
```

In addition to the framework's use of its container, you are encouraged to use it to register your own services, so they can be injected into consumers by the container, which will take responsibility for managing the lifetime (creation and destruction) of those services on your behalf. A key point to make here is that you are not *required* to use DI for your own services. However, you should at least have an understanding about how DI works in a Razor Pages application, so you can customize framework services as needed.

By the end of this chapter, you will understand what dependency injection is, how it is managed within a Razor Pages application, and the benefits of using DI for your own services. You will also have a clearer idea of what a service is in the context of a Razor Pages application. You will have created some services and registered them with the dependency injection container, so they are available throughout your application.

Services need to have their lifetime managed by the DI container, so your application doesn't run out of memory, for example. Neither should you instantiate services unnecessarily, especially if only one single instance is required by the application. In this chapter, you will learn the different lifetimes available and how to choose the correct one when registering your services.

7.1 The reason for dependency injection

Before we look at the fundamentals of dependency injection in ASP.NET Core, we need to be clear about the nature of the problem it solves. That discussion involves the use of terms the software engineering community has assimilated to describe principles and techniques. Many of the terms are quite abstract and are used to describe abstract ideas. Consequently, they can be difficult to grasp, especially for literal thinkers.

I have already used the term *loose coupling* as one of the primary targets a software engineer should strive for when designing a system. I've mentioned that this loose coupling should occur between components. Before looking at the nature of a component, I want to take a step back and look at the bigger picture in terms of software engineering design principles.

7.1.1 Single-responsibility principle

A key principle you should consider when designing a system is the *single-responsibility principle* (SRP). This is the *S* in SOLID, a set of principles designed to make software more understandable, flexible, and maintainable. Fundamentally, SRP states that any component, module, or service within an application should have only one reason to change: its single responsibility needs to change for some business reason. If you consider a `PageModel` class with this principle in mind, you can see its responsibility is to process the HTTP request for its page. Therefore, the only circumstances under which you should need to change any aspect of the code in the `PageModel` is if the logic required for processing the request should change.

If you look at the `PageModel` for the property manager's Create page you put together in the last chapter, you can see this principle is violated. The `PageModel` has *two* responsibilities: to process the request and to generate data for the `SelectList` in the form of a collection of cities (figure 7.1).

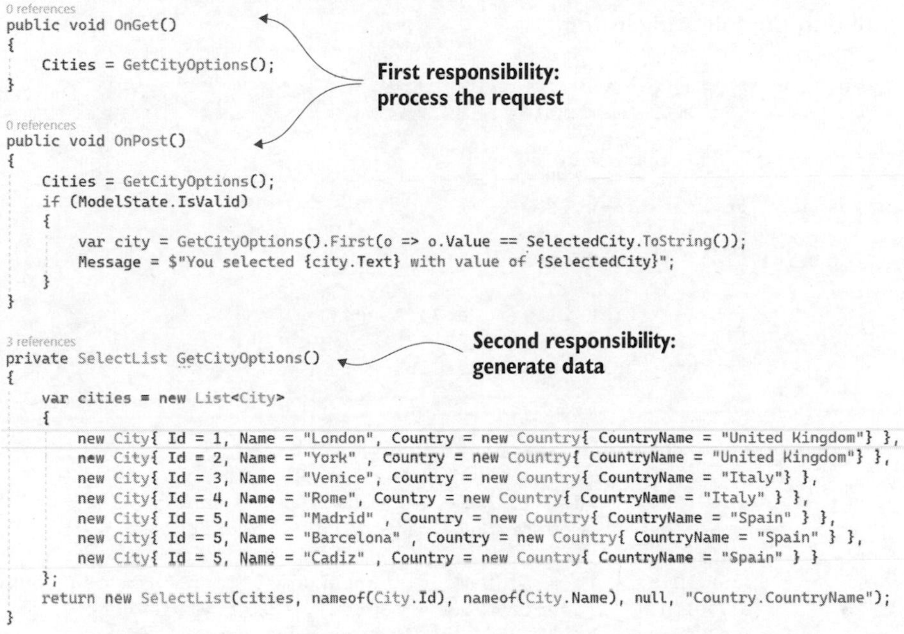
0 references
public void OnGet()
{
Cities = GetCityOptions();
}
First responsibility: process the request
0 references
public void OnPost()
{
Cities = GetCityOptions();
if (ModelState.IsValid)
{
var city = GetCityOptions().First(o => o.Value == SelectedCity.ToString());
Message = $"You selected {city.Text} with value of {SelectedCity}";
}
}
3 references
private SelectList GetCityOptions()
Second responsibility: generate data
{
var cities = new List<City>
{
new City{ Id = 1, Name = "London", Country = new Country{ CountryName = "United Kingdom"} },
new City{ Id = 2, Name = "York" , Country = new Country{ CountryName = "United Kingdom"} },
new City{ Id = 3, Name = "Venice", Country = new Country{ CountryName = "Italy"} },
new City{ Id = 4, Name = "Rome", Country = new Country{ CountryName = "Italy" } },
new City{ Id = 5, Name = "Madrid" , Country = new Country{ CountryName = "Spain" } },
new City{ Id = 5, Name = "Barcelona" , Country = new Country{ CountryName = "Spain" } },
new City{ Id = 5, Name = "Cadiz" , Country = new Country{ CountryName = "Spain" } }
};
return new SelectList(cities, nameof(City.Id), nameof(City.Name), null, "Country.CountryName");
}

Figure 7.1 The `PageModel` currently has two responsibilities.

In the next chapter, we will look at using databases in Razor Pages applications. You will want to change how the city options are generated by retrieving them from the database. That change has nothing to do with the primary role of a `PageModel` class—processing a request. However, as things are currently designed, the move to a database will require us to delve into the `CreateModel` class to alter the `GetCityOptions` method. In other words, a change of data access strategy currently provides an additional reason for changing the `PageModel` class. If you are to comply with SRP, you need to move the logic that generates the city data into its own component with the single responsibility of managing data for the `City` entity.

Think back to the don't repeat yourself (DRY) principle discussed in chapter 3, which encourages you to minimize code duplication. *Each piece of logic should only have one representation in the system,* the principle states. We have fallen foul of this principle too. We have code in the home page that generates cities for the list box example, effectively duplicating the `GetCityOptions` code just discussed in the `CreateModel`. This code should be centralized, and once again, moving it to its own component will address the fault.

Let's start by fixing this. You will build a component with the responsibility of generating a collection of `City` objects and making that available to any part of the application that needs it. Then you will use that component in the `PageModel` class to provide the source data for one of the select lists you have built so far.

Start by adding a new folder named Services to the root of the application. Within this, add a new C# class named SimpleCityService.cs. The content of the file is provided in the following listing.

Listing 7.1 The `SimpleCityService` code

```
using CityBreaks.Models;

namespace CityBreaks.Services
{
    public class SimpleCityService
    {
        public Task<List<City>> GetAllAsync()
        {
            return Task.FromResult(Cities);
        }

        private readonly List<City> Cities = new()
        {
            new City { Id = 1, Name = "Amsterdam", Country = new Country {
                Id = 5, CountryName = "Holland", CountryCode = "nl"
            } },
            new City { Id = 2, Name = "Barcelona", Country = new Country {
                Id = 7, CountryName = "Spain", CountryCode = "es"
            } },
            new City { Id = 3, Name = "Berlin", Country = new Country {
                Id = 4, CountryName = "Germany", CountryCode = "de"
            } },
            new City { Id = 4, Name = "Copenhagen", Country = new Country {
                Id = 2, CountryName = "Denmark", CountryCode = "dk"
            } },
            new City { Id = 5, Name = "Dubrovnik", Country = new Country {
                Id = 1, CountryName = "Croatia", CountryCode = "hr"
            } },
            new City { Id = 6, Name = "Edinburgh", Country = new Country {
                Id = 8, CountryName = "United Kingdom", CountryCode = "gb"
            } },
            new City { Id = 7, Name = "London", Country = new Country {
                Id = 8, CountryName = "United Kingdom", CountryCode = "gb"
            } },
            new City { Id = 8, Name = "Madrid", Country = new Country {
                Id = 7, CountryName = "Spain", CountryCode = "es"
            } },
```

```
            new City { Id = 9, Name = "New York", Country = new Country {
                Id = 9, CountryName = "United States", CountryCode = "us"
            } },
            new City { Id = 10, Name = "Paris", Country = new Country {
                Id = 3, CountryName = "France", CountryCode = "fr"
            } },
            new City { Id = 11, Name = "Rome", Country = new Country {
                Id = 6, CountryName = "Italy", CountryCode = "it"
            } },
            new City { Id = 12, Name = "Venice", Country = new Country {
                Id = 6, CountryName = "Italy", CountryCode = "it"
            } }
        };
    }
}
```

It really is a simple city service. All this code does is generate a collection of cities and the country they belong to and then make them available via a public method called `GetAllAsync`. You've included some unique identifiers that look like relational database primary keys. You might use code like this for a proof of concept application or as a test double (a replacement for a relational database) for unit testing. Or indeed, you could use code like this as part of a demonstration application for learning purposes if you ever write a book! The only slightly odd thing here is that the `GetAllAsync` method returns a `Task<List<City>>` rather than just a `List<City>`. This is because you will be migrating to using a database in the next chapter, so you want to emulate database calls, which are typically executed asynchronously within an ASP.NET Core application. I discuss this in more detail in the next chapter.

Now that you have centralized the creation of cities, you can use your new component in the PropertyManager\Create.cshtml.cs file. Open that, and change the existing handler methods and `GetCityOptions` method, leaving the various page properties as they are. You will also need to add a `using` directive for `CityBreaks.Services`.

Listing 7.2 Revised Create Property page using the new `SimpleCityService`

```
public async Task OnGetAsync()
{
    Cities = await GetCityOptions();
}

public async Task OnPostAsync()
{
    Cities = await GetCityOptions();
    if (ModelState.IsValid)
    {
        var city = Cities.First(o => o.Value == SelectedCity.ToString());
        Message = $"You selected {city.Text} with value of {SelectedCity}";
    }
}

private async Task<SelectList> GetCityOptions()
```

You amend the handler methods and the GetCityOptions methods to make them asynchronous.

```
{
    var service = new SimpleCityService();
    var cities = await service.GetAllAsync();
    return new SelectList(cities, nameof(City.Id),
    ➥ nameof(City.Name), null, "Country.CountryName");
}
```

Obtain the data from the SimpleCityService class instead of generating it in the PageModel.

Aside from the conversion to using asynchronous methods, the only real change here is that the responsibility for generating the collection of cities is no longer that of the `CreateModel` class. That job has been delegated to the new class: the `SimpleCity-Service`. The `CreateModel` class *depends* on the `SimpleCityService` for the data, making the `SimpleCityService` a *dependency* of the `CreateModel` class.

7.1.2 Loose coupling

I believe it was Steve Smith, aka "Ardalis," a well-known ASP.NET speaker, author, and trainer, who first coined the phrase "new is glue" (https://ardalis.com/new-is-glue/). He suggests that whenever you use the `new` keyword in C# code, you consider whether you are creating a *tight coupling* between a consumer (a "high-level module") and its dependencies ("low-level modules") and, if so, what ramifications that might have in the longer term. In this example, while shifting the logic for providing city data into its own component, you have effectively glued your `SimpleCityService component` to the `CreateModel` class. The relationship between these actors is shown in figure 7.2.

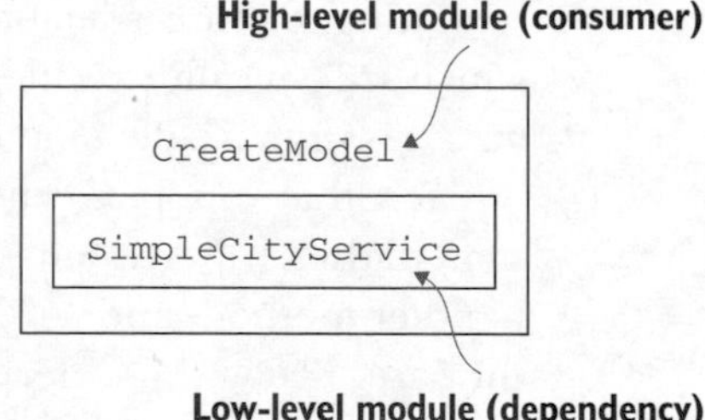

Figure 7.2 The `SimpleCityServices` is glued (tightly coupled) to the `Create-Model` class.

You are in breach of a software engineering principle here, the *explicit dependencies principle,* which states that "methods and classes should explicitly require (typically through method parameters or constructor parameters) any collaborating objects they need in order to function correctly" (http://mng.bz/9Vzj). Your collaborating object, the `SimpleCityService`, is an *implicit* dependency of the `CreateModel` class because it is only apparent that the `CreateModel` class depends on the `SimpleCityService` when you look at the source code of the consuming class. Implicit dependencies are to be avoided. They are difficult to test and make the consumer (the `CreateModel`) more brittle and resistant to change.

If you want to change the implementation of the data provider to another one, say that gets data from a database, you will have to go through all the places in the code where you call `new SimpleCityService()` and change it to reference your alternative implementation. And you *will* be changing the implementation in the next chapter. You might think using your development tool's Find and Replace feature makes this a relatively painless exercise, but that's not a sustainable way to build applications, especially when there are better options available for swapping implementations, which we will look at next.

7.1.3 Dependency inversion

So how do you achieve *loose coupling*? How can you redesign the consumer of your components or services, so they are no longer tightly coupled to a specific, or *concrete*, implementation? One solution is to rely on abstractions, rather than specific implementations. This approach is known as the *dependency inversion principle* (DIP), which is the *D* in the SOLID acronym. Dependency inversion is also known as *inversion of control* (IoC).

Abstract classes and interfaces represent abstractions in C#. As a rule of thumb, you will generally use interfaces as your abstraction, unless you have some common default behavior you want all implementations to share; in which case, you should choose an abstract class.

The dependency inversion principle states that "high-level modules should not depend on low-level modules. Both should depend on abstractions. Abstractions should not depend on details. Details should depend on abstractions" (Robert C. Martin: *Agile Software Development, Principles, Patterns, and Practices,* Pearson, 2002).

High-level modules tend to be consumers of services, and low-level modules tend to be the services themselves. So the first part of the DIP states that both the consumer and the service should depend on an abstraction, rather than the consumer depending on a specific service implementation. In the example, the abstraction will be an interface; the service will implement it, and the consumer will call it (figure 7.3).

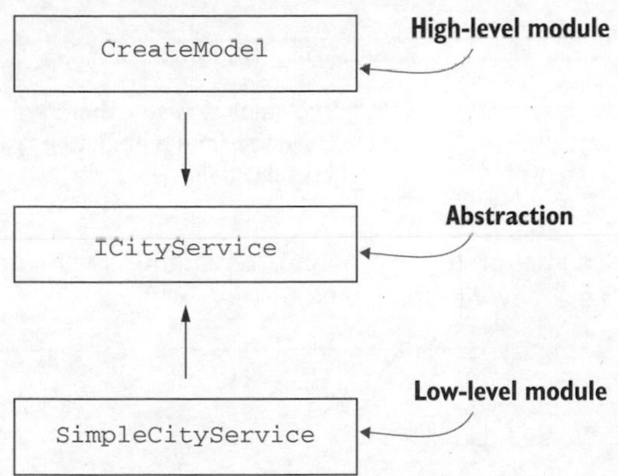

Figure 7.3 The `PageModel` and the `SimpleCityService` depend on an abstraction: the `ICityService` interface.

Now that the dependency chain is *inverted*, you need to design your `ICityService` interface. The second part of the DIP states that the interface should depend on abstractions too, not "details." That is, the interface should not be tied to specific implementations. So your interface should not return implementation-specific types, like a `DbDataReader`, which only works with relational databases. It should depend on more general-purpose types like a `List<T>`. Your `SimpleCityService` class already does that, fortunately. So you will create an interface based on its existing API.

Add a new C# code file to the Services folder, and name it ICityService.cs. Note that if you are using Visual Studio, the Add… New Item dialog includes Interface as an option. Replace the existing code with the following.

Listing 7.3 The ICityService interface

```
using CityBreaks.Models;

namespace CityBreaks.Services
{
    public interface ICityService
    {
        Task<List<City>> GetAllAsync();
    }
}
```

Easy interface generation for Visual Studio Users

There is an even quicker way to generate an interface for Visual Studio users. Place your cursor on the `SimpleCityService` class name, and press Ctrl-. (period). From the dialog that appears, select Extract Interface... .

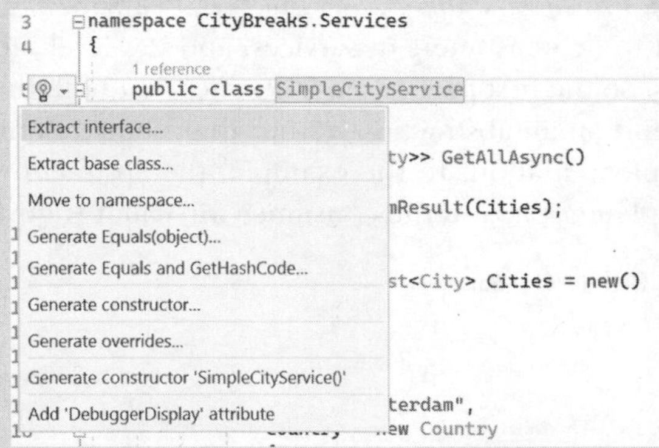

The quick way to generate a new interface from an existing type in Visual Studio

In the next dialog, change the name of the type, and leave the single method selected. Leave the destination as a new file, and click OK.

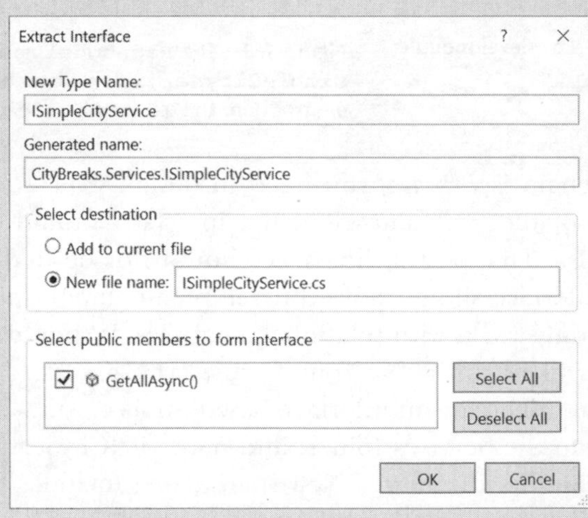

The Extract Interface dialog

Now you need to ensure that the low-level component depends on the abstraction. Change `SimpleCityService`, so it implements the following interface:

```
public class SimpleCityService : ICityService
```

Note that this step is not necessary if you used the Visual Studio wizard to extract the interface.

The final step is to get the high-level module, the `CreateModel` class, to also depend on the abstraction. How do you do that? Drum roll, please … you use dependency injection.

7.1.4 Dependency injection

Dependency injection is a technique that helps us to achieve dependency inversion. As its name suggests, you inject the dependency into the consuming module, typically via its constructor as a parameter, and assign it to a private field for use within the consuming class. Injecting dependencies as arguments to a constructor method, as you will recall, helps us conform to the explicit dependencies principle.

The following code listing shows the `CreateModel`, altered to include an explicit constructor that takes an `ICityService` as a parameter. It assigns it to a private field, so it can be referenced within the class where needed.

Listing 7.4 Injecting `ICityService` dependency via `CreateModel`'s constructor

```
public class CreateModel : PageModel
{
    private readonly ICityService _cityService;        // Add a private field to the class to store the dependency.
    public CreateModel(ICityService cityService)       // Inject the dependency via the constructor.
    {
        _cityService = cityService;                    // Assign the injected dependency to the private field.
    }
    ...
}
```

Now your dependency is explicit. The collaborating object (any type that implements the `ICityService` interface) needed by your `CreateModel` class is identified to the outside world by its presence in the class's constructor.

7.2 Inversion of control containers

Of course, in C#, you cannot instantiate an interface, so how can this code make any sense? The actual type passed in to the constructor argument can be any type that implements the specified interface. At run time, an implementation of the interface is provided to the constructor. A built-in dependency injection container provides the implementation. This is more commonly referred to in Microsoft documentation as a *service container*, although more widely, you might also see this type of component referred to as an IoC container or a DI container.

So that leaves just one question: how does the container know which implementation to provide? And the answer is you tell it by registering your services with the container.

7.2.1 Service registration

Service registration takes place in the `Program` class by adding registrations to the `WebApplicationBuilder`'s `Services` property. You may recall seeing this in chapter 2 when I discussed using the `IMiddleware` interface for building middlewares, although I didn't go into detail at the time. The standard web application template already includes a registration for Razor Pages through the `AddRazorPages` method, which is responsible for registering all the services Razor Pages depends on, including those that are responsible for generating and matching routes, handler method selection and page execution, as well as the Razor view engine itself.

The `Services` property is an `IServiceCollection`, which is the framework's service container. It contains a collection of `ServiceDescriptor` objects, each one representing a registered service. A basic registered service consists of the *service type*, the *implementation*, and the service *lifetime*. The following listing shows how you can register the `ICityService` as a new `ServiceDescriptor`.

Listing 7.5 Registering the `ICityService` with the service container

```
builder.Services.AddRazorPages();
builder.Services.Add(new ServiceDescriptor(typeof(ICityService),
    typeof(SimpleCityService), ServiceLifetime.Transient));
```

However, you are more likely to use one of the lifetime-specific extension methods available on the `IServiceCollection` that takes the service type and implementation as generic parameters (figure 7.4).

```
builder.Services.AddTransient<ICityService, SimpleCityService>();
```

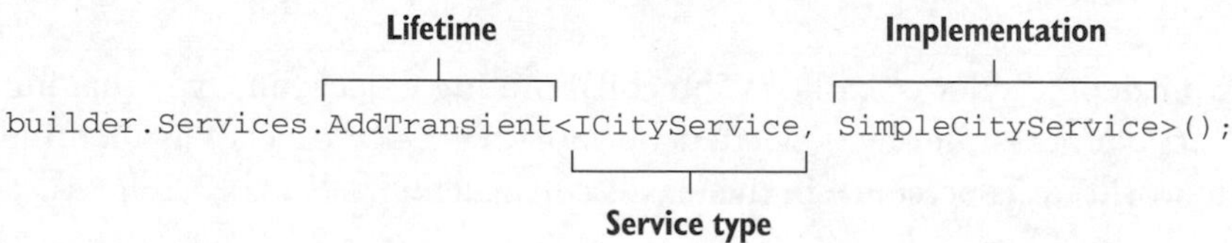

Figure 7.4 Registration results in a `ServiceDescriptor` object being added to the `IServiceCollection`, consisting of a service type, implementation, and lifetime.

The service container's job is to provide the correct implementation whenever a service type is requested—for example, being injected into a constructor. This process is also referred to as *resolving* the dependency. So when the container sees a request for an `ICityService`, it will provide an instance of `SimpleCityService` (figure 7.5).

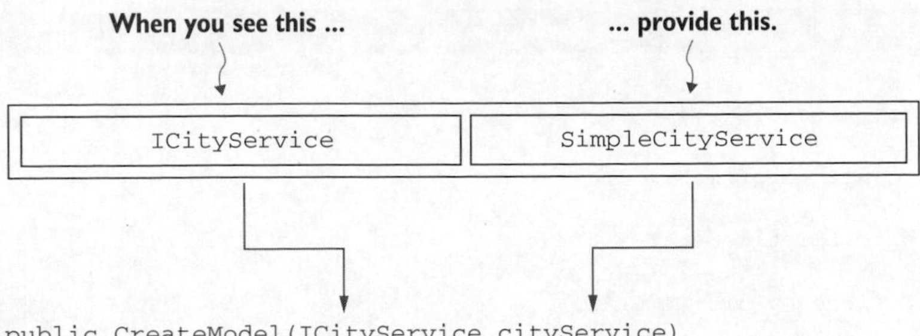

Figure 7.5 When the container sees a request for a service, it provides the implementation

7.2.2 Service lifetimes

The service container is not only responsible for resolving implementations. It is also responsible for managing the lifetime of the service. That is, the container is responsible for creating the service *and* destroying it, as determined by the lifetime the service is registered with. A service can be registered as having one of three lifetimes:

- Singleton
- Transient
- Scoped

For each lifetime, there is an extension method that starts with the word `Add`, followed by the name of the lifetime. For example, you have used the `AddTransient` method to register the `ICityService` with the transient lifetime.

SINGLETON SERVICES

Services registered with the `AddSingleton` method are instantiated as singletons when the service is first requested and retained for the duration of the container's lifetime, which is typically the same as the running application. As its name suggests, only one instance of a singleton can exist. It is reused for all requests. The vast majority of framework services—model binding, routing, logging, and so on—are registered as singletons. They all share the same characteristics in that they don't have any state and are thread safe, which means the same instance can be used across multiple threads; this may be required to process concurrent requests. The same characteristics must also apply to any dependencies the singleton services rely on that are instantiated along with the service.

I will briefly digress from the main direction of our current application to explore how this works with a simple demonstration. You will create a service that exposes a value that is set in its constructor, and then register that service as a singleton. You will use a GUID for the value because it is almost certain to be different each time it is generated. Then you will render that value to the browser. You will note that the value doesn't change when you refresh the page. Add a new C# class to the Services folder named `LifetimeDemoService` with the following code.

Listing 7.6 The `LifetimeDemoService` class

```
using System;
namespace CityBreaks.Services
{
    public class LifetimeDemoService
    {
        public LifetimeDemoService()
        {
            Value = Guid.NewGuid();
        }
        public Guid Value { get; }
    }
}
```

The public `Value` property is set whenever the class constructor is called, which is when the container instantiates the service. You will register this service as a singleton, which should ensure it is only ever instantiated once during the life of the application:

```
builder.Services.AddRazorPages();
builder.Services.AddTransient<ICityService, SimpleCityService>();
builder.Services.AddSingleton<LifetimeDemoService>();
```

The service is registered with a version of the `AddSingleton` method that takes a single generic parameter representing the implementation. You don't have an abstraction for this example. It's not needed because this is a simple demonstration, and an abstraction will provide an unnecessary distraction from the main point of the examples that follow. Create a new Razor page called LifetimeDemo.cshtml in the Pages folder with the following code in the `PageModel` class file.

Listing 7.7 The `LifetimeDemoModel` code for demonstrating how service lifetimes work

```
using CityBreaks.Services;
using Microsoft.AspNetCore.Mvc.RazorPages;

namespace CityBreaks.Pages
{
    public class LifetimeDemoModel : PageModel
    {
        private readonly LifetimeDemoService _lifetimeDemoService;
        public LifetimeDemoModel(LifetimeDemoService lifetimeDemoService)
        {
            _lifetimeDemoService = lifetimeDemoService;
        }

        public Guid Value { get; set; }
        public void OnGet()
        {
            Value = _lifetimeDemoService.Value;
        }
    }
}
```

Change the code in the Razor page itself by adding the highlighted lines from the following listing.

Listing 7.8 The `LifetimeDemo` Razor page

```
@page
@model CityBreaks.Pages.LifetimeDemoModel
@{
    ViewData["Title"] = "Lifetime demo";
}
<h2>Service Lifetime Demo</h2>
<p>The Singleton service returned @Model.Value</p>
```

Run the application, navigate to /lifetime-demo (remembering the effect of the `KebabPageRouteParameterTransformer`), and note the value rendered to the browser. Refresh the page, and confirm the value stays the same. Use a different browser to request the page. The value doesn't change. This is because the value was set when the service was first instantiated, and as a singleton, the same instance of the service is shared by all consumers across all requests.

Transient services

Services registered with the `AddTransient` method are given a transient lifetime, meaning they are created each time they are resolved. These types of services should be lightweight, stateless services for which the cost of instantiation is relatively low. They are destroyed when the service scope is destroyed. In the context of an ASP.NET Core application, the scope is destroyed at the end of an HTTP request. If you have a complex dependency graph where the same service type is injected into multiple constructors, each consumer will receive its own instance of the service. The `SimpleCityService` is a good candidate for the transient lifetime, as it meets the definition of a service that maintains no state and has a low instantiation cost.

To see this working, you will inject a second instance of the service into the `PageModel` and render its value to the browser. Make the following changes to the `LifetimeDemoModel` class.

Listing 7.9 Injecting a second service to the `PageModel`

```
private readonly LifetimeDemoService _lifetimeDemoService;
private readonly LifetimeDemoService _secondService;        <- Add a private field for the second service.
public LifetimeDemoModel(LifetimeDemoService lifetimeDemoService,
    LifetimeDemoService secondService)       <- Inject a second instance of the LifetimeDemoService.
{
    _lifetimeDemoService = lifetimeDemoService;
    _secondService = secondService;      <- Assign it to the private field.
}

public Guid Value { get; set; }
public Guid SecondValue { get; set; }     <- Add another public property to the PageModel.
public void OnGet()
```

```
{
    Value = _lifetimeDemoService.Value;
    SecondValue = _secondService.Value;   <-- Set its value to the second service's Value.
}
```

Next change the code in the Razor page that renders the service values as follows.

Listing 7.10 Rendering values from both services

```
<p>The first transient service returned @Model.Value</p>
<p>The second transient service returned @Model.SecondValue</p>
```

Finally, change the registration in Program.cs to use the transient lifetime:

```
builder.Services.AddTransient<LifetimeDemoService>();
```

Run the application, navigate to /lifetime-demo, and note that the values rendered to the browser are different. Every time you refresh the page, they change, confirming that each service is instantiated every time they are requested.

SCOPED SERVICES

The final lifetime option is the scoped lifetime. As mentioned previously, in ASP.NET Core web applications, a *scope* is an HTTP request, which means *scoped services* are created once per HTTP request. What actually happens is that an instance of the container is created for each HTTP request and is destroyed at the end of the request. Scoped services are resolved by this scoped container and are consequently destroyed when the container is destroyed at the end of the scope. Scoped services differ from transient services in that only one instance of a scoped service is resolved per scope, whereas multiple instances of a transient service can be instantiated.

Once instantiated, the scoped service is reused as many times as needed during the scope (request) and disposed of at the end of the request. Each request gets its own scoped container, so concurrent requests to the same resource will work with different containers.

To see how this works, all you need to do is change the registration of the `LifetimeDemoService` to use the `AddScoped` method:

```
builder.Services.AddScoped<LifetimeDemoService>();
```

Then change the Razor page to reference the scoped service values:

```
<p>The first scoped service returned @Model.Value</p>
<p>The second scoped service returned @Model.SecondValue</p>
```

Now when you run the application, you should see that both services produce the same value. Once the `LifetimeDemoService` is instantiated, it is reused wherever it is needed within the scope of the HTTP request. It is similar, in that respect, to a singleton, scoped to a request, rather than the application's lifetime.

Scoped lifetimes are most suitable for services that are expensive to instantiate and/or need to maintain state during a request. In a Razor Pages application, one of the most frequently used services that benefits from a scoped lifetime is the Entity Framework `DbContext`, which we will look at in more detail in the next chapter. The `DbContext` meets both criteria in that it is expensive to instantiate because it creates a connection to an external resource (the database), and it may need to maintain information about data that it has retrieved from the database.

7.2.3 Captive dependencies

When choosing a lifetime for your service, you should also take into account the lifetime of any dependency the service relies on. For example, if the dependency is a `DbContext` that has been registered with the scoped lifetime, you should ensure your service is also registered with a scoped lifetime. Otherwise, you could end up suffering from an issue known as *captive dependencies*. This issue arises when dependencies are registered with a shorter lifetime than their consumer. The DI container will raise an `InvalidOperationException` if you try to consume a scoped service from within a singleton, but you receive no such protection against consuming a transient service from within a singleton. If you inject a transient service into another service that is then registered as a singleton, the dependencies also effectively become singletons because the consuming service will only ever have its constructor called once during the lifetime of the application, and it will only ever be destroyed when the application stops.

Let's have a look at this, so you understand it clearly. Add the following code as a new C# class to the Services folder.

Listing 7.11 The `SingletonService` class

```
namespace CityBreaks.Services
{
    public class SingletonService
    {
        private readonly LifetimeDemoService _dependency;
        public SingletonService(LifetimeDemoService dependency)
        {
            _dependency = dependency;
        }
        public Guid DependencyValue => _dependency.Value;
    }
}
```

The code is simple; the `SingletonService` class takes your existing `LifetimeDemoService` as a dependency and uses it to generate a value. Now you need to register the `SingletonService` as a singleton, while leaving the `LifetimeDemoService` registered with a transient lifetime:

```
builder.Services.AddTransient<LifetimeDemoService>();
builder.Services.AddSingleton<SingletonService>();
```

Change the markup in the Razor page to output the following:

```
<p>The singleton service's transient dependency returned @Model.Value</p>
```

Run the page, and refresh it. Notice that the value never changes. You don't get a new instance of the `LifetimeDemoService` on each request because the consumer's constructor is not being called, since it is a singleton.

7.2.4 Other service registration options

The aforementioned examples use one of the `Add[LIFETIME]` methods that takes two generic arguments—the first representing the service type and the second representing the implementation. This is the pattern you are likely to use most often. We have also looked at the version of the `Add[LIFETIME]` method that takes an implementation. Here we'll review some other registration options that provide additional capabilities.

Imagine your `SimpleCityService` needs some constructor arguments passed to it. You can do this by passing in a factory that defines the arguments to be passed:

```
builder.Services.AddTransient<ICityService>(provider => new
➥ SimpleCityService(args));
```

If the constructor arguments include a dependency from the container, the factory provides access to the service, so you can resolve the dependency. The following example shows how this works if the `SimpleCityService` takes a dependency on an implementation of `IMyService` as well as `args`. You use the `IServiceProvider GetService` method to resolve the dependency. We will look at other ways to access services directly from the service provider at the end of the chapter:

```
builder.Services.AddTransient(provider =>
    new SimpleCityService(args, provider.GetService<IMyService>())
);
```

The factory option is preferred because it hands responsibility for newing up, or *activating*, the service to the service container. And if the container is responsible for service activation, it also takes responsibility for service disposal. There is an alternative method that applies to singleton services, which involves passing in the constructed service:

```
builder.Services.AddSingleton<IMyService>(new MyService(args));
```

When you register a service using this approach, you must take responsibility for its disposal too. The same is true if you pass in the constructed service using the implementation-only option:

```
builder.Services.AddSingleton(new MyService(args));
```

7.2.5 Registering multiple implementations

It is possible to register multiple implementations of a service by repeating the relevant `Add[LIFETIME]` method with the same service type but a different implementation:

```
builder.Services.AddTransient<ICityService, SimpleCityService>();
builder.Services.AddTransient<ICityService, CityService>();
```

This raises an obvious question: which one will get resolved when its abstraction is injected into a constructor? The answer to that question is the last one you registered. So another question arises: how is the capability to inject multiple implementations useful?

Imagine you have several different implementations of a service, but you rely on runtime data to determine which implementation to use. For example, you might want to calculate prices, taxes, and discounts based on the visitor's location. You could fill one service with conditional code for each location that you serve, but you can imagine that approach getting very messy very quickly, especially if the calculations are complex. And you can also imagine the maintenance issues if you need to update the code to reflect changes in laws in one territory, for example. That opens up the possibility of inadvertently changing code for other locations and introducing bugs unrelated to the change you needed to make.

Instead, you could provide a separate implementation for each location. Consider the following simple interface: `IPriceService`.

Listing 7.12 The `IPriceService` interface

```
public interface IPriceService
{
    string GetLocation();
    double CalculatePrice();
}
```

This interface defines two methods—one that returns the location that applies to any specific implementation and another that represents the logic for calculating prices. Let's assume each implementation of this service definition returns the ISO 3166-1 Alpha-2 code you already know about, except for a default price service, which returns `"XX"`. The US version is shown in listing 7.13. Others are available in the download that accompanies this section (http://mng.bz/o54p).

Listing 7.13 Example implementation for an `IPriceService` for the USA

```
public class UsPriceService : IPriceService
{
    public string GetLocation() => "us";
    public double CalculatePrice()
    {
```

```
        ...
    }
}
```

You register a variety of implementations with the service container:

```
builder.Services.AddScoped<IPriceService, FrPriceService>();
builder.Services.AddScoped<IPriceService, GbPriceService>();
builder.Services.AddScoped<IPriceService, UsPriceService>();
builder.Services.AddScoped<IPriceService, DefaultPriceService>();
```

If you were to inject `IPriceService` into a `PageModel` constructor, you would always get the `DefaultPriceService`, as established above, being that it is the last one registered. However, you can also inject an `IEnumerable<IPriceService>`, which resolves to a collection of all registered implementations. Then it is just a question of selecting the implementation that applies to the current request.

I'm a fan of Cloudflare (https://www.cloudflare.com/), which provides a range of web-related services, including geolocation (other geolocation service providers are available), whereby they identify the location of a request based on its IP address. The location is made available to application code in the request headers as an ISO-3166-1 Alpha-2 code, or `"XX"` where it is not possible to resolve the location. The following listing shows an example of how to use this header value to resolve the correct service to call based on the current request.

Listing 7.14 Resolving one from a number of registered services

```
public class CityModel : PageModel
{
    private readonly IEnumerable<IPriceService> _priceServices;
    public CityModel(IEnumerable<IPriceService> priceServices)
    {
        _priceServices = priceServices;
    }

    public void OnGet()
    {
        var locationCode = Request.Headers["CF-IPCountry"];
        var priceService = _priceServices.FirstOrDefault(s=> s.GetLocation()
        ➥ == locationCode);
        // do something with priceService
    }
}
```

Inject a collection representing all registered implementations.

Obtain the runtime data used to define the implementation applicable to this request.

Query the collection for a service that matches the predicate passed in to the FirstOrDefault method.

There are two clear benefits to adopting this pattern. The first is that each `IPriceService` implementation is location specific, which reduces the amount of code they require and results in a simpler maintenance experience. The second is that if you want to cater to additional locations, you just need to create a new service and register it along with the others. It will automatically be resolved as part of the injected collection.

There is another way to register services that will result in the first registration to be resolved in the situation where multiple implementations are registered, instead of the last. That is to use the `TryAdd<LIFETIME>` method. If you repeat the registration of the `IPriceService` implementations using `TryAddScoped` (as shown in the following listing), the first one will be resolved, unless you inject an `IEnumerable`.

Listing 7.15 `TryAdd<LIFETIME>` resulting in the first implementation being resolved

```
builder.Services.TryAddScoped<IPriceService, FrPriceService>();
builder.Services.TryAddScoped<IPriceService, GbPriceService>();
builder.Services.TryAddScoped<IPriceService, UsPriceService>();
builder.Services.TryAddScoped<IPriceService, DefaultPriceService>();
```

The implementation that was registered first is resolved.

So when would you use the `TryAdd` method for registering services? Typically, you would use this approach if you wanted to ensure additional registrations made accidentally are not used by default. This could happen if it is not clear what registrations are being made because they are hidden within an extension method—for example, the `AddRazorPages` method. The library authors might want to ensure their registration is used regardless of what consumers of the framework subsequently try to do.

7.3 Other ways to access registered services

Constructor injection is likely to be the most common way you work with registered services. However, there are other ways to access services you should be aware of. You will likely use some of these options at some stage, but they have their caveats. The options include injecting directly into Razor files, method injection, and retrieving services directly from the service container.

7.3.1 View injection

Some services provided by the framework are designed to assist with the generation of HTML. One example is the `IHtmlLocalizer` service, which is used for localizing snippets of HTML in web applications that need to handle multiple languages. It serves no purpose outside of a Razor page or view. It is possible to inject this service into the `PageModel` of a page that needs it and then assign it to a public property, so it is accessible via the `Model` in the Razor page itself. But a better solution is to simply inject the service directly into the page using the `@inject` directive.

Listing 7.16 Using the `@inject` directive to inject services into a Razor page

```
@page
@inject IHtmlLocalizer<IndexModel> htmlLocalizer
@model IndexModel
@{
    ViewData["Title"] = "Home page";
}
```

The IHtmlLocalizer<T> service is injected using the @inject directive and assigned to the variable htmlLocalizer.

```
<div class="text-center">
    <h1>Welcome</h1>
    <p>@htmlLocalizer["Intro"]</p>
</div>
```

The localizer service is used to localize a snippet of HTML identified as "Intro".

I should stress that this approach is fine when you are only using it for HTML-based services. You should not inject any services containing business logic directly into the page. We keep our business logic away from HTML, don't we?

7.3.2 Method injection

Out of the box, the default services container only supports constructor injection. However, ASP.NET Core adds method parameter injection in a couple of places. You have already seen an example of this in chapter 2, when we looked at creating conventional middleware. If you recall, you injected an `ILogger<T>` into the `InvokeAsync` method:

```
public async Task InvokeAsync(HttpContext context,
➥ ILogger<IpAddressMiddleware> logger)
```

But what about handler methods? After all, handler method parameters are seen as binding targets by the model binder. What happens when the model binder encounters an `IPriceService` parameter? Your application breaks. That's what happens, unless you prefix the service parameter with the `FromServices` attribute:

```
public async Task OnGetAsync([FromServices]IPriceService service)
{
    // do something with service
}
```

This is a useful pattern for services that are expensive to create but are only used a fraction of the time in a Razor page. It might be, for example, that you have a named handler in a page that needs a service that is not required by the `OnGet` and `OnPost` handlers, and the named handler is only called under certain circumstances. In this scenario, it makes little sense to inject the service into the `PageModel` constructor. The `FromServices` attribute lets you scope the service purely to the handler method that needs it, and it will only be resolved when it is needed.

7.3.3 Directly from the service container with GetService and GetRequiredService

Sometimes, you will need to access the service container directly for a service. This approach is known as the *service locator* pattern. That sounds like it's a good thing, being a design pattern and all, but it is generally considered an *anti-pattern* and should be avoided. However, sometimes you don't have a choice. You have already seen an example of this when you used a factory to register a service that takes another service as a dependency earlier in the chapter.

DEFINITION An anti-pattern is a commonly used solution to a recurring problem (a pattern), that is usually suboptimal in some way. This might be because the solution introduces new problems or because it simply moves the problem elsewhere.

The `IServiceProvider` service provides access to registered services. It has one method, `GetService`, which returns the specified service, or `null` if it is not found. In addition, there is an extension method, `GetRequiredService`, that throws an exception if the specified service is not found. The `IServiceProvider` is injected into the consumer, which then uses it to retrieve the services it needs.

Listing 7.17 Example usage of the service locator pattern

```
public class IndexModel : PageModel
{
    private readonly IServiceProvider _serviceProvider;

    public IndexModel(IServiceProvider serviceProvider) =>]
    ➥ _serviceProvider = serviceProvider;

    public List<City> Cities { get; set; }
    public async Task OnGetAsync()
    {
        var cityService =
        ➥ _serviceProvider.GetRequiredService<ICityService>();
        Cities = await cityService.GetAllAsync();
    }
}
```

Inject the IServiceProvider into the class constructor.

Recalling what I said about the explicit dependencies principle, you may be able to discern why the service locator is an anti-pattern. It is not clear from the code in listing 7.17 what the dependencies of the `IndexModel` are—apart from the service provider. In fact, it still depends on the `ICityService`, but that detail is no longer visible to code outside of the class.

The service provider is also available as a request feature (http://mng.bz/neE2), so you don't even need to inject the provider into classes that have access to the `HttpContext`. You could replace the line of code that resolves the city service in listing 7.17 with the following:

```
var cityService =
➥ HttpContext.RequestServices.GetRequiredService<ICityService>();
```

Dependency injection and the other terms that accompany it sound complicated, but the reality is that it is a pretty simple technique that helps to achieve high-quality code. The built-in service container should suffice for most use cases, but if you find yourself needing something more advanced, you can use one of the many (usually free and open source) third-party containers that support ASP.NET Core. Integration is usually quite straightforward and should be fully documented by the vendor.

In the next chapter, we will look at working with data in a Razor Pages application. While we do that, we will create a new service that obtains data from a database and seamlessly swap out the existing service for a new one, demonstrating one of the key advantages of using DI.

Summary

- Dependency injection (DI) is a key feature in ASP.NET Core.
- DI helps you implement inversion of control, a technique that promotes loose coupling of code.
- Services are injected into classes that depend on them as explicit dependencies.
- The dependency inversion principle (DIP) states that high-level classes and low-level classes should depend on abstractions, such as interfaces.
- You configure services in Program.cs via the WebApplication Services property, which represents the configured services for the application.
- Services are registered as a type and an implementation with a service container.
- Services are registered using one of three lifetimes: singleton, transient, or scoped.
- Only one instance of a singleton can exist. It lasts for the lifetime of the container.
- Transient services are resolved every time they are requested.
- Scoped services last for the duration of a web request in ASP.NET Core.
- Multiple implementations of the same service can be registered. The last one registered will be resolved.
- You can access all registered implementations by injection and IEnumerable<ServiceType>.
- You can inject into page handler methods by prefixing the service parameter with [FromServices].
- You can inject directly into Razor pages via the @inject attribute.

8 Working with data

This chapter covers

- Understanding the value of Entity Framework Core and how it works
- Managing the database schema with Entity Framework Core
- Using Entity Framework Core to query and manage data
- Scaffolding Razor Pages that work with Entity Framework Core and improving the output

So far we have concentrated our efforts on exploring features of the Razor Pages framework and how they work to generate HTML. This chapter takes a slight departure from that, focusing instead on a different framework known as Entity Framework Core (EF Core).

All but the simplest interactive web applications rely on the persistence and retrieval of data to support their dynamic content. That data is most often stored in and retrieved from a relational database of some kind. In the bad old days, the code required to manage these data access tasks was very repetitive. You would establish a connection to the database in code each time you wanted to communicate with the database, define the SQL query you wanted to execute, execute it, and capture the returned data in a low-level container, such as a `Recordset`, `DataTable`, or `DataReader`, and then process the data into some form your application could work with. The primary role of EF Core is to abstract that away, so you can concentrate on writing code to work with the data instead of code to retrieve it from a database. This chapter performs the basic CRUD operations with EF Core via its *context*, an object that derives from `DbContext`, which is central to working with EF Core.

EF Core is a lot more powerful than just replacing the boilerplate code required to execute commands against a database. We will explore how it can be used to generate a database from your application model and then keep your database schema in sync with the model with a feature called *migrations*. We will also look at the conventions EF Core uses to map your model to the database and how you can use configuration to customize those mappings if needed.

This chapter will also cover a feature known as *scaffolding*. This feature combines your application model and database knowledge to quickly generate working CRUD pages for specific objects within the model. You'll understand the limitations of the code generated by the scaffolding tools and see how to improve them to comply with some of the software engineering principles we looked at in the last chapter.

By the end of this chapter, you will understand the role of EF Core and how to use it to execute commands against a relational database, manage that database's schema, and generate CRUD pages. EF Core is, however, a massive topic; we'll only scratch the surface of its capabilities and use in this book. To get the best out of this fantastic tool, you should obtain a copy of the excellent *Entity Framework Core in Action* (2nd ed.) by Jon P. Smith (http://mng.bz/vXr4) and refer to the official documentation (https://docs.microsoft.com/en-us/ef/core/).

8.1 What is Entity Framework Core?

EF Core is an object-relational mapping (ORM) tool. Its role is to map between objects (your application model) and the relational world (your database). EF Core works with many databases, including the popular Microsoft SQL Server and MySQL database systems. This book will use EF Core with SQLite, an open source, cross-platform, file-based database. While lacking many advanced features you find in more powerful server-based systems, SQLite is easy to use, requiring no installation or configuration, and will suffice for the EF Core features we will explore in this chapter.

8.1.1 Why choose EF Core?

You could use low-level, old-school ADO.NET APIs to manage communication with the database, but the code required is repetitive (did I say that already?) and boring to write. One solution would be to write your own library of helpers to reduce the repetition. But then you would have to maintain that code yourself. Data access libraries are abundant, and unless you can see ways to improve on existing offerings, writing your own is likely to be a waste of time if you just need to get on with producing a web application.

You are free to use any library you like for managing data access in Razor Pages applications, so of all the abundant existing libraries, why choose EF Core? Being part of .NET, it is well supported and tested and enjoys a significant amount of official documentation. On top of the official docs, there are a huge number of community contributions, such as books, blog posts, and tutorial sites, that explore the more esoteric features of EF Core along with its most common workflows. If all else fails and you struggle to get something to work, you can post an issue to the EF Core GitHub repo (https://github.com/dotnet/efcore), where you might even get a response from one of the developers on the EF Core team.

EF Core enjoys tooling support within Visual Studio that can help you quickly generate CRUD pages based on your application model. While the results are not perfect, they provide a significant head start to developing the more mundane parts of your application. The scaffolding support is also available to non-Visual Studio users from the command line. You will see this in action later.

8.1.2 How does EF Core work?

At a fundamental level, EF Core creates a conceptual model of how your domain objects and their properties—your application model—map to tables and columns in a database. It also understands the associations between domain objects and can map those to database relationships. It is a drop-in data layer for your application, sitting between the domain (on the left-hand side of figure 8.1) and the data store (on the right-hand side of figure 8.1).

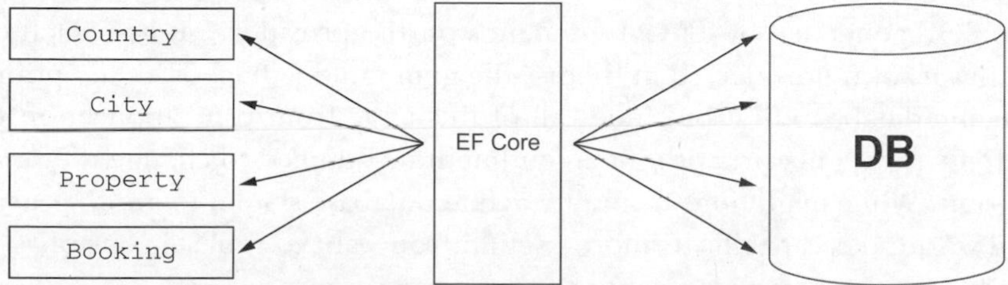

Figure 8.1 EF Core sits between the domain objects on the left and the database on the right and maps objects and their properties and associations to database tables, columns, and relationships.

EF Core manages communication between your business objects and the data store. Language-Integrated Query (LINQ) will help you create query specifications within your application code and provide those to EF Core. Your LINQ queries are translated into SQL commands by EF Core, which executes them against the database, as illustrated in figure 8.2. The SQL EF core generates is parameterized, meaning it is protected against potential *SQL injection* attacks (http://mng.bz/49qj). You will study SQL injection attacks in more detail in chapter 13 when you focus on securing your application against external threats.

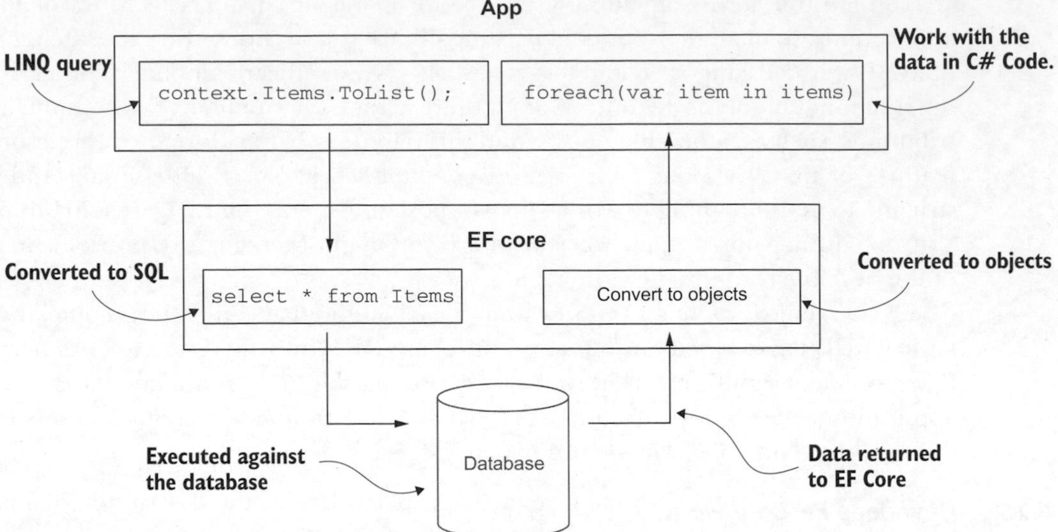

Figure 8.2 EF Core workflow, taking your LINQ query, converting it to SQL to execute against the database, and returning the results in a form you can work with in your application

If your query is designed to return data, EF Core takes care of converting the data from the database into your domain objects. If you are familiar with software design patterns, you may well recognize this as an implementation of the Repository pattern (http://mng.bz/QnYv).

The SQL generated by EF Core depends on the provider you use. Each database system has its own provider, so in theory, the generated SQL should be optimized for the specific database. EF Core hides all of this away from your application code, so your LINQ query will work without amendment if you need to change the provider at some point. While migrations from one actual database system to another are rare in the real world, this capability is more useful if you want to replace your physical database with an in-memory database for testing purposes.

The approach you take when working with EF Core is known as *code first* (as opposed to *database first*), meaning you concentrate your efforts on developing the application model and allow EF Core to use the model as the basis for maintaining the database schema, using a concept known as *migrations*. EF Core can also create the database itself if it doesn't exist. EF Core relies on several conventions to map objects and their properties to database tables and columns and create relationships. You will explore the most important conventions as you refine your domain model to work with EF Core. In addition to the conventions that "just work," EF Core provides extensive configuration options that enable you to control how your model maps to tables and columns in the database.

8.1.3 Managing relationships

Relational database systems exist solely to facilitate working with sets of data that relate to each other. Within the database, relationships between different entities are represented by the presence of foreign keys. In figure 8.3, `Country` and `City` are related in a one-to-many relationship by the `CountryId` foreign key on the `City` table.

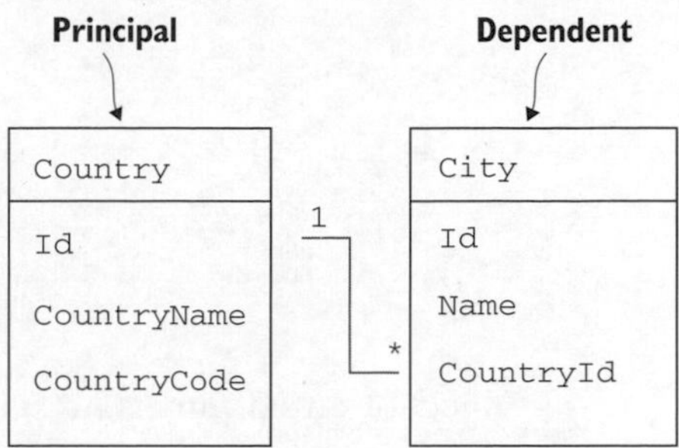

Figure 8.3 A one-to-many relationship exists between `Country` and `City`, where one country can have many cities.

By convention, relationships in an EF Core model are represented by *navigational properties*. These are properties in a class that cannot be mapped to a primitive or scalar value, such as a string, Boolean, integer, or `datetime` type. Your existing `City` class (see the next listing) already has a `Country` property that fits the description of a navigational property.

Listing 8.1 The `City` class with the `Country` navigational property

```
public class City
{
    public int Id { get; set; }
    public string Name { get; set; }
    public Country Country { get; set; }    <-- Country is a navigational property.
}
```

This is all that is needed for EF Core to infer a one-to-many relationship between the `Country` and `City` entities, where the `Country` is the principal in the relationship and the `City` is the dependent. In this example, the `Country` property is referred to as a *reference navigation property*, which has a *multiplicity* (the potential number of items at one end of a relationship) of zero or one. More commonly, EF Core relationships are *fully defined*, having properties representing each end of the relationship and a property representing the foreign key value. In listing 8.2, you add a property representing the `CountryId` foreign key to the `City` class and a collection navigation property to the `Country` class representing all the cities that could belong to a single country. As a best practice, you should always instantiate collection navigation properties as part of their declaration, so you can avoid having to test for `null` when accessing them in code.

Listing 8.2 Fully defined one-to-many relationship between `Country` and `City`

```
public class City
{
    public int Id { get; set; }
    public string Name { get; set; }
    public int CountryId { get; set; }    <-- Foreign key property
```

```
    public Country Country { get; set; }    ◁── Reference navigation property representing
}                                               the one country a city belongs to

public class Country
{
    public int Id { get; set; }
    public string CountryName { get; set; }
    public string CountryCode { get; set; }
    public List<City> Cities { get; set; } = new List<City>();
}
```

Collection navigation property representing the many cities that can belong to a country, instantiated to ensure that it can never be null

Object-oriented purists are generally not keen on the idea of including foreign key properties in domain classes because they see this as an example of the relational database world "bleeding" into the domain. If you omit the foreign key property, EF Core will create a *shadow foreign key* property (http://mng.bz/Xawa) as part of its conceptual model.

By convention, a property named `Id` or `<entity_name>Id` is seen as the primary key value, and EF Core will map it to an `IDENTITY` column. Both of your domain classes have an `Id` property, but EF Core will also see `CityId` in the city class or `CountryId` in the country class as representing the primary key. Foreign key properties should use the name of the reference navigation property followed by `Id`—`CountryId`, in our example.

You have yet to create a class in your model representing properties vacationers can rent. So using the information above to create a one-to-many relationship between cities and properties, the following listing shows the `Property` class that should be added to the Models folder.

Listing 8.3 The `Property` class

```
public class Property
{
    public int Id { get; set; }    ◁── The primary key property
    public string Name { get; set; }
    public string Address { get; set; }
    public int CityId { get; set; }          The foreign key and reference
    public City City { get; set; }           navigation property
    public int MaxNumberOfGuests { get; set; }
    public decimal DayRate { get; set; }
    public bool SmokingPermitted { get; set; }
    public DateTime AvailableFrom { get; set; }
}
```

You also need to amend the `City` class to include a collection navigation property representing the properties that belong to a city, bolded in the following listing.

Listing 8.4 Updating the `City` class to include a collection of `Properties`

```
public class City
{
    public int Id { get; set; }
```

```
    public string Name { get; set; }
    public int CountryId { get; set; }
    public Country Country { get; set; }
    public List<Property> Properties { get; set; } = new List<Property>();
}
```

Now that the model has been configured so that EF Core will recognize its relationships, you can start working with EF Core.

8.1.4 Installing Entity Framework Core

EF Core is not included in a web application project by default. You need to install it as an additional package from NuGet. The simplest way to install packages that doesn't depend on which IDE you are using is adding a new package reference to your project file: the CityBreaks.csproj file in the root of your application folder. The project file is visible in the explorer and is easily accessible if you are using VS Code. It is not visible in the Visual Studio Solution Explorer. You need to right-click the project name and choose Edit Project File from the context menu that appears. Once you have the file open, add a new `PackageReference` entry to an existing `ItemGroup`, or create a new `ItemGroup` node:

```
<ItemGroup>
   <PackageReference Include="Microsoft.EntityFrameworkCore.Sqlite"
    ➥ Version="6.0.0" />
</ItemGroup>
```

Visual Studio users should notice that when you add a package this way, VS automatically runs the `restore` command and fetches the required libraries from NuGet. Using VS Code, you need to execute the `dotnet restore` command yourself from the terminal. The C# extension should prompt you to do this.

Alternatively, you can use the `dotnet add` command to add a package in VS Code. The command is:

```
dotnet add package Microsoft.EntityFrameworkCore.Sqlite
```

VS Code will automatically restore all packages after that command has been executed.

Visual Studio users have built-in tools for managing packages. Go to Tools > NuGet Package Manager, and from there, you can choose to Manage NuGet Packages for Solution. This brings up a dashboard UI that allows you to manage previously installed packages as well as search for and install additional ones. Or you can invoke the Package Manager Console (PMC) and execute commands for managing packages. To add a package, you use the `install-package` command:

```
install-package Microsoft.EntityFrameworkCore.Sqlite
```

Once again, VS will automatically restore your packages after the package has been resolved.

8.1.5 Create the context

The entry point to working with EF Core in code is the *context*—an object derived from `DbContext`. It represents a session with a database and provides an API for communicating with the database to perform data operations, such as querying and data persistence. It also supports more advanced features, such as model building and data mapping, which we will touch on later, as well as transaction management, object caching, and change tracking, which aren't be covered in this book.

The steps required to deliver a working context to the application are

1. Create a class that derives from `DbContext`.
2. Provide a connection string.
3. Register the context with the service container.

Starting at step 1, add a new folder to the project named Data, and within that, add a new class file named CityBreaksContext.cs with the following code.

Listing 8.5 The `CityBreaksContext`

```
using Microsoft.EntityFrameworkCore;

namespace CityBreaks.Data
{
    public class CityBreaksContext : DbContext
    {
        public CityBreaksContext(DbContextOptions options) : base(options)
        {

        }
    }
}
```

The class has a constructor that takes a `DbContextOptions` object as a parameter. You will configure this object when registering the context as a service, providing a connection string. First, you need to add a connection string to the application. You will use the main configuration file for this purpose. If you recall from chapter 2, this is the appSettings.json file. You will add a property called `ConnectionStrings`. The naming of this property, or *section*, is important because it is a convention the configuration API relies on to locate connection strings. Then you will provide a name for the connection string and its value.

Listing 8.6 Adding a connection string to appSettings.json

```
{
  "Logging": {
    "LogLevel": {
      "Default": "Information",
      "Microsoft": "Warning",
      "Microsoft.Hosting.Lifetime": "Information"
    }
```

```
  },
  "AllowedHosts": "*",
  "ConnectionStrings": {
    "CityBreaksContext": "Data source=Data/CityBreaks.db"
  }
}
```

The connections strings section and the actual connection string

SQLite connection strings are nice and simple, representing the path to the database file. In your application, you will house the database file in the Data folder alongside the context. The file will be created by EF Core when you run your first migration a bit later.

The final step is to register the context with the service container. As you learned from the last chapter, you do this in the Program.cs file. You need to add some `using` directives to bring in `Microsoft.EntityFrameworkCore` and `CityBreaks.Data` before adding the following code.

Listing 8.7 Configuring the `CityBreaksContext`

```
builder.Services.AddDbContext<CityBreaksContext>(options =>
{
    options.UseSqlite(builder.Configuration.GetConnectionString
    ➥ ("CityBreaksContext"));
});
```

The `GetConnectionString` method locates the specified connection string within the `ConnectionStrings` section of appSettings.json, while the `UseSqlite` method sets up the correct database provider for EF Core to use.

You have your context and have registered it as a service. At the moment, it's pretty useless; it's like having an empty database. You will need some database tables represented in the context by `DbSet<TEntity>` properties, where `TEntity` is the entity you want the table to represent. Figure 8.4 illustrates the relationship between entities, `DbSet`s and the database.

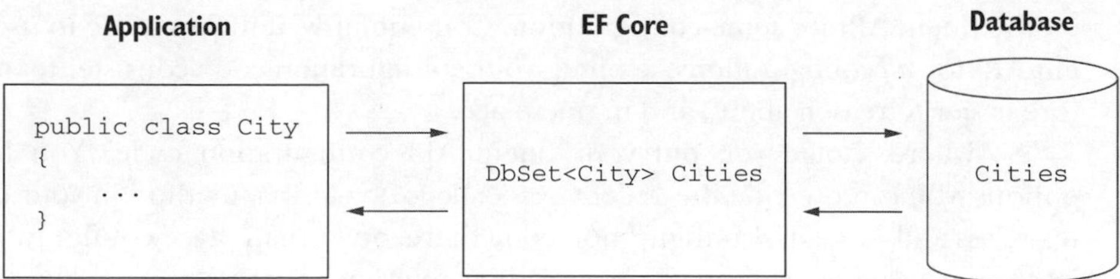

Figure 8.4 Each entity is represented by a `DbSet`, which is mapped to a table in the database.

8.1.6 Adding DbSets

First you will add a `DbSet` to the context for each entity you want to map to a database table. By convention, the table will take the name of the `DbSet` property. The next listing shows the three classes you have created in your model so far, each represented as a `DbSet<TEntity>`.

Listing 8.8 DbSet properties mapping to tables in a database

```
public class CityBreaksContext : DbContext
{
    public CityBreaksContext(DbContextOptions options) : base(options)
    {

    }
    public DbSet<City> Cities { get; set; }
    public DbSet<Country> Countries { get; set; }
    public DbSet<Property> Properties { get; set; }
}
```

8.1.7 Configuring the model

If you were to create a migration at this stage, it would generate a database with three tables, one for each `DbSet`, and it would use conventions to create columns based on the properties for each of the types represented by the `DbSet` type parameter. In most real-world applications, the default conventions will be acceptable for most of your model, especially if you are starting from scratch. For those cases in which the conventions aren't suitable or EF Core needs help understanding your intentions, EF Core provides configuration APIs that allow you to override the conventions.

Configuration targets three levels: the model, types, and properties. You can configure the schema EF Core uses for objects at the model level. Type configuration options enable you to configure the table's name that a type maps to or how relationships should be specified between types. Property configuration provides extensive options for managing how individual properties map to columns, including their name, data type, default values, and so on.

Configuration can be applied in two ways: by decorating classes and properties with attributes or by using a fluent API that consists of a collection of extension methods that can be chained together. Attributes only provide a subset of configuration options. Therefore, for any reasonably complex model, you are likely to need to rely on the fluent API for some configuration. Consequently, it makes sense to use the fluent API for *all* configurations, keeping your configuration code consistent, and therefore easier to reason about, and in one place.

So where should you put your fluent API configuration code? You have two options: you can override the `DbContext` `OnModelCreating` method in your own context class and place the configuration code there, or you can place configuration code in separate classes for each entity and then reference those classes in the `OnModelCreating` method. You will adopt the latter approach, since it is the recommended way to manage this aspect of your application.

Configuration classes derive from `IEntityTypeConfiguration<TEntity>`, which implements one method, `Configure`, which takes an `EntityTypeBuilder<TEntity>` as a parameter. It is in this method that you will place your configuration code.

Start by creating a new folder in the Data folder, naming it Configurations. Add a C# class file to the new folder, named CountryConfiguration, with the following code.

Listing 8.9 The CountryConfiguration class

```
using CityBreaks.Models;
using Microsoft.EntityFrameworkCore;
using Microsoft.EntityFrameworkCore.Metadata.Builders;

namespace CityBreaks.Data.Configuration;
public class CountryConfiguration : IEntityTypeConfiguration<Country>
{
    public void Configure(EntityTypeBuilder<Country> builder)
    {
        builder.Property(x => x.CountryName)
            .HasMaxLength(50);
        builder.Property(x => x.CountryCode)
            .HasColumnName("ISO 3166 code")
            .HasMaxLength(2);
    }
}
```

The class implements IEntityTypeConfiguration<TEntity>.

Implement the Configure method, as required by the interface.

Use the HasMaxLength method to constrain the length of the text field for the CountryName property.

Map the CountryCode property to a column named "ISO 3166 Code" and constrain its size.

String properties conventionally map to `nvarchar(max)` datatypes in SQL Server. You have used the `HasMaxLength` method to apply a limit to the size of a text-based column in databases that support it. SQLite doesn't support this method, so unless you are working with SQL Server instead, this configuration will have no effect. Nevertheless, the `HasColumnName` method will work in any database and map the `CountryCode` property to the `"ISO 3166 code"` column. You can see the fluent API with the `HasMaxLength` method chained to the `HasColumnName` method when configuring the `CountryCode` property.

8.2 Migrations

You are almost at the point where you can create a migration that keeps the database schema in sync with the model. The migration tooling examines the `DbSet` properties of the context and compares them to a snapshot generated by the previous migration if there was one. Any differences result in C# code being generated, which, when executed, is translated into SQL that applies changes to the actual database. The first migration will result in the database being created if it doesn't already exist. It is also possible to generate the migration SQL scripts on demand, so you can apply them to the database yourself. This is particularly useful for making the changes to your live database, where it is often difficult, if not impossible, to execute C# code.

One other aspect of configuration that can be very useful is the capability to specify seed data, which is used to populate the database during a migration. This feature has obvious uses in that it can get you started with a set of data without manually entering it. In the next section, you will look at using this feature with some country data, followed by some city data.

The migration download that comes with this chapter (http://mng.bz/jAra) also includes seed data for the `Property` type as well as some images (courtesy of https://unsplash.com/) for cities. I recommend you obtain the relevant code and images from the GitHub repo and use that for your migration, so your database content matches the examples going forward.

8.2.1 Seed data

You will use the Fluent API `HasData` method to specify seed data for an entity as part of its configuration. You must specify primary and foreign key values, so the migration can determine if any changes have been made to data outside of migrations. Such changes will be overwritten, so the seeding feature is most suitable for static data that will not change. If data is likely to change once it has been added using the seeding feature, you can comment out the relevant code, so it is not called in subsequent migrations. The following listing shows the `Configure` method in the `CountryConfiguration` class amended to include the `HasData` method call, which takes a collection of the relevant types.

Listing 8.10 `Country` seed data

```
public void Configure(EntityTypeBuilder<Country> builder)
{
    builder.Property(x => x.CountryName)
        .HasMaxLength(50);
    builder.Property(x => x.CountryCode)
        .HasColumnName("ISO 3166 code")
        .HasMaxLength(2);
    builder.HasData(new List<Country>
    {
        new Country {Id = 1, CountryName = "Croatia", CountryCode="hr" },
        new Country {Id = 2, CountryName = "Denmark", CountryCode = "dk" },
        new Country {Id = 3, CountryName = "France", CountryCode = "fr" },
        new Country {Id = 4, CountryName = "Germany", CountryCode = "de" },
        new Country {Id = 5, CountryName = "Holland", CountryCode = "nl" },
        new Country {Id = 6, CountryName = "Italy", CountryCode = "it" },
        new Country {Id = 7, CountryName = "Spain", CountryCode = "es" },
        new Country {Id = 8, CountryName = "United Kingdom",
        ➥ CountryCode = "gb" },
        new Country {Id = 9, CountryName = "United States",
        ➥ CountryCode = "us" }
    });
}
```

To add seed data for cities, you first need to add a property to the `City` class to represent an image. I will call this property `Photo`, but you will configure it to map to a column named `Image`.

Listing 8.11 Adding the `Photo` property to the `City` class

```
public class City
{
    public int Id { get; set; }
    public string Name { get; set; }
```

```
    public string Photo { get; set; }
    public int CountryId { get; set; }
    public Country Country { get; set; }
    public List<Property> Properties {  get; set; } = new List<Property>();
}
```

Now you need to add another `IEntityTypeConfiguration` class to the Configuration folder, this time named `CityConfiguration`, with the following code.

Listing 8.12 The `City` configuration class

```
using CityBreaks.Models;
using Microsoft.EntityFrameworkCore;
using Microsoft.EntityFrameworkCore.Metadata.Builders;

namespace CityBreaks.Data.Configuration;
public class CityConfiguration : IEntityTypeConfiguration<City>
{
    public void Configure(EntityTypeBuilder<City> builder)
    {
        builder.Property(x => x.Photo).HasColumnName("Image");
        builder.HasData(new List<City>
        {
            new City { Id = 1, Name = "Amsterdam", CountryId = 5,
            ➥ Photo = "amsterdam.jpg" },
            new City { Id = 2, Name = "Barcelona", CountryId = 7,
            ➥ Photo ="barcelona.jpg" },
            new City { Id = 3, Name = "Berlin", CountryId = 4,
            ➥ Photo ="berlin.jpg" },
            new City { Id = 4, Name = "Copenhagen", CountryId = 2,
            ➥ Photo ="copenhagen.jpg" },
            new City { Id = 5, Name = "Dubrovnik", CountryId = 1,
            ➥ Photo ="dubrovnik.jpg" },
            new City { Id = 6, Name = "Edinburgh", CountryId = 8,
            ➥ Photo ="edinburgh.jpg" },
            new City { Id = 7, Name = "London", CountryId = 8,
            ➥ Photo ="london.jpg" },
            new City { Id = 8, Name = "Madrid", CountryId = 7,
            ➥ Photo ="madrid.jpg" },
            new City { Id = 9, Name = "New York", CountryId = 9,
            ➥ Photo ="new-york.jpg" },
            new City { Id = 10, Name = "Paris", CountryId = 3,
            ➥ Photo ="paris.jpg" },
            new City { Id = 11, Name = "Rome", CountryId = 6,
            ➥ Photo ="rome.jpg" },
            new City { Id = 12, Name = "Venice", CountryId = 6,
            ➥ Photo ="venice.jpg" }
        });
    }
}
```

Note that you have used the `HasColumnName` method to map the `Photo` property to a column named `Image`.

The final configuration is for the `Property` type. This configuration consists purely of seed data, and the example in the book's downloads includes 50 fictitious property details. You can either generate your seed data based on what you have learned so far or copy the configuration file's contents from the book's GitHub repo: http://mng.bz/yaBd.

Once the configuration classes are done, you will need to register them with the `DbContext`. You can do this by overriding the `OnModelCreating` method in the `CityBreaksContext` class and then using the `ModelBuilder` `ApplyConfiguration` method to register each type. Since the `ApplyConfiguration` method returns a `ModelBuilder`, you can chain these calls.

Listing 8.13 Registering configurations in the `OnModelCreating` method

```
protected override void OnModelCreating (ModelBuilder builder)
{
    builder
        .ApplyConfiguration(new CityConfiguration())
        .ApplyConfiguration(new CountryConfiguration())
        .ApplyConfiguration(new PropertyConfiguration());
}
```

8.2.2 Adding migration tools

Before creating a migration, you need to add the necessary package to the project that contains the commands for managing them. Two packages are available, each one having a different set of commands. The one you use will depend on what tool you want to use to execute the migration commands.

If you are a Visual Studio user, you can use the Package Manager Console; in that case you will want the PowerShell commands contained in the `Microsoft.EntityFrameworkCore.Tools` package. Alternatively, you can use the cross-platform CLI commands available in the `Microsoft.EntityFrameworkCore.Design` package instead. Once you have selected your package, you can use whichever method you prefer from those covered earlier to add the package to your project. If you are using the CLI commands, you must also ensure that the `dotnet-ef` tools are installed globally, which you can do using the following command:

```
dotnet tool install --global dotnet-ef
```

8.2.3 Creating and applying a migration

Once the tools and relevant package are installed, you can create your first migration. You will use one of the following commands:

```
[Powershell]
add-migration Create
[CLI]
dotnet ef migrations add Create
```

The PowerShell command to be executed from within the Package Manager Console in Visual Studio

The CLI command to be executed from a command prompt located within the directory containing the csproj file

The migration is named `Create`. Successful execution of whichever command you used has resulted in a new folder being added to the project, named Migrations. Figure 8.5 shows the Migrations folder and its contents in the Visual Studio Code file explorer.

Migrations
20211004082658_Create.cs
20211004082658_Create.Designer.cs
CityBreaksContextModelSnapshot.cs

Figure 8.5 The generated Migrations folder, containing three files

The new folder contains three files:

1 *[Timestamp]_Create.cs*—Contains a class named `Create` with two methods: `Up` and `Down`. The `Up` method applies changes to the database, while the `Down` method reverts them.
2 *[Timestamp]_Create.Designer.cs*—Contains metadata used by EF Core.
3 *CityBreaksContextModelSnapshot.cs*—A snapshot of the model as it is currently. When you add another migration, this snapshot is used as the baseline to determine what has changed.

The first two files are specific to the migration. New ones will be added for additional migrations. The model snapshot file will be updated for each new migration. If you look at the contents of the `Up` method in the first file, the C# code should be self-explanatory. You are free to amend this as you see fit prior to applying the migration to the database. For example, in later migrations, you may want to be able to execute some custom SQL as part of the procedure, such as bringing in non-seed data. I don't cover that in this book, but it is useful to know that the capability is available should you need it. However, I usually take a look at the migration code to ensure that the changes I intend to apply are reflected there. More than once, I've realized by looking at the migration code that I have not configured a property correctly. When that is the case, you can adjust the model configuration and then use the `remove-migration` (PowerShell) or `dotnet ef migrations remove` (CLI) commands to remove the existing migration before adding it back again, using the same command as before.

Having generated the migration and checked that it does what you want, you will apply it using one of the following commands:

```
[Powershell]
update-database
[CLI]
dotnet ef database update
```

Once you have executed one of these commands, you should see that a SQLite database file has been created in the Data folder: CityBreaks.db. Using whichever tool you prefer (I use the cross-platform DB Browser for SQLite; https://sqlitebrowser.org/), take a look at the schema (figure 8.6). In addition to tables for each of your model classes, the database includes a table named __EFMigrationsHistory.

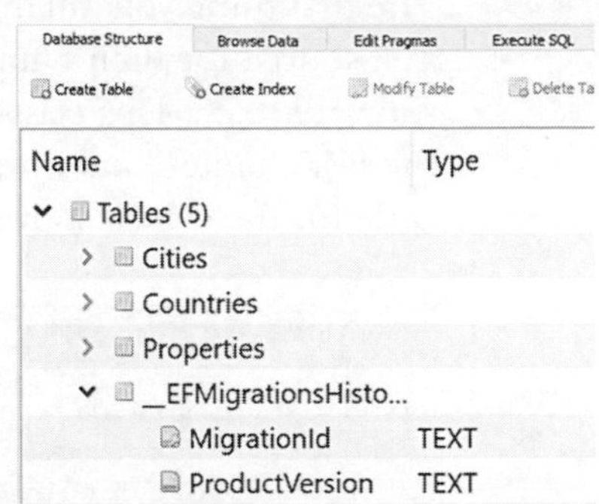

Figure 8.6 The new database includes a table named __EFMigrationsHistory.

This table keeps track of which migrations have been applied to the database. At the moment, it contains one record consisting of the name of the migration you just applied as well as the version of EF Core that was used.

8.3 Querying data

Your database is populated with the seed data, and it is about time you started working with it. You will use LINQ to express the commands you want EF Core to execute against the database. LINQ comprises a set of `extension` methods on the `IEnumerable` type that enable selection and filtering operations against collections. The collections you operate on are the `DbSet` objects in your context.

EF Core is responsible for translating the LINQ query into SQL to be executed against the database. The SQL generated is dependent on the provider used, taking into account database-specific features.

You can take one of two approaches when writing LINQ queries. You can use *query* syntax or *method* syntax. Query syntax looks similar to SQL statements, and some folk feel more comfortable with it. The following example shows query syntax being used to obtain all cities that belong to a country having a primary key value of `1`:

```
var data = from c in _context.Cities where c.CountryId == 1 select c;
```

However, much like how data annotation attributes only provide a subset of model configuration options, query syntax is not always enough. Some queries can only be expressed using method calls.

My preference is for method syntax, which consists of chaining calls to extension methods on the `IEnumerable` type (http://mng.bz/M0RB). Using query syntax, your code is translated to method calls when it is compiled, so there is no performance difference between the two approaches. We only use method syntax in this book. If you are interested in learning more about query syntax, the official LINQ documentation provides many examples: http://mng.bz/aPNm.

8.3.1 Retrieving multiple records

The first thing you will do is to create a new service for cities that will use the database as a source for their data. Add a new class file to the Services folder, calling this one CityService.cs. This class will implement the `ICityService` interface you created in the last chapter, and it will take the `CityBreaksContext` as a dependency. The initial code for the class is shown in the following listing.

Listing 8.14 The `CityService` class

```
using CityBreaks.Data;
using CityBreaks.Models;
using Microsoft.EntityFrameworkCore;

namespace CityBreaks.Services;
```

```
public class CityService : ICityService
{
    private readonly CityBreaksContext _context;
    public CityService(CityBreaksContext context) => _context = context;
    public async Task<List<City>> GetAllAsync()
    {
        var cities = _context.Cities
            .Include(c => c.Country)
            .Include(c => c.Properties);
        return await cities.ToListAsync();
    }
}
```

The entry point to a query is the DbSet.

Use the Include method to specify related data you want included in the query.

The ToListAsync method call causes query execution.

LINQ queries consist of two phases: the *specification* phase and the *execution* phase. In our example, the specification of the query takes place in the first three lines of the `GetAllAsync` method. The execution is deferred until the last line, where you call the `ToListAsync` method. It is only at that point that a call to the database is made. This ability to defer execution enables you to continue to compose the specification by adding additional criteria. For example, you might want to filter the query to only return cities in France, which you can do within a `Where` method call that takes a predicate representing the filter condition(s):

```
var cities = _context.Cities
    .Where(c => c.Country.CountryName == "France")
    .Include(c => c.Country)
    .Include(c => c.Properties);
```

You want to return all cities, including their related country and properties, so you can display details on the home page of the application. However, you only want to include currently available properties, so you apply the filter to the `Include` method:

```
var cities = _context.Cities
    .Include(c => c.Country)
    .Include(c => c.Properties.Where(p => p.AvailableFrom < DateTime.Now));
```

The next step is updating the Index.cshtml.cs file content and replacing the existing content with the following code, which injects the `ICityService` into the constructor and uses it to obtain city data.

Listing 8.15 Revised `IndexModel` code for the home page

```
using CityBreaks.Models;
using CityBreaks.Services;
using Microsoft.AspNetCore.Mvc.RazorPages;

namespace CityBreaks.Pages
{
    public class IndexModel : PageModel
    {
        private readonly ICityService _cityService;
```

```
        public IndexModel(ICityService cityService)
        {
            _cityService = cityService;
        }

        public List<City> Cities { get; set; }
        public async Task OnGetAsync() => Cities =
        ➥ await _cityService.GetAllAsync();
    }
}
```

Then you remove the list box from the home page (if it is still there from chapter 5) and replace it with the following.

Listing 8.16 Updated Razor code for the home page

```
<h1>City Breaks</h1>
<div class="container">
    <div class="row">
        @foreach (var city in Model.Cities)        // Loop through all of the cities.
        {
            <div class="col-4 p-3" style="text-shadow: rgb(0, 0, 0) 1px 1px
            ➥ 1px">
                <div class="card p-3 shadow"
                ➥ style="background:url(/images/cities/@city.Photo)
                ➥ no-repeat center;background-size: cover;height:240px;">
                    // Use the Photo property of each city to set a background image.
                    <h3>
                        <a class="text-white text-decoration-none"
                        ➥ asp-page="/City" asp-route-name="@city.Name">
                        ➥ @city.Name</a>
                        // Output the name of the city.
                        <img
                        ➥ src="/images/flags/@(city.Country.CountryCode).png"
                        ➥ aria-label="@($"{city.Name},
                        ➥ {city.Country.CountryName}")">
                        // Reference the city's Country property and use its CountryCode to render the appropriate flag icon.
                    </h3>
                    <h6 class="text-white">
                    ➥ @city.Properties.Count()properties</h6>
                    // Use the Count() method to render the total number of properties associated with each city.
                </div>
            </div>
        }
    </div>
</div>
```

Now you just need to replace the existing `SimpleCityService` registration in Program.cs with one that specifies the new `CityService` as the implementation to use for `ICityService`:

```
builder.Services.AddScoped<ICityService, CityService>();
```

Once this has been done, you can run the application and enjoy the new home page (figure 8.7).

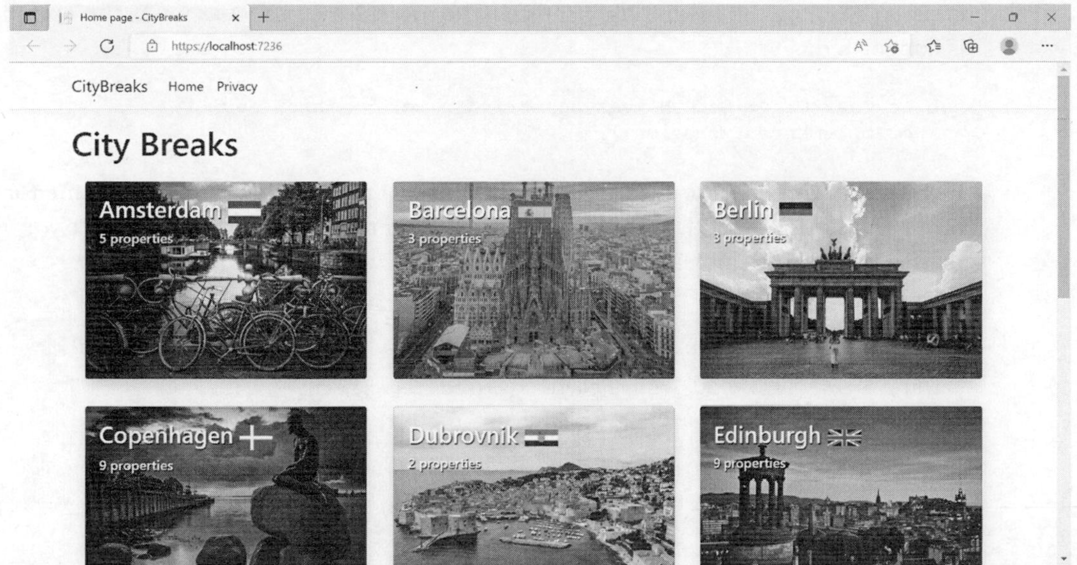

Figure 8.7 The home page displays data from the database.

Before you move on, navigate to /property-manager/create to ensure the select-city list is populated. Previously, that data came from the `SimpleCityService`, and now it originates from the database. Not only do you have a working database connected to your application, but you also have a great example of how loose coupling enables changes to be made to the application with a minimum of fuss. You haven't had to touch the code in either of the Create page's files to get it to work with a database. All you had to do was change the service registration.

8.3.2 Selecting single records

Now that you have a good working example of selecting multiple records, you will amend the City page to retrieve a single record based on a value passed in the URL. First, you need to update the `ICityService` to include a new method called `GetByNameAsync`, which takes a string as a parameter and returns a `Task<City>`.

Listing 8.17 Adding new method to the `ICityService`

```
public interface ICityService
{
    Task<List<City>> GetAllAsync();
    Task<City> GetByNameAsync(string name);
}
```

You have two services that implement this interface; you won't be using the `SimpleCityService` again, so you can safely delete it or use the `NotImplementedException` to create a stub for the method that satisfies the interface contract as far as the compiler is concerned:

```
public Task<City> GetByNameAsync(string name) => throw new
➥ NotImplementedException();
```

If you choose to take the latter route, you will need to remember to do the same for all other methods you add to the `ICityService` interface going forward. Next you will provide a working implementation in the `CityService` class.

Listing 8.18 Query that returns a single city using the name as the criteria

```
public async Task<City> GetByNameAsync(string name)
{
    return await _context.Cities
        .Include(c => c.Country)
        .Include(c => c.Properties.Where(p => p.AvailableFrom <
        ➥ DateTime.Now))
        .SingleOrDefaultAsync(c => c.Name == name);
}
```

The query differs from the previous one only in the method used to cause execution. This time, you use the `SingleOrDefaultAsync` method. This method expects there to be zero or one matching records in the database. If no records match, the method returns the default value, which is `null` in this case. If more than one record matches the criteria, an exception will be raised. If you expect there to be only one matching record, you can use the `SingleAsync` method, which returns an exception in the event of no matches. If you believe more than one record might match the criteria, you should use the `FirstAsync` or `FirstOrDefaultAsync` method, depending on whether there is a possibility of no matches. This will return the first match based on the default order of the database or the order you specify via an `OrderBy` method. For example:

```
return _context.Cities.OrderBy(c => c.Name).FirstAsync(c => c.Name == name);
```

You use the `SingleOrDefaultAsync` method here because you don't have total control over the value being passed in to the method. You may think you do because your code generates the links from data that comes from the database. However, you are exposing that data to the outside world when you include it as part of a URL and cannot trust it will not be changed, innocently or otherwise. Next you need to change the code for the `CityModel` class, so replace the content of \Pages\City.cshtml.cs with the following code.

Listing 8.19 Revised `CityModel` code

```
using CityBreaks.Models;
using CityBreaks.Services;
using Microsoft.AspNetCore.Mvc;
```

```
using Microsoft.AspNetCore.Mvc.RazorPages;

namespace CityBreaks.Pages;

public class CityModel : PageModel
{
    private readonly ICityService _cityService;
    public CityModel(ICityService cityService)
    {
        _cityService = cityService;
    }

    [BindProperty(SupportsGet = true)]
    public string Name { get; set; }
    public City City { get; set; }

    public async Task<IActionResult> OnGetAsync()
    {
        City = await _cityService.GetByNameAsync(Name);
        if(City == null)
        {
            return NotFound();
        }
        return Page();
    }
}
```

You inject the `ICityService` and use it to retrieve a city matching the name passed to the page in the URL. You should anticipate the result may be `null`, in which case, you will let the user know there is no matching page. All that remains now is displaying the details of the matching record if one is found.

To add some visual interest to the details, you are going to incorporate some free icons from Font Awesome (https://fontawesome.com). You will need to add a link to a CDN version of their icons in the Pages\Shared_Layout.cshtml file. Add the following line of code just before the closing </head> tag:

```
<link rel="stylesheet" href="https://cdnjs.cloudflare.com/ajax/libs/font-
➥ awesome/5.15.4/css/all.min.css" />
```

Now change the content of the Pages\City.cshtml file to the following.

Listing 8.20 Rendering details of the specified `City`

```
@page "{name}"
@model CityBreaks.Pages.CityModel
@{
    ViewData["Title"] = $"{Model.City.Name} Details";
}
<h3>@Model.City.Name</h3>
@foreach (var property in Model.City.Properties)
{
```

```
    <div class="mb-3">
        <h5>@property.Name</h5>
        <p class="mb-1">@property.Address</p>
        <i class="fas fa-euro-sign text-muted"></i>
        ➥ @property.DayRate.ToString("F2")<br>
        @if (!property.SmokingPermitted)
        {
            <i class="fas fa-smoking-ban text-danger"></i>
        }
        @for (var i = 1; i <= property.MaxNumberOfGuests; i++)
        {
            <i class="fas fa-bed text-info"></i>
        }
    </div>
}
```

The code loops through all the properties available in the city and renders their details, using Font Awesome icons to show a no smoking sign if smoking is not permitted and several bed icons representing the maximum allowed guests. You have also used the euro icon to represent a currency. All you have to do now is spin up the application and click one of the cities on the home page (figure 8.8).

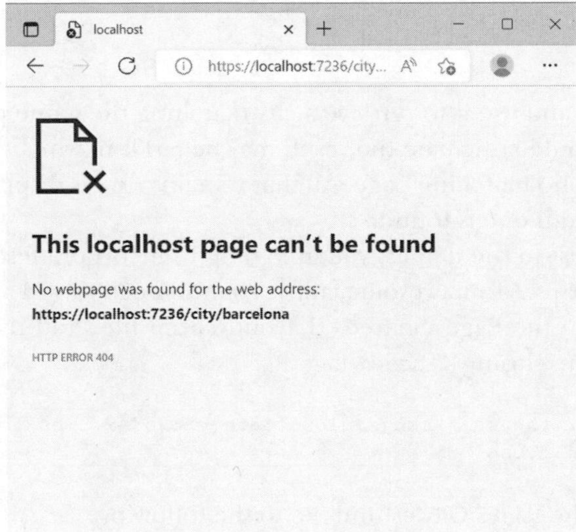

Figure 8.8 The City page returns a 404 Not Found.

Oh! What happened there? Well, chances are if you are using SQL Server instead of SQLite, you can see details of the selected city. The problem with SQLite is that, by default, string comparisons are case sensitive. You are passing a lowercase value from the URL to the service method, which compares it to a mixed case value in the database. To get around this, you can use the `EF.Functions.Collate` method to specify the collation SQLite should use for this comparison. `EF.Functions` contain a collection of useful methods that translate to database functions and only apply to LINQ queries used within EF Core. The documentation provides a comprehensive list of them (http://mng.bz/gRrv). Open up the CityService, and change the GetByNameAsync method as follows.

Listing 8.21 Specifying the collation to be used for the query

```
public async Task<City> GetByNameAsync(string name)
{
    name = name.Replace("-"," ");      ◁ Replace the hyphens added by the page
    return await _context.Cities          route parameter transformer with
                                          spaces, so they match database entries.
        .Include(c => c.Country)
        .Include(c => c.Properties.Where(p =>
        ➥ p.AvailableFrom < DateTime.Now))
        .SingleOrDefaultAsync(c =>
        ➥ EF.Functions.Collate(c.Name, "NOCASE") == name);   ◁ Use EF.Functions.Collate to specify
                                                                a collation of NOCASE for SQLite.
}
```

Once this correction is in place, you should be able to view details of your selected city (figure 8.9).

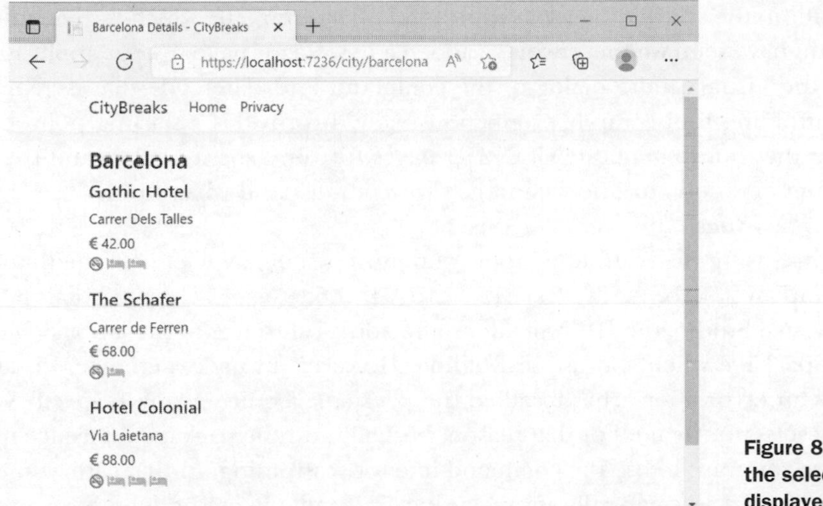

Figure 8.9 Details of the selected city are displayed.

Great! At this point, you have retrieved single instances of data as well as collections. You have also retrieved related data. Next we will concentrate on the other aspects of CRUD: creating new records, updating them, and deleting them. At the same time, we will look at another feature that will speed up the development of these examples: scaffolding.

8.4 Scaffolding CRUD pages

Scaffolding is a technique used to generate code at design time to support several common application scenarios when working with EF Core. The scaffolding tool supports the generation of Razor pages that interact with the database using the templates in table 8.1.

Table 8.1 The templates available to the scaffolding tool

Template	Description
`Create`	Generates a Razor page with a form for creating the specified model class and `PageModel` handlers complete with code for saving to a database
`Edit`	Generates a Razor page with a form for editing the specified model class and `PageModel` handlers complete with code for retrieving the specified entity and saving changes to a database
`Delete`	Produces a page that displays details of the selected entity and a form with a hidden field that passes the key value of the entity to a handler method that removes it from the database
`Details`	Produces a page that displays details of the selected entity
`List`	Produces a page that displays details of all instances of the selected entity in a table

In addition, the scaffolding tool supports an *empty* template, which is the equivalent of what you have seen whenever you've added a new Razor page to your application from either the Visual Studio dialog or the command line. The code that is generated by the scaffolding tool is rarely production ready. It provides a starting point only. You will use the tool to generate all CRUD pages for the `Property` class and then review the generated code to understand its shortcomings and what you will need to do to resolve any issues.

Before using the scaffolding tools, you must install a NuGet package that contains the templates: `Microsoft.VisualStudio.Web.CodeGeneration.Design`. If you are using Visual Studio, the IDE will attempt to add a reference to the latest stable version of this package when you use scaffolding. However, in my experience, Visual Studio reports an error after it has installed the package, requiring you to specify your scaffolding selection again. For that reason, I usually add the package reference manually. Suppose you want to use the command line for scaffolding. In that case, you will need to add the package manually anyway, using any available methods we have already covered for managing NuGet.

8.4.1 Visual Studio scaffold instructions

Scaffolding is built into Visual Studio and is accessible from the Add dialog. Right-click the Pages\PropertyManager folder, and choose Add from the context menu. Then choose New Scaffolded Item… from the second menu group. Select Razor Pages from the dialog that appears, and then select Razor Pages using Entity Framework (CRUD). Next click the Add button. In the next dialog, select Property (CityBreaks.Models) as the Model class and CityBreaksContext as the Data context class. Leave the other options as their defaults; that is, Reference Script Libraries and Use a

Layout Page should both be selected. Leave the layout page input empty. Refer to figure 8.10.

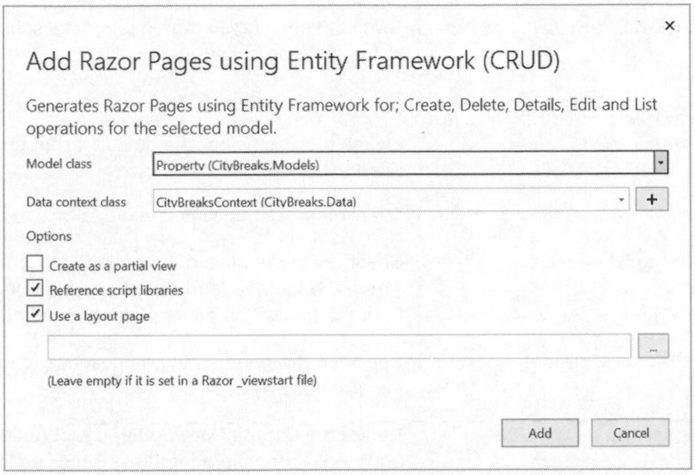

Figure 8.10 The scaffolding dialog in Visual Studio

Click the Add button. You will be prompted to replace the existing files related to the Create page. Click Yes. Then the code generator should run. You may find that the scaffolding tool adds a reference to the `Microsoft.EntityFrameworkCore.SqlServer` package. This is not needed for your application while using the SQLite database; only the scaffolding tools require it. Once you have completed scaffolding, you can remove this reference if you prefer. If you are working with SQL Server, this reference will already exist and is required by your application.

8.4.2 Scaffolding from the command line

To scaffold items from the command line, you must install the `dotnet-aspnet-codegenerator` tool first. This is a global tool, similar to the `dotnet-ef` tool you installed earlier. The tool is installed using the following command:

```
dotnet tool install --global dotnet-aspnet-codegenerator
```

Once the tool is installed, you can use it. The command name is the same as the tool: `dotnet-aspnet-codegenerator`. The command requires the name of the generator you want to use, followed by the options you want to apply. The name of the Razor Pages generator is `razorpage`. The Razor Pages generator options are detailed in table 8.2.

Table 8.2 Razor Pages generator options

Option	Description
`--model|-m`	Model class to use
`--dataContext|-dc`	`DbContext` class to use

Table 8.2 Razor Pages generator options *(continued)*

Option	Description
`--referenceScriptLibraries|-scripts`	Switch to specify whether to reference script libraries in the generated views
`--layout|-l`	Custom layout page to use
`--useDefaultLayout|-udl`	Switch to specify that the default layout should be used for the views
`--force|-f`	Overwrites existing files
`--relativeFolderPath|-outDir`	Specifies the relative output folder path from project where the file needs to be generated; if not specified, the file will be generated in the project folder
`--namespaceName|-namespace`	Specifies the name of the namespace to use for the generated `PageModel`
`--partialView|-partial`	Generates a partial view; other layout options (`-l` and `-udl`) are ignored if this is specified
`--noPageModel|-npm`	Switch to prevent generating a `PageModel` class for an empty template
`--useSqlite|-sqlite`	Flag to specify if `DbContext` should use SQLite instead of SQL Server

You can scaffold individual pages based on the existing templates by specifying a name for the Razor page as well as the name of the template to use, which is one of the following options: `Empty`, `Create`, `Edit`, `Delete`, `Details`, or `List`. Or you can omit the name and template; in which case, the generator will scaffold all except the empty template.

You want to scaffold all CRUD pages for the `Property` class, and you want to use the `CityBreaksContext` as the data context. You also want the generated files to be placed in the Pages\PropertyManager folder, and you want them to use the default layout page for that folder. You won't specify a namespace for the pages; instead the scaffolder will generate one based on the project name and the folder path: `CityBreaks.Pages.PropertyManager`. You want the unobtrusive validation scripts to be included, and you want to specify that your context uses SQLite. Putting all that together, your command is as follows:

```
dotnet aspnet-codegenerator razorpage -m Property
➥ -dc CityBreaksContext -outDir
➥ Pages\PropertyManager -udl -scripts -sqlite
```

This command must be executed within the folder that houses the project file. Once it has been completed, the pages appear in the specified folder shown in figure 8.11.

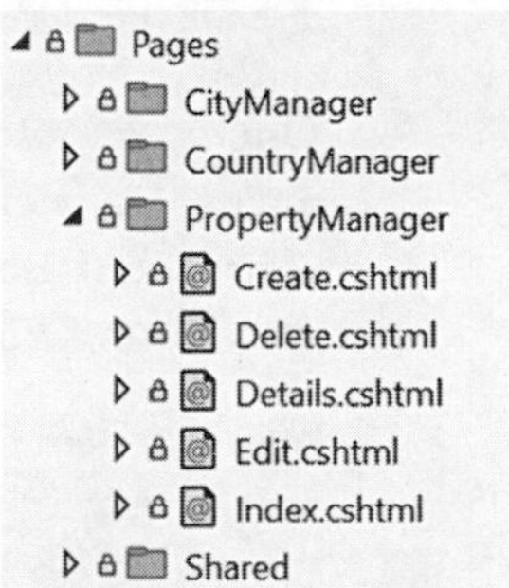

Figure 8.11 The scaffolded CRUD pages

8.4.3 Working with the scaffolded pages

Whichever approach you took to scaffolding the CRUD pages, you should now have the same results. The first thing you may notice is that they fail to build. At the time of writing, there is a bug in the scaffolding tool that results in the @ character (which cannot be used as a valid C# identifier) being applied as a parameter in the Include methods in the Edit, Delete, Details, and Index PageModel classes:

```
Property = await _context.Properties
    .Include(@ => @.City).FirstOrDefaultAsync(m => m.Id == id);
```

This needs to be replaced with another character—say, p:

```
Property = await _context.Properties
    .Include(p => p.City).FirstOrDefaultAsync(m => m.Id == id);
```

Once that change has been made, you can examine the code in the various pages and look to improve it. In this chapter, I focus on the files for the Edit page. Once you understand the range of issues that need to be addressed in this page, you will be in a good position to apply appropriate changes to the other pages.

I'll start by showing the first few lines of the EditModel code. The first thing you will notice is that EditModel takes a dependency on the EF Core context.

Listing 8.22 The scaffolded EditModel constructor

```
private readonly CityBreaks.Data.CityBreaksContext _context;

public EditModel(CityBreaks.Data.CityBreaksContext context)
{
    _context = context;
}
```

Referring to the previous chapter, this breaches the dependency inversion principle because the context is not an abstraction. Your PageModel class is tightly coupled to the data access technology you have chosen, and if you instantiate an instance of this class in a unit test, for example, it will call into whatever database is defined in the context's connection string. That's not a unit test. It's an integration test. Ideally, you should replace the context with a service or, rather, its abstraction.

The next major issue with the generated code opens up a potential attack vector. The generated code makes the entire Property class a binding target:

```
[BindProperty]
public Property Property { get; set; }
```

If you recall from chapter 5, you should limit the scope of the binding targets on your page to just those properties you want your users to set. If you expose more, your application is susceptible to overposting attacks. You do actually want to expose all the *current* properties of the `Property` class to the model binder, but that may not always be the case. In the future, you might add more properties to the class. They will be exposed to model binding by default because you decorated the entire class with the `BindProperty` attribute. So as a best practice, you should start by explicitly exposing properties individually or through an `InputModel`. The next listing shows the scaffolded `OnGetAsync` handler method.

Listing 8.23 The scaffolded `EditModel` `OnGetAsync` handler

```
public async Task<IActionResult> OnGetAsync(int? id)
{
    if (id == null)
    {
        return NotFound();
    }

    Property = await _context.Properties
        .Include(p => p.City).FirstOrDefaultAsync(m => m.Id == id);

    if (Property == null)
    {
        return NotFound();
    }
    ViewData["CityId"] = new SelectList(_context.Cities, "Id", "Id");
    return Page();
}
```

I'm not a fan of code that serves no purpose, and there is a great example of that at the beginning of this handler. The method takes a nullable parameter representing the identity of the item you want to edit. Then a block of code checks to see if a value has been passed, and it returns a 404 if not. You have a mechanism that ensures this page can *only* be reached if a number is provided. It's called *route constraints*, which you learned about in chapter 4. Instead, you can make the `id` a required route parameter of this page and constrain it to a number type, negating the need for the first code block because the framework will return a 404 if no number is provided.

This code block creates a `SelectList` populated with `City` data. The `SelectList` is assigned to `ViewData`, which, as you might recall from chapter 3, is a weakly typed dictionary. Objects retrieved from `ViewData` need to be cast to their correct type to be used again in code. Ideally, the `SelectList` should be a property of the `PageModel`, so you do not need to use casting when you use the object in the Razor page.

The code that obtains the city data is not asynchronous. As a performance best practice, you should always aim to use asynchronous APIs in an ASP.NET Core web application when they are available (http://mng.bz/epwV). Most libraries that make *out of process*, or I/O, calls, such as those that enable communication with databases, sending email, file handling, and so on, offer asynchronous APIs.

The reason for asynchronous code

Imagine you are installing a kitchen. You build the cabinets from DIY kits, but you get to a point at which one of the doors is missing a hinge. You decide you can't move forward until you get a hinge, so you drive down to the store to pick one up. All the time you spend driving to the store is wasted and adds a delay to your task. You are working synchronously, completing one task before moving to the next.

A more efficient approach to this scenario would be to call the store and have them deliver a hinge. That way, you can continue with other tasks while waiting for notification (the ringing of your doorbell) that the delivery task you delegated to the store has been completed. This is how asynchronous programming works.

A web server has a limited number of threads available, and in high-load situations, all of the available threads might be in use. When that happens, the server can't process new requests until the threads are freed up. With synchronous code, many threads may be tied up while they aren't actually doing any work because they're waiting for I/O, such as database calls, to complete. With asynchronous code, when a process is waiting for I/O to complete, its thread is freed up for the server to use for processing other requests. As a result, asynchronous code enables server resources to be used more efficiently, and the server is able to handle more traffic without delays.

The next major issue with the generated code may not be obvious at first glance, but it soon becomes clear when you run the application and navigate to /property-manager/edit?id=1, as figure 8.12 illustrates. The values appearing in the city select list are the key values, not the city names.

Figure 8.12 The key values appear in the select list, not the city names.

Your remediation plan will be to do the following:

1. Exchange the injected context for a service, enabling loose coupling.
2. Bind to individual properties to mitigate the security risk.
3. Reduce the reliance on `ViewData`.

4 Use asynchronous code wherever possible.

8.5 Creating, modifying, and deleting data

In this section, you will create a PropertyService to meet the requirements of the scenarios handled by the scaffolded pages. You will add methods to create and edit Property entities and retrieve single instances based on their key value. You won't generate a method for deleting entities just yet. You will take a quick look at the code required to remove an item from the database later, but for this application, you will use a *soft delete,* marking an item as deleted without actually removing it.

In EF Core, operations that result in adding, updating, or deleting data can be performed directly against the DbContext, using its Add, Update, and Remove methods, respectively. Each of these methods takes the entity to be operated on as a parameter and sets its state to one of Added, Modified, or Deleted. You will call the asynchronous SaveChangesAsync method of the DbContext to commit the changes to the database. The context will generate the appropriate SQL based on the state of the entity. This workflow is illustrated in figure 8.13.

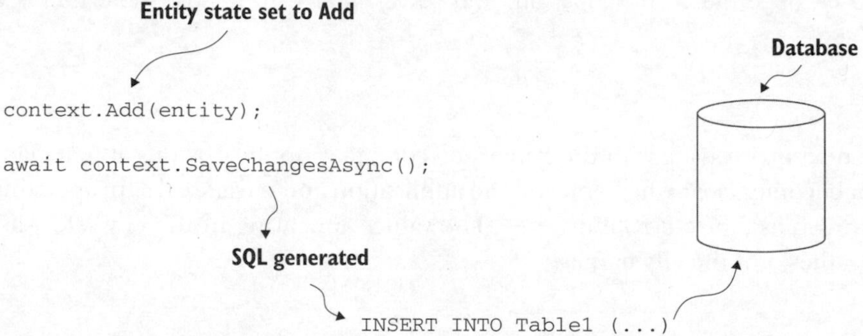

Figure 8.13 The Add method sets the state of the entity to Added. When SaveChangesAsync is called, EF Core generates an SQL INSERT statement and executes it against the database.

So let's begin by creating the service class for the Property entity that encapsulates these operations. The first step is adding a new interface named IPropertyService with the following code to the Services folder.

Listing 8.24 The IPropertyService interface with CRUD methods

```
using CityBreaks.Models;

namespace CityBreaks.Services
{
    public interface IPropertyService
    {
        Task<Property> CreateAsync(Property property);
        Task<List<Property>> GetAllAsync();
```

```
        Task<Property> FindAsync(int id);
        Task<Property> UpdateAsync(Property property);
        Task DeleteAsync(int id);
    }
}
```

Now add a new class to the Services folder named `PropertyService` that implements the interface.

Listing 8.25 Implementing the CRUD methods in the `PropertyService`

```
using CityBreaks.Data;
using CityBreaks.Models;
using Microsoft.EntityFrameworkCore;

namespace CityBreaks.Services;
public class PropertyService : IPropertyService
{
    private readonly CityBreaksContext _context;

    public PropertyService(CityBreaksContext context) =>
        _context = context;

    public async Task<Property> FindAsync(int id) =>
        await _context.Properties
        .FindAsync(id);

    public async Task<List<Property>> GetAllAsync() =>
        await _context.Properties
        .Include(x => x.City)
        .ToListAsync();

    public async Task<Property> CreateAsync(Property property)
    {
        _context.Add(property);
        await _context.SaveChangesAsync();
        return property;
    }

    public async Task<Property> UpdateAsync(Property property)
    {
        _context.Update(property);
        await _context.SaveChangesAsync();
        return property;
    }
}
```

The first method uses the `FindAsync` method to retrieve a single entity. This method is different from the methods that begin with `First` and `Single` you have looked at so far. It takes a value representing the key of the entity to retrieve, but you cannot use it with the `Include` method. When you edit an item, you don't necessarily need its associated data; you only need the foreign key values. The `FindAsync` method is perfect for this purpose.

The `CreateAsync` method uses the `DbContext.Add` method to get the context to begin *tracking* the property entity. An `EntityState` is applied to all entities tracked by the context, which is an enumeration specifying the entity's current state. When you use the `Add` method, the `EntityState.Added` value is assigned. This tells the context that the entity should be added as a new record, and the generated SQL is an `INSERT` statement.

The `DbContext.Add` method was introduced in EF Core. In previous versions of EF, data operations were performed against the relevant `DbSet`, with the equivalent being

```
_context.Properties.Add(property)
```

The `UpdateAsync` method uses the `DbContext.Update` method, which tells the context to begin tracking the entity in the `EntityState.Modified` state. The `DbContext.Update` method is also new in EF Core. In previous versions of EF, you had to attach a modified entity to the context and explicitly set its state to `EntityState.Modified`, which is similar to the pattern that has been applied to the existing `OnPostAsync` handler in the scaffolded code:

```
_context.Attach(Property).State = EntityState.Modified;
```

When an entity is in the `Modified` state, EF Core generates an SQL `UPDATE` statement that results in all the entity's non-key values being modified. We will look at how to control the SQL, so it only updates individual property values when you implement the soft delete later.

Both the `CreateAsync` and `UpdateAsync` method include the same line:

```
await _context.SaveChangesAsync();
```

The `SaveChangesAsync` method causes all the pending changes to data to be written to the database. It returns an `int`, representing the number of rows affected by the operation. When you use the `Add` method to create a new record, the generated SQL retrieves the primary key value of the newly created record, and EF Core assigns that to the tracked entity. Your database operations are very simple and only involve one command. It is possible to set up multiple operations and have them all committed at the same time with one call to `SaveChangesAsync`. By default, EF Core uses a transaction to perform these operations, so if any of them fail, all the others are rolled back, thereby leaving the database unmodified.

The service is almost ready to replace the `DbContext` operations in the `PageModel`. Before you can use the service in code, you must register it with the service container. Go to Program.cs, and add the following registration:

```
builder.Services.AddScoped<IPropertyService, PropertyService>();
```

8.5.1 Modifying data

Turning to the scaffolded EditModel class, you will make the following alteration to replace the existing private field with new ones for an IPropertyService and an ICityService. The injected context is replaced with the services. You also need to add a using directive to reference CityBreaks.Services.

Listing 8.26 Injecting the IPropertyService in place of the DbContext

```
private readonly IPropertyService _propertyService;
private readonly ICityService _cityService;

public EditModel(IPropertyService propertyService, ICityService cityService)
{
    _propertyService = propertyService;
    _cityService = cityService;
}
```

In the step shown in listing 8.27, you replace the Property binding target with individual binding targets representing the values you want to expose to the user. You also add a public SelectList property to replace the ViewData approach currently being taken for the city dropdown. Finally, you replace the OnGet handler parameter (id) with a public property that enables you to use the value in both handler methods, and you will ensure it can be bound to when the request uses the GET method.

Listing 8.27 Replacing binding to entity with binding to properties

```
public SelectList Cities { get; set; }
[BindProperty(SupportsGet = true)]
public int Id { get; set; }
[BindProperty, Display(Name = "City")]
public int CityId { get; set; }
[BindProperty, Required]
public string Name { get; set; }
[BindProperty, Required]
public string Address { get; set; }
[BindProperty, Display(Name = "Maximum Number Of Guests")]
public int MaxNumberOfGuests { get; set; }
[BindProperty, Display(Name = "Daily Rate")]
public decimal DayRate { get; set; }
[BindProperty, Display(Name = "Smoking?")]
public bool SmokingPermitted { get; set; }
[BindProperty, Display(Name = "Available From")]
public DateTime AvailableFrom { get; set; }
```

You need to populate the Cities SelectList property in the OnGetAsync handler and again in the OnPostAsync handler if there are ModelState errors. You have already established a pattern for this that reduces duplication. In listing 8.28, you add a private method that returns a SelectList that uses asynchronous code to the end of the PageModel class.

Listing 8.28 The reusable private method for populating `SelectList` objects

```
private async Task<SelectList> GetCityOptions()
{
    var cities = await _cityService.GetAllAsync();
    return new SelectList(cities, nameof(City.Id), nameof(City.Name));
}
```

You will have lots of squiggly red lines indicating compiler errors now. You tackle those in the `OnGetAsync` method first by replacing the entire method block with the following code, which uses the service to obtain the `Property` instance to be edited and assigns its values to the public `PageModel` properties.

Listing 8.29 The amended `OnGetAsync` method

```
public async Task<IActionResult> OnGetAsync()
{
    var property = await _propertyService.FindAsync(Id);

    if (property == null)
    {
        return NotFound();
    }
    Address = property.Address;
    AvailableFrom = property.AvailableFrom;
    CityId = property.CityId;
    DayRate = property.DayRate;
    MaxNumberOfGuests = property.MaxNumberOfGuests;
    Name = property.Name;
    SmokingPermitted = property.SmokingPermitted;

    Cities = await GetCityOptions();
    return Page();
}
```

The code that maps values from the entity you retrieved from the database to `PageModel` properties is manageable for your relatively simple entity. You can imagine this type of code will be laborious to write and maintain for entities with more properties. Tools that can help reduce this code significantly—to a single line, in many cases—are available, such as the popular AutoMapper (https://automapper.org/), which is my preferred option. You won't be using such a tool in this book, but I recommend exploring this massive time saver for your own applications.

That just leaves the `OnPostAsync` method to tidy before moving the Razor part of the page. The scaffolded code catches a `DbUpdateConcurrencyException` if one is raised, which indicates the item you are editing no longer exists; someone else has deleted it between the time you retrieved it from the database and submitted your amendments. That is not a scenario you need to worry about because you won't be removing entries from the database. So your task is straightforward. You check `ModelState`, and if it is valid, you will pass the posted values as a `Property` instance to the service's `UpdateAsync` method.

Listing 8.30 The updated `OnPostAsync` method

```
public async Task<IActionResult> OnPostAsync()
{
    if (!ModelState.IsValid)
    {
        Cities = await GetCityOptions();
        return Page();
    }

    var property = new Property
    {
        Address = Address,
        AvailableFrom = AvailableFrom,
        CityId = CityId,
        DayRate = DayRate,Id = Id,
        MaxNumberOfGuests = MaxNumberOfGuests,
        Name = Name,
        SmokingPermitted = SmokingPermitted
    };
    await _propertyService.UpdateAsync(property);

    return RedirectToPage("./Index");
}
```

You've reached the final part of the transformation: the Razor page itself. There aren't many changes required here. All you need to do is

- Add a route template.
- Remove the `Property` prefix from the tag helper model expressions.
- Update the source of city data in the cities select list.

You don't want this page to be reachable unless a number is passed in the URL, so the route template must include a constraint. So you add the following template to the `@page` directive:

```
@page "{id:int}"
```

You have the `id` in the URL, and you have enabled binding to the route parameter in the `PageModel`, so you no longer need the hidden field in the form:

```
<input type="hidden" asp-for="Property.Id" />
```

You can comment it out or remove it altogether. Next locate the section of HTML for the cities select list, shown in the following listing.

Listing 8.31 The scaffolded select list HTML

```
<div class="form-group">
    <label asp-for="Property.CityId" class="control-label"></label>
    <select asp-for="Property.CityId" class="form-control"
    ➥ asp-items="ViewBag.CityId"></select>
    <span asp-validation-for="Property.CityId" class="text-danger"></span>
</div>
```

All of the references to `Property` should have red squiggly lines under them, indicating a compiler error. You need to remove them all, as well as those in other tag helpers in the page. You also need to update the `asp-items` attribute to reference `Model.Cities` instead of `ViewBag.CityId`. The modified version is shown in the following listing.

Listing 8.32 The modified select list

```
<div class="form-group">
    <label asp-for="CityId" class="control-label"></label>
    <select asp-for="CityId" class="form-control"
    ➥ asp-items="Model.Cities"></select>
    <span asp-validation-for="CityId" class="text-danger"></span>
</div>
```

Now you are ready to test the revisions. Run the application, and navigate to /property-manager. You will be taken to the scaffolded Index page, which lists all properties (figure 8.14).

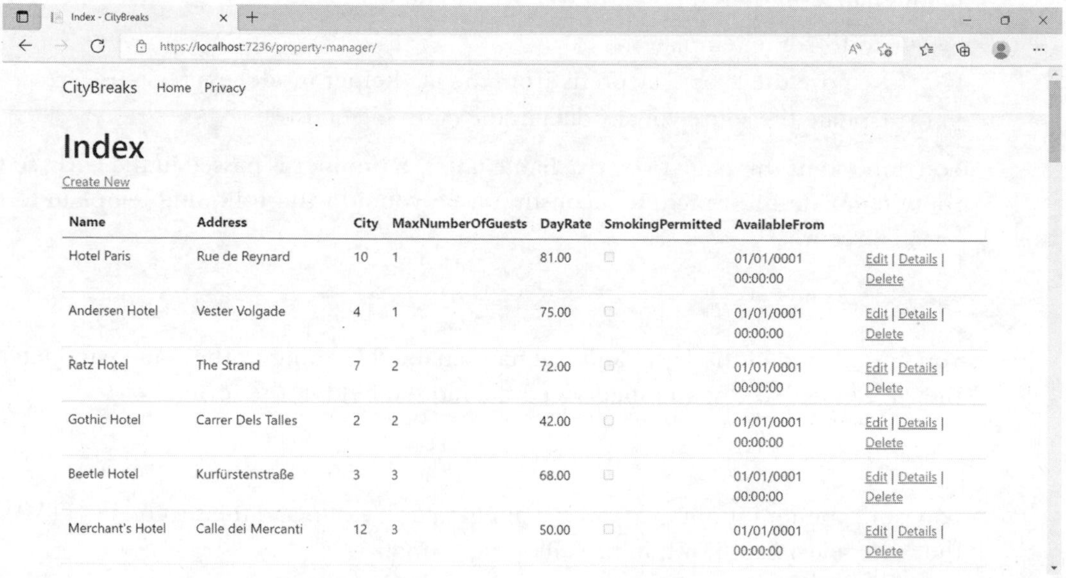

Figure 8.14 The original scaffolded Index page

Remember, this is the unmodified scaffolded version, so it displays the key values in the City column, not the Name column. The key values are also displayed in the select list on the Create page, which you can reach by clicking the Create New link just below the page heading. They are also displayed on the Details page for each property. Click the Edit link of one of the properties to see how it differs from the scaffolded Create page. The names of the cities appear in the select list, and the form labels are user friendly (figure 8.15).

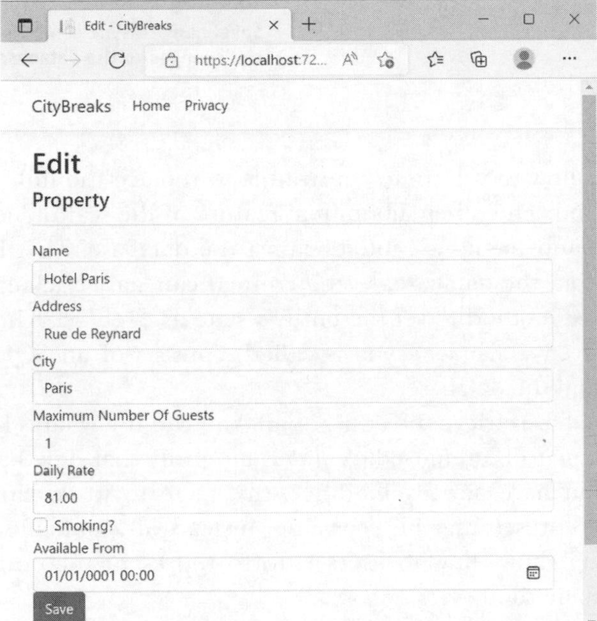

Figure 8.15 The amended Edit page

Make a change to the property by setting its Available From date to one in the future. Submit those changes, and confirm that your revisions work when you are redirected to the Index page, which should show the revised date. Then navigate to the home page, and confirm that the number of properties for the specified city has dropped by one.

8.5.2 Deleting data

The scaffolded pages include one that enables you to delete an entity. The `OnPostAysnc` method in the `DeleteModel` class contains the code that actually removes the entry from the database. It is important to understand how it works because it is suboptimal.

Listing 8.33 The scaffolded `OnPostAsync` method in the `DeleteModel`

```
public async Task<IActionResult> OnPostAsync(int? id)
{
```

```
    if (id == null)
    {
        return NotFound();
    }

    Property = await _context.Properties.FindAsync(id);

    if (Property != null)
    {
        _context.Properties.Remove(Property);
        await _context.SaveChangesAsync();
    }

    return RedirectToPage("./Index");
}
```

Checks that a key value was passed to the method

This retrieves the matching entry from the database. The context starts tracking it.

The DbSet.Remove method sets the entity's state to Deleted.

SaveChangesAsync commits the changes to the database.

We have already discussed how to use route constraints to replace the null check at the beginning of this method. The other suboptimal feature of the scaffolded code is that it results in *two* commands being executed against the database. The first command retrieves the item from the database, so the context can start tracking it. The code uses the `DbSet.Remove` method to set the entity's state as `Deleted`. The second command, executed when `SaveChangesAsync` is called, consists of an SQL `DELETE` statement that deletes it from the database.

There is actually no need to retrieve the entity at all. You can use what is known as a stub to represent the entity to be removed. A *stub* is an entity that only has its key value assigned. Assume you have already modified this page to work with a constrained route parameter representing the key value, instead of a nullable handler parameter. The next listing shows how to use a stub to represent the entity to be deleted in the `OnPostAsync` method.

Listing 8.34 Deleting an entity represented by a stub

```
public async Task<IActionResult> OnPostAsync()
{
    var property = new Property { Id = Id };
    _context.Remove(property );
    await _context.SaveChangesAsync();

    return RedirectToPage("./Index");
}
```

Create a stub, only assigning its key value.

Pass the stub to the DbContext.Remove method, which marks the entity as Deleted.

Taking this approach, you significantly reduce the complexity of the code and halve the number of database calls required to achieve your objective. Note that you have also used the `DbContext.Remove` method instead of the `DbSet.Remove` method the scaffolder generates. Like the `DbContext Add` and `Update` methods, the `Remove` method is new to EF Core and helps you reduce code.

When you delete an entity, all dependent data is either lost or orphaned. Depending on how your foreign keys are set up, the delete operation cascades to all dependent data, and it is either also removed, or its foreign key values are updated to `null`, resulting in orphaned data. If the dependent data is business critical, such as orders, this is not desirable. You would clearly want to retain historical data about bookings at a property, despite the fact that it has since been bulldozed, for example. You may even need to restore it if it has been deleted accidentally. For this reason, you will more often employ a *soft delete*, whereby a record is flagged in some way as deleted, rather than removing the record entirely, which is what the `DbContext.Remove` method results in. In the final section of this chapter, you will add a new property to the `Property` class representing the date and time an entity was marked as deleted. You will add a new migration to update the database schema, and then modify the Delete pages to accommodate your revised strategy for managing deletes.

The first step is to add a nullable `DateTime` property to the `Property` class:

```
public DateTime? Deleted { get; set; }
```

I usually use a `DateTime`, rather than a `bool`, for this purpose because someone will inevitably ask *when* the item was deleted. In the absence of more sophisticated logging, at least this can help me answer that question.

I'll take this opportunity to reinforce the point about overposting attacks. You have just added a new property to your class that you do not want users to set directly. If you allow the model binder to bind directly to an instance of the class, you will expose this property to users. By specifying only individual properties as binding targets, you prevent the user from being able to set the `Deleted` property's value.

Having added the `Deleted` property, you can add a new migration using either the package manager console or the command line, which will detect the changes you have made to the model and will reflect those changes by amending the database schema accordingly. Both the Powershell and command-line options are shown in the following listing.

Listing 8.35 Add migrations

```
[Powershell]
add-migration AddedDeleteToProperty
[CLI]
dotnet ef migrations add AddedDeleteToProperty
```

The Powershell command to be executed from within the Package Manager Console in Visual Studio

The CLI command to be executed from a command prompt located within the directory containing the csproj file

Once executed, you can check the `Up` method in the migration code to ensure it will add a nullable `Delete` column. In SQLite, this will be a `TEXT` type.

Listing 8.36 The `Up` method of your new migration

```
protected override void Up(MigrationBuilder migrationBuilder)
{
    migrationBuilder.AddColumn<DateTime>(
```

```
        name: "Deleted",
        table: "Properties",
        type: "TEXT",
        nullable: true);
}
```

Now you can apply the migration using one of the following commands:

```
[Powershell]
update-database
[CLI]
dotnet ef database update
```

Once that has completed, add a new method to the `IPropertyService` interface:

```
Task DeleteAsync(int id);
```

Then add an implementation to the `PropertyService` class.

Listing 8.37 The `Delete` method implementation

```
public async Task DeleteAsync(int id)
{
    var property = new Property { Id = id, Deleted = DateTime.Now };
    _context.Attach(property).Property(p => p.Deleted).IsModified = true;
    await _context.SaveChangesAsync();
}
```

Create a stub to represent the item to be modified.

Attach the entity to the context, and specify which property should be modified.

Commit the changes.

This method provides another example where stubs are useful. You only want to update the `Deleted` column in the database for this entity. If you pass the entire entity to the `Update` method, all properties are included in the generated SQL `UPDATE` statement. To avoid this, you can use `Attach` to tell the context to start tracking your entity with its state set to `Unchanged`. Then you explicitly set the `Deleted` property as modified. When you set individual properties as modified, only those properties are included in the `UPDATE` statement. You utilize this method by replacing the injected context in the `DeleteModel` with the `IPropertyService`.

Listing 8.38 Modified `DeleteModel` takes a dependency on `IPropertyService`

```
public class DeleteModel : PageModel
{
    private readonly IPropertyService _propertyService;

    public DeleteModel(IPropertyService propertyService)
    {
        _propertyService = propertyService;
    }

    public Property Property { get; set; }
```

The injected context is replaced with the IPropertyService.

Remove the unnecessary BindProperty attribute from the Property property.

```
    [BindProperty(SupportsGet = true)]
    public int Id { get; set; }

    public async Task<IActionResult> OnGetAsync()
    {
        Property = await _propertyService.FindAsync(Id);

        if (Property == null)
        {
            return NotFound();
        }
        return Page();
    }

    public async Task<IActionResult> OnPostAsync()
    {
        await _propertyService.DeleteAsync(Id);
        return RedirectToPage("./Index");
    }
}
```

Add a bound property for the key value, replacing the handler parameters.

Remove the null check against the key value because you will use a route constraint instead.

Use the service to "delete" the entity.

Just as with the Edit page, you only want the Delete page to be reached if an integer value is included in the URL, so you turn to the Delete.cshtml and add a route constraint as part of a route template:

```
@page "{id:int}"
```

There are two more things to do before you can test this out. The first is altering the `GetAllAsync` method in the `PropertyService` to exclude properties that have a value assigned to their `Deleted` property.

Listing 8.39 Excluding deleted properties from the result set

```
public async Task<List<Property>> GetAllAsync() =>
    await _context.Properties
    .Where(p => !p.Deleted.HasValue)
    .Include(x => x.City)
    .ToListAsync();
```

Then you alter the `IndexModel` class in the PropertyManager\Index.cshtml.cs file to take a dependency on `IPropertyService` instead of the context, so you can use your new method to populate the page.

Listing 8.40 The revised `PropertyManager IndexModel`

```
public class IndexModel : PageModel
{
    private readonly IPropertyService _propertyService;

    public IndexModel(IPropertyService propertyService)
    {
```

```
        _propertyService = propertyService;
    }

    public IList<Property> Property { get;set; }

    public async Task OnGetAsync()
    {
        Property = await _propertyService.GetAllAsync();
    }
}
```

Now run the application, and navigate to /property-manager. Observe the first property in the list. If you are using the seed data provided with the last chapter's downloads, the first property in the listing should be Hotel Paris. Clicking the Delete link should take you to the Delete page, which asks for confirmation that you want to delete this item (figure 8.16).

CityBreaks Home Privacy

Delete

Are you sure you want to delete this?

Property

Name	Hotel Paris
Address	Rue de Reynard
City	
MaxNumberOfGuests	1
DayRate	81.00
SmokingPermitted	
AvailableFrom	01/01/0001 00:00:00

Delete | Back to List

Figure 8.16 The Delete page

Click the Delete button, and then observe that Hotel Paris is no longer in the list. As a final check, use whichever database tool you are comfortable with to look at the data in the Properties table to confirm the relevant record still exists—albeit now with a value in the Deleted column (figure 8.17).

This has been a long chapter, but we have only really scratched the surface of what EF Core can do. I'll once again recommend Jon P. Smith's *Entity Framework Core in Action* (2nd ed.; http://mng.bz/WMeg) as an excellent resource for learning more about how to use EF Core, as well as the official documentation (https://docs.microsoft.com/en-us/ef/).

Table: Properties

	Id	Name	Address	CityId	nberC	)ayRate	ıgPer	AvailableFrom	Deleted
	Fil...	Filter	Filter	Fi...		F...		Filter	Filter
1	1	Hotel Paris	Rue de Reynard	10	1	81.0	0	0001-01-01 0...	2022-07-22 09:55:38.2814745
2	2	Andersen Hotel	Vester Volgade	4	1	75.0	0	0001-01-01 0...	NULL
3	3	Ratz Hotel	The Strand	7	2	72.0	0	0001-01-01 0...	NULL
4	4	Gothic Hotel	Carrer Dels Ta...	2	2	42.0	0	0001-01-01 0...	NULL
5	5	Beetle Hotel	Kurfürstenstra...	3	3	68.0	0	0001-01-01 0...	NULL

Figure 8.17 The database view shows that the "deleted" record still exists.

You have moved your application forward in that it can now interact with a database. However, anyone visiting the site can add and modify data if they know the URLs for the CRUD pages. Over the next two chapters, we will look at authenticating users, so you know who they are, and then protecting access to those pages from unauthorized users.

Summary

- Entity Framework Core is an object-relational mapping (ORM) tool from Microsoft, which acts as a drop-in data layer, abstracting away the boilerplate code required to work with a relational database.
- The main entry point to working with EF Core is via a context, an object that derives from `DbContext`.
- The EF Core context tracks objects and generates SQL based on their state.
- Entities map to database tables via `DbSet` objects.
- EF Core translates LINQ queries to SQL, which it executes against a database.
- Conventions drive EF Core mappings between objects and the database.
- You can customize the mapping using configuration.
- EF Core migrations enable you to keep your model and database schema in sync with each other.
- You can use seeding to add data to the database as part of a migration.
- Scaffolding enables you to quickly generate CRUD pages based on EF Core's mappings.

9 Managing users with authentication

This chapter covers

- Implementing basic authentication
- Installing and configuring ASP.NET Core Identity
- Scaffolding and customizing the Identity UI

This and the next chapter look at managing users within a Razor Pages application. They look at two closely related topics: authentication and authorization. *Authentication* is the process of identifying who your user is. *Authorization* is part of the process of securing your application by limiting your user's access to only those parts of the application they are allowed to access.

This chapter concentrates on the nature of a user and how you can authenticate their identity, or ensure they are who they claim to be. Authentication is hard to get right. From a practical point of view, you need to provide mechanisms to capture and store a user's personal information, including something only they know, such as a password. Then you need to be able to *remember* the user on subsequent visits. Your application might also require you to use a secondary authentication mechanism, two-factor authentication (2FA), like a code sent by SMS. You might need to provide the user with features to reset their password if they have forgotten it or manage their profile information. What about verifying email addresses? Or managing account lockouts in the event of repeated incorrect attempts to log in? And you need to do all of this in a cryptographically secure manner.

To be truly secure, you need to keep up with ever-changing cryptographic standards and have a deep knowledge of potential attack vectors that allow bad actors (hackers) to hijack or clone a user's identity. For this reason, unless you are an expert in the field, you should never try to implement your own authentication solution. Your users won't be admiring your technical endeavors if their personal data ends up on Pastebin for the world to see.

Instead, we will explore the ready-made ASP.NET Core Identity library, written and tested by experts, that solves the problem of managing users securely. We will look at its default implementation as well as opportunities it provides for customization. You will then learn about the Identity UI package, which includes ready-made pages covering a wide range of user management scenarios. You will use scaffolding to generate versions of some of these pages to customize them to your requirements, and you will implement an email confirmation service for new registrations.

By the end of the chapter, you will have an understanding of the authentication basics and will have used ASP.NET Core Identity to extend your existing database to handle user information storage. You will know how to customize various aspects of the Identity framework to cater to your business needs and will have installed the Identity UI package and learned how to modify it for your application requirements.

9.1 Authentication basics

While the bulk of this chapter concentrates on the ASP.NET Core Identity library, you will begin by understanding the basics behind authentication within an ASP.NET Core application. You will look at how to add authentication services to a Razor Pages application, enable them, and use them to assign an identity to a user, so they are no longer anonymous to you.

9.1.1 How authentication works

If you have ever been to a trade convention, you are likely to have been challenged to identify yourself at the door, maybe by completing some kind of paper or electronic form. You get yourself signed in and are given a badge to wear around the convention halls to save you from having to reidentify yourself again and again. The badge will include your information encoded as a barcode or a QR code, so those who need to know your identity can use a decoder (scanner) to access it quickly without having to ask you for it. The badge will expire at some point—perhaps at the end of the day or convention.

Authentication in a web application follows a similar process. A Razor Pages application visitor is challenged to provide their identification by completing some kind of sign-in form. Once signed in, authentication services serialize information about the user into an encrypted cookie, which is the equivalent to the badge that you wear around a convention. The cookie is passed between the client and server for all subsequent requests, until the cookie expires. Authentication middleware reads values from this cookie and uses them to hydrate the `User` property of the `HttpContext`. Thereafter, any service that needs information about the current user can check the `User` property, which is a `ClaimsPrincipal` type. The equivalent to a trade convention visitor is represented within a Razor Pages application by this instance of the `ClaimsPrincipal`.

9.1.2 Adding simple authentication

This section shows the minimum steps required to add cookie-based authentication to the CityBreaks application. You will add authentication services to the service container, specifying some default information about how the authentication service should work. Then you will add authentication middleware enabling authentication capabilities. Finally, you will add a simple login form to obtain the user's credentials and authenticate them.

First you need to add a using directive to Program.cs to make `Microsoft.AspNetCore.Authentication.Cookies` available to your code. Then you use the `AddAuthentication` method to add authentication services.

Listing 9.1 Adding authentication services to the service container

```
builder.Services.AddAuthentication(CookieAuthenticationDefaults
➥ .AuthenticationScheme)
    .AddCookie();
```

That's it. You have added very basic cookie authentication. You must specify the name of a default *scheme*, which represents the registered authentication handler and its options. In this case, you have used `CookieAuthenticationDefaults.AuthenticationSchxme` to represent the name of the scheme. It is a constant that resolves to `Cookies`.

The next stage is to add the authentication middleware. You will do this by calling `app.UseAuthentication()` in the request pipeline. However, the positioning of this call is crucial to authentication working properly. It must be placed *after* routing is added but *before* endpoints are added by the `MapRazorPages` call. The default template includes a call to `UseAuthorization`, which adds authorization middleware. You must add authentication before that too; the end result is shown in the following listing.

Listing 9.2 Adding authentication middleware after routing and before authorization

```
app.UseRouting();

app.UseAuthentication();    <-- Add authentication after routing and before
app.UseAuthorization();         authorization and endpoint middleware.

app.MapRazorPages();
```

We will explore authorization in more detail in the next chapter, but for the time being, authorization middleware needs to have information about the current user (produced by the authentication middleware) and the current endpoint (selected by routing middleware) to know whether to short-circuit the pipeline if the current user doesn't have authority to access the selected endpoint or allow the request to flow to endpoint middleware, so the selected endpoint can be executed. Next, you will create a new Razor page in the Pages folder, named Login. You will add a very simple form that captures just the name, using the code in the following listing.

Listing 9.3 The simple login form

```
@page
@model CityBreaks.Pages.LoginModel
@{
}
<div class="col-4">
    <form method="post">
        <div class="mb-3">
            <label class="form-label" asp-for="UserName"></label>
            <input class="form-control" asp-for="UserName" />
        </div>
        <div class="mb-3">
            <button class="btn btn-outline-primary">Sign in</button>
        </div>
    </form>
</div>
```

Now, turning to the `PageModel`, you will need to add the using directives shown in the next listing.

Listing 9.4 The using directives required by the LoginModel class

```
using Microsoft.AspNetCore.Authentication;
using Microsoft.AspNetCore.Authentication.Cookies;
using System.Security.Claims;
using System.ComponentModel.DataAnnotations;
```

The `PageModel` class itself (`LoginModel`) features a bound property for the `UserName`, and an asynchronous `OnPost` handler, where you sign the user in with the username supplied.

Listing 9.5 The `LoginModel` class

```
public class LoginModel : PageModel
{
    [BindProperty, Display(Name="User name")]
    public string UserName { get; set; }

    public async Task OnPostAsync()
```

The UserName property is assigned as a binding target.

```
    {
        var claims = new List<Claim>
        {
            new Claim(ClaimTypes.Name, UserName)
        };
        var identity = new ClaimsIdentity(claims,
        ➥ CookieAuthenticationDefaults.AuthenticationScheme);
        var principal = new ClaimsPrincipal(identity);
        await HttpContext.SignInAsync(principal);
    }
}
```

Assign the username to a claim.

Create an identity based on the claim.

Use the identity to create a ClaimsPrincipal.

Sign the principal in.

Concentrating on the `OnPostAsync` handler in listing 9.5, you first create a claim. *Claims* are pieces of information about the user stored consistently: the name of the claim and, optionally, a value. This is the basis of *claims-based authentication*, which is what ASP.NET Core uses. For example, I claim to have the name Mike Brind. I also claim to be an author (albeit an accidental one). And I claim to be able to drive a car … better than Lewis Hamilton. OK, so some of my claims might not stand up to scrutiny, but we will look at that a bit later.

You will use the claim to create an *identity*. The identity is a specific type that supports claims: a `ClaimsIdentity`. As you may well deduce from the fact that the claim used to construct this identity is part of a collection, an identity can support multiple claims. This identity is used to construct a `ClaimsPrincipal`, representing the user logging in. The `ClaimsPrincipal` is capable of supporting multiple identities, which also makes sense because, in real life, we actually have multiple forms of identity. I have a driver's license and a passport, for example. Both forms of identity share similar claims: my name and address. My driver's license also includes claims about the class of vehicle I am permitted to drive. I have a season ticket to go and watch my favorite football team. This is another form of identity with claims including the entrance I am permitted to use to access the stadium, the seat I am allocated, and the season for which the pass is valid. The concept is illustrated in figure 9.1.

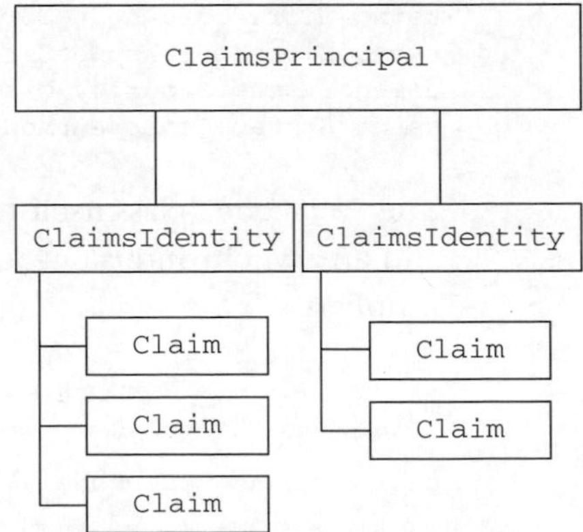

Figure 9.1 A `ClaimsPrincipal` supports multiple identities, each supporting multiple claims.

Once your principal has been created, you sign them in using the `SignInAsync` extension method on the `HttpContext`. This method uses the registered authentication handler to create a cookie, establishing that the user is authenticated.

Next you will add some code to the layout page that will display the authenticated user's name or a link to the login page if they are not authenticated. Place the code block in listing 9.6 just after the `div` containing the `ul` element that houses the navigation links in the `nav` element.

Listing 9.6 Displaying the user's name or a link to sign in

```
<div class="align-content-end">
    @if (User.Identity.IsAuthenticated)    <-- Check to see if the user is authenticated.
    {
        <p>@User.Identity.Name, you are logged in</p>    <-- Use the User.Identity.Name property to access the user's name.
    }
    else
    {
        <a asp-page="/login">Sign in</a>
    }
</div>
```

The ClaimsPrincipal is accessed via the page's User property. Its Identity property provides access to the primary claims identity for the user. It exposes two useful properties: IsAuthenticated, to enable you to establish whether the current request is from an authenticated user or an anonymous one, and Name, which gets the value assigned to the Name claim.

There are two more steps to take. The first is to force the user to sign in. You will do that by issuing a *challenge*, using an action result I didn't cover in chapter 3: the ChallengeResult. When used with cookies, a challenge redirects the anonymous user to the configured loginpath, which is /Account/Login by default. You are working with a different path, so you need to configure that first. Navigate to Program.cs, and amend the authentication service registration to include cookie options as follows.

Listing 9.7 Configuring the default login path

```
builder.Services.AddAuthentication(CookieAuthenticationDefaults
➥ .AuthenticationScheme)
.AddCookie(options =>
{
    options.LoginPath = "/login";
});
```

Finally, you amend the OnGetAsync handler in the home page IndexModel to return a ChallengeResult if the user is not authenticated. You also need to add a using directive for Microsoft.AspNetCore.Mvc.

Listing 9.8 Adding a ChallengeResult to the OnGetAsync handler

```
public async Task<IActionResult> OnGetAsync()    <-- Change the method to return Task<IActionResult>.
{
    if (User.Identity.IsAuthenticated)    <-- Check to see if the user is authenticated before showing the content.
    {
        Cities = await _cityService.GetAllAsync();
        return Page();
    }
    return Challenge();    <-- If not, issue a challenge.
}
```

In addition to the Razor page, the `PageModel` class exposes the current user via a `User` property. You will access that to establish whether the current user is authenticated, and if not, you will use the `Challenge` helper method to return a new `ChallengeResult`.

Now that everything is in place, you can run the application. You should automatically be redirected to the configured login path when the application launches, but notice that the URL in the browser address bar also includes a query string: `/login?ReturnUrl=%2F`. The `ReturnUrl` query string value represents the page that issued the challenge—in this case, the home page. `%2F` is a URL-encoded forward slash. Once you have authenticated by entering a username and submitting the login form, the `SignInAsync` method will redirect you back there. Try entering any name you like, and notice that you are authenticated (figure 9.2).

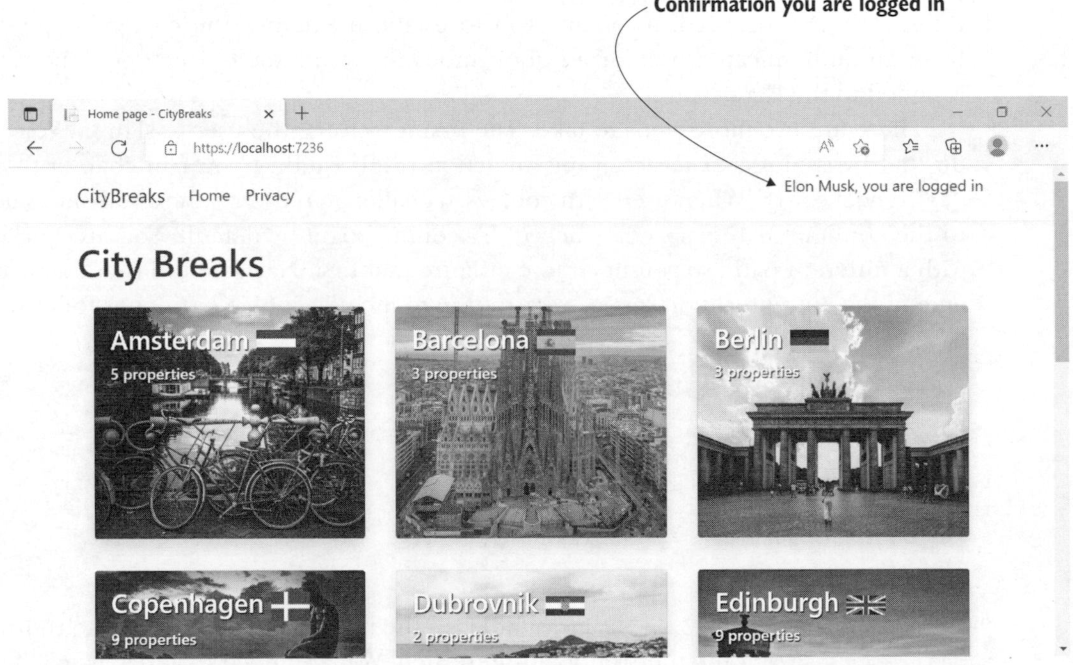

Figure 9.2 You are successfully authenticated, as confirmed by the message in the nav bar.

Move around the site, and notice you stay logged in. You can only get yourself logged out when you close the browser—not just the tab. That's not very secure. Nor is the fact that you can pretend to be anyone when you log in.

I logged in as one of the richest people on the planet (Elon Musk), just because I could. There is currently no code in the application to verify my claim to be Mr. Musk. Imagine if you could just walk up to Elon's bank and say you are him. Of course, the bank would demand that you verify your claim by providing additional information, such as a secret that only Mr. Musk would know. In most cases, this takes the form of a password, at the very least.

To make your login more secure, you need a way to securely capture and store the password for a user. You also need to compare submitted credentials to those you have stored to ensure the person logging in is who they say they are. Ideally, you also need to provide the user with a way to register an account, log out, and reset their password if they forgot it or believe it to be compromised. That is a lot of work to undertake from scratch, especially when ASP.NET Core Identity does most of it for you.

9.2 ASP.NET Core Identity

ASP.NET Core Identity (Identity) is a framework that supports authentication (determining who a visitor is) and authorization (determining what they are allowed to do). The default implementation uses EF Core to store user details, including their credentials in a database. It also provides a customizable UI for many common scenarios, including registering users; logging them in; resetting passwords; managing their profiles; generating account validation tokens; working with external authentication providers, such as Google, Microsoft, Facebook, Twitter; and more.

Identity is available as NuGet packages. When you first create a web application using the new project wizard in Visual Studio, you can configure it to include Identity at the outset by specifying Individual Accounts as the authentication type (figure 9.3).

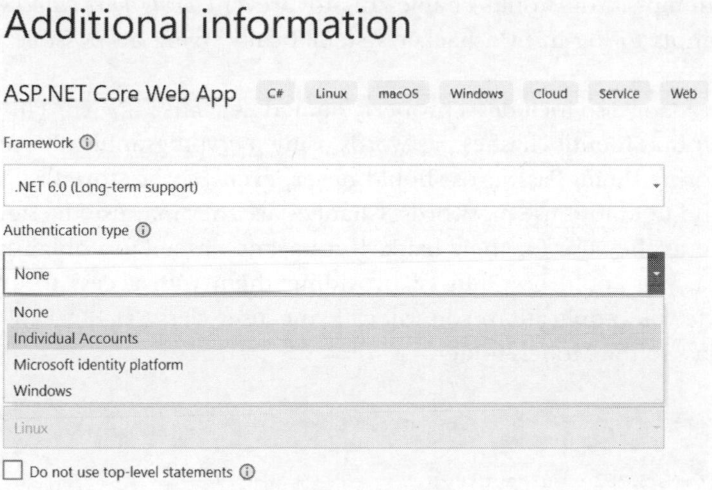

Figure 9.3 Select Individual Accounts to include Identity within the project.

If you create your application using the CLI, you can use the `--auth` or `-au` switch to specify that the new project uses individual accounts:

```
dotnet new webapp --auth Individual
```

However, you already have a project. There are certain steps you need to take to set it up to work with Identity. You need to add the required packages, add a class to represent your user, configure the existing database so it works with Identity, and then configure the services Identity relies on. Once those steps are completed, you can add a new migration that will update your existing database to act as an Identity store.

Storage is separate to Identity itself. You are free to choose your own storage mechanism and create a custom provider to work with it if one doesn't already exist. The default implementation of Identity storage relies on the `Microsoft.AspNetCore.Identity.EntityFrameworkCore` NuGet package, which works with relational databases. You add that to the project using `dotnet add package` if you are using the CLI, or `install-package` for the Package Manager Console, by adding a reference to the project file directly or using the Visual Studio tool for managing NuGet packages in the solution. The Identity UI is in a package called `Microsoft.AspNetCore.Identity.UI`, so that needs to be added too. Once both packages have been added, ensure that `dotnet restore` is executed.

9.2.1 Creating a user

The next step requires you to create a class to represent your user. A key feature of this class is that it must derive from `IdentityUser` if it is to work with the Identity framework. The `IdentityUser` type has several properties already defined, including `UserName`, `Email`, `PhoneNumber`, and some authentication workflow–specific properties, such as `LockoutEnabled`. This indicates whether the lockout feature has been enabled, whereby accounts are automatically locked after a specified number of invalid login attempts. You would enable this to prevent *brute force attacks*—usually automated attempts to log in by a hacker systematically trying all possible password combinations.

The `IdentityUser` also includes a property named `HashedPassword`. This provides a clue to the fact that Identity hashes passwords using a cryptographically secure algorithm before storing them. Passwords should never, ever, *ever* be stored as plain text. Users are lazy and tend to reuse passwords. Chances are they may use the same one in your application as they use for their bank. If a hacker was able to obtain a copy of your users' data, you could be guilty of providing them with access to all sorts of resources outside your application. You will call your user class `CityBreaksUser`. Add the following class to the Models folder.

Listing 9.9 The `CityBreaksUser` class

```
using Microsoft.AspNetCore.Identity;

namespace CityBreaks.Models
{
    public class CityBreaksUser : IdentityUser     <-- Your user class derives from IdentityUser.
    {
    }
}
```

At this stage, we will only work with the default properties of the `IdentityUser`. We will look at customizing this class a bit later.

9.2.2 Configuring the DbContext

The next stage involves adapting the existing `CityBreaksContext` to work with Identity. Two amendments are required for this (listing 9.10). The first is to derive your context class from `IdentityDbContext<TUser>`, instead of `DbContext`, where `TUser` represents the user class you just created. The `IdentityDbContext` includes some `DbSet` properties, representing database tables Identity uses to store various aspects of user data. You also need to include a `using` directive for `Microsoft.AspNetCore.Identity.EntityFrameworkCore`.

Listing 9.10 Adapting the DbContext to work with Identity

```
using CityBreaks.Data.Configuration;
using CityBreaks.Models;
using Microsoft.AspNetCore.Identity.EntityFrameworkCore;
using Microsoft.EntityFrameworkCore;

namespace CityBreaks.Data
{
    public class CityBreaksContext :
    ➥ IdentityDbContext<CityBreaksUser>
    {
        public CityBreaksContext(DbContextOptions options) :
        ➥ base(options)
        {
            ...
```

- Add the relevant using directive to bring Identity into scope.
- Derive the CityBreaksContext from IdentityDbContext<TUser> instead of DbContext, specifying the CityBreaksUser as the type parameter.

You need to ensure you call `base.OnModelCreating` in your overridden `OnModelCreating` method; otherwise, model configuration for `IdentityDbContext` will not take place, resulting in errors when you attempt to create a migration. This is shown in the bold line in the following listing.

Listing 9.11 Calling base.OnModelCreating in the overridden OnModelCreating

```
protected override void OnModelCreating(ModelBuilder builder)
{
    builder
        .ApplyConfiguration(new CityConfiguration())
        .ApplyConfiguration(new CountryConfiguration())
        .ApplyConfiguration(new PropertyConfiguration());
    base.OnModelCreating(builder);
}
```

CONFIGURING IDENTITY SERVICES

You will need to configure the application to include Identity services and use the `CityBreaksContext` as a store. Replace the existing call to `AddAuthentication` with the following call to `AddDefaultIdentity<TUser>` in Program.cs, passing in your `CityBreaksUser`.

Listing 9.12 Adding Identity services to the application

```
builder.Services.AddDefaultIdentity<CityBreaksUser>()
    .AddEntityFrameworkStores<CityBreaksContext>();
```

This service registration configures Identity with its default settings. You will see what those settings are and how to customize them a bit later.

9.2.3 Adding migration

Finally, you are at the stage where you can add a migration that will scaffold the tables required in the database. Like in the last chapter, you create a migration either through the Package Manager Console using the `add-migration` command or through `dotnet ef migrations add` via the CLI. You will name this migration `AddedIdentity`:

```
[PMC]
add-migration AddedIdentity
[CLI]
dotnet ef migrations add AddedIdentity
```

Once this command has been executed, take a moment to examine the code in the migration's `Up` method. If all has gone according to plan, you should have code that will create seven tables, each one representing a `DbSet` in the `IdentityDbContext` class. Apply the migration using the `update-database` command or `dotnet ef database update` via the CLI, and then take a look at the revised schema of your database. Sure enough, seven tables have been added to the database (figure 9.4), each one's name prefixed with `AspNet`.

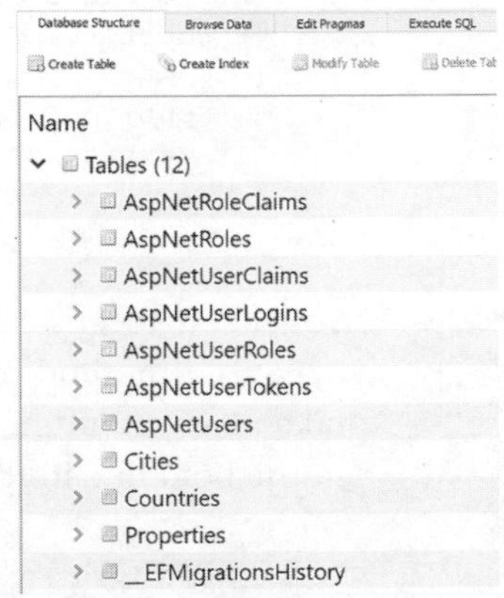

Figure 9.4 Identity adds seven tables prefixed with `AspNet`.

The primary table is the `AspNetUsers` table. This is where user profile data is stored. The other tables are optional. Three of them relate to the management of *roles*, which is a mechanism for managing different levels of authorization; we will explore these in the next chapter. The `AspNetUserClaims` table is for storing additional information about a user as a collection of claims to support authorization scenarios. The `AspNetUserLogins` table is for storing information about a user's external login, such as Google or Facebook, if you choose to implement third-party authentication. The `AspNetUserTokens` table is where external login authorization tokens are saved. I don't cover third-party authentication in this book, but you can refer to the official documentation for guidance on integrating with the most popular social login services: http://mng.bz/p6QK.

There is just one last thing you need to do before you can run the application. You need to replace the code you added to the layout in the previous section with a partial because the default Identity UI expects one name: _LoginPartial. So add a new Razor

View > Empty to the Pages\Shared folder named _LoginPartial.cshtml. Cut the following section of code from the layout, and paste it into the new partial file. Add the `Sign out` anchor tag helper, and amend the `Sign in` anchor tag helper.

Listing 9.13 Extracting from the layout and pasting into _LoginPartial.cshtml

```
<div class="align-content-end">
    @if (User.Identity.IsAuthenticated)
    {
        <p>@User.Identity.Name, you are logged in
        <a asp-area="Identity" asp-page="/Account/Logout">Sign out</a>
        </p>
    }
    else
    {
        <a asp-area="Identity" asp-page="/Account/Login">Sign in</a>
    }
</div>
```

Add an anchor tag helper for signing out.

Change the anchor tag helper to specify the Identity area and Account/Login page.

At the point where you cut the code from the layout, replace it with

```
<partial name="_LoginPartial" />
```

Once this is done, you can launch the application. This time, the challenge in the `IndexModel OnGet` method should redirect you to Identity's default login path, /Identity/Account/Login, illustrated in figure 9.5.

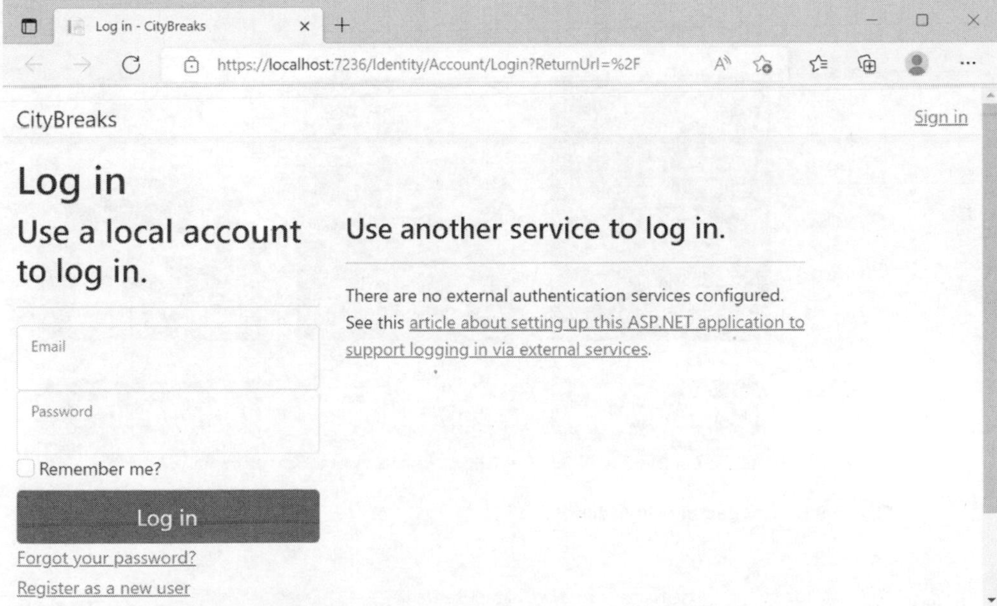

Figure 9.5 The default Identity login UI

If you were expecting an award-winning theme at this point, you are likely feeling a bit disappointed. The good news is that the default UI works; but it is not great to look at, and like the scaffolded CRUD pages you created in the previous chapter, it needs some customization before you can deploy it as part of a working application. Your users won't have much use for the content on the right, which links to an article about configuring external authentication providers, such as Facebook or Google.

For the time being, you will register a new account and use it to log in. Click the Register as a New User link, and enter an email address along with a password. The default password requirements are that it should consist of the following:

- A minimum of six characters
- At least one non-alphanumeric character (e.g., *!)
- At least one lowercase character
- At least one uppercase character
- At least one digit

As soon as you submit the registration form, you should find you are automatically logged in to the application (figure 9.6). You should also see there is a single entry in the `AspNetUsers` table (figure 9.7).

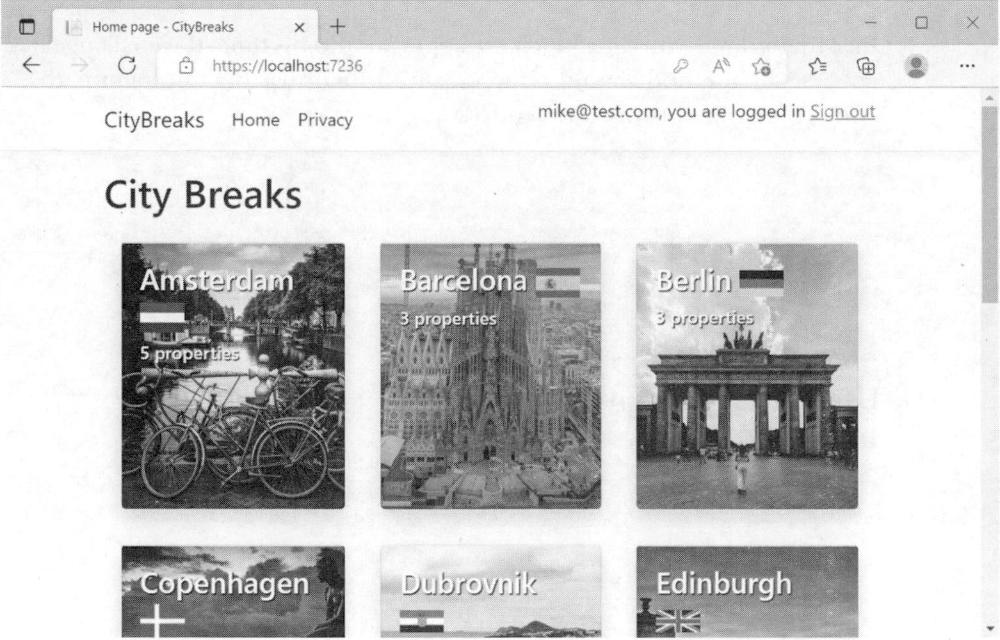

Figure 9.6 Logged in using Identity

	Id	UserName	NormalizedUserName	Email
	Filter	Filter	Filter	Filter
1	3991dab1-1ae...	mike@test.com	MIKE@TEST.COM	mike@test.com

Figure 9.7 A new entry has been added to the `AspNetUsers` table.

While you are looking at the data within the `AspNetUsers` table, you can take a quick look at the schema for the table, which mirrors the `IdentityUser` class properties. Some of the fields are related to account status, while others relate to the user's profile. The profile fields are limited to those required for account management—name, email, and phone number—so tokens and confirmations can be sent by email or SMS. If you are operating an e-commerce site, you will also want to store the user's address for delivery and, possibly, a different billing address. You might want to store their date of birth, so you can send them a card or limit sales of age-restricted products and services. You will look at how to customize your `IdentityUser` to enable that, along with other Identity-related customizations, in the remainder of this chapter. Before you do that, click the Sign Out link, and follow the instructions to sign out of the application to confirm the sign-out feature works.

9.3 Customizing Identity

Now that you have Identity and its UI working, we can look at some options for customizing various aspects to suit your own application requirements. You have already seen the default password options; now we will explore how to control those and other options related to how Identity works. Then we will look at customizing your implementation of the `IdentityUser`, so you can store more information than the base type caters for. Finally, we will look more closely at the default UI and understand how you can control its look, feel, and behavior.

9.3.1 Customizing Identity options

The `IdentityOptions` class represents all the options you can use to configure the Identity system. It has a number of properties providing access to options that relate to specific areas of Identity. The properties you are most likely to work with are shown in table 9.1.

Table 9.1 Select `IdentityOptions` properties

Property	Type	Description
`User`	`UserOptions`	Provides access to the options for user validation
`Password`	`PasswordOptions`	Enables customization of your application's password policy
`SignIn`	`SignInOptions`	Represents configurable account confirmation options
`Lockout`	`LockoutOptions`	The options for managing your application's policy for locking accounts in the event of failed login attempts

Additional properties enable you to configure token generation for email confirmation, password reset, and so on, as well as a couple of options related to the storage of key values and personal data. You are unlikely to touch these for the majority of applications.

You will configure `IdentityOptions` via an overload of `AddDefaultIdentity<TUser>` that takes an `Action<IdentityOptions>` as an argument. The following listing illustrates this by showing how to configure specific options of the `User` and `Password` properties.

Listing 9.14 Setting Identity options

```
builder.Services.AddDefaultIdentity<CityBreaksUser>(options => {
    options.User.RequireUniqueEmail = false;      <-- Set user options through the User property.
    options.Password.RequiredLength = 8;          <-- Set password options though the Password property.
})
```

CONFIGURING USER OPTIONS

Table 9.2 shows the two properties of the `UserOptions` class that represent configurable user options. The default Identity UI package uses email addresses as usernames, which must be unique. Bearing this in mind, if you were to restrict the allowed characters further and remove the symbols, users would not be able to register because email addresses require at least two symbols. These options will only take effect if you change the way users are registered—which is relatively easy to do, as you will see later.

Table 9.2 The `UserOptions` properties

Property	Description
`AllowedUserNameCharacters`	Specifies the range of characters permitted in a user's name. Defaults to a–z, A–Z, 0–9, and the symbols -._@+.
`RequireUniqueEmail`	Boolean. If set to true, email addresses must be unique.

CONFIGURING PASSWORD OPTIONS

Passwords are becoming a hot topic. Microsoft has been moving away from passwords in favor of biometrics (e.g., fingerprints and facial and speech pattern recognition) along with security codes sent to users via SMS for a while. Nevertheless, passwords are still central to the default implementation of Identity. As already hinted at, there are a number of options for configuration via the `PasswordOptions` object (table 9.3).

Table 9.3 The `PasswordOptions` properties

Name	Default	Description
`RequireDigit`	`true`	Specifies whether the password must include a digit.
`RequiredLength`	`6`	Specifies the minimum number of characters in a password.
`RequireLowercase`	`true`	Determines whether passwords must contain a lowercase ASCII character.
`RequireNonAlphanumeric`	`true`	Indicates whether passwords must contain a non-alphanumeric character.

Table 9.3 The PasswordOptions properties *(continued)*

Name	Default	Description
RequiredUniqueChars	1	Specifies the number of unique characters required in the password.
RequireUppercase	true	If true, the password must contain an uppercase ASCII character.

Within Identity, passwords are hashed before they are stored. The hashing process also includes a *salt*—a randomly generated value that is added to the password to ensure the resulting hash for two identical passwords is unique. Then the salt and the hashed password are stored together in the PasswordHash column of the AspNetUsers table.

When a user submits a password as part of the login process, the PasswordHash value is retrieved for the username, and the salt is extracted and used to hash the submitted password. Hashing is deterministic in that, given the same input, hashing will always result in the same output. So the salted and hashed version of the submitted password should match what is stored in the database, assuming the correct password was submitted. Hashing is also one-way, unlike encryption. You cannot reverse a hashed value to retrieve the original value.

This might sound complicated, and the algorithms that take care of processing the password for storage certainly are, which emphasizes the point that you should not attempt to replace the existing implementation, unless you know what you are doing.

Within your application, you will remove most of the restrictions, so you can use simple passwords for testing. Apply the following options, which eliminate the need to use special characters.

Listing 9.15 Configuring password options

```
builder.Services.AddDefaultIdentity<CityBreaksUser>(options =>{
    options.Password.RequireDigit = false;
    options.Password.RequireLowercase = false;
    options.Password.RequireNonAlphanumeric = false;
    options.Password.RequireUppercase = false;
}).AddEntityFrameworkStores<CityBreaksContext>();
```

NOTE If you change the RequiredLength value, you will also need to update the StringLength validation that has been applied to the UserName property in the RegisterModel used in the Identity UI registration form. You will get to that a bit later when you scaffold and customize the UI itself.

CONFIGURING SIGNINOPTIONS

The SignInOptions enables configuration of various account confirmation requirements, detailed in table 9.4. The IUserConfirmation<TUser> interface is provided to enable you to set your own conditions for allowing users to sign in. I don't cover this in any detail here, but the interface has one member: IsConfirmedAsync, which returns a `Task<bool>`, wherein you apply your custom logic to determine whether the user is permitted to sign in. You then register your implementation as a service in line with the guidance provided in chapter 7.

Table 9.4 The `SignInOptions` properties

Name	Default	Description
`RequireConfirmedAccount`	`false`	Determines whether conditions specified by the `IUserConfirmation<TUser>` interface need to be met to enable sign-in. The default implementation of this interface specifies that an email address is required.
`RequireConfirmedEmail`	`false`	Determines whether a confirmed email is needed to enable the user to log in.
`RequireConfirmedPhoneNumber`	`false`	Specifies whether a confirmed phone number is needed to enable the user to log in.

The Identity UI package does not support phone number confirmations by default. So if you set this to `true`, you will lock all users out of the application. If you want to enable password reset or other features that rely on email addresses, it is a good idea to enable `RequireConfirmedEmail`. We will look at how you can enable and test this locally without requiring access to an email provider a bit later.

CONFIGURING LOCKOUTOPTIONS

Primarily as a defense against brute force attacks, you can enable account lockout in the event of multiple failed attempts to sign in. The configurable options are detailed in table 9.5.

Table 9.5 The `LockoutOptions` properties

Name	Default	Description
`AllowedForNewUsers`	`true`	Determines the value applied to the `LockoutEnabled` column for newly created users
`DefaultLockoutTimeSpan`	5	Sets the duration for the lockout (in minutes)
`MaxFailedAccessAttempts`	5	Specifies the maximum number of failed attempts to sign in before the account is locked out

The options in table 9.5 configure account lockout if it is used. You will see how this is managed later in the chapter when you customize the UI. Before that, we will look at customizing the user.

9.3.2 *Customizing the user*

Your user class, `CityBreaksUser`, derives from `IdentityUser`. As I have discussed, this has a limited number of properties relating to the user's profile. If you want to allow your user to book somewhere to stay, you need some additional information from them, such as their name and address, at the very least. Remember that the default data access technology behind Identity is EF Core, so rather than modifying the database schema manually to accommodate this data, you can add new properties to your user entity and then use a migration to propagate those changes to the database. First, you will modify the `CityBreaksUser` to include three properties.

Listing 9.16 Customizing the `IdentityUser`

```
public class CityBreaksUser : IdentityUser
{
    public string FirstName { get; set; }
    public string LastName {  get; set; }
    public string Address { get; set; }
}
```

Then, you will create a new migration:

```
[Powershell]
add-migration CustomizeIdentityUser
[CLI]
dotnet ef migrations add CustomizeIdentityUser
```

Once you have applied the migration (`update-database` or `dotnet ef database update`), you can check the schema of the `AspNetUsers` table to confirm the new columns have been added successfully, as shown in figure 9.8.

Figure 9.8 The amended `AspNetUser` table following the migration

Now that you can accommodate additional user data, you need to capture it at registration. So in the next section, you will see how that is done.

9.3.3 Scaffolding and customizing the UI

The Identity UI is developed as a *Razor class library* (RCL), enabling it to be deployed as a NuGet package and plugged into applications that want to use it. RCLs can contain Razor pages, static assets, and even MVC controllers and views. Developing RCLs is an advanced topic not covered in this book, but you can refer to the official documentation for more details: http://mng.bz/O6Vw. The contents of an RCL are overridable, as long as you replicate the file structure within the RCL. Physical files on disk take precedence over the content of the RCL.

The Identity UI includes support for scaffolding to generate physical copies of some, if not all, of the Identity pages. The scaffolded pages replicate the file structure within the RCL, which means they automatically override the default UI. Identity scaffolding depends on the same package you installed when you generated the CRUD pages in chapter 8: `Microsoft.VisualStudio.Web.CodeGeneration.Design`. If you are using Visual Studio, the Identity scaffolder is accessible via the Add... New Scaffolded Item dialog (figure 9.9). When you click the Add button, you are presented with a selection of files to scaffold (figure 9.10).

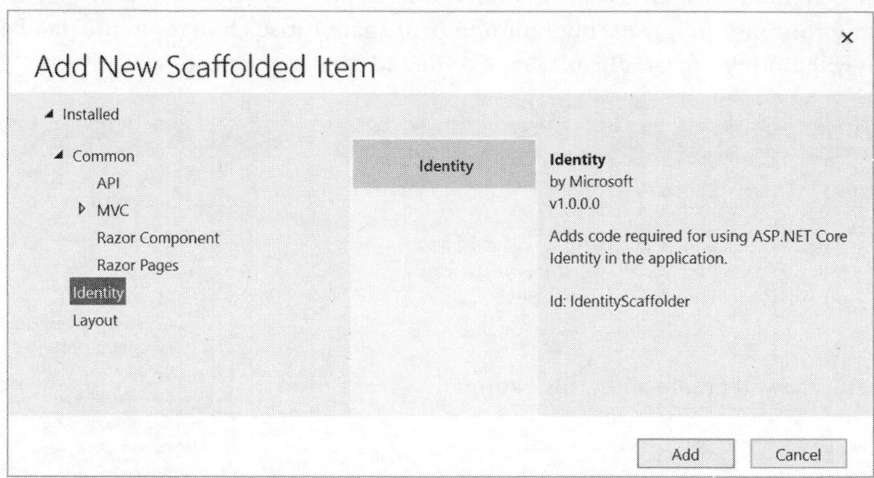

Figure 9.9 The New Scaffolded Item dialog

Add Identity
Select an existing layout page, or specify a new one:
/Areas/Identity/Pages/Account/Manage/_Layout.cshtml
(Leave empty if it is set in a Razor _viewstart file)
Override all files
Choose files to override
Account\StatusMessage
Account\AccessDenied
Account\ConfirmEmail
Account\ConfirmEmailChange
Account\ExternalLogin
Account\ForgotPassword
Account\ForgotPasswordConfirmation
Account\Lockout
Account\Login
Account\LoginWith2fa
Account\LoginWithRecoveryCode
Account\Logout
Account\Manage\Layout
Account\Manage\ManageNav
Account\Manage\StatusMessage
Account\Manage\ChangePassword
Account\Manage\DeletePersonalData
Account\Manage\Disable2fa
Account\Manage\DownloadPersonalData
Account\Manage\Email
Account\Manage\EnableAuthenticator
Account\Manage\ExternalLogins
Account\Manage\GenerateRecoveryCodes
Account\Manage\Index
Account\Manage\PersonalData
Account\Manage\ResetAuthenticator
Account\Manage\SetPassword
Account\Manage\ShowRecoveryCodes
Account\Manage\TwoFactorAuthentication
Account\Register
Account\RegisterConfirmation
Account\ResendEmailConfirmation
Account\ResetPassword
Account\ResetPasswordConfirmation
Data context class <Required>
Use SQLite instead of SQL Server
User class
Add
Cancel

Figure 9.10 The Identity UI scaffold selection dialog

This dialog lists every page in the Identity UI. The purpose of most of them is relatively easy to figure out from their names. However, you can always tick the Override All Files option to generate every file and inspect their content if you want to see what they do. I recommend doing this in a separate project, which you can use for reference. Once you scaffold a page, you take responsibility for managing its code.

If you are using VS Code, the scaffold dialog is not available to you. Instead, you can use the CLI to scaffold pages. First, you can list all the available files using the `-lf` or `--listFiles` option, as with the following command, executed from within the project folder:

```
dotnet aspnet-codegenerator identity --listFiles
```

Note that the `listFiles` options are case sensitive, and the tool name must include the hyphen: `aspnet-codegenerator`. When scaffolding CRUD pages, you may recall you did not need to include the hyphen. The output shows the filenames using dot notation in place of the path separator you see in the Visual Studio version of the file list (figure 9.11).

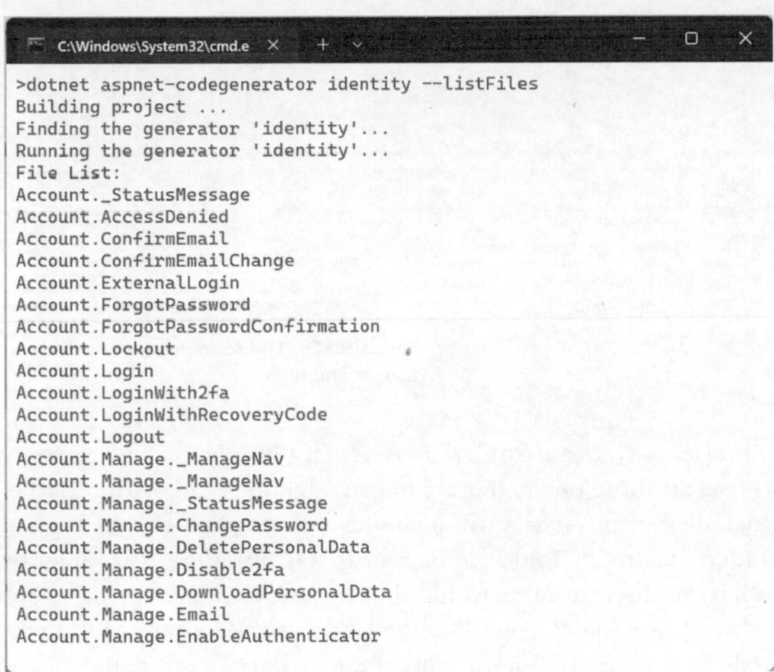

Figure 9.11 The Identity files listed using the CLI for scaffolding

Depending on the tool you use to scaffold, select the Account\Login and Account\Register files in the dialog, and select the `CityBreaksContext` as the data context class, or use the following command from the CLI:

```
dotnet aspnet-codegenerator identity -dc CityBreaks.Data.CityBreaksContext
➥ -sqlite -fi "Account.Login;Account.Register"
```

To fully understand the options you have set in this command and their longer alternative versions, you can execute `dotnet aspnet-codegenerator identity --help` at any time from the CLI.

Click Add in the dialog, or execute the command. Once completed, the code generator should have created a new folder named Areas, containing a series of nested folders and files (figure 9.12).

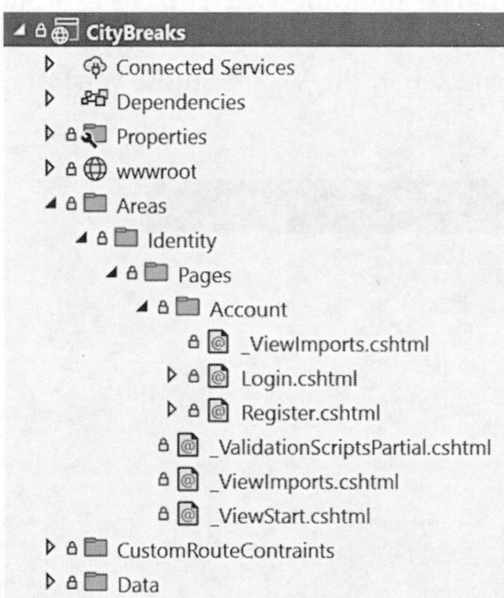

Figure 9.12 The scaffolded folders and files

Razor class libraries use a feature called *areas*, which I briefly touched on when discussing the `asp-area` attribute on anchor tag helpers. If you recall, earlier in the chapter, you had to include the `asp-area` attribute in the login tag helper, which pointed to an area named Identity. Any subfolder defines an area within the Areas folder by convention. So you have an Identity area; within that, you store the Razor pages in the individual area's own Pages folder. As well as the Login and Register pages, the scaffolder has produced the ViewStart, ViewImports, and a partial for managing validation scripts. All of these override the matching content in the RCL. This is your code now. You own it. Before you start working with the code, you will quickly review its content to better understand two of the principal Identity actors: the `UserManager` and the `SignInManager`.

THE USERMANAGER AND SIGNINMANAGER

The Identity UI is optional. Whether you use it or not, if you build an application based on Identity itself, you will find that you need to customize your authentication workflows to a greater or lesser degree. When you do, you will have to work with the `UserManager` and the `SignInManager`.

The `SignInManager` class provides an API for managing signing a user in. Table 9.6 summarizes the methods you are most likely to use when working with this class.

Table 9.6 Commonly used `SignInManager` methods

Method	Description
`SignInAsync`	Signs the user in and assigns an Identity cookie
`SignOutAsync`	Signs the user out and removes the Identity cookie
`PasswordSignInAsync`	Attempts to sign the user in with the specified password

In addition, the `SignInManager` provides a range of methods that help you work with external login providers, two-factor authentication, lockouts, and so on. When reviewing the `PageModel` code in the Register and Login pages, you can see that the `SignInManager` is injected as a service into the constructors and only used to sign the user in as well as obtain a list of possible registered external login providers (e.g., Twitter and Google). The `SignInManager` class is fully documented at http://mng.bz/m2z4.

The `UserManager` provides an API for managing the user with a database or other registered persistence store. Accordingly, it includes a wide range of methods for saving and retrieving user data, including the methods in table 9.7.

Table 9.7 Select `UserManager` methods

Method	Description
`CreateAsync`	Adds a user to the database
`UpdateAsync`	Updates the user details in the database
`DeleteAsync`	Removes the user from the database
`GetUserAsync`	Gets the user corresponding to the `ClaimsPrincipal` passed in to the method
`FindByIdAsync`	Retrieves the user with the specified `Id`
`FindByNameAsync`	Retrieves the user with the specified `Name` claim
`AddClaimAsync`	Adds a claim to the user
`AddToRoleAsync`	Adds the user to the specified `Role`

In addition, there are methods for managing passwords, confirmation tokens, two-factor authentication, lockouts, and so on. The last two methods in the table are more likely to be used as part of an authorization workflow, and we will look at them in a little more detail in the next chapter. Like the `SignInManager`, the `UserManager` is injected as a service wherever it is required. For details on the wide range of other methods and properties on the `UserManager` class, you can refer to the documentation: http://mng.bz/5mYa.

Returning to customizing the UI, first you will modify the Login page, so it no longer features guidance on wiring up external authentication services. Open the scaffolded Login.cshtml file, and locate the `div` element that starts with the following code:

```
<div class="col-md-6 col-md-offset-2">
    <section>
        <h3>Use another service to log in.</h3>
```

Comment the entire `div` out, or eradicate it. Then run the application. This time, the login page should appear without the content that previously occupied the right-hand side of the page (figure 9.13). Next you will change the Registration page to remove the same content about external logins and capture the additional information you added to the user class.

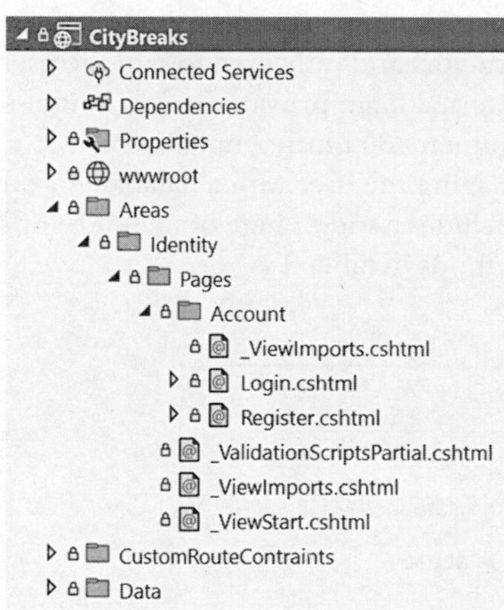

Figure 9.13 The modified Login page

AMENDING THE REGISTRATION PAGE

The `RegisterModel` class, located in Areas\Identity\Pages\Account\Register.cshtml.cs, uses the input model pattern to encapsulate the binding targets for the username and email. You need to add properties for the first name, last name, and address, so add the following lines of code to the `InputModel` class declared within the `RegisterModel`.

Listing 9.17 Adding properties for the additional registration data you want to capture

```
[Required]
[Display(Name ="First Name")]
public string FirstName { get; set; }
[Required]
[Display(Name = "Last Name")]
public string LastName { get; set; }
[Required]
public string Address { get; set; }
```

At this stage, if you changed the `RequiredLength` value when configuring the password options, you should adjust the `MinimumLength` property value on the `StringLength` attribute that has been applied to the `Password` property of the `InputModel` accordingly.

Next you need to assign the bound values of your new properties to the user. This happens in the `OnPostAsync` method, which contains a lot of code. However, at this stage, you should only be interested in the bit where the user is created if `ModelState` is valid.

Listing 9.18 Creating the user if `ModelState` is valid

```
if (ModelState.IsValid)
{
    var user = CreateUser();    <- An instance of the user is created by the private CreateUser method at the bottom of the file.

    await _userStore.SetUserNameAsync(user, Input.Email,
    ➥ CancellationToken.None);    <- The username is assigned to the user.
    await _emailStore.SetEmailAsync(user, Input.Email,
    ➥ CancellationToken.None);    <- The email is assigned to the user.
    var result = await _userManager.CreateAsync(user,
    ➥ Input.Password);    <- The user is saved to the data store by the UserManager.
```

In previous versions of the Identity UI, the user was created with its email and usernames in one line of code:

```
var user = new CityBreaksUser { UserName = Input.Email, Email = Input.Email };
```

The updated version released as part of .NET 6 is a lot more verbose. Creation is delegated to a private method named `CreateUser` that uses `Activator.CreateInstance` with error handling for some edge cases the scaffold developers couldn't foresee. You don't have to stick with this. You can replace the code with the simpler version instead. After all, this is your code now.

There are other differences from previous versions. The username and email properties are assigned via the `IUserStore.SetUserNameAsync` and `IUserEmailStore.SetEmailAsync` methods, respectively. These APIs provide a consistent way to get and set the username and email for the user. There is also a similar API for managing phone numbers: the `IUserPhoneNumberStore` interface. I don't go into any real detail on these interfaces in this book. It is enough to know that the default implementations simply assign the specified value (`Input.Email`) to the user's `UserName` and `Email` properties. All you need to do for the time being is assign incoming values to the user's new properties.

Listing 9.19 Assigning values to the Identity user's custom properties

```
if (ModelState.IsValid)
{
    var user = CreateUser();

    user.FirstName = Input.FirstName;
    user.LastName = Input.LastName;
    user.Address = Input.Address;

    await _userStore.SetUserNameAsync(user, Input.Email,
    ➥ CancellationToken.None);
    await _emailStore.SetEmailAsync(user, Input.Email,
    ➥ CancellationToken.None);
    var result = await _userManager.CreateAsync(user, Input.Password);
```

Here you assign the bound values to the custom properties you added to your implementation of the IdentityUser.

You make two modifications to the Razor page—the first to comment out or remove the same block of code about external logins you dealt with in the Login page and the second to add the following form fields at the beginning of the form, just below the validation summary tag helper.

Listing 9.20 The forms fields for the additional `IdentityUser` properties

```
<div class="form-floating">
    <input asp-for="Input.FirstName" class="form-control" />
    <label asp-for="Input.FirstName"></label>
    <span asp-validation-for="Input.FirstName" class="text-danger"></span>
</div>
<div class="form-floating">
    <input asp-for="Input.LastName" class="form-control" />
    <label asp-for="Input.LastName"></label>
    <span asp-validation-for="Input.LastName" class="text-danger"></span>
</div>
<div class="form-floating">
    <textarea asp-for="Input.Address" class="form-control"></textarea>
    <label asp-for="Input.Address"></label>
    <span asp-validation-for="Input.Address" class="text-danger"></span>
</div>
```

Now you can run the application and click the Register as a New User link on the Login page, which should take you to the revised form shown in figure 9.14. Complete it (with a different email address), and submit. You should find yourself logged in, and you should also see that the additional fields were populated in the `AspNetUsers` table.

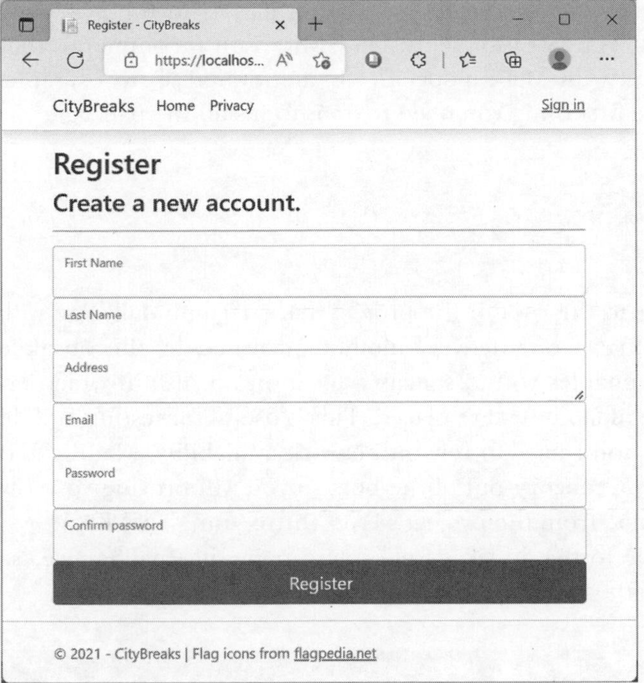

Figure 9.14 The revised register form

9.3.4 Enabling email confirmation

Identity supports some scenarios that utilize email. For example, you can require a user to confirm they have control over the email address they use to register with by sending them an email containing a link they must click to validate their registration. Password reset features also rely on email. The Identity UI incorporates an email service represented by the `IEmailSender` interface. It has one method, `SendEmailAsync`, which in the default implementation does nothing at all.

Listing 9.21 The default `EmailSender` service

```
internal class EmailSender : IEmailSender
{
    public Task SendEmailAsync(string email, string subject, string
     htmlMessage)
    {
        return Task.CompletedTask;
    }
}
```

You don't have to use the `IEmailSender` interface. You can use whatever you like, but in this example, you will provide your own implementation that generates an email using an open source email management library called MailKit (http://mng.bz/69GA). Countless examples all over the internet (and on my sites) demonstrate how to send email from ASP.NET applications by using classes in the `System.Net.Mail` class, but this approach is now obsolete. Instead, Microsoft recommends that you use more modern libraries, with MailKit specifically mentioned as an example in their documentation. So the first thing you need to do is to install the package:

```
[CLI]
dotnet add package MailKit
[Package Manager Console]
install-package MailKit
```

Next add a new folder to the root of the project named TempMail. You will emulate the `SpecifiedPickupDirectory` delivery method provided by the obsolete `System.Net.Mail` class. This enables you to specify a location on disk in which email messages generated by the mail library are placed. This is useful for testing and debugging because it means you don't have to rely on network availability. MailKit doesn't support `SpecifiedPickupDirectory` out of the box, so you will provide your own implementation based on code from the project's FAQ (http://mng.bz/YK8z).

Add a new class file to the Services folder, and name it EmailService.cs. Replace any existing content with the code in the following listing.

Listing 9.22 The `EmailService` class

```
using MailKit.Net.Smtp;
using Microsoft.AspNetCore.Identity.UI.Services;
using MimeKit;
using MimeKit.IO;

namespace CityBreaks.Services
{
    public class EmailService : IEmailSender       <-- The class implements the IEmailSender interface.
    {
        private readonly IHostEnvironment _environment;
        public EmailService(IHostEnvironment environment)
        {
            _environment = environment;
        }
        // Inject the IHostEnvironment interface in, so you can use it to generate a path for the email folder.
        public async Task SendEmailAsync(string email, string subject,
            string htmlMessage)
        {
            // Generate the folder path.
            var pickupDirectory = Path.Combine(_environment.ContentRootPath,
                "TempMail");
            var message = new MimeMessage();
            message.From.Add(MailboxAddress.Parse(
                "test@test.com"));
            message.To.Add(MailboxAddress.Parse(email));
            message.Subject = subject;

            message.Body = new TextPart("html")
            {
                Text = htmlMessage
            };
            // Construct a message from the arguments sent in to the SendEmailAsync method.
```

```
            Await SaveToPickupDirectory(message, pickupDirectory);  <-- "Send" the email.
            await Task.CompletedTask;
        }
    }
    // SaveToPickupDirectory method here
}
```

Take the code for the `SaveToPickupDirectory` method from the MailKit project's FAQ, or from the download for this section (http://mng.bz/G18D), and insert it at the point indicated in the comment in listing 9.22.

> **NOTE** This implementation is hardcoded to dump email messages into a folder on disk. While that is convenient when running the application locally, it is not much use when the application is live in production. In the final chapter, we will look at ways to manage this, so the behavior of the mailing service depends on the environment in which the application is running.

Now that you have an implementation of the `IEmailSender` service, you need to register your implementation with the service container:

```
builder.Services.AddTransient<IEmailSender, EmailService>();
```

Remember, by default, Identity does not require the user to confirm their account. The email service is only used if account confirmation is required, so you need to change the `SignIn` options in Program.cs. Add the bolded line shown in the following listing.

Listing 9.23 Making account confirmation required

```
builder.Services.AddDefaultIdentity<CityBreaksUser>(options => {
    options.Password.RequireDigit = false;
    options.Password.RequireLowercase = false;
    options.Password.RequireNonAlphanumeric = false;
    options.Password.RequireUppercase = false;
    options.SignIn.RequireConfirmedAccount = true;
}).AddEntityFrameworkStores<CityBreaksContext>();
```

Run the application, and go through the registration process again. This time, you are not automatically logged in when you complete the form. You should receive a message to check your email (figure 9.15).

At this stage, if you have not configured your email service correctly, you will see a message to that effect with a link in the page that you should click to confirm your account.

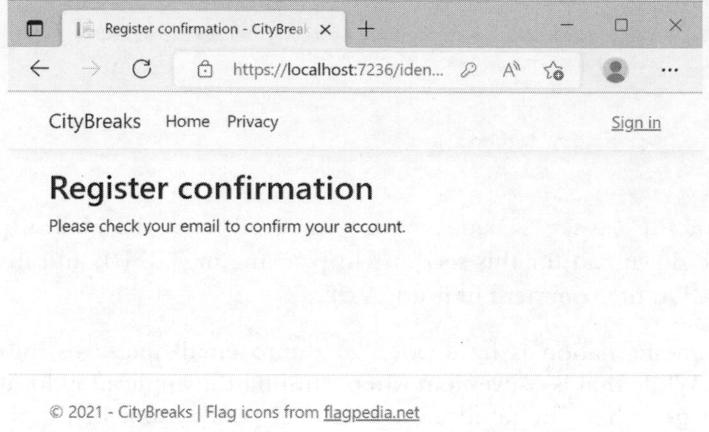

Figure 9.15 The Register Confirmation page

Hopefully, you got things right, however, and now have an EML file in your TempMail folder (figure 9.16).

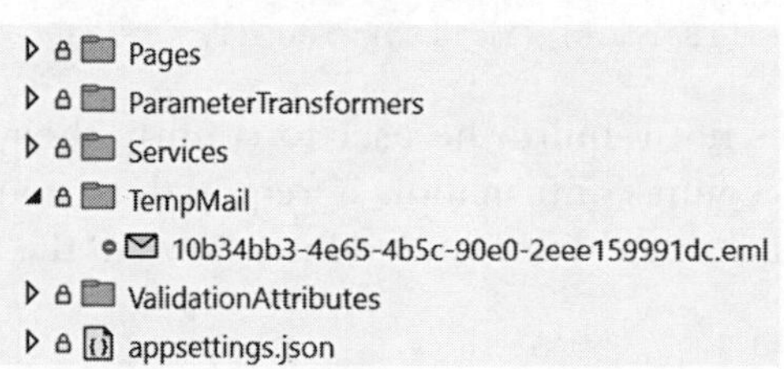

Figure 9.16 The email was generated and placed in the specified pickup directory.

Open the EML file with a suitable application (email client), and click the link (figure 9.17).

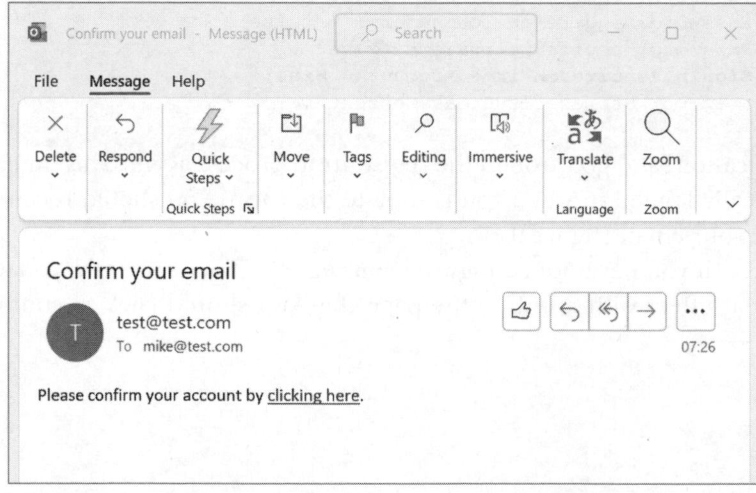

Figure 9.17 The confirmation email

You should be directed back to the application and rewarded with a message that your email is confirmed. Now you can sign in to the application. You can access all of the Identity UI when you do—even parts that provide workflows you do not intend to implement. For example, several pages at the identity/account/manage endpoint allow users to change their personal data, get a copy of it, delete it, manage 2FA, and so on. We will look at ways to manage these in the next section.

Before we move on, there is one thing you should bear in mind about how this feature works. The link in the generated email includes a validation token within the query string. The token is encoded using Base64 URL encoding (http://mng.bz/09YJ). The resulting value includes mixed-case characters. If you have `LowercaseQueryStrings` set to `true` within your routing options, the encoded value will be altered to all lowercase, breaching the token's integrity. In this scenario, the token will always fail validation.

9.3.5 Disabling UI features

When you include the UI package, you opt in to all of it. There will, undoubtedly, be parts you don't want to implement. You have a choice of how you want to disable these features. You can use authorization to prevent unauthorized access, while maintaining the functionality of the pages, which we will look at in the next chapter.

It is, of course, possible to remove links to any pages you don't want users to access. However, that is not a foolproof solution. Other savvy developers may well recognize the Identity UI URL scheme when they visit or use your application and could be tempted to poke around. Instead, you can scaffold the pages you don't want to implement and alter their code to disable them.

In this example, you will scaffold the LoginWith2Fa page and disable it. If you are using Visual Studio, use the Add... New Scaffolded Item option to generate Account\LoginWith2fa. Or, using the CLI, execute the following command:

```
dotnet aspnet-codegenerator identity -dc CityBreaks.Data.CityBreaksContext
➥ -sqlite -fi Account.LoginWith2fa
```

Having scaffolded the page, open the `PageModel` file, and comment out both the existing `OnGetAsync` and `OnPostAsync` methods. Once you have done that, replace them with the following implementations:

```
public IActionResult OnGet() => NotFound();
public IActionResult OnPost() => NotFound();
```

I have chosen to return a 404 Not Found message if a user attempts to reach this endpoint either by a `GET` or `POST` request. You can provide an alternative response if you prefer. You might want to redirect the user somewhere else; for example, you can use a `RedirectToPage` method. The important thing is to replace both the `OnGet` and `OnPost` handlers. When disabling other pages that only have an `OnGet` handler, it is still wise to implement the `OnPost` handler as well.

You have completed the task of identifying who your users are, so they are no longer anonymous. Armed with this information, you can now determine what they are authorized to do while on the site. At the moment, you have a management area open to everyone. You don't want just anyone to have access to the property management pages, for example. They could set their vacation price, and that would never do. In the next chapter, you will learn how to use authorization to restrict access to select visitors based on what you know about them.

Summary

- Authentication is the process of identifying site users, so they are no longer anonymous.
- You need to add authentication services and middleware to enable authentication in your application.
- Authentication in a browser-based web application relies primarily on cookies that hold the current user's identity in an encrypted format.
- ASP.NET Core Identity is a framework for managing authentication and users. It uses EF Core to store user data in a database.
- You can customize the `IdentityUser` through migrations.
- Identity UI is a package that provides pages for many authentication scenarios.
- You can use scaffolding to generate your versions of Identity UI pages and customize them for your needs.

10 Controlling access with authorization

This chapter covers

- Enabling authorization services within a Razor Pages application
- Using roles and claims to authorize endpoints
- Creating authorization policies from requirements and handlers
- Authorizing access to resources

In the last chapter, you learned how to identify your users by asking them to authenticate themselves. Once authenticated, the user is no longer anonymous; they have an identity, which we can use to restrict access to various parts of the application. This process is known as *authorization*, and it is vital for securing parts of your application against users who should not have access to them.

Even the simplest dynamic web application is likely to include an area where the owner maintains the content—an admin area. That will need securing against unauthorized access, unless you want random users to start posting their own content, or worse: defacing or removing your existing content. More complex applications can require complex access policies where different users have different levels of authority over parts of the application. For example, you might allow a select number of users to add to the range of vacation locations offered by your website but further restrict who can manage prices. Customers will be able to book vacations and see details of their own orders, but only administrators can see details of all orders. Super admins might be the only people who can change parts of an order.

At the simplest level, you can secure parts of your application, so only authenticated users can access them. You will start off by learning how to do that for single pages, or endpoints. You will also look at securing all pages in a specific folder or across the entire application. Then you will explore some of the features provided by ASP.NET Core Identity for managing authorization on a more granular level. You will look at grouping users together according to their role and managing access to endpoints on that basis. Then you will explore the notion of claims, introduced in the last chapter, in more detail and establish how you can formulate authorization policies based on claims and apply them for managing access to endpoints. Preventing access to endpoints is known as *request-based* authorization. While you learn how to create policies, you will understand how they are based on requirements and their handlers. You will write your own requirements and handlers and use them to formulate some policies.

Finally, you will look at implementing fine-grained authorization within a page. For example, many users may be authorized to access a page that lists properties to rent, but only selected users will be authorized to edit them. In that scenario, you do not want to present the Edit navigation to those users who do not have sufficient permissions. Applying authorization policies within a page like this is known as *resource-based* authorization.

I've always thought that authorization shares something in common with dependency injection. Both are actually relatively simple topics to understand, but both are shrouded in a fog of abstract concepts. Just as I hope to have lifted the fog in the chapter on dependency injection, I'm going to start by explaining some of the concepts surrounding authorization you will be working with.

10.1 Basic authorization in Razor Pages

Authorization within a Razor Pages application is provided by a number of services, including an `IAuthorizationService`. These must be added to the service container at application startup. A convenience method, `AddAuthorization`, takes care of adding all the required services:

```
builder.Services.AddAuthorization();
```

Authorization middleware is enabled by default in the web application template by the inclusion of `app.UseAuthorization()` in the `Program` class.

Authorization depends on knowing who the user is and what they are trying to do as well as, in the case of request-based authorization, which page they are trying to reach. As established in chapter 4, `EndpointRouting` middleware, which is added to the pipeline by `UseRouting`, is responsible for determining which page the user is trying to reach. In the last chapter, you learned that authentication middleware (added with `UseAuthentication`) is responsible for establishing who the user is. Finally, `MapRazorPages` is where the selected page is executed. This middleware flow is illustrated in figure 10.1.

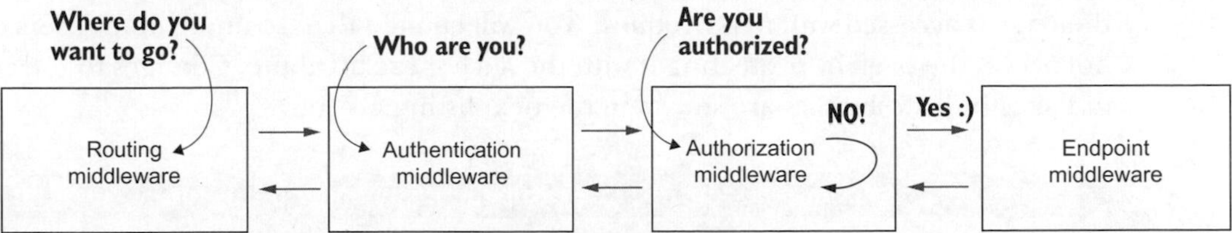

Figure 10.1 Middleware authorization order depends on knowing who the user is and where they are trying to go. If the user is not authorized, the pipeline is short-circuited. Otherwise, the request flows through to endpoint middleware, and the page is executed.

Given that you do not want to execute pages the current user is not authorized to access, the only logical position within the pipeline to place `UseAuthorization` is *after* `UseRouting` and `UseAuthentication` and *before* `MapRazorPages`. For that reason, authorization middleware must be placed after the authentication middleware and before the call to `MapRazorPages` (listing 10.1).

Listing 10.1 The position of `app.UseAuthorization` is critical

```
app.UseRouting();
app.UseAuthentication();
app.UseAuthorization();
app.MapRazorPages();
```

Routing and authentication middleware must be placed *before* authorization middleware.

Endpoint middleware must be placed *after* authorization middleware.

10.1.1 Applying simple authorization

You will use the `AuthorizeAttribute` to apply authorization to endpoints. The attribute has some properties, among which are `Roles` and `Policy`, which you will explore in more detail as you work through the chapter. At its most basic, when you apply the attribute to an endpoint, it prevents access to that endpoint to anonymous users. Users must authenticate to become authorized to proceed.

There are a number of ways you can apply the attribute to an endpoint. The simplest way to add it to the `PageModel` class.

NOTE Readers who are familiar with the MVC framework may be used to assigning the `Authorize` attribute to action methods within controllers. While `PageModel` handler methods are analogous to controller action methods, Razor Pages does not support assigning the `Authorize` attribute to handler methods. This makes sense if you think about it because you are authorizing the endpoint, regardless of the HTTP method used to access it. A Razor page represents a single endpoint, whereas an MVC controller, more often than not, is responsible for processing multiple endpoints.

At the moment, your Index page returns a `ChallengeResult` to anonymous users if the page is accessed with a `GET` request. You will change that, so anonymous users cannot access the page by protecting it with the `Authorize` attribute. Changes to the code in Pages\Index.cshtml.cs are shown in the next listing.

Listing 10.2 Applying the `Authorize` attribute to the home `PageModel`

```
using CityBreaks.Models;
using CityBreaks.Services;
using Microsoft.AspNetCore.Authorization;     <-- Add a using to bring in the Authorization API.
using Microsoft.AspNetCore.Mvc.RazorPages;

namespace CityBreaks.Pages
{
    [Authorize]     <-- Add the Authorize attribute to the PageModel class.
    public class IndexModel : PageModel
    {
        private readonly ICityService _cityService;

        public IndexModel(ICityService cityService) =>
            _cityService = cityService;

        public List<City> Cities { get; set; }
        public async Task OnGetAsync() =>
            Cities = await _cityService.GetAllAsync();     <-- Remove the check to see if the user is authenticated.
    }
}
```

When you launch the application, you will be directed to the login page, just as before. The authorization service is able to access the endpoint metadata for the requested page and determines that it requires an authorized user. It is also able to determine the current user is not authenticated, so the service itself returns a `ChallengeResult` (401 status code), resulting in the user being directed to log in. The `ChallengeResult` is one of three possible outcomes. If the user is authenticated but doesn't meet the specified authorization policy requirements, the authorization service returns a `ForbidResult` (403 status code). If the user is authorized, the middleware passes the request on to the next middleware in the pipeline (figure 10.2).

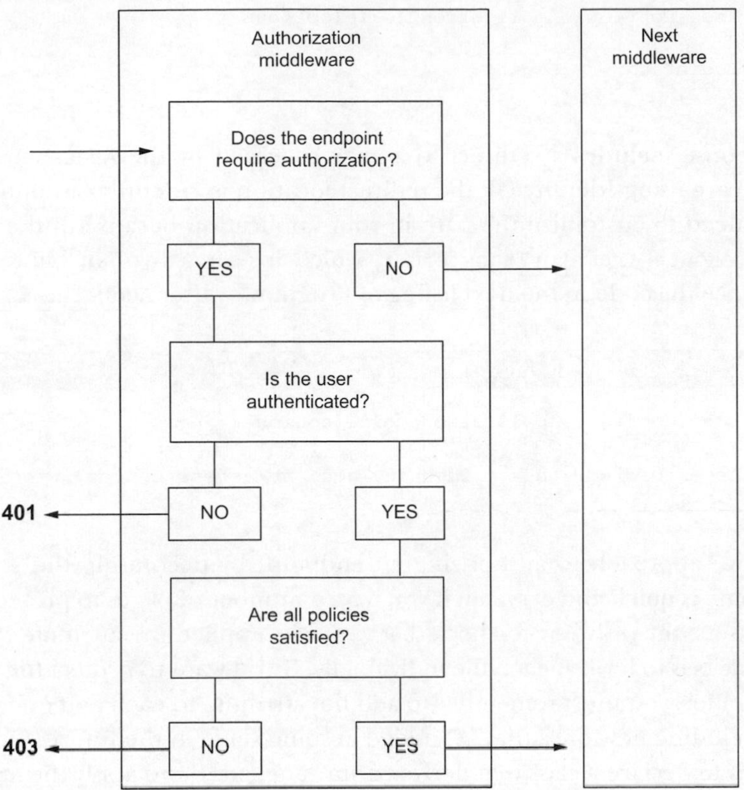

Figure 10.2 The decision making within the authorization middleware has one of three possible outcomes: 401 Challenge, 403 Forbidden, or pass the request on to the next middleware in the pipeline.

In a Razor Pages application, the 401 response includes an instruction to the browser to redirect to the login page, which, by default, is configured to be at /identity/account/login. If you are not using Identity, you can customize this using the `LoginPath` cookie option, as you saw in the last chapter:

```
builder.Services.AddAuthentication(CookieAuthenticationDefaults
➥ .AuthenticationScheme)
    .AddCookie(options =>
{
    options.LoginPath = "/Login";
});
```

When you are using Identity, you can customize the login path through the application cookie configuration. This customization should be placed after Identity services have been added to the container:

```
builder.Services.ConfigureApplicationCookie(options =>
{
    options.LoginPath = "/Login";
});
```

The 403 response includes a redirect to a page specified by the `AccessDeniedPath` option. If you are using Identity UI, the redirect location is /identity/account/access-denied. You need to customize the path in your application because of the effect of the `KebabPageRouteParameterTransformer`, which inserts a hyphen between *access* and *denied*. Place the code in the next listing in Program.cs after `AddDefaultIdentity`.

Listing 10.3 Customizing the `AccessDenied` path

```
builder.Services.ConfigureApplicationCookie(options =>
{
    options.AccessDeniedPath = "/identity/account/access-denied";
});
```

The declarative approach to authorizing an endpoint by decorating the `PageModel` with an attribute is quick and easy, but if you have a number of pages to protect against anonymous users, the only way to check that you have applied the attribute to the relevant `PageModels` is to look at each file individually. If you want to protect the contents of an entire folder, you must remember to add the attribute to each and every page in the folder, including new ones that get added at some stage in the future. One way to mitigate this is to declare a class that derives from `PageModel` and apply the `Authorize` attribute to it and then get all the pages in the folder to inherit from it. The following illustrates how you can achieve this with a class named `AdminPageModel`.

Listing 10.4 Using a `BasePage` to restrict access to derivatives

```
using Microsoft.AspNetCore.Authorization;
using Microsoft.AspNetCore.Mvc.RazorPages;

namespace CityBreaks.Pages
{
    [Authorize]
    public class AdminPageModel : PageModel
    {
    }
}
```

When you create a page that needs to be protected, you simply change the type it inherits from, so it derives from `AdminPageModel` and is automatically protected by the `Authorize` attribute:

```
public class CreateModel : AdminPageModel
```

This base-page approach is quite common, especially in older versions of .NET, but it still suffers from the problem that you need to remember to change your generated code to ensure the Razor page derives from your custom type rather than `PageModel`. You can always write unit tests that help enforce this (and they would be a good idea in any event).

Ideally, you want to centralize the code that applies authorization to endpoints, so you can tell, at a glance, which parts of the application are protected and to what degree. In chapter 4, you used some extension methods on the `PageConventionCollection` type to add new routes and page route model conventions to the routing system. Additional extension methods exist that enable you to apply authorization to individual pages and whole folders via conventions. Using these, you can establish your authorization rules in one place: the `Program` class. The key methods are

- `AuthorizePage`—Adds authorization to a single page
- `AuthorizeFolder`—Adds authorization to all pages in the specified folder
- `AuthorizeAreaFolder`—Adds authorization to all pages in the specified folder within the specified area

Each of these methods takes the name of the page, folder, and/or area and also includes an overload that takes the name of a *policy*. We will explore policies in detail a bit later. For now, you can think of policies as representing authorization requirements beyond just being authenticated. You can use the `AuthorizePage` method in Program.cs to replace the `Authorize` attribute you applied to the home page earlier.

Listing 10.5 Using the `AuthorizePage` method to apply authorization to a specific page

```
builder.Services.AddRazorPages(options => {
    options.Conventions.AuthorizePage("/Index");
    options.Conventions.Add(new CultureTemplatePageRouteModelConvention());
    options.Conventions.Add(new PageRouteTransformerConvention(new
     KebabPageRouteParameterTransformer()));
});
```

Using AuthorizePage with no policy has the same effect as applying a plain Authorize attribute to the endpoint PageModel.

You only want authorized users to be able to reach your CRUD admin pages in the various *Manager folders in the Pages directory. You can use the `AuthorizeFolder` method to immediately bar unauthenticated users from access, as in the following listing.

Listing 10.6 Authorizing folders with the `AuthorizeFolder` method

```
builder.Services.AddRazorPages(options => {
    options.Conventions.AuthorizeFolder("/CityManager");
    options.Conventions.AuthorizeFolder("/CountryManager");
    options.Conventions.AuthorizeFolder("/PropertyManager");
});
```

10.1.2 Allowing anonymous access

There may well be occasions when you want to bar anonymous access to most of an application's content but enable it for the odd page. For example, you might be developing an internal line-of-business application that needs to be locked down to prevent anonymous users from gaining access. You can do this by specifying a `FallbackPolicy` that requires authentication as part of configuring authorization services:

```
builder.Services.AddAuthorization(options => {
    options.FallbackPolicy = new AuthorizationPolicyBuilder().
        RequireAuthenticatedUser().Build();
});
```

The `FallbackPolicy` becomes the default authorization policy for the application wherever no other authorization policies are specified, such as through an attribute or a convention.

You still need users to be able to reach the login page to authenticate. For those instances, you can use the `AllowAnonymousAttribute`. Just like the `AuthorizeAttribute`, you can apply this to the `PageModel` class of the target endpoint:

```
[AllowAnonymous]
public class LoginModel : PageModel
```

Alternatively, you can combine the `AuthorizeFolder` method's application with the `AllowAnonymousToPage` method, which overrides the authorization for the specified page, allowing users to access it without having to be authenticated.

Listing 10.7 Allowing anonymous access to individual endpoints

```
builder.Services.AddRazorPages(options => {
    options.Conventions.AuthorizeFolder("/");                    // Prevent anonymous access to the application by default.
    options.Conventions.AllowAnonymousToPage("/Login");          // Allow anonymous access to the Login page in the protected folder.
});
```

So far we have looked at authorization that depends solely on whether the user is authenticated or not. In the real world, anything more than the simplest application will require finer-grained access controls. In the rest of the chapter, we will explore strategies to express those requirements and apply them to users.

10.2 Working with roles

Roles provide a simple mechanism for grouping together users who have the same level of access. They are most useful in applications that are unlikely to grow in complexity and where it is easy to differentiate the access needs of different groups of users. Identity includes support for roles, but it must be enabled by adding role-related services to the container with the AddRoles<TRole> method. IdentityRole is the default implementation representing a role:

```
builder.Services.AddDefaultIdentity<CityBreaksUser>(options => {
    options.Password.RequireDigit = false;
    options.Password.RequireLowercase = false;
    options.Password.RequireNonAlphanumeric = false;
    options.Password.RequireUppercase = false;
})
    .AddRoles<IdentityRole>()    <-- Use the AddRoles method to add role-related services to the application.
    .AddEntityFrameworkStores<CityBreaksContext>();
```

There is no UI for managing roles, so you have to build your own. The primary API for working with roles is the RoleManager<TRole> service, which was one of the services added to the service container by the AddRoles method. The RoleManager includes the following CRUD methods:

- CreateAsync
- UpdateAsync
- DeleteAsync

The RoleManager also includes a property, Roles, which returns all of the roles from the RoleStore. The RoleStore represents the storage mechanism for roles. In your case, that's the SQLite database. You won't work directly with the RoleStore, generally; you will use the RoleManager for that. In the next couple of sections, you will look at creating a simple admin area for creating and viewing roles with the RoleManager and assigning them to users.

10.2.1 Viewing roles

Start by adding a folder to the Pages folder named RolesManager. Within that, add a new Razor page named Index.cshtml. You will inject the RoleManager service into the PageModel class constructor and use its Roles property to populate a public List<IdentityRole> property.

Listing 10.8 The RolesManager IndexModel class

```
using Microsoft.AspNetCore.Identity;
using Microsoft.AspNetCore.Mvc.RazorPages;

namespace CityBreaks.Pages.RolesManager
{
    public class IndexModel : PageModel
    {
        private readonly RoleManager<IdentityRole> _roleManager;
        public IndexModel(RoleManager<IdentityRole> roleManager)
        {
            _roleManager  = roleManager;
        }
```

Inject the RoleManager<TRole> service into the IndexModel via its constructor, and assign it to a private field for later use.

```
        public List<IdentityRole> Roles { get; set; }
        public void OnGet()
        {
            Roles = _roleManager.Roles.ToList();
        }
    }
}
```

Declare a public List<IdentityRole> property, and use the RoleManager service to populate it with all your existing roles.

In the Razor page itself, check to see if there are any roles, and if so, display them in a table. The code for this is shown in the following listing.

Listing 10.9 Listing roles and displaying them in a table

```
@page
@model CityBreaks.Pages.RolesManager.IndexModel
@{
    ViewData["Title"] = "Roles";
}
<a asp-page="/RolesManager/Create">New</a>
@if (Model.Roles.Any())
{
    <table class="table">
        @foreach(var role in Model.Roles)
        {
            <tr>
                <td>@role.Name</td>
            </tr>
        }
    </table>
}
```

The code here shouldn't need any explanation by now. If you run the page, you will only see a link to create a new role. It goes nowhere because the page does not exist yet. That's your next job.

10.2.2 Adding roles

Add a new Razor page to the RolesManager folder, named Create. This will contain a form for creating a new role. The only piece of data you need for the role is a name. You inject the `RoleManager` service into the page and use its `CreateAsync` method to add the new role. Once again, the code should look similar to the CRUD pages you have already created. The following listing shows the code for the `PageModel` class.

Listing 10.10 The `CreateModel` for the RolesManager

```
using Microsoft.AspNetCore.Identity;
using Microsoft.AspNetCore.Mvc;
using Microsoft.AspNetCore.Mvc.RazorPages;

namespace CityBreaks.Pages.RolesManager
{
```

```
    public class CreateModel : PageModel
    {
        private readonly RoleManager<IdentityRole> _roleManager;
        public CreateModel(RoleManager<IdentityRole> roleManager)
        {
            _roleManager = roleManager;
        }

        [BindProperty]
        public string Name { get; set; }
        public async Task<IActionResult> OnPostAsync()
        {
            if (ModelState.IsValid)
            {
                var role = new IdentityRole { Name = Name };
                await _roleManager.CreateAsync(role);
                return RedirectToPage("/RolesManager/Index");
            }
            return Page();
        }
    }
}
```

Next you add a form to the Razor page itself.

Listing 10.11 The Create Role form

```
@page
@model CityBreaks.Pages.RolesManager.CreateModel
@{
    ViewData["Title"] = "Create Role";
}
<h4>Create Role</h4>

<div class="row">
    <div class="col-md-8">
        <form method="post">
              <div class="form-group mb-3">
                <label asp-for="Name" class="control-label"></label>
                <input asp-for="Name" class="form-control" />
                <span asp-validation-for="Name" class="text-danger"></span>
            </div>
            <div class="form-group">
                <input type="submit" value="Assign" class="btn btn-primary" />
            </div>
        </form>
    </div>
</div>

@section scripts{
<partial name="_ValidationScriptsPartial" />
}
```

Now run the application, and navigate to /roles-manager/create. Add a role named `Admin`, and once you are happy that works, add two more roles named `CityAdmin` and `PropertyAdmin`.

10.2.3 Assigning roles to users

Before you can assign roles to users, you need some users. Register three users in the application with the following email addresses and, for simplicity, the same password. I have used *password* in the code download that accompanies this chapter:

- anna@test.com
- colin@test.com
- paul@test.com

Next, add a new Razor page to the RolesManager folder named Assign. In this page, you will obtain a list of all users and a list of all roles and present them in select lists that will be used to assign the selected user to the selected role. Change the `AssignModel` code to the code in the following listing.

Listing 10.12 The `AssignModel` code

```
using CityBreaks.Models;
using Microsoft.AspNetCore.Identity;
using Microsoft.AspNetCore.Mvc;
using Microsoft.AspNetCore.Mvc.RazorPages;
using Microsoft.AspNetCore.Mvc.Rendering;
using Microsoft.EntityFrameworkCore;
using System.ComponentModel.DataAnnotations;

namespace CityBreaks.Pages.RolesManager
{
    public class AssignModel : PageModel
    {
        private readonly RoleManager<IdentityRole> _roleManager;
        private readonly UserManager<CityBreaksUser> _userManager;
        public AssignModel(RoleManager<IdentityRole>
        ➥ roleManager, UserManager<CityBreaksUser> userManager)
        {
            _roleManager = roleManager;
            _userManager = userManager;
        }
        public SelectList Roles { get; set; }
        public SelectList Users { get; set; }
        [BindProperty, Required, Display(Name ="Role")]
        public string SelectedRole { get; set; }
        [BindProperty, Required, Display(Name ="User")]
        public string SelectedUser { get; set; }
        public async Task OnGet()
        {
            await GetOptions();
        }
```

Inject the UserManager and RoleManager services into the PageModel class.

```
    public async Task<IActionResult> OnPostAsync()
    {
        if (ModelState.IsValid)
        {
            var user = await _userManager.FindByNameAsync(SelectedUser);
            await _userManager.AddToRoleAsync(user, SelectedRole);
            return RedirectToPage("/RolesManager/Index");
        }
        await GetOptions();
        return Page();
    }

    public async Task GetOptions()
    {
        var roles = await _roleManager.Roles.ToListAsync();
        var users = await _userManager.Users.ToListAsync();
        Roles = new SelectList(roles, nameof(IdentityRole.Name));
        Users = new SelectList(users, nameof(CityBreaksUser.UserName));
    }
  }
}
```

Get the user with the selected name.

Assigns the selected user to the selected role.

Declare a private method that assigns users and roles to SelectList object.

The Razor page itself contains two select elements within a form, shown in the following listing.

Listing 10.13 Assigning users to the Role form

```
@page
@model CityBreaks.Pages.RolesManager.AssignModel
@{
}
<h4>Assign User To Role</h4>

<div class="row">
    <div class="col-md-8">
        <form method="post">
            <div class="form-group mb-3">
                <label asp-for="SelectedUser" class="control-label"></label>
                <select asp-for="SelectedUser" asp-items="Model.Users"
                ➥ class="form-control">
                    <option></option>
                </select>
                <span asp-validation-for="SelectedUser"
                ➥ class="text-danger"></span>
            </div>
            <div class="form-group mb-3">
                <label asp-for="SelectedRole" class="control-label"></label>
                <select asp-for="SelectedRole"
                ➥ asp-items="Model.Roles" class="form-control">
                    <option></option>
                </select>
                <span asp-validation-for="SelectedRole"
                ➥ class="text-danger"></span>
            </div>
```

```
            <div class="form-group">
                <input type="submit" value="Assign"
                ➥ class="btn btn-primary" />
            </div>
        </form>
    </div>
</div>

@section scripts{
<partial name="_ValidationScriptsPartial" />
}
```

Once this is done, launch the application, and navigate to /roles-manager/assign. Assign anna@test.com to the `Admin` role. Having done that, go back to the Assign .cshtml file and add a `using` directive for `Microsoft.AspNetCore.Authorization`. Then add an `Authorize` attribute to the `AssignModel` class, but this time, assign `"Admin"` as the value in the `Roles` property:

```
[Authorize(Roles = "Admin")]
public class AssignModel : PageModel
{
```

Rerun the application, and this time, sign in using either colin@test.com or paul@test.com. Then attempt to navigate to /roles-manager/assign. You should find you are redirected to the Access Denied page.

Log out, and then sign in with anna@test.com. This time, when you navigate to roles-manager/assign, you should access the page. Anna can access the page because she is a member of the role specified in the `Roles` property, whereas Paul is not. Although you have only passed one role name in, the `Roles` property takes a comma-separated list of role names, which provides an element of flexibility when using roles. In addition, users can belong to more than one role.

10.2.4 Using policies to apply role checks

You have extended the `Authorize` attribute to check that the current user belongs to the specified role. If you want to apply this check over the contents of an entire folder, you can use an overload of the `AuthorizeFolder` method that takes a *policy*; we will look at policies in more detail soon. Still, you can consider a policy as representing the requirements that need to be satisfied to determine whether the current user is authorized to access the requested endpoint.

For relatively simple policies, you can use `AuthorizeOptions` within the `AddAuthorization` method to configure a role-based policy. The `AddPolicy` method takes the name of the policy and an `AuthorizationPolicyBuilder`, which has a `RequireRole` method, enabling you to state which roles are required.

Listing 10.14 Configuring a role-based policy in Program.cs

```
builder.Services.AddAuthorization(options =>
{
    options.AddPolicy("AdminPolicy",
    ➥ policyBuilder => policyBuilder.RequireRole("Admin"));
});
```

Having configured the policy named `AdminPolicy`, you can apply it to the `AuthorizeFolder` method to ensure only members of the `Admin` role can access the content:

```
builder.Services.AddRazorPages(options => {
    options.Conventions.AuthorizeFolder("/RolesManager", "AdminPolicy");
});
```

As I noted at the beginning of this section, roles are useful for relatively simple authorization requirements, where access policies can be applied to groups of users. Users either are members of a role or they aren't. Roles have a benefit in that they are easy to configure and manage.

If your application's authorization requirements increase in complexity, you will begin to find an increasingly complex collection of roles difficult to manage. At that point, rather than managing authorization based on predefined groups of users, you will want to control authorization based on what you know about the individual user. The mechanism you will use to determine this is called *claims*.

10.3 Claims-based authorization

We touched on claims in the last chapter, but as a refresher, claims are simply name-value pairs that represent items of data you know about the user. They are attached to a `ClaimsIdentity`, which is then attached to the `ClaimsPrincipal` (see figure 10.3).

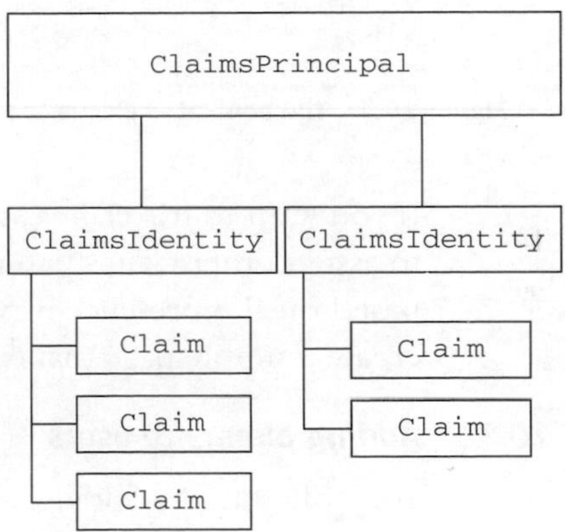

Figure 10.3 A `ClaimsPrincipal` supports multiple identities, each supporting multiple claims.

Within .NET claims are represented by the `Claim` class. Among its properties are `Type`, `Value`, and `Issuer`. The last of these, the `Issuer`, is the authority that issued the claim. When you assign claims to users in your application, the issuer is `LOCAL_AUTHORITY`, by default. If you incorporate external authentication providers, like Google or Facebook, in your application, they will issue any claims they add to the identity they authenticate. You can choose which version of a claim to use, based on how much weight you give the issuer. For example, an external authentication service like Facebook may well prove an email claim, but the email address may not exist.

There is no limit imposed on what the `Type` represents. Widely used claim types are represented by URIs at the domain schemas.xmlsoap.org. It would be unreasonable to expect developers to use these URIs in their code, so for convenience, they are represented in .NET by a collection of constants in the `ClaimTypes` class. Table 10.1 shows the claim types you are most likely to find yourself working with.

Table 10.1 Commonly used claim types

Claim type	Description
`ClaimTypes.Name`	Represents the username of the user
`ClaimTypes.Email`	Used for the user's email address
`ClaimTypes.GivenName`	The user's first name
`ClaimTypes.Surname`	The user's last name
`ClaimTypes.NameIdentifier`	The user's unique identifier

When the user is authenticated in your application and has a `ClaimsIdentity` assigned to it, the authentication system adds various claims to it. These include the `Name`, `Email` and, `NameIdentifier` (figure 10.4).

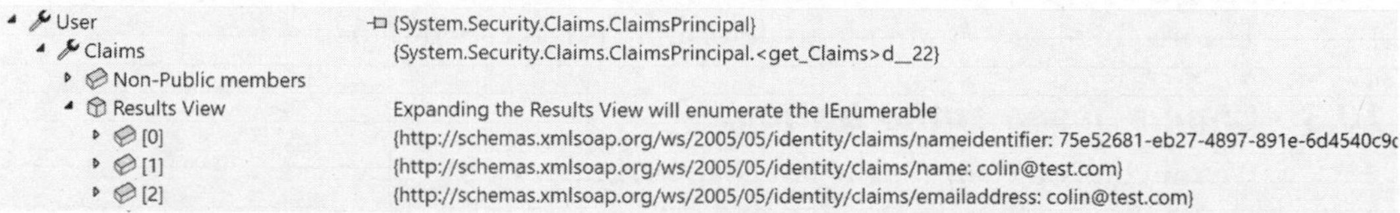

Figure 10.4 The populated claims of an authenticated user

If you want to use claims as the basis for managing authorization, you need some way to assign other claims that relate to levels of access and test whether the user qualifies based on the presence or value of the claims they have. In the next section, you will create a simple page that enables adding new claims to users.

10.3.1 *Adding claims to users*

You will start by adding a new folder to the Pages folder named ClaimsManager. Within that, you will add a new Razor page named Index. This will list all users who have additional claims assigned to them and details of the claims that have been assigned.

The `PageModel` code for the ClaimsManager Index page takes the `UserManager` as an injected dependency and assigns it to a `public` property, so it is accessible to the Razor part of the page via its `Model` property. It is also used within the `OnGetAsync` method to populate a collection of `CityBreaksUser` objects.

Listing 10.15 The `IndexModel` class for the claims manager section of the application

```
using CityBreaks.Models;
using Microsoft.AspNetCore.Identity;
using Microsoft.AspNetCore.Mvc.RazorPages;
using Microsoft.EntityFrameworkCore;

namespace CityBreaks.Pages.ClaimsManager
{
    public class IndexModel : PageModel
    {
        public UserManager<CityBreaksUser> UserManager { get; set; }
        public IndexModel(UserManager<CityBreaksUser> userManager)
        {
            UserManager = userManager;
        }
        public List<CityBreaksUser> Users { get; set; }
        public async Task OnGetAsync()
        {
            Users = await UserManager.Users.ToListAsync();
        }
    }
}
```

The Razor page iterates over the collection of users and obtains their claims via the `UserManager.GetClaimsAsync` method. This method communicates with the data store, so it only returns claims that have been stored in the database within the `AspNetUserClaims` table. The resulting data does not include the claims assigned by, for example, the authentication service. If any stored claims are found, details of them are rendered to the screen.

Listing 10.16 The `ClaimsManager` index page

```
@page
@model CityBreaks.Pages.ClaimsManager.IndexModel
@{
    ViewData["Title"] = "User Claims";
}
<h4>User Claims</h4>
<a class="btn btn-success" asp-page="/ClaimsManager/Assign">New</a>
@foreach (var user in Model.Users)
{
    var claims = await Model.UserManager.GetClaimsAsync(user);
    if (claims.Any())
    {
        <h5>@user.UserName</h5>
        <table class="table-striped col-12">
            <tr>
                <th>Type</th>
                <th>Value</th>
                <th>Issuer</th>
            </tr>
            @foreach (var claim in claims)
            {
```

```
                <tr>
                    <td>@claim.Type</td>
                    <td>@claim.Value</td>
                    <td>@claim.Issuer</td>
                </tr>
            }
        </table>
    }
}
```

It is worth noting that the preceding code includes something you should avoid for your production application. That is an example of the *N + 1 problem*—so called because the code makes one database call for the users (in the `OnGetAsync` method) and then *N* further calls to the database, where *N* represents the number of results retrieved in the first call. Each time `GetClaimsAsync` is executed, a database query is issued. Depending on your application, that could hurt performance terribly if you have a lot of data and/or concurrent users. If you ever find yourself needing to iterate over the claims of all users, you should consider writing your own SQL to obtain all the relevant data in one call.

When you run this page for the first time, all the database calls are made, but there is no data to be displayed, so you will only be presented with the button inviting you to add a new claim. It goes nowhere at the moment because you have yet to create the page.

Add a new page to the ClaimsManager folder named Assign. This page will feature a list of users in a select list and inputs for a claim type and value. You will use this page to create claims and assign them to users. The `UserManager` is injected into the `AssignModel` constructor and used to populate a `SelectList` containing the `Id` and `name` of each user. The selection will be bound to the `SelectedUserId` property. Two further bound properties are added, representing the claim type and value.

Listing 10.17 The `AssignModel` code for adding claims to users

```
using CityBreaks.Models;
using Microsoft.AspNetCore.Identity;
using Microsoft.AspNetCore.Mvc;
using Microsoft.AspNetCore.Mvc.RazorPages;
using Microsoft.AspNetCore.Mvc.Rendering;
using Microsoft.EntityFrameworkCore;
using System.ComponentModel.DataAnnotations;
using System.Security.Claims;

namespace CityBreaks.Pages.ClaimsManager
{
    public class AssignModel : PageModel
    {
        private readonly UserManager<CityBreaksUser> _userManager;
        public AssignModel(UserManager<CityBreaksUser> userManager)
        {
            _userManager = userManager;
        }
```

```
        public SelectList Users { get; set; }
        [BindProperty, Required, Display(Name = "User")]
        public string SelectedUserId { get; set; }
        [BindProperty, Required, Display(Name ="Claim Type")]
        public string ClaimType { get; set; }
        [BindProperty, Display(Name = "Claim Value")]
        public string ClaimValue { get; set; }
        public async Task OnGetAsync()
        {
            await GetOptions();
        }

        public async Task<IActionResult> OnPostAsync()
        {
            if (ModelState.IsValid)
            {
                var claim = new Claim(ClaimType, ClaimValue ?? String.Empty);
                var user = await _userManager.FindByIdAsync(SelectedUserId);
                await _userManager.AddClaimAsync(user, claim);
                return RedirectToPage("/ClaimsManager/Index");
            }
            await GetOptions();
            return Page();
        }

        public async Task GetOptions()
        {
            var users = await _userManager.Users.ToListAsync();
            Users = new SelectList(users,
            ➥ nameof(CityBreaksUser.Id), nameof(CityBreaksUser.UserName));
        }
    }
}
```

You use the AddClaimAsync method of the UserManager to assign additional claims to the user. It takes a user and a claim as arguments. You use the bound properties to construct those. This time, because you are binding the user's unique identifiers to the select list, you use the FindByIdAsync method to get the user from the UserManager. Remember, you used FindByNameAsync previously. You construct a new claim from the type and value passed in. Claims don't have to have a value assigned, but the value cannot be null, so you pass in String.Empty if no value is provided. Once the claim is added, you are directed to the Index page, where you can see your new claim displayed.

Run the application, and navigate to /claims-manager/assign. Add a new claim to anna@test.com. The type should be Admin, and the value should be left empty (figure 10.5). Having assigned a claim, the next step is to use it as part of an authorization policy.

anna@test.com

Type	Value
Admin	
Joining Date	2018-3-9
Permission	View Roles

colin@test.com

Type	Value
Joining Date	2020-8-22

paul@test.com

Type	Value
Joining Date	2021-9-15
Permission	View Roles

Figure 10.5 List of claims assigned to the user

10.3.2 Using policies to enforce claims-based authorization

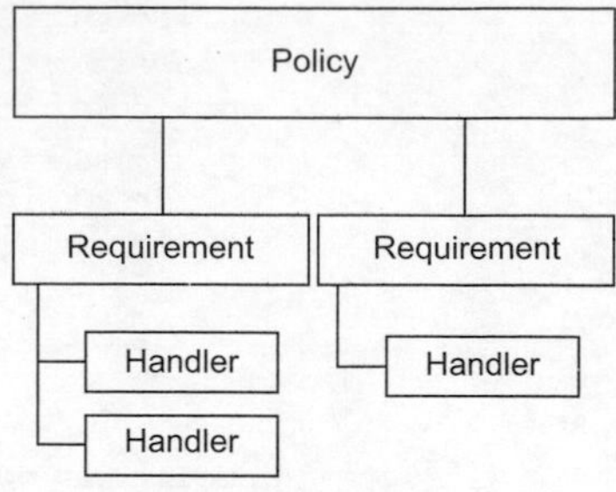

Figure 10.6 Policies consist of one or more requirements, each having one or more handlers.

Claims-based authorization is dependent on *policies,* which I've touched on before. A policy consists of one or more *requirements.* Authorization is granted when all of the requirements in a policy have been met. It is the job of one or more *authorization handlers* to evaluate whether each requirement within the policy has been satisfied (figure 10.6).

Using this pattern, it is possible to build complex authorization policies that enable fine-grained control over who can reach which parts of an application. In addition to protecting endpoints, it is also possible to apply authorization policies within a Razor page itself, so, for example, you can toggle the visibility of parts of the UI, depending on the current user's claims.

When you used the `AuthorizationPolicyBuilder.RequireRole` method earlier, a requirement of type `RolesAuthorizationRequirement` was created that specifies that the nominated role is required. Other methods are available on the `AuthorizationPolicyBuilder` that enable you to express common policies simply by using other built-in requirements and handlers (table 10.2).

Table 10.2 Common methods for building simple policies

Method	Description
`RequireClaim(string claimtype)`	The user must have the specified claim.
`RequireClaim(string claimtype, params string[] allowedValues)` or `RequireClaim(string claimtype, IEmumerable<string> allowedValues)`	The user must have the specified claim with one of the specified values.
`RequireUserName`	The user must have the specified name.
`RequireAuthenticatedUser`	The user must be authenticated.
`RequireAssertion`	Takes a delegate that represents an assertion to be tested to determine authorization status.

The variations of the `RequireClaim` method create a `ClaimsAuthorizationRequirement` with a handler that returns `true` if the specified claim exists and, if values are specified, that at least one of them is found. You can test this by changing the code for the existing policy to use the `RequireClaim` method instead of `RequireRole`:

```
builder.Services.AddAuthorization(options =>
{
```

```
    options.AddPolicy("AdminPolicy", policyBuilder =>
    ➥ policyBuilder.RequireClaim("Admin"));
});
```

You can also apply this policy to pages individually by passing the name of the policy to the Policy property of the AuthorizeAttribute:

```
[Authorize(Policy="AdminPolicy")]
public IndexModel : PageModel
{
    ...
}
```

10.3.3 Using assertions for more complex requirements

The RequireAssertion method is provided to handle more complex requirements than the other methods can handle. For example, let's say you want to implement a requirement stating a user can access the roles management area if they have a claim with a particular value, but only if they have been with the business for more than six months. To be able to determine this, you will record the user's joining date as a claim. Then you need to convert the value to a DateTime and compare it to the current date to determine how long the user has been with the business.

To demonstrate this, examine the claims illustrated in figure 10.7. Note that, at the time of writing, Paul's joining date is less than six months ago, whereas the other users' joining dates are more than six months ago. If you want to replicate this exercise, it is important that you enter dates that meet the same criteria. Only Anna and Paul have a Permission claim with the value View Roles.

The RequireAssertion method takes an AuthorizationHandlerContext as a parameter, as shown in listing 10.18. This type provides you with access to the current user through its User property. From that, you can examine their claims. In the following code, you ensure the user has a claim named Permission and that its value is View Roles. Then you attempt to retrieve the value of a claim named Joining Date and convert it to a DateTime, so you can test its value based on your authorization requirement.

anna@test.com

Type	Value
Admin	
Joining Date	2018-3-9
Permission	View Roles

colin@test.com

Type	Value
Joining Date	2020-8-22

paul@test.com

Type	Value
Joining Date	2021-9-15
Permission	View Roles

Figure 10.7 The joining date and permission claims assigned to the users

Listing 10.18 RequireAssertion for more complex authorization requirements

```
builder.Services.AddAuthorization(options =>
{
    options.AddPolicy("ViewRolesPolicy", policyBuilder =>
        policyBuilder.RequireAssertion(context =>
        {
```

Use the RequireAssertion method, which takes an AuthorizationHandlerContext as a parameter providing access to the current user.

```
        var joiningDateClaim = context.User.FindFirst(c =>
        ➥ c.Type == "Joining Date")?.Value;
        var joiningDate = Convert.ToDateTime(
        ➥ joiningDateClaim);
        return context.User.HasClaim("Permission",
        ➥ "View Roles") &&
            joiningDate > DateTime.MinValue &&
            joiningDate < DateTime.Now.AddMonths(-6);
    }));
});
```

Use the FindFirst method to access a claim and obtain its value (if there is one) and convert it to a DateTime.

Use the HasClaim method to establish that a claim with the specified value exists.

Compare the joining date value with DateTime.MinValue and the current date to ensure the claim is not null and the date is earlier than six months ago.

The built-in requirements and handlers should cover most common authorization requirements. If you have a lot of complex authorization policies you want to apply to your application, your `Program` class will fill up pretty quickly with multiple assertions. At that point, you can move the code out of authorization configuration and into separate classes by writing your own custom requirements and handlers.

10.3.4 Custom authorization requirements and handlers

Authorization requirement classes implement the `IAuthorizationRequirement` interface. It is an empty marker interface, defining no members. Handlers are represented by the `IAuthorizationHandler` interface, which defines the `HandleAsync` method that takes an `AuthorizationHandlerContext` object as a parameter and returns a `Task`. The logic for handling the requirement is placed in this method.

Requirements can have multiple handlers, but where there is a one-to-one relationship between the requirement and a handler, it is common to see the code for both placed in the same class, which implements both interfaces. The following example illustrates how to migrate the assertion you created earlier into such a class, which takes a parameter representing the number of months. Add a new folder to the project with the name AuthorizationRequirement, and then add a new class named `ViewRolesRequirement` with the code in the following listing.

Listing 10.19 A custom requirement with in-built handler

```
using Microsoft.AspNetCore.Authorization;

namespace CityBreaks.AuthorizationRequirements
{
    public class ViewRolesRequirement :
    ➥ IAuthorizationRequirement, IAuthorizationHandler
    {
        public int Months { get; }
        public ViewRolesRequirement(int months)
        {
            Months = months > 0 ? 0 : months;
        }

        public Task HandleAsync(
        ➥ AuthorizationHandlerContext context)
```

The class implements both the IAuthorizationRequirement and IAuthorizationHandler interfaces.

The constructor takes an int as a parameter and ensures it is not a positive number.

The HandleAsync method is implemented as required by the IAuthorization-Handler interface.

```
        {
            var joiningDateClaim = context.User.
            ➥ FindFirst(c => c.Type == "Joining Date")?.Value;
            if(joiningDateClaim == null)
            {
                return Task.CompletedTask;
            }
            var joiningDate = Convert.ToDateTime(
            ➥ joiningDateClaim);
            if(context.User.HasClaim("Permission",
            ➥ "View Roles") &&
                joiningDate > DateTime.MinValue &&
                joiningDate < DateTime.Now.AddMonths(
                ➥ Months))
            {
                context.Succeed(this);
            }
            return Task.CompletedTask;
        }
    }
}
```

The user is checked to see if they have a joiningDateClaim. If not, the handler is exited.

The joining date is assessed to see if it exists and if its value is older than the age passed in.

If the requirement is not satisfied, Task.CompletedTask is returned to satisfy the HandleAsync method signature.

The requirement is satisfied if it is marked as being successfully evaluated. This is achieved by calling the `Succeed` method of the `AuthorizationHandlerContext` class. This class also offers a `Fail` method, which you can call to ensure authorization is not successful. You would use this method if your handler allowed all users *except* those that meet the specified condition, for example. You use the `PolicyBuilder` to register the policy, passing in a suitable value for the `months` parameter.

Listing 10.20 Registering a custom requirement

```
builder.Services.AddAuthorization(options =>
{
    options.AddPolicy("ViewRolesPolicy", policyBuilder =>
        policyBuilder.AddRequirements(new ViewRolesRequirement(months: -6)));
});
```

CREATING A SEPARATE HANDLER CLASS

Building a combined requirement and handler is fine for simple use cases, but more often, you may want to create your handler as a separate class to enable reuse. When you do this, there are a couple of changes you need to make to your general approach. The existing requirement itself is trimmed down to just an implementation of `IAuthorizationRequirement`.

Listing 10.21 The standalone requirement class

```
public class ViewRolesRequirement : IAuthorizationRequirement
{
    public int Months { get; }
```

```
    public ViewRolesRequirement(int months)
    {
        Months = months > 0 ? 0 : months;
    }
}
```

Create a new folder named AuthorizationHandlers, and add a new class to it named `ViewRolesHandler`. This is the separate handler class. It implements `IAuthorizationHandler`. Since the handler class itself isn't scoped to a specific requirement, you have to access the `PendingRequirements` property of the `AuthorizationHandlerContext` to filter to the right type of requirement. The `PendingRequirements` property gets all the requirements that have yet to be marked as succeeded.

Listing 10.22 The `ViewRolesHandler` separated into a class

```
public class ViewRolesHandler : IAuthorizationHandler
{
    public Task HandleAsync(AuthorizationHandlerContext context)
    {
        foreach (var requirement in
        ➥ context.PendingRequirements.ToList())
        {
            if (requirement is ViewRolesRequirement req)
            {
                var joiningDateClaim =
                ➥ context.User.FindFirst(c => c.Type ==
                ➥ "Joining Date")?.Value;
                if (joiningDateClaim == null)
                {
                    return Task.CompletedTask;
                }
                var joiningDate = Convert.ToDateTime(joiningDateClaim);

                if (context.User.HasClaim("Permission", "View Roles") &&
                        joiningDate < DateTime.Now.AddMonths(req.Months))
                {
                    context.Succeed(requirement);
                }
            }
        }
        return Task.CompletedTask;
    }
}
```

The PendingRequirements return all unsatisfied requirements. They need to be assigned to a list, so you can execute operations against them.

Use pattern matching to identify ViewRolesRequirements and assign them to a local variable.

The final difference between this approach and the combined requirement-handler is that you need to register the handler with the service container as an implementation of `IAuthorizationHandler`:

```
builder.Services.AddSingleton<IAuthorizationHandler, ViewRolesHandler>();
```

Once you have done this, the authorization policy works in the same way as the previous approach that employed the combined requirement-handler combo.

USING MULTIPLE HANDLERS FOR A REQUIREMENT

As I mentioned before, requirements can have multiple handlers. This is usually the case when there are alternative ways of satisfying the requirement. Suppose users can view roles if they have the `Permission` claim with the value `View Roles` and have been with the business for at least six months, *or* they're in the `Admin` role. Now you have two alternative ways to authorize the user. You could add more code to the existing handler to check whether the user is in the specified role, but there would be a possibility of that code growing into a mess as more alternatives arise over time. Instead, you will implement an additional handler for your `ViewRolesRequirement`. This time, however, you will take an alternative approach to crafting the handler that types it specifically to the requirement and, therefore, negates the need to filter all pending requirements.

You will derive from the abstract `AuthorizationHandler<TRequirement>` class, where `TRequirement` represents the requirement type the handler is designed for. The handler logic is placed in an overridden `HandleRequirementAsync` method which, in addition to an `AuthorizationHandlerContext`, takes the requirement type as a parameter. The following listing shows the claims check refactored into an `AuthorizationHandler<TRequirement>` class named `HasClaimHandler`, which is placed in a folder named AuthorizationHandlers.

Listing 10.23 Handling authorization requirements

```
using CityBreaks.AuthorizationRequirements;
using Microsoft.AspNetCore.Authorization;

namespace CityBreaks.AuthorizationHandlers
{
    public class HasClaimHandler : AuthorizationHandler<ViewRolesRequirement>
    {
        protected override Task
     HandleRequirementAsync(AuthorizationHandlerContext context,
            ViewRolesRequirement req)
        {
            var joiningDateClaim =
            ➥ context.User.FindFirst(c => c.Type == "Joining Date")?.Value;
            if (joiningDateClaim == null)
            {
                return Task.CompletedTask;
            }
            var joiningDate = Convert.ToDateTime(joiningDateClaim);

            if (context.User.HasClaim("Permission", "View Roles") &&
                joiningDate < DateTime.Now.AddMonths(req.Months))
            {
                context.Succeed(req);
            }
            return Task.CompletedTask;
```

```
            }
        }
    }
```

Next you add a new class named `IsInRoleHandler`, which is responsible for handling the additional condition for authorization. The code is very similar to the previous handler.

Listing 10.24 The `IsInRoleHandler`

```
using CityBreaks.AuthorizationRequirements;
using Microsoft.AspNetCore.Authorization;

namespace CityBreaks.AuthorizationHandlers
{
    public class IsInRoleHandler : AuthorizationHandler<ViewRolesRequirement>
    {
        protected override Task
        ➥ HandleRequirementAsync(AuthorizationHandlerContext context,
            ViewRolesRequirement req)
        {
            if (context.User.IsInRole("Admin"))
            {
                context.Succeed(req);
            }
            return Task.CompletedTask;
        }
    }
}
```

Both handlers need to be registered with the service container:

```
builder.Services.AddSingleton<IAuthorizationHandler, IsInRoleHandler>();
builder.Services.AddSingleton<IAuthorizationHandler, HasClaimHandler>();
```

These registrations should replace the existing handler registration; otherwise, it will be evaluated as well. Handlers that implement `IAuthorizationHandler` are processed for every requirement, whereas those typed to a specific requirement only execute for that type of requirement.

To test this new arrangement out, remove the `Permission` claim from Anna, so she only has the `Admin` role and the `Joining date` claim. You can do this directly using a database management tool. Then run the application, and log in as her. You should find she is still able to access the Roles folder contents.

10.3.5 Roles or claims?

We've explored two ways to establish whether a user is authorized: based on the role they are in or the claims they possess. But which approach should you favor? Roles have been part of ASP.NET since before the release of Identity, when the user management system revolved around a `Membership` framework. They are a pretty simple concept to grasp, but they are designed to work with groups of users and are intended to represent what those groups of users can do. The emphasis shifted to one that is claims-based when Identity was introduced. Claims describe what a user is, rather than what they can do. Even the `IsInRole` method you have been using checks for a specific claim.

The general advice is to favor claims over roles. Claims offer much more flexibility than roles, which were primarily included in Identity for backward compatibility reasons. Having said that, there is at least one area where roles can still provide value: as a mechanism for bulk-assigning claims to users.

We looked at the schema of the Identity tables last chapter. One of the created tables we didn't explore at the time is the `AspNetRoleClaims` table. This table holds claims and their values that have been assigned to a role rather than an individual user. Any user placed in the specified role automatically acquires all the related claims.

The `RoleManager` class has an `AddClaimsAsync` method, which takes an `IdentityRole` object and a `Claim` as arguments and adds them to this table. Using the existing ClaimsManager/Assign page as a basis, create an additional page called AssignToRole that uses this method to add claims to a role. The main differences between the original Assign page and this new one is that the new one will take a `RoleManager<IdentityRoles>` as a dependency instead of a `UserManager<CityBreaksUser>`. You will use the `RoleManager.Roles` property to get a list of roles for the select list and the `FindByIdAsync` method to hydrate a role from the selected identity value. The rest is up to you, dear reader. If you get stuck, check the downloads for this chapter for a working version.

10.4 Authorizing resources

So far we have concentrated on authorizing endpoints (pages). A user is either authorized to access an endpoint, or they aren't. Sometimes you will want to perform authorization based on a resource that is exposed at the endpoint. For example, you might have a situation in which any authorized user can add a new property (the resource), but only the creator can edit a property. That means both you and I can add properties, but you cannot edit mine, and I cannot edit yours. To apply this kind of authorization, you need to know who created the property. That can only be done by executing the endpoint and loading the property from the database. In this section, you will look at how to approach this task using an authorization handler that takes the resource as a parameter.

Before you can do that, you need to assign creators to properties. Open the `Property` class, and add the following two properties:

```
public string CreatorId { get; set; }
public CityBreaksUser Creator { get; set; }
```

The `CreatorId` is a string property because it will hold the user's identity value. By default, that is a GUID. Add a new migration named `AddedCreatorToProperty`:

```
[Powershell]
add-migration AddedCreatorToProperty
[CLI]
dotnet ef migrations add AddedCreatorToProperty
```

Apply the migration, and then update a number of properties in the database, so the `CreatorId` column contains the `Id` value of your users. I manually applied the `Id` of my three users to the first 20 records in the database table (figure 10.8). Once this has been done, you are ready to go.

Table: Properties

	Id	Address	AvailableFrom	CityId	CreatorId
	Filter	Filter	Filter	Filter	Filter
1	1	Rue de Reynard	0001-01-01 0...	10	beed5675-3a02-4e58-893c-72a2d823f558
2	2	Vester Volgade	0001-01-01 0...	4	75e52681-eb27-4897-891e-6d4540c9c85a
3	3	The Strand	0001-01-01 0...	7	beed5675-3a02-4e58-893c-72a2d823f558
4	4	Carrer Dels Ta...	0001-01-01 0...	2	54e7e011-a0eb-4e72-9337-075a629985d7
5	5	Kurfürstenstra...	0001-01-01 0...	3	54e7e011-a0eb-4e72-9337-075a629985d7
6	6	Calle dei Merc...	0001-01-01 0...	12	beed5675-3a02-4e58-893c-72a2d823f558
7	7	Calle del Amp...	0001-01-01 0...	8	75e52681-eb27-4897-891e-6d4540c9c85a
8	8	Cowgate	0001-01-01 0...	6	beed5675-3a02-4e58-893c-72a2d823f558
9	9	Magstraede	0001-01-01 0...	4	75e52681-eb27-4897-891e-6d4540c9c85a
10	10	Beursstraat	0001-01-01 0...	1	beed5675-3a02-4e58-893c-72a2d823f558

Figure 10.8 Update properties, so the `CreatorId` column is populated with the `Id` values of existing users.

10.4.1 Creating a requirement and a handler

Resource authorization is more or less identical to other authorization. It needs a requirement and a handler. For the requirement, I'm going to use the `OperationAuthorizationRequirement` class that comes with ASP.NET Core authorization. This is a helper class that has a single property: `Name`. The class is intended to represent authorization requirements specific to the most common operations performed on data. Create an instance of this class for each operation you want to authorize, and then set the `Name` property accordingly. Listing 10.25 shows a number of instances, representing the basic CRUD operations, grouped together within a class named `PropertyOperations`. This class is placed in the AuthorizationRequirements folder.

Listing 10.25 Implementing `OperationAuthorizationRequirements`

```
using Microsoft.AspNetCore.Authorization.Infrastructure;

namespace CityBreaks.AuthorizationRequirements
{
```

The OperationAuthorizationRequirement helper class is in the Microsoft.AspNetCore.Authorization.Infrastructure namespace.

```
    public static class PropertyOperations
    {
        public static OperationAuthorizationRequirement Create =
            new () { Name = nameof(Create) };
        public static OperationAuthorizationRequirement Read =
            new () { Name = nameof(Read) };
        public static OperationAuthorizationRequirement Edit =
            new () { Name = nameof(Edit) };
        public static OperationAuthorizationRequirement Delete =
            new () { Name = nameof(Delete) };
    }
}
```

PropertyOperations is a wrapper class for multiple authorization requirements relating to operations on the Property type.

An instance of OperationAuthorizationRequirement is instantiated with its Name set to Create. Others are instantiated with their names set to other CRUD operations.

Now that you have your requirement classes, you can create handlers. In fact, because the requirement type is the same for all operations (a key benefit to using the `OperationAuthorizationRequirement` class), you only need to create one handler—one that is based on `AuthorizationHandler<TRequirement, TResource>`, where `TResource` represents the type of the resource being authorized.

The handler class is named `PropertyAuthorizationhandler` and is placed in the AuthorizationHandlers folder. For brevity, it only contains checks for two of the operations: `Edit` and `Delete`. Since the handler will be invoked for all property authorization requirements, check the `Name` property of the requirement to determine which specific requirement is being evaluated. If the `Edit` requirement is being evaluated, check the current user's `NameIdentifier` claim for their `Id`, and compare it to the resource's `CreatorId` property. If there is a match, the current user created the resource, so you should mark the requirement as succeeded.

You have also decided that only users who are in the `Admin` role can delete a property. So if the current requirement is the `Delete` requirement, only mark it as successful under those circumstances. You don't actually need to access the resource to make this evaluation, but it makes sense to keep all the authorization logic for a resource in one place. The handler's code is as shown in the following listing.

Listing 10.26 The `PropertyAuthorizationHandler` class

```
using CityBreaks.AuthorizationRequirements;
using CityBreaks.Models;
using Microsoft.AspNetCore.Authorization;
using Microsoft.AspNetCore.Authorization.Infrastructure;
using System.Security.Claims;

namespace CityBreaks.AuthorizationHandlers
{
    public class PropertyAuthorizationHandler :
        AuthorizationHandler<OperationAuthorizationRequirement, Property>
    {
```

TRequirement is OperationAuthorizationRequirement, and TResource is Property.

```
    protected override Task
    ➥ HandleRequirementAsync(AuthorizationHandlerContext context,
      OperationAuthorizationRequirement requirement, Property resource)
    {
        if(requirement.Name == PropertyOperations.Edit.Name)
        {
            if (resource.CreatorId ==
            ➥ context.User.FindFirst(c => c.Type ==
            ➥ ClaimTypes.NameIdentifier).Value)
            {
                context.Succeed(requirement);
            }
        }
        if(requirement.Name == PropertyOperations.Delete.Name)
        {
            if (context.User.IsInRole("Admin"))
            {
                context.Succeed(requirement);
            }
        }
        return Task.CompletedTask;
    }
  }
}
```

The HandleRequirementAsync method takes both the requirement and the resource as well as the AuthorizationHandlerContext.

Check the current requirement's Name property. If it is the same as the Edit requirement's name, you process the authorization check.

Access the resource's CreatorId property and check its value against the current user's Id. If they match, the requirement is successful.

If the requirement is the Delete requirement, you check whether the current user is an Admin.

At this stage, you have a choice. You can either register formal policies for your requirements like you did previously, or you can choose to evaluate against the requirement directly. Since the latter involves less work, take that option.

The `Edit` authorization check will take place in the property manager Edit page's `OnGetAsync` handler, after the property to be edited has been retrieved from the database. You will use the `IAuthorizationService` directly to perform the check. It has an `AuthorizeUserAsync` method that takes a user, a resource, and a requirement as arguments and returns an `AuthorizationResult` object that has a Boolean `Succeeded` property. You will pass in the current user, the property to be edited, and the `Edit` requirement. If `Succeeded` is `true`, the current user is authorized. If not, you return a `Forbid` result, which will redirect the user to the Access Denied endpoint. First, you need to inject the `IAuthorizationService` and capture it in a private field.

Listing 10.27 Injecting `IAuthorizationService` into the `EditModel`

```
public class EditModel : PageModel
{
    private readonly IPropertyService _propertyService;
    private readonly ICityService _cityService;
    private readonly IAuthorizationService _authService;

    public EditModel(IPropertyService propertyService,
                     ICityService cityService,
                     IAuthorizationService authService)
    {
        _propertyService = propertyService;
```

```
        _cityService = cityService;
        _authService = authService;
    }
...
```

Then you modify the OnGetAsync method to perform the authorization check.

Listing 10.28 Using AuthorizeUserAsync to evaluate user, resource, requirement

```
public async Task<IActionResult> OnGetAsync()
{
    var property = await _propertyService.FindAsync(Id);

    if (property == null)
    {
        return NotFound();
    }
    var result = await _authService.AuthorizeAsync(User,
    ➥ property, PropertyOperations.Edit);
    if (!result.Succeeded)
    {
        return Forbid();
    }
```

In my version of the application, Paul is the user who has an Id starting with beed. As you can see from figure 10.8, he is the creator of the property with an Id of 1. If I log in as Paul and navigate to /property-manager/edit/1, I have access to the Edit form. If I attempt to replace the 1 in the URL with a 2, I am presented with the Access Denied page because Paul is not the creator of the property with an Id of 2.

If you prefer to check against a policy, rather than the requirement directly, you would register the policy like this:

```
builder.Services.AddAuthorization(options =>
{
    options.AddPolicy("EditPropertyPolicy", policyBuilder =>
        policyBuilder.AddRequirements(PropertyOperations.Edit));
});
```

Then you would pass the name of the policy in to the AuthorizeUserAsync method instead of the name of the requirement:

```
var result = await _authService.AuthorizeAsync(User, property,
➥ "EditPropertyPolicy");
```

As well as requiring a bit more work, checking against a policy entails the use of strings, which you can get around by using constants, but that would require even more work.

There is still one thing to be attended to. At the moment, the property manager Index page lists all properties with links to see their details, edit, and delete them. It seems pointless presenting a user with a link to edit or delete a property when they are not authorized to do so. Ideally, you would only provide edit links if the user created the property and delete links if they are in the `Admin` role. In the final section of this chapter, you will use the `IAuthorizationService` to manage the presentation based on the current user and resource.

10.4.2 Applying authorization to the UI

When you want to evaluate authorization in the UI based on resources, use the same `AuthorizeAsync` method on the `IAuthorizationService` as you just used within the `EditModel` within the property manager. You need to make the service available to the Razor page, so you inject it using the `inject` directive. Then you display Edit and Delete links based on the result of the method calls.

The code changes to the PropertyManager\Index.cshtml file are detailed in the following listing. It requires a couple using directives at the top of the page along with the `inject` directive to make the `IAuthorizationService` available.

Listing 10.29 Injecting the `IAuthorizationService` into the index page

```
@page
@model CityBreaks.Pages.PropertyManager.IndexModel
@using CityBreaks.AuthorizationRequirements
@using Microsoft.AspNetCore.Authorization
@inject IAuthorizationService authService
```

The only other required change takes place in the `td` element containing the links. Replace the element with the code in the following listing.

Listing 10.30 Using the IAuthorizationService

```
<td>
    <a asp-page="./Details" asp-route-id="@item.Id">Details</a>
    @{
        var result = await authService.AuthorizeAsync(User,
        ➥ item, PropertyOperations.Edit);
        if (result.Succeeded)
        {
            @:|
            <a asp-page="./Edit" asp-route-id="@item.Id">Edit</a>
        }
        result = await authService.AuthorizeAsync(User,
        ➥ item, PropertyOperations.Delete);
        if (result.Succeeded)
        {
                @:|
                <a asp-page="./Delete" asp-route-id="@item.Id">Delete</a>
        }
    }
</td>
```

Here you are using the same method with the same parameters as you did with the `EditModel`'s `OnGetAsync` method. This time, if authorization evaluation succeeds, you render a link.

When Paul is logged in, he sees some Edit links but no Delete links at all because he is not in the `Admin` role. When Anna logs in, she is able to delete any property but only has an Edit link available for properties for which you assigned her as the creator (figure 10.9).

paul@test.com, you are logged in Sign out

DayRate	SmokingPermitted	AvailableFrom	
81.00	☐	01/01/0001 00:00:00	Details | Edit
75.00	☐	01/01/0001 00:00:00	Details
72.00	☐	01/01/0001 00:00:00	Details | Edit
42.00	☐	01/01/0001 00:00:00	Details
68.00	☐	01/01/0001 00:00:00	Details
50.00	☐	01/01/0001 00:00:00	Details | Edit

anna@test.com, you are logged in Sign out

		ıbleFrom	
		/0001 00:00:00	Details | Delete
		/0001 00:00:00	Details | Delete
		/0001 00:00:00	Details | Delete
42.00	☐	01/01/0001 00:00:00	Details | Edit | Delete
68.00	☐	01/01/0001 00:00:00	Details | Edit | Delete
50.00	☐	01/01/0001 00:00:00	Details | Delete

Figure 10.9 The operation links differ, depending on who is logged in.

There is still one important thing to bear in mind. While you have removed the Delete links from the page, it is still possible for someone with knowledge of the URLs of the application to submit a request to the Delete endpoint. You need to apply an authorization check to only allow users in the `Admin` role to be able to do that. Whether you use an `Authorize` attribute or a page convention to apply the authorization check is your decision, but a check needs to be added. You can consider UI-based authorization in the same way as client-side input validation, which we covered in chapter 5: it's nice to have, but you must still apply the checks on the server, and endpoint authorization is equivalent to server-side input validation.

With this chapter, you have completed your review of all the major framework features. The final four chapters cover a range of topics you need to know to troubleshoot your application, secure it, and get it published. Before that, we will take a look at some aspects of client-side development as they pertain to the Razor Pages framework, particularly the use of AJAX technologies, in the next chapter.

Summary

- Authorization is the process of determining what a user is allowed to do.
- Authorization is added as a service via `AddAuthorization` and enabled as middleware via `UseAuthorization`. This should be placed after authentication. You cannot authorize a user if they are not authenticated.
- You can apply authorization to endpoints (pages) and to resources.
- The `Authorize` attribute enables you to apply simple authorization to endpoints. By default, it only allows authenticated users.
- Alternatively, you can use page conventions to add authorization to pages, folders, and areas, allowing you to centralize your authorization configuration.
- ASP.NET Identity supports roles-based authorization, which enables you to group together users who have the same permissions.
- You can use the current user's claims as the basis for authorization, which represent data about the user and form part of their identity.
- Authorization is built on requirements, handlers, and policies. Each policy is formed of one or more requirements, and each requirement has one or more handlers.
- A requirement handler contains the logic for determining whether the current user is authorized. The handler calls `context.Succeed(requirement)` to mark the requirement as succeeded.
- Only one handler needs to succeed for a requirement to succeed. All requirements must be met for authorization to be granted.
- You can ensure authorization fails by calling the `context.Fail` method within a handler.
- Authorization includes a number of built-in policies, including ones that require one or more roles, one or more claims, an authenticated user, and a specific username.
- You can create your own custom requirements, handlers, and policies. Custom handlers must be registered as services.
- Resource authorization enables you to apply fine-grained control over access to elements of your application model.
- The `OperationAuthorizationRequirement` helper class is intended to be used to help define handlers for authorizing specific operations on resources.
- You can inject the `IAuthorizationService` into your Razor page to apply authorization to the rendering of UI.

11 Client-side technologies and AJAX

This chapter covers

- Choosing your client-side technology
- Calling page handlers from client-side code
- Working with JSON in Razor Pages
- Isolating CSS styles on a per-page basis

All the code examples we have worked with have relied on the HTML for the page being generated in full on the server, except in one area: client-side validation. The validation error messages were generated using client-side libraries, specifically Microsoft's jQuery Unobtrusive Validation library. As a feature, client-side validation enhances the usability of the website. It gives users instant feedback on form validation errors, without waiting for the entire form to be submitted to the server for processing.

Usability is critical if you want to keep your users happy, and usability can be improved dramatically in server-side applications using client-side technologies. In this chapter, we will look at how to implement some common patterns that use client-side technologies within a Razor Pages application. Since it is included as part of the default project template, we will look at jQuery for DOM manipulation and making asynchronous HTTP requests initiated by the browser. We will also explore alternatives, using plain JavaScript, and consider the future of jQuery.

Asynchronous HTTP requests (commonly known as AJAX) enable you to obtain data from the server without a full-page postback, so they are invisible to the user. You can do what you want with that data. You can use it to perform calculations or update parts of a page. Or you can provide the data as a file download. The data itself can be in many forms. It can be HTML or structured as XML or, more commonly, as JSON. In this chapter, you will look at how to use page handler methods to generate HTML and JSON data from AJAX requests and learn about the limitations of this approach. You will also look at how to post data to page handlers successfully.

If you want to work with JSON extensively, the recommended path is building Web API controllers into your application, which provide the foundation for RESTful HTTP services. I don't cover API controllers in this book, but we will explore a newly simplified request-handling feature introduced in .NET 6 (based on the minimal API) that offers a similar bang for your buck with considerably less ceremony. We will also look at another new feature in .NET 6 that enables you to isolate CSS styles to the scope of a single page without increasing the number of HTTP requests. Before we get into some code examples, we will discuss how you might approach your client-side development.

11.1 Choosing your client-side technology

The jQuery library is, without a doubt, the most used JavaScript library of all time. Introduced in 2006, it quickly became the de facto way to manipulate the DOM, handle events, manage CSS transitions, and perform asynchronous HTTP requests (AJAX). When jQuery was launched, implementations of these APIs differed widely across browsers. jQuery acted as an adapter, providing a set of APIs that worked the same way across all supported browsers.

Many other client-side libraries took dependencies on jQuery, including the leading UI framework library, Bootstrap, which is bundled into the default ASP.NET Core web application templates. The latest version of Bootstrap (version 5) included in the new templates from .NET 6 onwards dropped its dependency on jQuery. These days, most browsers adhere to standards much more closely than they used to. Many of them share the same underlying technology. The problem jQuery was designed to solve has largely disappeared.

Despite that, jQuery is still included in the default Razor Pages applications template to provide support for client-side validation. In the longer term, this may well change because there is an open issue on GitHub that discusses the potential replacement of client-side validation so that it no longer depends on jQuery (https://github.com/dotnet/aspnetcore/issues/8573). Nevertheless, jQuery is still widely used, so in this chapter, we will look at implementing client-side solutions using both jQuery and plain JavaScript.

Other client-side libraries exist. Probably the most widely used among them are React and Angular. Angular is more accurately referred to as an application framework, but both are primarily used for building single-page applications (SPAs) for which workflow logic executes in the browser rather than on the server. They *can* be used as part of a Razor Pages application, but they are overkill if all you want to do is add isolated instances of client-side functionality.

11.2 Calling page handlers from JavaScript

This section focuses on calling named page handler methods from client-side code. We will cover how to use a partial page to return a snippet of HTML you can use to update a section of a page. Then we will explore how to post a standard form to a page handler and standalone data. We will pay particular attention to request verification when we do this, remembering it is baked into the Razor Pages framework by default. Finally, we will cover how to work with JSON when interacting with page handlers from client code.

11.2.1 Using a partial page to return HTML

In the first example, you will look at loading snippets of HTML into a page asynchronously. Specifically, you will load details of a property into a Bootstrap modal when the user clicks on the name of a property in a list. You will use partial pages for this exercise. One partial will contain the outline HTML for the modal, the head and foot, which will be included in the existing City page. The modal body will be loaded from the server when the user clicks on a property listing on the city page. You will add client-side code that identifies which property was clicked and then makes a request to a page handler that returns a `PartialResult`, which, if you remember from chapter 3, represents the processing of a partial page. It is perfect for generating fragments of HTML, such as those that might be used for updating regions of pages.

You will create the outline of the modal to start. Add a new cshtml file to the Pages\Shared folder. Remember, there is no template for partial views, so if you are using Visual Studio, you can choose the Razor View > Empty template and then remove the default content. Name the partial file _PropertyModalPartial.cshtml, and replace any existing content with the following code.

Listing 11.1 The `PropertyModalPartial` content based on Bootstrap 5 modal

```
<div class="modal fade" id="property-modal">
  <div class="modal-dialog">
    <div class="modal-content">
      <div class="modal-header">
        <h5 class="modal-title">Property Details</h5>
        <button type="button" class="btn-close"
        ➥ data-bs-dismiss="modal" aria-label="Close"></button>
      </div>
      <div class="modal-body">
```

```
      </div>
      <div class="modal-footer">
        <button type="button" class="btn btn-secondary"
        ➥ data-bs-dismiss="modal">Close</button>
      </div>
    </div>
  </div>
</div>
```

This code is more or less lifted straight out of the Bootstrap 5 documentation for modals. It is a standard modal with no content in its body. You have changed the title to be more relevant to your application and added an `id` attribute, so you can identify the modal from client code. You have also added the `fade` class to the modal, so it animates when appearing and disappearing.

Now you need some content for your modal. This will be placed in another partial named _PropertyDetailsPartial.cshtml, which is also placed in the Pages\Shared folder. Its content is simple. You pass a `Property` in as the model for the Razor file and render details of the property as follows.

Listing 11.2 The partial containing the property details that will be loaded

```
@model Property
<h3>@Model.Name</h3>
<address>
    @Model.Address
</address>
<p>Availability: @(Model.AvailableFrom < DateTime.Now ?
➥ "Immediate" : Model.AvailableFrom.ToShortDateString())</p>
<p>Day Rate: @Model.DayRate.ToString("c")</p>
<p>Max Guests: @Model.MaxNumberOfGuests</p>
<p>Smoking permitted? @(Model.SmokingPermitted ? "Yes" : "No")</p>
```

Next you need a page handler that uses this partial to generate HTML. Add the following handler method to the City.cshtml.cs file after the existing `OnGetAsync` method.

Listing 11.3 The named handler that generated HTML as a `PartialViewResult`

```
public async Task<PartialViewResult> OnGetPropertyDetails(int id)
{
    var property = await _propertyService.FindAsync(id);
    return Partial("_PropertyDetailsPartial", property);
}
```

This is a named handler method. It takes an `int` as a parameter, representing the identity of the chosen property. It uses the property service to obtain the property details from the database and then passes it to the partial file, returning the rendered result. You need to inject the property service into the constructor of the PageModel.

Listing 11.4 Injecting the property service into the CityModel constructor

```
private readonly ICityService _cityService;
private readonly IPropertyService _propertyService;

public CityModel(ICityService cityService, IPropertyService propertyService)
{
    _cityService = cityService;
    _propertyService = propertyService;
}
```

The final steps involve some changes to the City.cshtml file. Iterate a collection of properties within the selected city, and render their details in this file. The name of the property is presented in an h5 heading, which has role="button" assigned to it, so the cursor becomes a pointer when the user hovers over the heading. You need to modify the heading to add some data attributes. One will help you identify the specific property, and others are used to trigger the modal. I've broken the resulting declaration of the h5 element over several lines in the following listing, so it is easier to annotate the code.

Listing 11.5 The amended h5 element designed to trigger a modal

```
<h5 role="button"
data-id="@property.Id"
data-bs-toggle="modal"
data-bs-target="#property-modal"
>@property.Name</h5>
```

- The data-id attribute has the property Id assigned to It. You will retrieve this value and pass it to the named page handler you just added.
- This Bootstrap custom attribute makes the element a trigger for a modal.
- This attribute takes the Id of the target modal.

Finally, include the modal partial in the page (listing 11.6), and use the scripts section to add a block of JavaScript. The client-side code uses jQuery to add a click event handler to all h5 elements. Within the click handler, the id of the specified property is retrieved from the data-id attribute. A URL is constructed, with query string parameters representing the name of the page handler method and its id parameter. This is used in the jQuery load method that uses the GET method to make an HTTP request and then loads the response into the specified element.

Listing 11.6 Adding a partial and the script block to the page

```
<partial name="_PropertyModalPartial" />
@section scripts{
<script>
$(function(){
    $('h5').on('click', function() {
        const id = $(this).data('id');
```

- Use a partial tag helper to include the modal partial.
- Add a click event handler to all h5 elements.
- Within the handler, retrieve the Id of the selected property from the data-id attribute.

```
        $('.modal-body').load(`?handler=propertydetails&id=${id}`);
    });
});
</script>
}
```

The jQuery load method uses the GET method to call the specified URL and inserts the response into the element specified in the selector. In this case, that's the modal body.

Run the application, click a city on the home page, and then click the property's name in the resulting list. The details should appear in the modal.

Removing the reliance on jQuery, you can use the Fetch API instead, which is supported by all modern browsers. The only change you need to make is to the `scripts` section.

Listing 11.7 Calling a named handler with the Fetch API

```
@section scripts{
<script>
document.querySelectorAll('h5').forEach(el => {
    el.addEventListener('click', (event) => {
        const id = event.target.dataset.id;
        fetch(`?handler=propertydetails&id=${id}`)
        .then((response) => {
            return response.text();
        })
        .then((result) => {
            document.querySelector('.modal-body').innerHTML = result;
        });
    });
});
</script>
}
```

Add a click event handler to all h5 elements.

Within the handler, retrieve the Id of the selected property from the data-id attribute.

Make the requests to the specified URL, as before.

Call the text() method on the Response object to obtain the returned content as a string.

Assign it to the modal body.

If you make these changes and run the application, you should not see any difference in behavior. The Fetch example is a little more verbose than the jQuery example, but it is not that complicated once you understand what's going on within the code.

Fetch works with *promises*, which are similar to .NET tasks. They represent the future result of an asynchronous operation. The Fetch HTTP call returns a response as a stream. Use the `text()` method to read the stream into a string, and then use the resulting string to update the modal body. If you are unfamiliar with it and would like to learn more about Fetch, I recommend the Mozilla Developer Network docs as a good starting point: http://mng.bz/vXO4.

Before we move on, it is essential to understand what goes on behind the scenes when these asynchronous calls are being made. You will use the browser developer tools to view the actual request being made and examine its response. The browser developer tools are an essential aid whenever you do client-side work because they reveal what is going on in the browser. You should refer to your browser's documentation for more information on how to access the tools and use them, but for Chrome and Edge users, all you have to do is press your F12 key when you have your browser open. Once the tools are exposed, click the Network tab that shows details of network traffic (requests), shown in figure 11.1. Then navigate to one of the city pages, and click a property name. You should see details of the request appear.

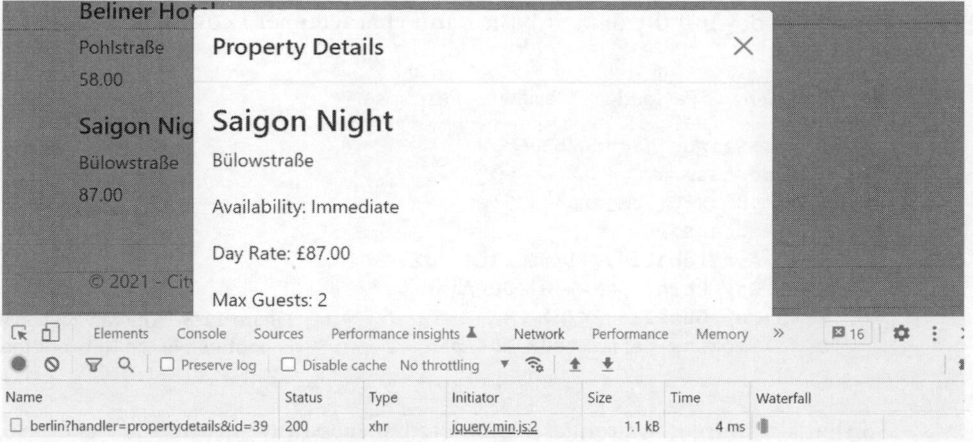

Figure 11.1 The request is recorded in the Network tab.

In this example, the request URL is `berlin?handler=properydetails&id=39`. The HTTP response status code is 200, and the type is specified as Fetch because my screengrab was taken using the Fetch example. If I had taken the grab using the jQuery code, the type would be recorded as `xhr`, representing the browser's Xml-HttpRequest object that jQuery relies on for making AJAX calls. You may have different headings depending on your configuration, but you can right-click any of the headings to customize your view. If you click the name of the request in the Network tab, you can see more details of the actual request (figure 11.2), including the request and response headers and details of any data being passed in the request.

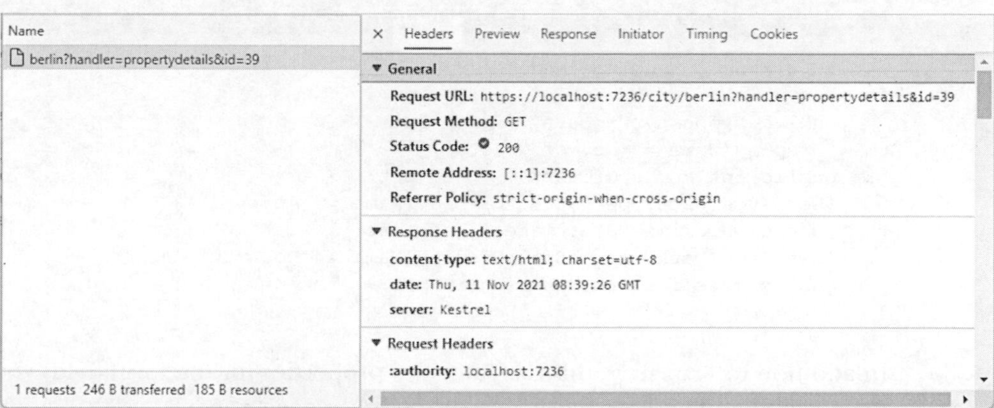

Figure 11.2 Click the request to see more details.

You can use the Response tab to see the actual response returned from the server on the right-hand side. In the example shown in figure 11.3, you can immediately tell from the existence of unicode characters that I have not configured any additional encodings beyond the default Basic Latin character set I covered in section 3.1.5.

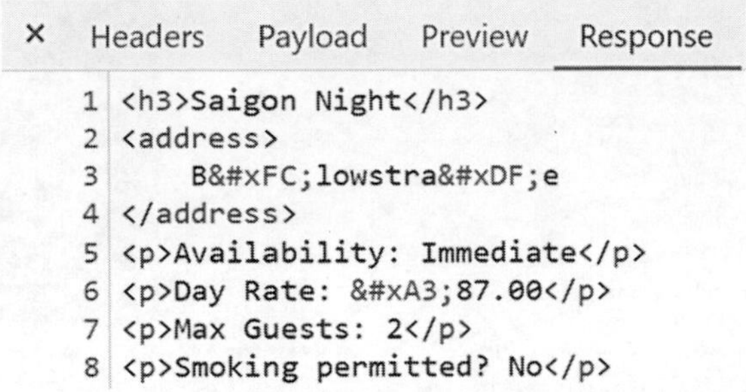

× Headers Payload Preview Response

```
<h3>Saigon Night</h3>
<address>
    B&#xFC;lowstra&#xDF;e
</address>
<p>Availability: Immediate</p>
<p>Day Rate: &#xA3;87.00</p>
<p>Max Guests: 2</p>
<p>Smoking permitted? No</p>
```

Figure 11.3 The raw response is captured in the Network tab.

So that's a simple `GET` request completed successfully. In the next exercise, you will attempt to post the content of a form to a page handler.

11.2.2 Posting to a page handler

Once you have the details of the selected property in the modal, it would be useful to select arrival and departure dates, specify the number of guests in your party, and obtain a total cost for a stay. In this section, you will add a form to the modal that enables you to do that and then post the content of the form to another handler method, which will return the total cost of the stay.

First, you need an input model to wrap a `Property` instance and the form values. Add the class declaration in the following listing to the `CityModel` class, so it is nested within it.

Listing 11.8 `BookingInputModel` added as a nested class to `CityModel`

```
public class BookingInputModel
{
    public Property Property { get; set; }
    [Display(Name = "No. of guests")]
    public int NumberOfGuests { get; set; }
    [DataType(DataType.Date), Display(Name = "Arrival")]
    public DateTime? StartDate { get; set; }
    [DataType(DataType.Date), Display(Name = "Departure")]
    public DateTime? EndDate { get; set; }
}
```

In addition to `Property`, this class includes properties for the form fields you will add to the modal. The `BookingInputModel` will replace `Property` as the model for the modal. You haven't included any `BindProperty` attributes because you will pass `BookingInputModel` as a parameter to the handler method that processes the request.

The code for the handler method follows in listing 11.9. It calculates the total cost of a stay, based on the number of days, the day rate, and the number of guests. This is also added to the CityModel.

Listing 11.9 The OnPostBooking handler method

```
public ContentResult OnPostBooking(BookingInputModel model)
{
    Var numberOfDays = (int)(model.EndDate.Value -
    ➥ model.StartDate.Value).TotalDays;
    var totalCost = numberOfDays * model.Property.DayRate *
    ➥ model.NumberOfGuests;
    return Content(totalCost.ToString("c"));
}
```

This handler method returns a ContentResult, which is a way of returning a string as a response. It is not something you are likely to use very often in real-world apps. However, it helps simplify this example. In addition, the fundamental logic for calculating the cost would usually belong in a service in a business logic layer. But again, I want to keep the example simple. The next listing shows the form added to the _PropertyDetailsPartial.cshtml file. I have not included validation, again, to keep the example simple.

Listing 11.10 The booking form added to the property details partial

```
<form id="booking-form">
    <input type="hidden" asp-for="Property.DayRate" />    ◁ Include a hidden field containing the selected property's day rate.
    <div class="form-group">
        <label asp-for="StartDate" class="control-label"></label>
        <input asp-for="StartDate" class="form-control" />    ◁ Add inputs for arrival and departure dates.
    </div>
    <div class="form-group">
        <label asp-for="EndDate" class="control-label"></label>
        <input asp-for="EndDate" class="form-control" />    ◁
    </div>
    <div class="form-group">
        <label asp-for="NumberOfGuests" class="control-label"></label>
        <input asp-for="NumberOfGuests" class="form-control"
     max="@Model.Property.MaxNumberOfGuests" />    ◁ Use the max attribute to limit the numeric input to the maximum number of guests the selected property can accommodate.
    </div>
</form>
```

You also need to change the model type for the partial. Currently it is a Property. You will be changing that to a BookingInputModel, so replace the first line of _PropertyDetailsPartial.cshtml with the following:

```
@model CityModel.BookingInputModel
```

Next add a new button to the property modal partial; the partial that acts as a frame for the dynamically loaded property details. Add the bold line in the following listing to the footer element.

Listing 11.11 The Book button added to the modal partial

```
<div class="modal-footer">
    <button type="button" class="btn btn-secondary"
    ➥ data-bs-dismiss="modal">Close</button>
    <button type="button" class="btn btn-success"
    ➥ data-bs-dismiss="modal">Book</button>
</div>
```

Finally, you need to wire the new button up to a click handler that posts the form to the page handler method. The jQuery version is shown in the following listing.

Listing 11.12 Adding a new handler to the new button using jQuery

```
$('.btn-success').on('click', function(){
    const data = $('#booking-form').serialize();
    $.post('?handler=booking', data, function(totalCost){
        alert(`Your stay will cost ${totalCost}`);
    });
});
```

- Use the jQuery serialize method to convert the form field values into a URL-encoded string for posting.
- Post to the page handler and define a callback function that takes the response as a parameter.
- Incorporate the response into a string that is displayed in a browser alert.

You are ready to test this out. Once you have the new version of the City page in your browser, make sure you have your developer tools open on the network tab. Then click a property, enter a start and an end date for the booking, and then specify the number of guests. Click the Book button. You should now see a 400 error code in the Network tab (figure 11.4).

Name	Status	Type
☐ amsterdam?handler=booking	400	xhr

Figure 11.4 The request fails with a 400 error code.

The 400 HTTP status code represents a malformed client request. In Razor Pages, this error occurs most commonly because a `POST` request is missing a request verification token. If you recall from chapter 6, the token is generated as a hidden field when the form tag helper has its `method` set to `post`. If you check the code you added in listing 11.10, there is no `method` attribute on the form element; hence, the hidden input was not generated.

The fix is straightforward in this case. You just add `method="post"` to the form element and rerun the application. The hidden field will be generated and will be included in the serialized values posted to the server. However, it is not uncommon to have no form element at all when you post values with AJAX. You might want to post the result of a calculation, for example, rather than the content of a form field. So in those cases, what are your options?

First, you could consider disabling request verification. This has to be done at the `PageModel` level by adding the `IgnoreAntiforgeryToken` attribute on the handler class. You cannot disable request verification at the page handler level (unlike an MVC action method), so if you have other handlers on your page that process `POST` requests, you will disable request verification for those too. That is probably not acceptable, and disabling this security feature is generally not advisable anyway. That leaves you with generating a token value and including it within the AJAX request.

You can render a hidden input with a token value using the `AntiForgeryToken` method on the `Html` helper property of the Razor page:

```
@Html.AntiForgeryToken()
```

Alternatively, you can use the `@inject` directive to inject the `IAntiforgery` service into the page and use its `GetAndStoreTokens` method to generate a token set and access the resulting `RequestToken` property.

Listing 11.13 Generating a request verification token from the `IAntiforgery` service

```
@using Microsoft.AspNetCore.Antiforgery
@inject IAntiforgery antiforgery
@{
    var token = antiforgery.GetAndStoreTokens(HttpContext).RequestToken;
}
```

This approach is only suitable if your JavaScript code is embedded in the Razor page because you need to render the C# token variable within the script. You cannot include C# code in external JavaScript files, so if you prefer to keep the script out of your pages, you will have to use the `AntiForgeryToken` method to render the hidden field.

Next include the token within the request, either as a form field (posting form values) or as a request header value. The default name of the form field is `__RequestVerificationToken` (with two leading underscores), and the default name of the request header is `RequestVerificationToken` (with no leading underscores). Redo this example without the form element to illustrate. First, remove the form tags from the property details partially, so the inputs are no longer enclosed within a form. Next, add a call to the `Html.AntiForgeryToken` method to the City Razor page. I placed mine just above the partial tag helper:

```
@Html.AntiForgeryToken()
<partial name="_PropertyModalPartial" />
@section scripts{
```

You only need to change how the data is assigned in the script block. You can no longer serialize a form because there isn't one, so create an object with properties that mirror the input model the page handler expects as a parameter. You only need to specify property values required by the page handler. The following listing shows the altered button click event handler.

Listing 11.14 Altering the button click event handler to use an object

```
$('.btn-success').on('click', function(){
    const data = {
            startdate: $('#StartDate').val(),
            enddate: $('#EndDate').val(),
            numberofguests: $('#NumberOfGuests').val(),
            __requestverificationtoken:
      $('[name="__RequestVerificationToken"]').val(),
            property:{
                dayrate: $('#Property_DayRate').val()
            }
        }
    $.post('?handler=booking', data, function(totalCost){
        alert(`Your stay will cost ${totalCost}`);
    });
});
```

Create an object.

Use the jQuery val() method to get the form field values and assign them to properties.

The token's hidden field doesn't have an id attribute, so you use its name as the jQuery selector.

The Property property of the input model is nested.

The jQuery library takes care of converting the JavaScript object represented by the data variable into a URL-encoded string for posting and assigning the correct content-type header to the request (`x-www-form-urlencoded`). In the plain JavaScript version of the button click handler, which is available in the chapter downloads, you flatten the input model by including a top-level `DayRate` property. This is so you can use the browser's `URLSearchParams` interface (http://mng.bz/49vj) to generate a URL-encoded string of values suitable for posting easily. This interface is not capable of serializing objects that have nested properties.

11.2.3 Working with JsonResult

Up to now, you have passed simple values and JavaScript objects to the page handler. This section will begin to look at working with JSON, which has become the de facto data format for exchanging data between the client and the server in web applications. You will use plain JavaScript for this example and serialize the JavaScript object you constructed from the form fields to JSON before posting it to the page handler. Then you will convert the page handler method to return a `JsonResult` rather than a `ContentResult`.

When you specify `x-www-form-urlencoded` as the content type for a request, the framework knows it should parse the request body for the posted name-value pairs that constitute the data you are sending to the server. You let the framework know when you post JSON by setting the content type to `application/json`. But you also tell the page handler where to get the data. You do this by applying the `FromBody` attribute to the page handler parameter. Listing 11.15 shows how the page handler method looks with the changes needed to work with JSON. In the code, you create an anonymous type to represent the returned data. While this works fine for ad hoc situations, a more robust approach would involve declaring classes or records for your return types, so they are testable.

Listing 11.15 Using `JsonResult` and the `FromBody` attribute

```
public JsonResult OnPostBooking([FromBody]BookingInputModel model)
{
    var numberOfDays = (int)(model.EndDate.Value -
    ➥ model.StartDate.Value).TotalDays;
    var totalCost = numberOfDays * model.Property.DayRate *
    ➥ model.NumberOfGuests;
    var result = new  { TotalCost = totalCost };
    return new JsonResult(result);
}
```

Change the return type to JsonResult and add the [FromBody] attribute to the handler parameter to tell the framework where to find the JSON data.

Create an object to represent the returned data.

Pass the object to the JsonResult constructor, serializing it appropriately.

Listing 11.16 shows the plain JavaScript version of the button click event handler that generates the JSON, posts it to the server, and processes the result. There are some essential points to note. You must pass the request verification token in the header this time. You cannot include it within the JSON in the request body because request verification takes place before the framework parses the JSON. In addition, you must specify the content type of the request as `application/json`. Finally, when you use the Fetch API, you use the `json()` method on the response (as opposed to the `text()` method you used previously) to deserialize the response, so you can work with it. The default JSON serializer generates property names using camel case, so the `TotalCost` property of the anonymous object you passed to the `JsonResult` constructor becomes `totalCost`.

Listing 11.16 The button click handler that posts JSON using the Fetch API

```
document.querySelector('.btn-success')
    .addEventListener('click', () => {
        const token = document.querySelector(
        ➥ '[name="__RequestVerificationToken"]').value;
        const data = {
            startdate: document.getElementById('StartDate').value,
            enddate: document.getElementById('EndDate').value,
            numberofguests: document.getElementById(
            ➥ 'NumberOfGuests').value,
            property: {
                dayrate: document.getElementById(
                ➥ 'Property_DayRate').value
            }
        };
        fetch('?handler=booking', {
```

```
        method: 'post',
        headers: {
            "Content-type": "application/json",
            "RequestVerificationToken" : token
        },
        body: JSON.stringify(data)
    }).then((response) => {
        return response.json();
    }).then((result) => {
        alert(`Your stay will cost ${result.totalCost}`);
    });
});
```

You must specify the content type as application/json.

You must pass the request verification token as a request header.

Use the json method on the response, which parses the return JSON into an object.

Use the JSON.stringify method to serialize your JavaScript object to JSON format.

Access the totalCost property of the resulting object.

Note that the header's name for the token does not have leading underscores. If you get a 400 error code when working with JSON, check the header's name once you have checked it is present. If you don't specify the content type as `application/json`, it will default to `text/plain`, and your handler will error because it will not attempt to parse the request body.

The jQuery version (listing 11.17) uses the `ajax` method rather than the shorthand `post` method to request because the `ajax` method enables you to set headers. The request's content type is specified using one of the `contentType` options in the settings rather than explicitly setting a header value.

Listing 11.17 Posting and processing JSON with jQuery and a page handler

```
$('.btn-success').on('click', function(){
    const token = $('[name="__RequestVerificationToken"]').val();
    const data = {
            startdate: $('#StartDate').val(),
            enddate: $('#EndDate').val(),
            numberofguests: $('#NumberOfGuests').val(),
            property:{
                dayrate: $('#Property_DayRate').val()
            }
        }
    $.ajax({
        url: '?handler=booking',
        method: "post",
        contentType: "application/json",
        headers: {
            "RequestVerificationToken" : token
        },
        data: JSON.stringify(data)
    })
    .done(function(response){
        alert(`Your stay will cost ${response.totalCost}`);
    });
});
```

Get the token value.

Set the content type via the contentType option.

Pass the token in a header.

Use the JSON.stringify method to serialize the JavaScript object to JSON format.

The key points to working with page handlers and JSON are as follows:

- Remember to apply the `FromBody` attribute to handler parameters.
- Set the content type of the request to `application/JSON`.
- Pass the request verification token in the request header.
- Use the Network tab in the browser developer tools to diagnose issues.

In my opinion, using a page handler method to process and return JSON is acceptable in moderation. Remember that every time a page handler is executed, an instance of the `PageModel` is instantiated, and all of its dependencies are resolved. If you find you are injecting additional dependencies that are only needed for a JSON-processing page handler, that suggests a bit of a code smell. At that point, or if your needs are more extensive, you should consider using *minimal request-handling APIs*, a new feature introduced in .NET 6.

11.3 Minimal request-handling APIs

Before .NET 6, the recommended way to handle extensive services over HTTP in ASP.NET Core, such as those that consume and produce JSON, was to use the Web API framework that forms part of the MVC framework. To do that, you create classes that derive from `ApiController`, add the required action methods to them for processing requests, add the relevant services to your application, and map the controller action methods as endpoints. Incorporating Web API controllers in your application involves a degree of ceremony.

If you recall from chapter 1, a larger part of the motivation behind the introduction of Razor Pages was to reduce the ceremony required by the existing MVC framework to generate HTML on the server. The effort to reduce ceremony has continued in .NET 6. You have already seen how application bootstrapping and configuration have been simplified down to one file, in chapter 2, based on a new minimal hosting API. As part of an overall *minimal APIs* feature, a slimmed-down approach to handling requests was also introduced that allows you to map a route to a function, and it *just works.*

You register minimal API request handlers with the `Map[HttpMethod]` method on `WebApplication`—`MapPost`, `MapGet`, `MapPut`, and so on—using the same convention with which you register page handler methods in a `PageModel` class. Recall that an instance of the `WebApplication` type is returned from the `builder.Build` method call in Program.cs. You pass in a route template and a *route handler*, a standard .NET `Delegate` that executes when the route matches. This can be a named function or a lambda expression that can take parameters (figure 11.5).

The route handler can be configured to return one of many built-in response types, including JSON, text, and files. The obvious omission from the built-in return types is HTML. That's what Razor Pages is for.

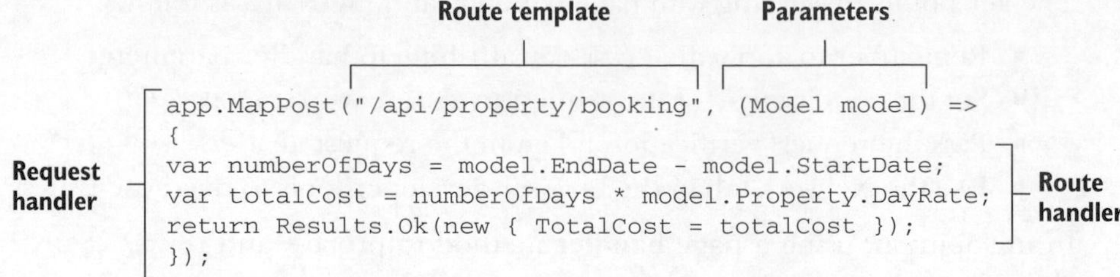

Figure 11.5 Anatomy of a minimal API request handler. This is a nonoperational, slimmed-down version of the actual request handler you will build, designed purely to illustrate the moving parts.

11.3.1 An example minimal API

In the next exercise, you will migrate the current booking page handler to the minimal API approach. You will define an endpoint that responds to `POST` requests at /api/property/booking. It takes a `BookingInputModel` as a parameter and returns a JSON response. Open the Program.cs file, and just before `app.Run()`, add the lines of code from the following listing.

Listing 11.18 Migrating a page handler to a minimal API

```
app.MapPost("/api/property/booking", (BookingInputModel model) =>
{
    var numberOfDays = (int)(model.EndDate.Value -
    ➥ model.StartDate.Value).TotalDays;
    var totalCost = numberOfDays * model.Property.DayRate *
    ➥ model.NumberOfGuests;
    return Results.Ok(new { TotalCost = totalCost });
});
```

Use the MapPost method to map a POST request to the specified route, accepting a BookingInputModel as a parameter.

Use the Results.Ok method to serialize the data to JSON and return it.

Next you'll modify the client script to call this new endpoint. By default, browsers do not allow scripts to make HTTP requests to another domain in a web page. This security feature is designed to mitigate cross-site request forgery, so request verification is not needed and is, therefore, not enabled for APIs. Listing 11.19 shows the client-side code amended accordingly. It only includes the Fetch request section, and the remainder is the same as the previous example. The URL for the request is modified to reflect the template passed to the `MapPost` method, and the request verification header is removed.

Listing 11.19 The Fetch request to the minimal API

```
fetch('/api/property/booking', {
    method: 'post',
    headers: {
        "Content-type": "application/json",
    },
    body: JSON.stringify(data)
```

Change the URL to point to the one specified in the API registration.

No need to include the request verification token

The code for the route handler itself is not that different from the `OnPostBooking` page handler you were working with before. However, the route handler itself performs better, not least because a `PageModel` does not need to be instantiated. Notice also that you don't have to tell the request handler where to find the data for the `BookingInputModel` parameter. We will look at the parameters in more detail in the next section.

The route template you passed to the request handler is similar to those discussed in chapter 4. You can specify route parameters and use constraints in the same way. The resulting template will be added to the collection of endpoints along with your pages.

11.3.2 Parameters in minimal APIs

Minimal API parameters are bound from a number of sources. They are (in order)

- Route values
- Query string
- Headers
- Body
- Services
- Custom

You can use one of the `From*` attributes to let the framework know which source to target explicitly:

- `FromRoute`
- `FromQuery`
- `FromHeader`
- `FromBody`
- `FromServices`

When binding parameters from the body, minimal APIs expect the parameter format to be JSON and attempt to deserialize it. Binding from forms is not supported in .NET 6. If you are working with a later release of .NET, you should check the documentation to see if this has changed, although, as you have seen, it is easy enough to serialize a form to JSON on the client before you pass it to the API.

In the following example, you will migrate the booking calculation to a service you will register with the dependency injection system and then add as a parameter to the request handler. This is the recommended way to separate the application logic because it makes it easier to debug and test. First add a new class to represent a booking to the Models folder. The class is named `Booking`, and its properties represent the data required to calculate a booking.

Listing 11.20 The Booking class

```
namespace CityBreaks.Models
{
    public class Booking
    {
        public DateTime StartDate { get; set; }
        public DateTime EndDate { get; set; }
        public int NumberOfGuests { get; set; }
        public decimal DayRate { get; set; }
    }
}
```

Add the following interface to the Services folder. It specifies a method that returns a decimal and takes an instance of the `Booking` class.

Listing 11.21 The IBooking interface

```
using CityBreaks.Models;

namespace CityBreaks.Services
{
    public interface IBookingService
    {
        decimal Calculate(Booking booking);
    }
}
```

Add the following implementation of the `IBooking` interface to the Services folder. The code for the `Calculate` method is essentially the same as that currently within the request handler.

Listing 11.22 The BookingService class

```
using CityBreaks.Models;

namespace CityBreaks.Services
{
    public class BookingService : IBookingService
    {
        public decimal Calculate(Booking booking)
        {
            var numberOfDays = (int)(booking.EndDate -
            ➥ booking.StartDate).TotalDays;
            var totalCost = numberOfDays * booking.DayRate *
            ➥ booking.NumberOfGuests;
            return totalCost;
        }
    }
}
```

Now you register the service in Program.cs:

```
builder.Services.AddSingleton<IBookingService, BookingService>();
```

Finally, you amend the request handler to take the service as a parameter and the route handler to utilize it to perform the calculation.

Listing 11.23 The request handler taking the `BookingService` as a parameter

```
app.MapPost("/api/property/booking",
    (BookingInputModel model, IBookingService bookingService) =>
{
    var booking = new Booking {
        StartDate = model.StartDate.Value,
        EndDate = model.EndDate.Value,
        NumberOfGuests = model.NumberOfGuests,
        DayRate = model.Property.DayRate
    };
    var totalCost = bookingService.Calculate(booking);
    return Results.Ok(new { TotalCost = totalCost });
});
```

The handler takes the IBookingService as a parameter.

An instance of the Booking class is instantiated from the input model.

It is passed to the service as a parameter, and the returned value is sent back to the client.

In this example, the binding sources are inferred. The framework will search for them from all sources, until a matching one is found. To make them explicit, and thereby narrow the search, you add `From*` attributes accordingly:

```
app.MapPost("/api/property/booking",
    ([FromBody]BookingInputModel model,
     [FromServices]IBookingService bookingService)
```

11.3.3 Minimal API return types

In the example so far, you have used the `Results.Ok` method to return the data serialized to JSON with a 200 status code. This is one of several return types you can use with a minimal API request handler. The static `Results` class, introduced in .NET 6, includes other methods for different return types, which all implement `IResult`. The ones you will use most often in a Razor Pages application are detailed in table 11.1.

Table 11.1 The commonly used methods in the `Results` class

Method	Response type	Description
`Results.Ok`	`application/json`	Produces JSON
`Results.Json`	`application/json`	Produces JSON and enables you to set various options including serializer options
`Results.Text`	`text/plain` (default)	Produces a text response, with a configurable content type

Table 11.1 The commonly used methods in the `Results` class *(continued)*

Method	Response type	Description
`Results.File`	`application/octet-stream` (default)	Writes a file to the response, with a configurable content type
`Results.Bytes`	`application/octet-stream` (default)	Writes a byte array to the response, with a configurable content type

In addition to these options, you can return a plain string or a more complex type. For example, your handler can obtain the total cost from the service and simply return that:

```
return bookingService.Calculate(booking);
```

The response will consist of just the value, with a content type set to `text/plain`. Note that you will need to adjust your Fetch code on the client to use the `text()` method instead of the `json()` method, and you will supply the entire response to the interpolated string in the alert:

```
}).then((response) => {
    return response.text();
}).then((result) => {
    alert(`Your stay will cost ${result}`);
});
```

If you return a complex type, the value will be serialized to JSON, and the content type will be set to `application/json`:

```
var totalCost = bookingService.Calculate(booking);
return new { TotalCost = totalCost };
```

These options might be handy in some cases, but they only save a few keystrokes compared to using one of the `IResult` options, which are strongly typed and lend themselves to being tested.

ROUTE HANDLER AUTHORIZATION

Route handlers can take part in authorization along with your pages. You can pass the `Authorize` attribute in before any parameters. For example,

```
app.MapPost("/api/property/booking", [Authorize](BookingInputModel model) =>
```

Alternatively, you can chain the `RequireAuthorization` method to the handler:

```
app.MapPost("/api/property/booking", (BookingInputModel model) => {
    ...
}).RequireAuthorization();
```

The RequireAuthorization method takes a params string[] as a parameter, enabling you to pass in the name or names of any authorization policies that should be applied to the route handler.

11.4 CSS Isolation in Razor Pages

In chapter 2, I briefly mentioned the Layout.cshtml.css file in the Shared folder, which contains CSS style declarations that are applied to the _Layout.cshtml file. I mentioned that the slightly odd name for the stylesheet is part of a convention used by CSS Isolation, which was introduced to Razor Pages in .Net 6. This section discusses what CSS isolation is and how it works.

First, have a look at the kind of problems CSS isolation is intended to mitigate. As you build a web application, you will generally place CSS style declarations in a global stylesheet that is referenced in the main layout file. That way, the declarations within the stylesheet are available to all pages that make use of the layout, whether they are needed in a specific page or not. As you continue to develop the application, new styles will be added that relate to specific pages or even sections. You might want to change the default font for a single page, for example, so you add a new CSS selector to your stylesheet that you can use to target elements on that page only and update the class attributes of the target elements accordingly. Your global stylesheet grows and grows. You find yourself relying more and more on your editor's search feature to locate the declaration for a particular style you might want to update. Over time, you forget which style declarations are actually being used and which can safely be removed.

Let's say, for example, you want to apply some CSS to the h5 headings on the City page. They are currently targeted by an event handler that listens for a click event and populates the modal dialog with the property details. Typically, users expect the cursor to change from an arrow to a pointing finger when they hover over clickable elements on a web page. So it makes sense to apply the cursor:pointer rule to all the h5 elements on the page. You don't want to apply this change to all other h5 elements in the application, so you need to narrow down the applicable scope for the CSS rule. You could add a CSS class to the h5 elements and then use that to target the headings selectively:

```
h5.clickable{
    cursor: pointer;
}
```

Add this to the global stylesheet, and you are in business. Obviously, you have to remember the purpose of the clickable class, and you have to remember to apply it to all h5 elements on the page. It may be that you want to modify the style on different pages. You can do this by adding further CSS classes to act as filters. Alternatively, you can use the sections featured in Razor to include a page-specific stylesheet:

```
@section styles{
<link href="/css/city.css" rel="stylesheet">
}
```

The downside to this approach is that you increase the number of HTTP requests for the site, especially if you add page-specific stylesheets for multiple pages. You can't really use bundling to combine all these page-specific stylesheets because that defeats the object of the exercise.

CSS isolation in Razor Pages facilitates page-specific stylesheets that do not rely on sections and are bundled into one single file. The feature is enabled by default in Razor Pages, so there is no need to add additional packages or configure any services or middleware. All you have to do is place a stylesheet alongside the page it is intended to affect. You just need to follow a specific naming convention: the Razor page filename with *.css* on the end.

Taking the example above, add a file named City.cshtml.css to the Pages folder, and in it, place the style declaration to affect clickable `h5` elements:

```
h5{
  cursor: pointer;
}
```

The reference to the stylesheet goes on the layout page. The filename you use in the reference is in the following format: `[name_of_application].styles.css`. The name of your application is CityBreaks, and you should already find the reference on the layout page. It was placed there as part of the project template:

```
<link href="~/CityBreaks.styles.css" rel="stylesheet" />
```

When you run the application and navigate to the City page, you can see that the cursor changes to a pointer when you hover over the names of the properties (figure 11.6). If you navigate to /claims-manager, you can see that the `h5` elements used to display the usernames are not affected by the same CSS rule, despite the fact that the stylesheet you just added is referenced globally in the layout file.

Figure 11.6 The isolated CSS style declaration is applied to level-3 headings on this page only.

So how does it work? Well, if you look at the rendered source for the City page, you can see that an additional attribute (`b-jbmzjjkv6t`) has been injected into every HTML element in the City.cshtml template (figure 11.7).

This attribute, the *scope identifier*, uniquely identifies elements within City.cshtml. Notice that the `main` and `div` elements with the `container` CSS class have different scope identifiers injected. They belong to the _Layout.cshtml file. Each Razor file that has an accompanying isolated stylesheet gets its identifier.

At build time, all the isolated stylesheets are combined into one, and their style declarations are altered, so they only apply to elements with the identifier associated with the page they target. Here's a snippet that shows the first few lines of the generated

```
            </div>
        </nav>
    </header>
    <div b-wjjjhz4rtp class="container">
        <main b-wjjjhz4rtp role="main" class="pb-3">

<h3 b-jbmzjjkv6t>Amsterdam</h3>
    <div b-jbmzjjkv6t class="mb-3">
        <h5 b-jbmzjjkv6t role="button" data-id="10"
        data-bs-toggle="modal"
        data-bs-target="#property-modal">
            Dam Hotel
```

Figure 11.7 An additional attribute (`b-jbmzjjkv6t`) is injected into each HTML element in the City page.

stylesheet for my example, which includes the City.cshtml.css file content along with the _Layout.cshtml.css content.

Listing 11.24 Combining all isolated stylesheets into one at build time

```
/* _content/CityBreaks/Pages/City.cshtml.rz.scp.css */
h5[b-jbmzjjkv6t]{
    cursor:pointer;
}
/* _content/CityBreaks/Pages/Shared/_Layout.cshtml.rz.scp.css */

a.navbar-brand[b-wjjjhz4rtp] {
  white-space: normal;
  text-align: center;
  word-break: break-all;
}
```

A comment is injected that shows which page the following style applies to.

The style is isolated to elements that have the specific attribute injected into them.

The scope identifier is generated by the framework, using the format `b-{10 character string}`, and by default, each file gets its unique string, guaranteeing isolation of styles. You might, however, want to share styles across a small number of pages. You can achieve this by customizing the generated identifier, so multiple pages get the same value. This is done in the project file. The following example results in both the Layout and City pages sharing the same identifier: `shared-style`.

Listing 11.25 Customizing the isolation identifier for selected pages

```
<ItemGroup>
    <None Update="Pages/Shared/_Layout.cshtml.css" CssScope="shared-style" />
    <None Update="Pages/City.cshtml.css" CssScope="shared-style" />
</ItemGroup>
```

Given that CSS isolation is a build-time feature, it isn't supported for tag helpers because they generate their output at run time.

This chapter wraps up our look at application development in Razor Pages. The final chapters concentrate more on configuring and publishing your application and ensuring it is safe against hostile activity. We'll start in the next chapter with a look at approaches to minimize errors in your application, how to handle them gracefully when they occur, and how to use logging to understand what is happening once your application is live.

Summary

- Client-side technologies can help you to improve the usability of your application.
- While it is still a great library, the case for using jQuery for manipulating the DOM and making asynchronous (AJAX) requests is diminishing as more and more browsers align behind standards.
- You can use a `PartialResult` for returning blocks of HTML to an AJAX call.
- You must ensure you include a request verification token when posting form values via AJAX to a page handler method.
- The request verification token can be included in the header or within the request body when the request content type is `x-www-form-urlencoded`.
- You must include the token as a header when posting JSON in the request body.
- When posting JSON to a page handler, you must mark the handler parameter with the `FromBody` attribute to tell the framework which binding source to use.
- Request handers are a new feature in .NET 6 and form part of the minimal API.
- Request handlers map routes to functions and can take parameters.
- Request handler parameter binding sources can be implicit or made explicit using the `From*` attribute, where the wildcard * represents the source—`Body`, `Services`, `Route`, and so on.
- Request handlers return `IResult`, strings, or other types serialized to JSON.
- Request handlers can partake in authorization via the `Authorize` attribute or the `RequireAuthorization` method.
- CSS isolation for Razor Pages is new in .NET 6.
- CSS isolation enables you to maintain styles scoped to a page in separate files for easier maintenance, without increasing the number of HTTP requests across your application.
- CSS isolation injects attributes into HTML elements at build time and uses them to scope CSS declarations to the page.
- Only one stylesheet is generated, which includes all scoped styles, reducing HTTP requests.
- Scoped styles only affect HTML elements, not tag helpers.

12 Troubleshooting your application

This chapter covers

- Understanding the nature of an exception
- Using StatusCodePages middleware to control the display of client error messages
- Implementing logging within a Razor Pages application

By now, you've probably written a fair amount of code as you have worked your way through the chapters. Chances are you have encountered an error or two while doing so. Some of these will be compile-time errors your development tool will have caught, so you can fix them as you work. Others will have surfaced only at run time, raising exceptions that result in an error page of some kind being displayed. As you build more complex applications, other types of errors creep in: logical errors. These kinds of errors won't stop your application from running, but they will result in unpredictable behavior. Coding errors, whether they are simply typos or logical errors, are a fact of a developer's life.

In this chapter, we will explore the nature of errors in a bit more detail, so that you can understand what you're dealing with. Ideally, you should code to prevent errors in the first place, but it is the nature of development that bugs will creep in and that forces outside of your control will affect things such as the availability of databases, mail servers, and other external services. We will look at how the application behaves at runtime when an error happens that results in an exception being raised and what opportunities there are to take control over that behavior.

Errors can also originate from the client. We will look at what happens when a client makes a request for a page that doesn't exist, for example. You will learn how to use middleware—StatusCodePages middleware—to manage how your application responds to this very common event and how to control what the user sees.

Unless your users report back to you, you may never know that an error has taken place. Often, when a user does report a fault, they cannot remember precisely what they were doing, so you spend a lot of time trying to replicate the issue but lack the knowledge required to do so successfully. Ideally, you would like someone to watch over the user's shoulder who can report every detail of what they were doing when something went wrong. Clearly, that's not feasible, but the next best thing is including a mechanism to record user actions at the time an error occurred. This mechanism is called *logging*, and we will explore how it is supported within an ASP.NET Core application. You will learn how to categorize the information the logs capture, so that you can more easily control what is recorded, and we will explore the options for controlling where log output goes.

The default support for logging in ASP.NET Core is limited in terms of where logs are written. In the event you want to output logs to a different medium, you may need to implement your own log provider. This chapter covers the basic steps required to implement a simple provider that writes logs to email. Alternatively, rather than write and maintain your own logging solution, you might prefer to use a tried and trusted solution from a third party. There are plenty available that support ASP.NET Core applications. See http://mng.bz/Qngv for more details. You could use any of the solutions listed in the documentation, but in this book, I will walk you through installing and using one called Serilog.

Logging isn't just useful for error reporting. It can be used for tracking user behavior and auditing activity as well. The standard output format for most logging systems is an unstructured string. Consequently, anything more than very simple analysis of the output is difficult. Ideally, you want to be able to query logs in the same way you can query the contents of a database. The solution to this problem is structured logging, which is supported by Serilog. *Structured logging* involves generating logs in a structured data format that enables advanced querying and filtering. In the final section of this chapter, you will learn more about this approach to logging and understand the benefits it brings.

12.1 Exception management

Exceptions are raised when a .NET application encounters an error condition. As a developer, you can choose to attempt to handle exceptions or not. If you don't handle an exception, your application stops execution of the current operation. What happens by default in a Razor Pages application at that point depends on whether the application is running in Development mode or not. This is determined by examining the application's `IWebHostEnvironment`, which we will look at in more detail in the final chapter when we explore environments. If the application is not running in Development mode, the default configuration results in `ExceptionHandlerMiddleware` intervening and executing the Error.cshtml page included in the initial project. This page is designed to provide no more than a bland message that an error has occurred. If the application is in Development mode, middleware invokes the *Developer Exception page,* which provides as much detail of the exception as possible.

12.1.1 The Developer Exception page

The purpose of the Developer Exception page is to help the developer to identify, locate, and fix any errors. Commonly, the Developer Exception page includes the exception type, its message, the filename, the line or lines of code where the exception was raised, and its stack trace. It also includes some information about the request, including details about cookies, request headers, the query string, and information about the route that was invoked. You can see this in action by removing the check for null in the `CityModel`'s `OnGetAsync` method and then navigating to the page, passing in a nonexistent city name in the URL. Change the `OnGetAsync` method in City.cshtml.cs to comment out the null check.

Listing 12.1 Commenting out the null check

```
public async Task<IActionResult> OnGetAsync()
{
    City = await _cityService.GetByNameAsync(Name);
    //if (City == null)
    //{
    //    return NotFound();
    //}
    return Page();
}
```

Comment out the null check.

Rebuild the application, and navigate to /city/mikebrind. The Developer Exception page should appear, informing you that an unhandled exception occurred while processing the request (figure 12.1).

There is no `City` named `mikebrind`, so when the page tries to access a property of the `Model.City` variable, you get a `NullReferenceException` because the value returned from the city service, which is assigned to the `City` property of the `PageModel`, is `null`. The error page shows all of this in detail. On the second line, it tells

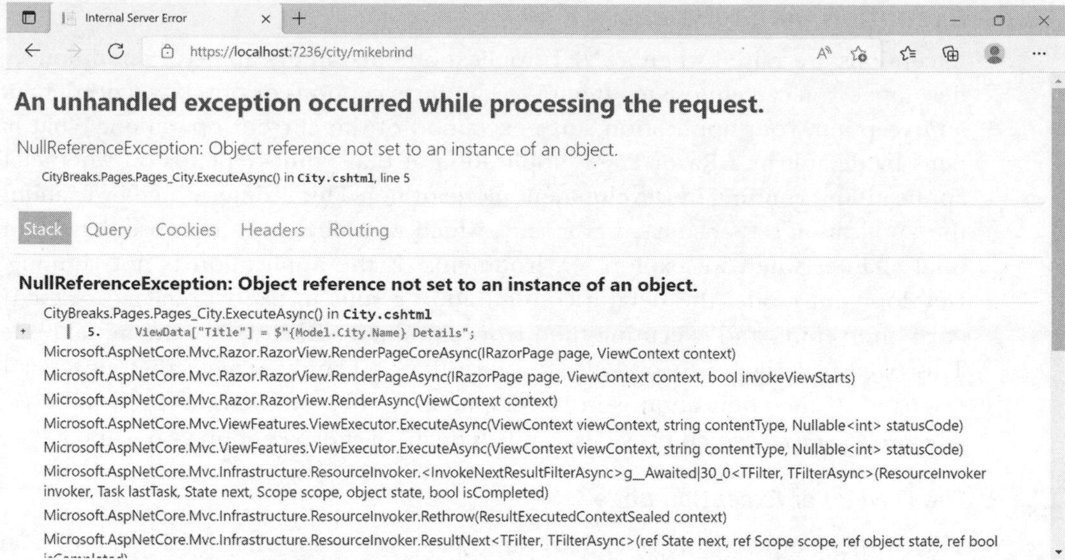

Figure 12.1 The Developer Exception page with tabs showing the stack trace and request details, including the query string, cookies, headers, and routing

you the type of the exception, followed by the actual exception message. This is repeated in bold at the top of the Stack tab content, followed by the name of the method that was called at the point the exception was raised:

```
CityBreaks.Pages.Pages_City.ExecuteAsync() in City.cshtml
```

The `ExecuteAsync` method belongs to the compiled Razor page. It is called at run time. The following listing shows how the start of it looks for your compiled City page.

Listing 12.2 The `ExecuteAsync` method for the compiled City page

```
public override async Task ExecuteAsync()
{
    this.WriteLiteral("\r\n");
    this.ViewData["Title"] =
    ➥ string.Concat(this.Model.City.Name, " Details");
    this.WriteLiteral("<h3 b-jbmzjjkv6t>");
    this.Write(this.Model.City.Name);
    this.WriteLiteral("</h3>\r\n");
```

This line of code caused the exception to be raised.

> **NOTE** In previous versions of Razor Pages, it is possible to easily see the C# code that is generated from a Razor page by navigating to /obj/Debug/[.Net app version]/Razor/Pages, where you will find a collection of files with a .g.cs extension. Each of these contains the generated source code for the matching Razor page. In .NET 6, the Razor compilation system was changed to support hot reload, and these intermediate files are no longer generated. Tools are

available, such as the free JustDecompile from Telerik (https://www.telerik.com/products/decompiler.aspx), that enable you to decompile the generated assembly (.dll file) created by the build process. You can find the assembly in \bin\Debug\[.NET app version]\.

The `string.Concat` method in the `ExecuteAsync` method was generated by the Razor parser from your original interpolated string:

```
ViewData["Title"] = $"{Model.City.Name} Details";
```

The Developer Exception page is clever enough to work out where in the original source code the exception was raised and points to the offending line of code in City.cshtml, highlighting it in red (figure 12.2).

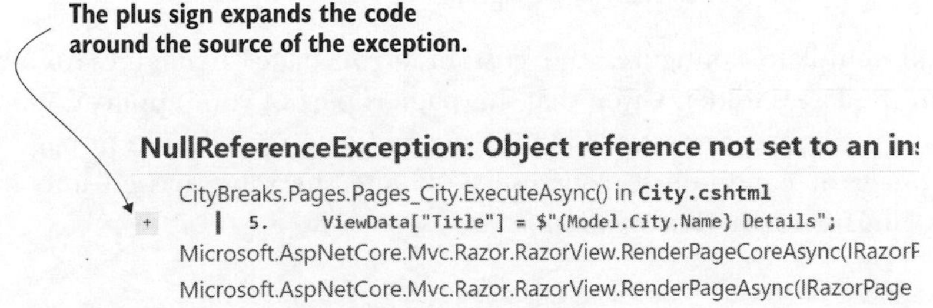

Figure 12.2 The original source code that generates the exception is indented, displayed in a red color, and has a plus sign to the left.

To make things clearer, you can click the plus sign to the left of the single line of code to show more code. From a developer's point of view, all this information is pure gold. You know exactly what broke, and you know which line or lines of code you need to focus on to fix it. If you are puzzled by the sometimes-obtuse error messages, you can always copy and paste them into a search engine. You'll probably find you are not alone in your puzzlement and that lots of developers before you have posted questions in technical communities about the same error and got good answers that can likely help you.

From a user's point of view, this is not gold at all. It doesn't help them one bit, unless the source code revealed by clicking the plus icon includes some interesting tidbits, such as a helpline phone number. Chances are that the source code is more likely to include some comments you don't want the world to see or, perhaps, the credentials for a mail server or database. For this reason, you are advised to use a generic page to report an error condition to the user.

12.1.2 ExceptionHandlerMiddleware

Use the `UseExceptionHandler` method within the application pipeline configuration to add `ExceptionHandlerMiddleware` to the application for capturing and displaying details of exceptions. The default template includes this middleware only if the application is not running in Development mode (listing 12.3). The middleware is positioned right at the start of the pipeline, so it can catch all exceptions. The method optionally takes a string representing the path to the page that should be displayed in the event of an unhandled exception occurring. When an exception happens, the middleware catches it, logs it, and reexecutes the request, so the configured error page can be displayed.

Listing 12.3 `ExceptionHandlerMiddleware`

```
if (!app.Environment.IsDevelopment())     <-- The condition checks whether the environment is Development.
{
    app.UseExceptionHandler("/Error");    <-- If it is not, you include the ExceptionHandlerMiddleware in the pipeline.
}
```

The default template configures the custom error page, named Error, which is included in the Pages folder. Given that this page is part of your application, it is easy to customize the content to your liking. If you prefer to use a different page to communicate an error condition to your users, change the value passed into the `UseExceptionHandler` method in Program.cs:

```
app.UseExceptionHandler("/Errors/MyCustomErrorPage");
```

The default setup has a built-in flaw. It is automatically assigned a layout page via the _ViewStart file that sits in the same folder. Consequently, if the exception is generated by an error condition within the layout, you will get a potentially recursive situation in which the exception occurs and the framework tries to display the error page, resulting in the exception again. For this reason, one of the first steps I usually take when starting a new application is setting the `Layout` to `null` in the error page and ensuring its content is not reliant on anything that could result in another exception being raised.

Listing 12.4 Setting the `Layout` property to `null` in the custom error page

```
@page
@model ErrorModel
@{
    Layout = null;     <-- Set Layout to null.
    ViewData["Title"] = "Error";
}
```

As might be obvious from its name, the exception-handler middleware only works when an unhandled exception—a server error—occurs within the application, resulting in an HTTP 500 status code. Other kinds of errors can occur while a user is visiting your application. For example, before you commented it out, you called the `NotFound` method if the city name passed into the City page could not be found in the database. You might recall from chapter 3 when we looked at handler method return types that the `NotFound` method is a helper result that returns a `NotFoundResult`. The `NotFoundResult` returns an HTTP 404 status code, indicating a client error. When client errors occur, ASP.NET Core returns the status code and an empty response body. The browser is left to display some kind of notification to the user (although it is not obliged to). You can take control of what is displayed to the user yourself by adding StatusCodePages middleware to the request pipeline, which you will test out in the next section.

12.2 StatusCodePages

StatusCodePages middleware is designed to enable you to provide a response body in the event of a client error occurring. The default implementation generates a plain text response, but you can produce a custom HTML-based error page and configure the middleware to return the contents of that instead. This enables you to fully control the appearance of the error message, maintain your site branding if so desired, and give the user helpful information on what happened and what they can do next.

Use the `UseStatusCodePages` extension method (set in bold) to enable StatusCodePages middleware. Ideally this method call should be registered early in the pipeline, before any request handling components:

```
app.UseHttpsRedirection();
app.UseStatusCodePages();
app.UseStaticFiles();
```

The primary processing logic within StatusCodePages middleware comes after the `await _next(context)` call, which, if you remember from chapter 2, happens on the *return leg* of the pipeline, once the response status code has been set by other middleware—usually the Razor Pages middleware (figure 12.3).

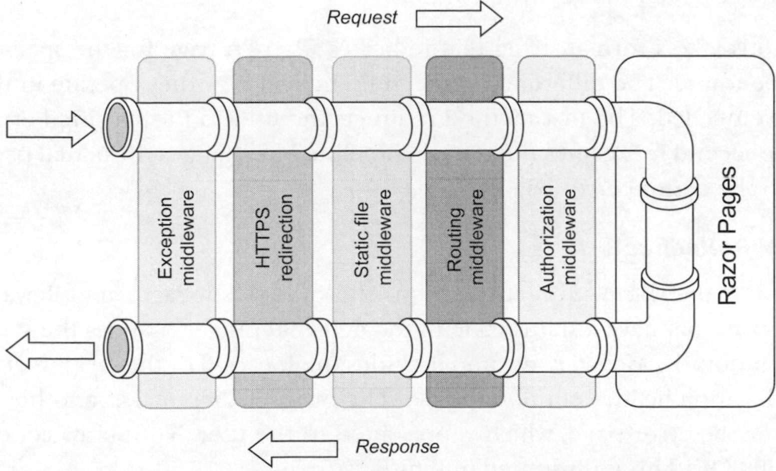

Figure 12.3 StatusCodePages operates on the return journey (the bottom part of the pipeline in the diagram) after the HTTP status code has been set.

The default behavior of StatusCodePages middleware is to return a plain text response when the status code is between 400 and 599 (but not for unhandled exceptions) and the response is empty. For example, having implemented `StatusCodePage` middleware, if you navigate to /city/mikebrind, the response is very plain, as shown in figure 12.4.

Figure 12.4 The default implementation of StatusCodePages middleware returns a plain text response.

A number of alternative methods exist, enabling you to register `StatusCodePages` middleware and take control over what is presented to the user. For example, you can pass in a string representing the content type and a body formatted accordingly:

```
app.UseStatusCodePages("text/html", "<h1>Error!</h1>");
```

Within a Razor Pages application, you will most likely want to return different content based on the status code, and you will also want to use Razor Pages to generate the HTML, rather than having one HTML message returned for all status codes. There are two methods for registering `StatusCodePages` middleware that enable this:

- `UseStatusCodePagesWithRedirects`
- `UseStatusCodePagesWithReExecute`

Both methods take a format string that indicates where a page for the specific status code is to be found. The difference between them is in how they operate in the event that they are needed. The first method redirects the user to the specified error page, whereas the second reexecutes the request pipeline but changes the actual page being executed to the custom error page.

12.2.1 Exploring WithRedirects

When you use the `WithRedirects` version, the StatusCodePages middleware intercepts responses that have a status code in the 400–599 range, changes the status code to a 302 Temporarily Moved code, and includes the location of the custom error page within the location header of the response. The browser then makes another request, this time, for the error page, which is presented to the user. The status code for this request is 200 OK. This is illustrated in figure 12.5.

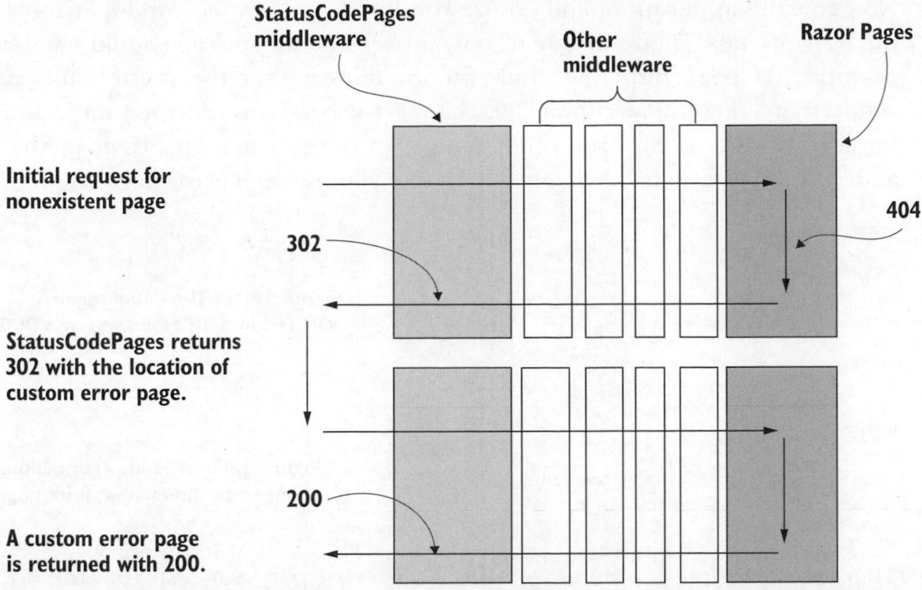

Figure 12.5 The flow of execution when using StatusCodePages middleware with redirects. The initial request for the nonexistent page results in a 404, which is then replaced with a 302 by the middleware. The browser is redirected to the custom error page, which is returned successfully.

You can examine this behavior in your application. First add a new folder to the Pages folder named Errors. Within that, add a new Razor page named 404.cshtml. The content of the Razor page is shown in the following listing.

Listing 12.5 The content for the custom error page

```
@page
@model CityBreaks.Pages.Errors._404Model
@{
}
<h1>Sorry</h1>
<p>The page you are looking for doesn't exist on this site.
    Check the URL and try again. </p>
```

Next register StatusCodePages middleware with redirects in Program.cs. The format string passed into the registration method in listing 12.6 includes a placeholder for the status code. At run time, in the event of an error resulting in a 404 status code, the middleware will redirect to /errors/404 if it exists.

Listing 12.6 Registering StatusCodePages middleware with redirects

```
app.UseHttpsRedirection();
app.UseStatusCodePagesWithRedirects("/errors/{0}");
app.UseStaticFiles();
```

The registration method takes a format string representing the HTTP status code.

Now run the application, and ensure you have the browser developer tools open in the Network tab. Then navigate to /city/mikebrind again. You should see the content of your 404 page displayed, and you should see that the request for `mikebrind` resulted in a 302 followed by a 200, as the error page was returned successfully to the browser (figure 12.6). One other thing to notice is that the URL in the browser address bar has also been changed to that of your custom error page (figure 12.7).

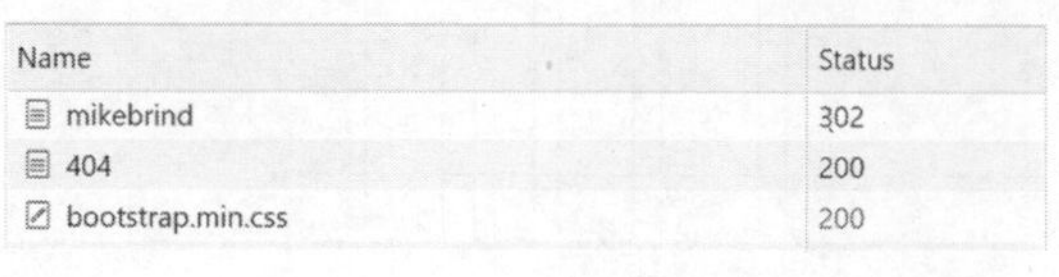

Figure 12.6 The initial request resulted in a 302 followed by a 200.

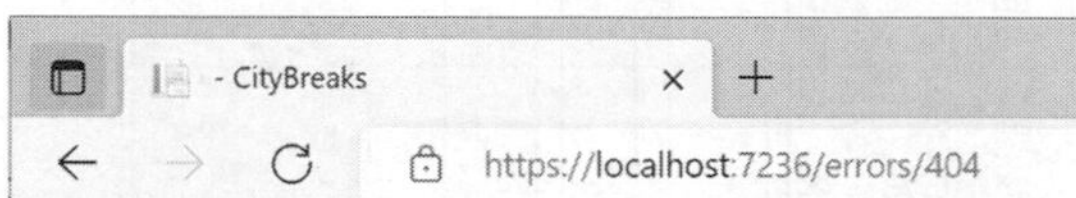

Figure 12.7 The browser address is changed to the custom error page.

There are a couple problems with this. Your error page suggests that the user checks the URL and tries again. However, the original request URL has been lost (unless they know how to use the developer tools). The second issue concerns search engines. Imagine if someone copies a link to the Paris city page, /city/paris, but omits the last character and pastes the result into something indexed by a search engine: /city/pari. The result of following that link is a 302 followed by a 200. The search engine will continue to index the resource, and users will be directed to the error page.

12.2.2 StatusCodePages WithReExecute

Ideally, you want the search engine to drop listings of any pages that cannot be found. If you are using Google webmaster tools, you can also get a report of requests that result in a 404, which enables you to act on them, such as setting up permanent redirects if they are the result of a typo in a URL, for example. So you need to allow the original 404 status code to reach the user agent. And this is what the second method for registering StatusCodePages middleware supports. Rather than sending a redirect to the user agent, the StatusCodePages middleware intercepts the response with the 404 status code and reexecutes the request using the specified custom error page, while retaining the status code and original request URL (figure 12.8).

To register the reexecute option, use the `UseStatusCodePagesWithReExecute` method that takes a format string for the path and, optionally, another format string for a query string (shown in bold):

```
app.UseHttpsRedirection();
app.UseStatusCodePagesWithReExecute("/errors/{0}");
app.UseStaticFiles();
```

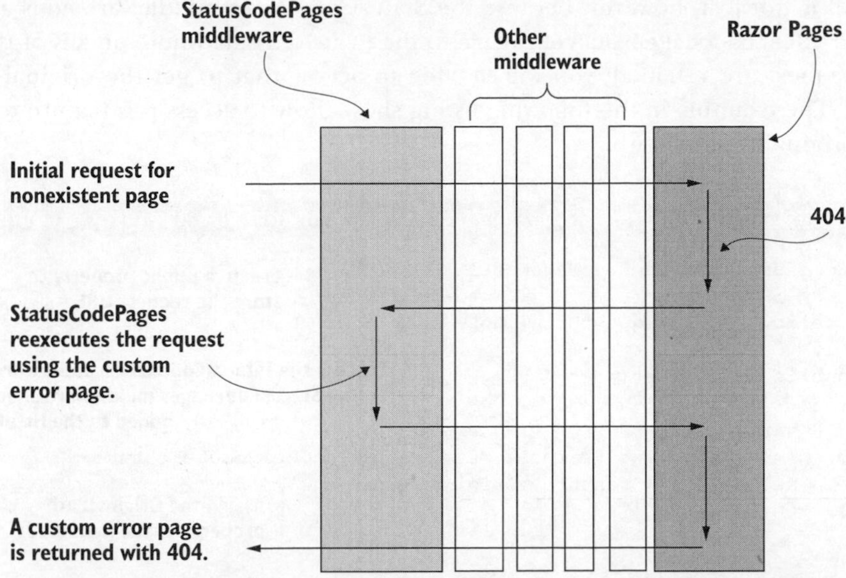

Figure 12.7 `WithReExecute` **results in the request being reexecuted within the application using the custom error page, while the status code and original request URL are retained.**

Run the application again, and navigate to /city/mikebrind. This time, you can see that the URL is preserved in the browser address bar, and the 404 status code is preserved (figure 12.9).

Name	Status	Type
mikebrind	404	document
jquery.min.js	200	script

Figure 12.8 The URL is preserved in the browser along with the 404 status code when using the reexecute method.

You can clearly see the original request URL in the browser address bar in figure 12.9, but sometimes it's not possible to check the URL in a browser address bar. Browsers on smaller devices, such as cell phones, don't show the complete URL. To get around this, you might want to display the incorrect URL to the user as part of the error message you provide them, so they can see if there is anything obviously wrong with it. When doing so, you would usually render `Request.Path` or similar, but the StatusCodePages middleware changes the request to the custom error page, so `Request.Path` will resolve to /errors/404.

All is not lost, however, because the StatusCodePages middleware adds a feature called `IStatusCodeReExecuteFeature` to the `HttpContext`, where details of the original request are retained; you will be able to access that to get the original request URL. The example in the following listing shows how to access this feature to extract the original request path.

Listing 12.7 Accessing the original request path when the request is reexecuted

```
public class _404Model : PageModel
{
    public string RequestUrl { get; set; }

    public void OnGet()
    {
        var feature =
        ➥ HttpContext.Features.Get<IStatusCodeReExecuteFeature>();
        RequestUrl = feature?.OriginalPath;
    }
}
```

- Create a public property to store the request URL.
- Access the IStatusCodeReExecuteFeature, which the StatusCodePages middleware should have added to the HttpContext.
- Assign the OriginalPath property to the RequestUrl.

In addition to the `OriginalPath` property, you can obtain details of any query string values via the `OriginalQueryString` property or route values from the `RouteValues` property. Finally, amend the content of the custom 404 page as follows.

Listing 12.8 The custom error page including the original request URL

```
<h1>Sorry</h1>
<p>
    The page you are looking for:
    <span class="fw-bold">@Model.RequestUrl</span>
    doesn't exist on this site.
</p>
```

Table 12.1 Redirect compared to reexecute

	Redirect	Reexecute
Preserves original request URL	No	Yes
Retains HTTP status code	No	Yes
Displays custom error page content	Yes	Yes
Results in additional HTTP requests	Yes	No

Table 12.1 recaps the differences between the reexecute and redirect options provided by the StatusCodePages middleware. Going by the summary provided in table 12.1, it should be clear that `WithReExecute` should be the default choice when implementing StatusCodePages middleware in a Razor Pages application. If the error occurred because the requested resource could not be found, the user can check the

original URL they requested in the browser address bar. The status code is preserved, so user agents can act accordingly, updating indexes if necessary.

You now know how to use StatusCodePages middleware or the DeveloperExceptionPage middleware to control the message the user sees when client or server errors occur within the application. However, you won't know these errors have occurred in the application when it is running live on the web server, unless a user makes the effort to inform you. Ideally, you need to be notified whenever an error has occurred, and you want that notification to include sufficient detail about the error, so you can attempt to identify the cause, locate it, and fix it, if at all possible.

You can satisfy these requirements by implementing *application logging*, which generates a record of events that take place within the running application. You can then refer to these log records to identify what happened, when it happened, and where it happened.

12.3 Logging

Logging is supported as a first-class citizen within ASP.NET Core. Several logging providers are enabled as part of the preconfigured defaults when the `WebApplication.CreateBuilder` method call is made in the `Program` class. A *logging provider* is responsible for the actual generation and output of log messages. Each one targets one or more different sources. The built-in providers enabled by default are the following:

- `Console`—Writes to the console
- `Debug`—Writes to the debug window in your IDE
- `EventSource`—Uses the operating system's event-tracing mechanism
- `EventLog`—Writes to the event log (Windows only)

In addition to these, you can enable your own logging provider. We will explore how to do that later in the chapter when you create a custom logger that gives you immediate notification that something has gone wrong in the application by outputting the log to email. You will learn about *structured*, or *semantic*, logging, which gives you rich data about the log and enables useful scenarios like querying and filtering of log messages. We will also look at integrating a third-party logging solution that includes support for ASP.NET Core and structured logging.

12.3.1 Logging basics

If you have been implementing the examples in this book so far, you may already have noticed the console logger at work, either in the console window that opens when you run your application from Visual Studio or the integrated terminal in VS Code. Various parts of the ASP.NET Core and EF Core frameworks are instrumented to output informational logs as a result of normal running of applications. You can see this in figure 12.10, which shows the integrated terminal in VS Code, while the application is running.

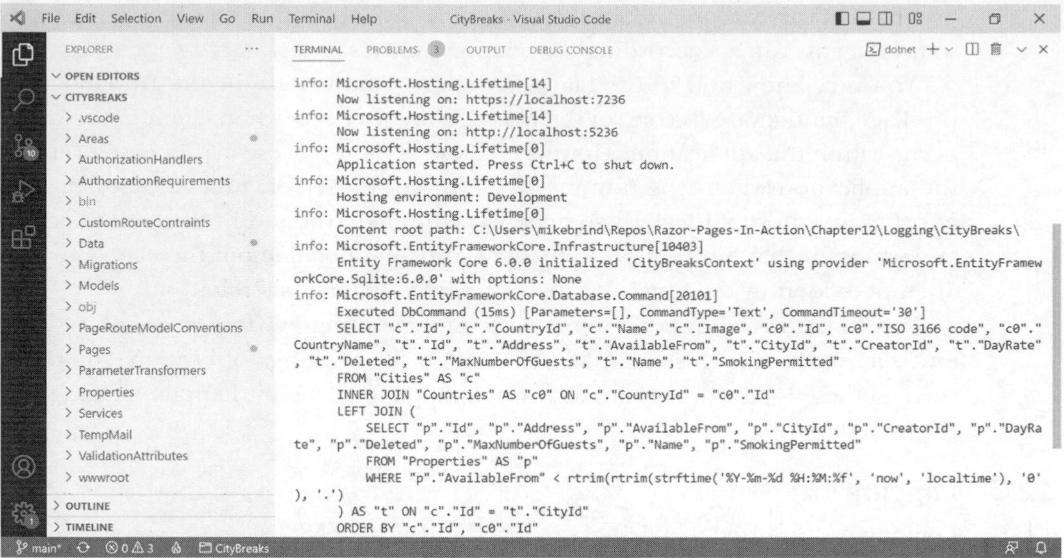

Figure 12.9 Logs (on the right) are output to the terminal window in VS Code.

Have a look at the structure of an individual log. It is composed of four elements:

- Level
- Category
- Event ID
- Message

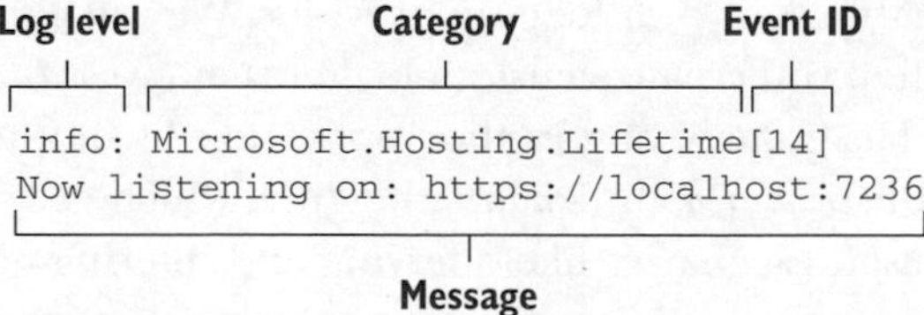

Figure 12.10 The log output comprises a level, category, event ID, and message.

In the next few sections, we will explore each of these elements in more detail.

12.3.2 Log levels

Log levels are used to convey the severity of the event that caused a log to be written. Table 12.2 lists the log levels used by .NET Core logging in order of severity, ranging from least severe to most severe.

The `ILogger` interface is the primary abstraction for logging within .NET. It has a number of extension methods that determine the level of the log generated. They are nice and predictable in that they take the form `Log[Level]`, so to generate an informational log, you use the `LogInformation` method.

Table 12.2 Log levels

Log level	Description
`Trace`	The lowest level of logging, which results in all logs being output. This level is rarely used and should not be enabled in a production application, as it may contain sensitive information.
`Debug`	This level is intended to be used for writing messages that are useful while developing the application. For example, you might want to log the value of variables or the processing time of an operation. You are unlikely to log at this level in a live application.
`Information`	The information level is used for logging normal operations within the application. For example, you might want to log details of changes made to a `Property` record in the database, such as who changed the details and what the changes were.
`Warning`	Warning logs are used to record details of events that are unexpected or abnormal but don't raise an exception. For example, within the `CityModel OnGet` method, you might want to log a warning when route values don't match an existing record.
`Error`	This level is used for recording details of errors that stop the current request from processing—typically unhandled exceptions. The `ExceptionHandlerMiddleware` automatically creates a log when an exception occurs.
`Critical`	This level is used for recording details of catastrophic events that prevent normal operation of the application for all users, such as the server running out of disk space.

The next code examples show how to generate logs based on the name of the city passed in to the City page. If it is found in the database, you log an informational message. If not, you log a warning. First, you need to get a reference to the logger. You do that by injecting `ILogger<T>` into the `PageModel` constructor.

Listing 12.9 Making loggers available using dependency injection

```
public class CityModel : PageModel
{
    private readonly ICityService _cityService;
    private readonly IPropertyService _propertyService;
    private readonly ILogger<CityModel> _logger;          <-- Add a field for an ILogger<T>.

    public CityModel(ICityService cityService,
        IPropertyService propertyService,
        ILogger<CityModel> logger)     <-- Inject the ILogger<T> into the constructor.
    {
        _cityService = cityService;
        _propertyService = propertyService;
        _logger = logger;              <-- Assign the parameter to the field.
    }
```

The `Logger<T>` takes a generic parameter representing the category of the logger. We will look at categories in more detail soon, but for now, pass in the name of the class that uses the logger.

The next listing shows the amended `OnGetAsync` method in the `CityModel` class. In it, you use the logger instance to log a warning if the city passed in the URL is not found and an informational message if it is.

Listing 12.10 The amended `OnGetAsync` class incorporating logging

```
public async Task<IActionResult> OnGetAsync()
{
    City = await _cityService.GetByNameAsync(Name);
    if (City == null)
    {
        _logger.LogWarning("City \"{name}\" not found", Name);   <- Log a warning if the city is not found.
        return NotFound();
    }
    _logger.LogInformation("City \"{name}\"
    ➥ found", Name);   <- Log an informational message if the city is found.
    return Page();
}
```

When you run the application normally and click a city on the home page, the log is output to the console with the log level specified at the start (`info`):

```
info: CityBreaks.Pages.CityModel[0]
      City "amsterdam"  found
```

When you try to navigate to /city/mikebrind, the warning is recorded, prefixed with `warn`:

```
warn: CityBreaks.Pages.CityModel[0]
      City "mikebrind" not found
```

Now that you have a basic understanding of log levels, we will move on to the next element: the log category.

12.3.3 Log categories

Log categories provide a way to label a log with an arbitrary string, which can be useful when you want to perform some kind of filtering on log entries. As you saw in the previous example, the `ILogger<T>` takes a parameter, which is used to generate the category. You can pass in any type you want to the `T` parameter, but the convention is to pass in the name of the consumer. In this example, that's the `CityModel` class. Its full name is then used as the category: `CityBreaks.Pages.CityModel`.

The type you pass in to the `Ilogger<T>` to generate the category name is constrained to only those types that your application recognizes. That doesn't fit the *label a log with an arbitrary string* definition. There is another way to instantiate loggers that allows you to provide any string you like as the category name. You can use `IloggerFactory` to create instances of loggers instead. Using this approach, you inject `IloggerFactory` into the consuming class and then use its `CreateLogger` method to instantiate an instance of `Ilogger` as needed. The `CreateLogger` method takes a string to represent the logger category. The following listing shows the relevant amendments to the CityModel in bold. The constructor of the CityModel class is amended to accommodate an Ilogger-Factory, which is assigned to a field. The factory is used within the OnGetAsync method to instantiate an instance of Ilogger for use within that method only, with a suitable category name.

Listing 12.11 Using an IloggerFactory to customize the category name

```
private readonly IcityService _cityService;
private readonly IpropertyService _propertyService;
private readonly IloggerFactory _loggerFactory;

public CityModel(IcityService cityService,
    IpropertyService propertyService,
    IloggerFactory loggerFactory)
{
    _cityService = cityService;
    _propertyService = propertyService;
    _loggerFactory = loggerFactory;
}

[BindProperty(SupportsGet = true)]
public string Name { get; set; }
public City City { get; set; }

public async Task<IactionResult> OnGetAsync()
{
    var logger = _loggerFactory.CreateLogger("City page OnGetAsync");
    City = await _cityService.GetByNameAsync(Name);
    if (City == null)
    {
        logger.LogWarning(404, "City \"{name}\" not found", Name);
        return NotFound();
    }
    logger.LogInformation("City \"{name}\"  found", Name);
    return Page();
}
```

Inject the ILoggerFactory into the constructor.

Use the CreateLogger method to instantiate a logger with a custom category name.

When you navigate to the City page, the log output differs in view of the fact that your customized category name is used:

```
info: City Page OnGetAsync[0]
      City "amsterdam"  found
```

This approach can be useful if you want to create logger categories at the method level, for example, but otherwise, you will most likely use an ILogger<T> within your application.

12.3.4 Using EventIds

Event IDs provide another way to filter log messages. For example, you might want to filter all logs that are recorded when a page cannot be found, so if necessary, you can redirect the user (and search engines) to a new permanent address. Accordingly, you might decide to associate warning logs for missing pages with an `EventId` of `404`. In this case, you pass an `EventId` in as the first parameter to one of the `Log*` methods. The `EventId` type is a struct, so you can associate an `EventId` with a log as follows:

```
_logger.LogWarning(new EventId(404), "City \"{name}\" not found", Name);
```

However, there is an implicit conversion between an `int` and an `EventId`, so you are more likely to use the following approach:

```
_logger.LogWarning(404, "City \"{name}\" not found", Name);
```

Event IDs are not required as part of a log. If you don't provide a value, the event ID defaults to zero.

12.3.5 Formatting the log message

The string you pass to the various `Log*` methods is referred to as a *template*. It can contain placeholders for variable values, which are supplied as a `params` array argument. Your examples so far include only one parameter, `{name}`, representing the city name, the value for which is passed in after the template. When constructing a template, you are advised to use named placeholders in this way. This is primarily so you can take advantage of the benefits of *structured logging*. Some third-party logging libraries are able to store the parameter names and values separately, which makes it easier to query logs for more detailed analysis. This is known as *structured*, or *semantic*, logging.

The log message template looks similar to a standard format string, but it does not behave in the same way. Parameter values are inserted into the template according to their position in the parameter array, not according to their name. You must provide at least as many arguments to the parameter array as there are placeholders in the template; otherwise, a runtime exception occurs. This means if you want to repeat a value within the message template, you must include it in the parameter array again, like this:

```
_logger.LogWarning("{name} searched for. {name} not found", Name, Name);
```

Now that you have a basic understanding of logging within ASP.NET Core, you will look at how to configure logging within your application.

12.3.6 Applying log filter rules

I've discussed filtering logs according to their level, category, and so on. Now it's time to look at ways to specify *rules* you can apply to filtering logs. The recommended way to specify log-filtering rules is via the application's main configuration file—appSettings .json—within the `Logging` section. Take a look at the default template version of the relevant section (listing 12.12).

Listing 12.12 The `Logging` section in the appSettings.json file

```
"Logging": {
  "LogLevel": {
    "Default": "Information",
    "Microsoft.AspNetCore": "Warning"
  }
}
```

This is the log level property. (→ `"LogLevel"`)

The default minimum log level is Information. (→ `"Default"`)

The minimum log level for the Microsoft.AspNetCore category is Warning. (→ `"Microsoft.AspNetCore"`)

The `LogLevel` property within the `Logging` section is where you define defaults for all logging providers. In this example, the minimum default log level is set to `Information`. That means only logs at `Information` level or above will be generated by all providers in all categories, unless a different rule is specified elsewhere. In the very next line, a different rule is indeed specified for all loggers in the `Microsoft.AspNetCore` category. This states that any logger that has a category name starting with `Microsoft.AspNetCore` will only generate logs at the `Warning` level or above.

You can override the rules specified in the `LogLevel` section by specifying new rules that apply to individual providers. In the next listing, add a section for the `Console` provider that results in logs being generated at `Debug` level and above, except for those in the Microsoft category, where you are only interested in seeing errors or critical events being recorded.

Listing 12.13 Adding a provider-specific filter rule

```
"Logging": {
  "LogLevel": {
    "Default": "Information",
    "Microsoft.AspNetCore": "Warning"
  },
  "Console": {
    "LogLevel": {
      "Default": "Debug",
      "Microsoft": "Error"
    }
  }
}
```

New rules that only apply to the Console logger (→ `"Console"`)

The default minimum logging level is set to Debug. (→ `"Default"`)

The minimum logging level for categories starting with Microsoft is Error. (→ `"Microsoft"`)

The `Console` section applies only to the console logger. Other loggers—the debug logger and the event source logger, for example—do not have specific rules, so their behavior is governed by the settings in the `LogLevel` section.

We have looked at working with the default logging implementations, but they are limited in terms of their application. When your website is live, you need to know when a show-stopping error has occurred. You also need details of the error. As discussed previously, you cannot rely on users giving you this information in a timely, accurate manner—if at all. The default logging providers won't give you immediate notification that an error has occurred (unless you spend your day watching a console window on a server), so you need another provider that does. In the next section, you will learn the steps required to create your own logging provider.

12.3.7 Custom email logger

In this section, you will implement a simple logging provider that writes to email. The primary purpose of this exercise is to gain an understanding of the moving parts involved in implementing your own logging provider. For more robust solutions, you should consider implementing a reputable third-party logging solution. Most of them are capable of supporting multiple targets, including email. We will look at implementing one such solution in the next section.

The component responsible for generating the log output implements the `ILogger` interface. The contract defined by the interface requires three methods to be implemented:

- `BeginScope`—This method enables the grouping of a set of logging operations within a scope and sharing of data between the operations. Your logger won't support scopes, but we will explore this feature in more detail later.
- `Log`—This method takes a number of parameters and is responsible for outputting the log.
- `IsEnabled`—This method takes a `LogLevel` as a parameter and determines whether the logger is enabled for the specified `LogLevel`.

The email logger implementation takes the `IEmailSender` used in chapter 9 as a dependency and will use its `SendEmailAsync` method to generate and send the email. First, create a folder for the logger code files named Logging. This is created in the root of the project. Then add a class file named EmailLogger.cs with the following code.

Listing 12.14 The `EmailLogger` implementation

```
using Microsoft.AspNetCore.Identity.UI.Services;

namespace CityBreaks.Logging
{
    public class EmailLogger : ILogger
    {
        private readonly IEmailSender _emailSender;
        public EmailLogger(IEmailSender emailSender)
        {
            _emailSender = emailSender;
        }
        public IDisposable BeginScope<TState>(TState state) => null;

        public bool IsEnabled(LogLevel logLevel) =>
            logLevel == LogLevel.Error || logLevel == LogLevel.Critical;

        public void Log<TState>(LogLevel logLevel, EventId eventId,
            TState state, Exception exception, Func<TState,
            Exception, string> formatter)
        {
            if (!IsEnabled(logLevel))
                return;
            var htmlMessage = state.ToString() + "<br><br>" +
```

A using directive is needed to bring the IEmailSender into scope.

Implement the ILogger interface.

Inject an IEmailSender and assign it to a field.

This logger will not support scopes.

If the log level is Error or Critical, this logger is enabled.

Within the Log method, you establish whether the logger is enabled. If not, you return. Otherwise, you construct some HTML from the state and any exception that is passed in.

```
            exception?.Message + "<br><br>" +
            exception?.StackTrace;
        Task.Run(() => SendLog(htmlMessage));
    }

    private async Task SendLog(string htmlMessage)
    {
        var subject = "Error in application";
        var to = "test@example.com";
        await _emailSender.SendEmailAsync(to, subject, htmlMessage);
    }
  }
}
```

Within the Log method, you establish whether the logger is enabled. If not, you return. Otherwise, you construct some HTML from the state and any exception that is passed in.

The SendLog method uses the IEmailSender to send the email.

The Log method takes a number of parameters. The first is the LogLevel of the log. You will use this to determine if the logger is enabled. If it is, you ignore the EventId because you are not interested in it. Instead, you are interested in the state that contains any values passed in to the log, and you are interested in the exception, if there is one. The state can be cast to an IEnumerable<KeyValuePair<string, object>>, with each entry containing the name of a placeholder as its key and an object representing its value. When the framework logs an exception, it adds one entry to the collection, which has a key of {OriginalFormat} and a value of An unhandled exception has occurred while executing the request. You can get this value simply by calling ToString() on the state variable. Then you attempt to reference the message and stack trace of the exception and include those in the email message.

The next component you need to create is an implementation of ILoggerProvider, which is responsible for creating the logger on demand. Add another class file to the Logging folder named EmailLoggerProvider with the code shown in the following listing.

Listing 12.15 The EmailLoggerProvider class

```
using Microsoft.AspNetCore.Identity.UI.Services;

namespace CityBreaks.Logging
{
    public class EmailLoggerProvider : ILoggerProvider
    {
        private readonly IEmailSender _emailService;

        public EmailLoggerProvider(IEmailSender emailService)
        {
            _emailService = emailService;
        }

        public ILogger CreateLogger(string categoryName)
        {
            return new EmailLogger(emailService);
        }
```

```
            public void Dispose() { }
        }
    }
```

The `ILoggerProvider` interface defines one method: `CreateLogger`. This method is responsible for instantiating an instance of the logger. Your logger takes a dependency on the `IEmailSender`, so you inject that and assign it to a field. The `ILoggerProvider` implements `IDisposable`, so you also need to include a `Dispose` method, although it does nothing in this example.

You register the `ILoggerProvider` with the service container:

```
builder.Services.AddTransient<ILoggerProvider, EmailLoggerProvider>();
```

Now it is ready to be used and will start writing any logs that have a log level of `Error` or `Critical`. To test this, you can manufacture an unhandled exception in the `OnGetAsync` method of the home page's `IndexModel`.

Listing 12.16 Adding an unhandled exception to the application

```
public async Task OnGetAsync()
{
    Cities = await _cityService.GetAllAsync();
    throw new ApplicationException("Testing the logger");
}
```

Run the application, and you should find a new email has been generated in the TempMail folder you created in chapter 9. The email includes the state, the error message, and the stack trace, including the line of code where the error occurred (figure 12.11).

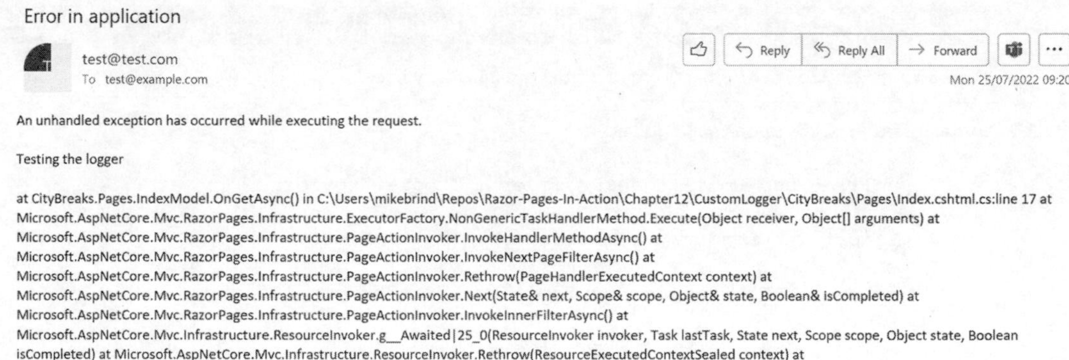

Error in application

test@test.com
To test@example.com

Reply | Reply All | Forward

Mon 25/07/2022 09:20

An unhandled exception has occurred while executing the request.

Testing the logger

at CityBreaks.Pages.IndexModel.OnGetAsync() in C:\Users\mikebrind\Repos\Razor-Pages-In-Action\Chapter12\CustomLogger\CityBreaks\Pages\Index.cshtml.cs:line 17 at Microsoft.AspNetCore.Mvc.RazorPages.Infrastructure.ExecutorFactory.NonGenericTaskHandlerMethod.Execute(Object receiver, Object[] arguments) at Microsoft.AspNetCore.Mvc.RazorPages.Infrastructure.PageActionInvoker.InvokeHandlerMethodAsync() at Microsoft.AspNetCore.Mvc.RazorPages.Infrastructure.PageActionInvoker.InvokeNextPageFilterAsync() at Microsoft.AspNetCore.Mvc.RazorPages.Infrastructure.PageActionInvoker.Rethrow(PageHandlerExecutedContext context) at Microsoft.AspNetCore.Mvc.RazorPages.Infrastructure.PageActionInvoker.Next(State& next, Scope& scope, Object& state, Boolean& isCompleted) at Microsoft.AspNetCore.Mvc.RazorPages.Infrastructure.PageActionInvoker.InvokeInnerFilterAsync() at Microsoft.AspNetCore.Mvc.Infrastructure.ResourceInvoker.g__Awaited|25_0(ResourceInvoker invoker, Task lastTask, State next, Scope scope, Object state, Boolean isCompleted) at Microsoft.AspNetCore.Mvc.Infrastructure.ResourceInvoker.Rethrow(ResourceExecutedContextSealed context) at

Figure 12.11 The email logger output

This example is designed to illustrate the basic steps required to implement your own custom logger. It is not an example of best practices and is certainly not production ready. For example, the `Log` method is not asynchronous, but you are calling an asynchronous API within it—hence the use of the `Task.Run` method. The best practice for writing logs to email, databases, or other *slow* (asynchronous) log stores is writing to an intermediate store, such as a buffer or message queue and then processing the queue separately. (See http://mng.bz/XaAa for more guidance.) In more complex applications, the general advice is to look for a third-party logger that offers all the features you need rather than trying to roll your own.

12.3.8 Structured logging with Serilog

Having explored the desirability of using a proven, tested, third-party logging solution, in this section, we will look at the steps required to implement logging with Serilog (https://github.com/serilog) in a Razor Pages application. The default implementation of Serilog includes logging providers (or *sinks*, in Serilog parlance) for console, file, and debug. The file option writes to a *rolling* log file, which means you can configure the logging system to create a new log file for each day, each hour, or after the file has reached a certain size, for example. In addition, you can specify that the file output is formatted as JSON, so you can see the structure of the logs, which will hopefully give you some idea of the usefulness of structured logging.

As well as the default sinks, there is a massive ecosystem of alternative sinks (http://mng.bz/ya2d) that target a wide variety of outputs, including email, databases, message queues, cloud-based service providers, and more. Just like .NET Core logging, Serilog outputs to all configured sinks. In this walk-through, you will configure Serilog to output to the console and a file as JSON.

The recommended version of Serilog for ASP.NET Core application logging is Serilog.AspNetCore (http://mng.bz/M0WB). So use your preferred method for installing that package from NuGet. Your project file should be updated with a new package reference accordingly, although the version number might differ:

```
<PackageReference Include="Serilog.AspNetCore" Version="4.1.0" />
```

CONFIGURATION

Serilog recommends the logger to be configured prior to the `WebApplication.CreateBuilder` method call in Program.cs, so it can log any application startup errors. Serilog supports two configuration strategies:

- You can use the appSettings.json file to configure Serilog, just as you have done with the default logging.
- Alternatively, you can use a fluent API. This is the recommended approach and the one that you will adopt in the chapter.

The main reason for recommending the fluent API approach is the appSettings.json configuration is not available until after the `WebApplication.CreateBuilder` method has been called. If you want to use appSettings.json for logging configuration, you will either need to create two loggers—one for application start (that will use the fluent

API anyway) and another that reads its config from appSettings.json after the `CreateBuilder` call—or create just one logger and forego logging details of application start errors.

To begin, you will add three additional `using` directives at the top of the Program.cs file, the first of which you will always need when working with Serilog; the other two are optional, depending on what you want to configure. They enable you to refer to the `LogEventLevel` and the `JsonFormatter` during configuration, respectively.

Listing 12.17 The using directives required for Serilog

```
using Serilog;
using Serilog.Events;
using Serilog.Formatting.Json;
```

You will always need this. (using Serilog;)

Optional—enables you to refer to LogEventLevel during configuration (using Serilog.Events;)

Optional—enables you to refer to the JsonFormatter during configuration (using Serilog.Formatting.Json;)

The next block of code is placed immediately after the `using` directives and before the `WebApplication.CreateBuilder` call.

Listing 12.18 Example Serilog configuration using the fluent API

```
Log.Logger = new LoggerConfiguration()
    .MinimumLevel.Override("Microsoft.AspNetCore", LogEventLevel.Warning)
    .MinimumLevel.Override("Microsoft.EntityFrameworkCore",
    LogEventLevel.Warning)
    .WriteTo.Console()
    .WriteTo.File(path: "Logs\\log.json",
    ➥ formatter: new JsonFormatter(), rollingInterval: RollingInterval.Day)
    .CreateLogger();
Log.Information("Starting up");
```

You use the static `Log.Logger` method to create a logger with the specified configuration. Your configuration specifies a minimum log level of `Warning` for the `Microsoft AspNetCore` and `EntityFramework` categories to reduce log verbosity. You use the `WriteTo` method to configure sinks. Your chosen sinks are the console and the file. You will use the default settings for the console output, but you have configured the file logger to output using JSON. You have also specified that a new file should be created each day via the `rollingInterval` parameter. Your log file will be written to a folder within the application named Logs. You don't need to create the folder yourself because Serilog will create it if it doesn't exist.

The existing content in Program.cs is placed in a `try-catch` block, so any exceptions raised during the startup phase are caught and logged. Listing 12.19 shows the code from the `CreateBuilder` method call all the way down to the final `app.Run` call being placed in a `try` block, with the addition of the `UseSerilog` method call, which removes existing logging providers and enables Serilog as their replacement.

Listing 12.19 Handling and logging any potential startup exceptions

```
try                                                  ◁── Place a try block around the existing code in Program.cs.
{
    var builder = WebApplication.CreateBuilder(args);
    builder.Host.UseSerilog();                       ◁── Add a call to UseSerilog on the Host property of the WebApplicationBuilder.
    builder.Services.AddRazorPages(options =>
    ...
    app.Run();
}
catch (Exception ex)                                 ◁── Log any exceptions encountered during app configuration and start.
{
    Log.Fatal(ex, "Application start failed");
}
finally                                              ◁── Flush any buffered log messages to their destination.
{
    Log.Information("Shut down complete");
    Log.CloseAndFlush();
}
```

Serilog log levels are mostly identical to those provided by the .NET logging system, except the lowest level is called `Verbose` (instead of `Trace`), and the highest level is called `Fatal` (instead of `Critical`). You will use the `Log.Fatal` method to record details of any exceptions that prevented the application from starting.

Now that you have replaced the existing log providers with Serilog, it's time to test that the replacement works. Remove the line that throws the exception in the `OnGetAsync` method of the main `IndexModel`, and then run the application. You should see something along the lines of the following listing in the console.

Listing 12.20 The Serilog console logger output

```
[08:35:58 INF] Starting up
[08:35:59 INF] Now listening on: https://localhost:7236
[08:35:59 INF] Now listening on: http://localhost:5236
[08:35:59 INF] Application started. Press Ctrl+C to shut down.
[08:35:59 INF] Hosting environment: Development
[08:35:59 INF] Content root path: D:\repos\
➥ Razor-Pages-In-Action\Chapter12\Serilog\CityBreaks\
[08:36:00 INF] 12 Cities retrieved
```

Notice the difference from the default loggers. There is no category included in the log message. You can change that by passing a string to the `outputTemplate` parameter of the `WriteTo.Console` method (http://mng.bz/M0WB). Serilog refers to the category as the `SourceContext`. The following template includes the category and uses the `NewLine` property to place the log message over multiple lines:

```
"[{Timestamp:HH:mm:ss} {Level:u3}]
➥ {SourceContext}{NewLine}{Message:lj}{NewLine}{Exception}"
```

Of more interest from a structured log point of view is the contents of the log file created in the Logs folder. This should now contain a number of logs in JSON format, each one on a separate line. The file content as a whole is not true JSON, but each standalone entry is. The following listing shows how the last entry looks once it has been formatted in a more friendly way.

Listing 12.21 The Serilog default JSON formatter output

```
{
  "Timestamp": "2022-01-08T08:42:50.6276136+00:00",
  "Level": "Information",
  "MessageTemplate": "{count} Cities retrieved",
  "Properties": {
    "count": 12,
    "SourceContext": "CityBreaks.Pages.IndexModel",
    "ActionId": "cda34ae3-2c8f-457a-964b-d7200a0f64df",
    "ActionName": "/Index",
    "RequestId": "0HMEIGBD156VF:00000001",
    "RequestPath": "/",
    "ConnectionId": "0HMEIGBD156VF"
  }
}
```

Note the level of detail here. The property bag, represented by the `Properties` node, includes more information than the console logger. As well as request details and the log category, it includes a property named `count`, which has been taken from your log message template. This enables querying of the property by tools that can parse the JSON log and illustrates why you should use named placeholders in your log message templates instead of interpolation or plain string concatenation.

It is not unusual for users to make mistakes when they modify data within an application. Sadly, I've also found it is not unusual for some users to evade responsibility, blaming someone else or *the system* for their mistake. What would be really useful in these situations would be to show the state of the data before they made an update and then again after the update was made, so there is clear evidence of the changes made and when they were made. In other words, you want a kind of transaction log.

Serilog enables capturing this level of information very simply, preserving an object's structure when it is logged. To see how powerful this can be, add another logging call to the application. Amend the `OnGetPropertyDetails` handler in the City.cshtml.cs file as follows. Note that the placeholder name is prefixed with your old friend the `@` symbol, known in Serilog as the *destructuring operator.*

Listing 12.22 The @ destructuring operator preserving object structure

```
public async Task<PartialViewResult> OnGetPropertyDetails(int id)
{
    var property = await _propertyService.FindAsync(id);
    _logger.LogInformation("Property {@property}
```

```
➥ retrieved by {user}", property, User.Identity.Name);
    var model = new BookingInputModel { Property = property };
    return Partial("_PropertyDetailsPartial", model);
}
```

Log details of the property that was retrieved and who it was retrieved by.

This time, the rendered log message (the relevant part of which is shown in the following listing) includes a destructured version of the property variable.

Listing 12.23 The rendered log including full details of the property

```
"Level": "Information",
"MessageTemplate": "Property {@property} retrieved by {user}",
"Properties": {
  "property": {
    "_typeTag": "Property",
    "Id": 38,
    "Name": "Hotel Colonial",
    "Address": "Via Laietana",
    "CityId": 2,
    "City": null,
    "MaxNumberOfGuests": 3,
    "DayRate": 88.0,
    "SmokingPermitted": false,
    "AvailableFrom": "0001-01-01T00:00:00.0000000",
    "Deleted": null,
    "CreatorId": null,
    "Creator": null
  },
  "user": "anna@test.com",
  "SourceContext": "CityBreaks.Pages.CityModel",
```

While it is possible to write your own log-querying tools for working with structured logs, there are existing tools out there already, such as Seq (pronounced *seek*) and Elasticsearch, both of which Serilog includes sinks for. These third-party services may not be free; you should check their cost against the likely cost of developing and maintaining your own solution.

In this chapter, we've covered the main ways you can control how your application behaves in the event of errors occurring that you did not anticipate in code. We've also explored logging, primarily as a mechanism for capturing as much information about exceptions that get raised as possible, although it can be used to capture details of any kind of activity for any purpose. In the next chapter, we will look at protecting your application against external threats.

Summary

- During development, the Developer Exception page is displayed in the event of an unhandled exception, providing details of the exception and the line of code where it was raised.

- When the application is exposed to users, you should use `ExceptionHandlerMiddleware` to show a generic error page to hide details of errors.
- `ExceptionHandlerMiddleware` should be placed very early in the application pipeline.
- StatusCodePages middleware is designed to control how the application behaves when client errors occur.
- With StatusCodePages middleware, you can incorporate the HTTP status code into the path or query string of the custom error page that is presented.
- Use the `WithRedirects` approach if you want StatusCodePages middleware to issue a redirect to the browser. The original status code and request path are replaced.
- Use the `WithReExecute` approach to retain the HTTP status code and the original path in the browser address bar.
- Logging is supported as a first-class citizen in Razor Pages applications.
- Default logging providers include `Console` and `Debug`.
- Log levels are used to denote log severity.
- Log categories help you identify the class that generated the log.
- Event IDs can be used to add metadata to logs.
- Recommended practice is to use named placeholders in format strings (templates) to generate log messages, so structured logging can extract their properties and values.
- Custom loggers consist of implementing the `ILogger` and `ILoggerProvider` interfaces, then registering the `ILoggerProvider` with the service container.
- Many third-party logging providers are available for ASP.NET Core applications.
- Structured logging generates logs in a structured format that facilitates advanced querying and filtering.

13 Protecting your application against external attacks

This chapter covers

- Configuring your application for HTTPS
- Ensuring you apply good access control
- Avoiding common cryptographic failures
- Preventing injection attacks

Once your application is published, it will come under attack. Most of these attacks will be automated, probing for well-known vulnerabilities. You will probably be surprised to see requests being logged for URLs that include *phpmyadmin*, or the names of popular third-party component libraries you don't even use. The HTTPS protocol underpins the security of any website. We will begin this chapter with a reminder of the importance of HTTPS and learning how to configure your application to use HTTPS.

Then we will look at the threats posed to your application in more detail, focusing on the most common of these according to the Open Web Application Security Project (OWASP) (https://owasp.org/). You will learn how the Razor Pages framework has been designed specifically to protect you from various threats and how to maintain security should you find the need to bypass these safeguards.

The OWASP categorizes vulnerabilities under a number of headings. We will look at some of the specific threats under the top three headings:

- Broken access control
- Cryptographic failures
- Injection attacks

We will examine vulnerabilities grouped under the broken access control heading, which includes issues affecting authentication and authorization. Then, you will learn about some common cryptographic failures, such as storing passwords in plain text, and how to avoid them. Finally, we will look at the two types of injection attack: SQL injection, a vulnerability that can result in arbitrary SQL commands being executed against your database; and cross-site scripting (XSS), where a malicious user can cause havoc and steal data by injecting client-side scripts into your pages.

Many threats can be mitigated simply by implementing HTTPS. In 2014, Google announced it would include HTTPS as a ranking signal (http://mng.bz/aP4m). The intention behind this announcement was to persuade as many site owners as possible to improve site security by running their application over encrypted connections backed up by valid certificates. To begin our look at application security, you will learn about the importance of HTTPS and learn how you can configure your application to work with it.

13.1 HTTPS

I'll start with a review of the basics. What is HTTPS, and why would you want to use it? HTTPS is a protocol that ensures a secure connection between your website and your users. HTTPS provides security in three ways:

- *Authentication*—Users can be sure they are interacting with your site rather than a spoofed copy hosted under a different domain.
- *Encryption*—All communication between the user and your website is encrypted, ensuring it cannot be stolen.
- *Data integrity*—Users are guaranteed the content they receive has not been modified by a third party.

Communication over an unsecured connection (HTTP) is conducted in plain text. Anyone who has access to the network you are using can see the content of your communications, including posted form values, such as your username and password, for example. They can also insert their own content into the response before it reaches you. Some of us are old enough to remember the free WiFi services offered by hotels that would insert their own advertising or branding into the web page you were trying to reach. Now imagine someone with less clear motives inserting their own links into pages you felt you could trust, and you will begin to understand the potential harm that can come from interacting with unsecured websites.

13.1.1 SSL/TLS certificates

Server authentication is guaranteed by the presence of a valid SSL or TLS certificate issued by a trusted *certificate authority* (CA). A list of all trusted CAs is built into your operating system or device, and clients such as web browsers use this list to verify the certificate issuer. The certificate issuer is responsible for ensuring the person who requests the certificate has control over the domain they are requesting the certificate for. This can be achieved in a number of ways, depending on the type of certificate being requested. The most common type of certificate is the *domain validation* (DV) certificate, which is used solely to validate who has control over the domain. Domain control can be verified by the addition of a specific DNS record or by using software on the server where the domain's IP address is assigned to request the certificate. These days, it is relatively easy to obtain DV certificates at no cost. More and more hosting companies offer them, or you can get them directly from an organization, such as Let's Encrypt (https://letsencrypt.org/).

> **NOTE** SSL, or Secure Sockets Layer, was the original protocol used for encrypting HTTP messages. Some time ago, it was deprecated in favor of the newer Transport Layer Security (TLS) protocol, which is what is used these days. The term *SSL* is still used to refer to authentication certificates, although SSL itself is no longer used anywhere.

Other types of TLS certificate are available, known as *organization validation* (OV) and *extended validation* (EV). They validate your business and, in the case of EV certification, its ownership. If you use Cloudflare (https://www.cloudflare.com/) as a reverse proxy, they offer OV certificates for free, although the organization they authenticate is their own. Cloudflare encrypts traffic between the user and its services. You have to take extra steps to encrypt traffic between the origin server (where you host your site) and Cloudflare. EV certificates are usually the most expensive. If an EV was used, browsers used to display details of the business that owned the domain in the address bar (a so-called *EV UI*), but that is no longer the case (http://mng.bz/gRYv). The value proposition of an EV over that of a DV certificate centers around degrees of trust and identity assurance, although whether that is something a site visitor even understands is debatable (http://mng.bz/epRV).

When you visit a site over a secure connection that has a valid certificate of any kind, the browser displays a small padlock at the beginning of the address, shown in figure 13.1. The appearance of the padlock differs from browser to browser, but each padlock confirms the connection is secure and the certificate is valid. If you click the padlock, you can see further details of the certificate, such as the domain it validates, its expiry date, and who the issuer is.

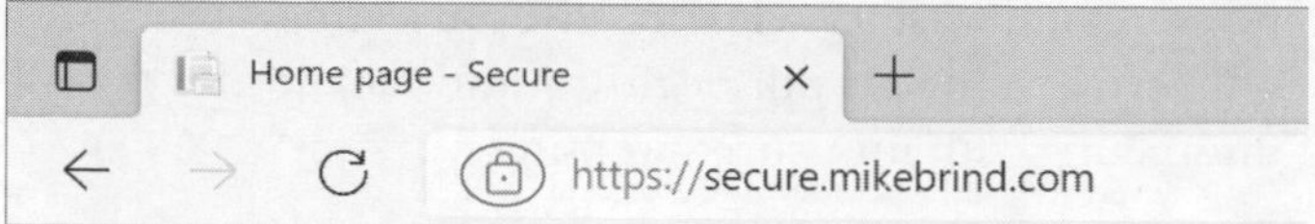

Figure 13.1 The padlock provides visible confirmation that the connection is secure.

When you visit a site over an unsecured connection, most browsers provide a warning instead of a padlock. The warning consists of a triangular sign and the words *Not secure*, which can be seen in figure 13.2.

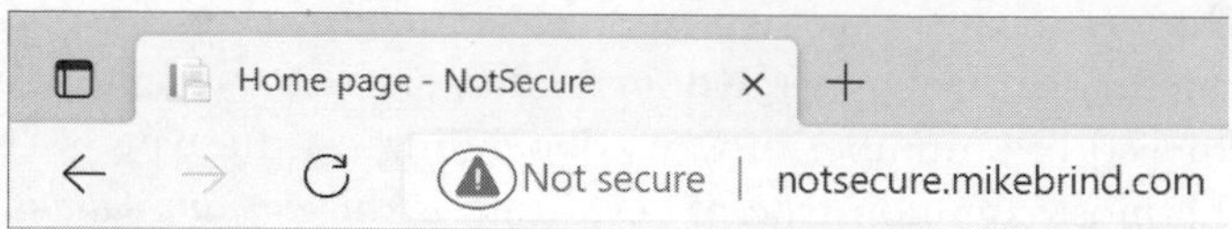

Figure 13.2 The warning triangle and words *Not secure* confirm this is an unsecured connection.

When you deploy your website to a public web server, you will obtain your TLS certificate from a trusted issuer, so that browsers accept it. How you go about this process depends on the issuer that you use. You should check their documentation or support. When developing and testing your application locally, you also need a certificate the browser trusts to run the application over HTTPS.

13.1.2 Using HTTPS in development

When you install the .NET 6 SDK, it installs a TLS certificate for development purposes (the ASP.NET Core HTTPS development certificate), which is used by the Kestrel server. By default, this certificate is not trusted. When you first run any application using Visual Studio on its configured HTTPS port, you are prompted to trust the certificate. If you are not a Visual Studio user, you can use the `dotnet` tool to trust the certificate, using the following command:

```
dotnet dev-certs https --trust
```

This should be a one-time step. Once you have granted trust to the development certificate, you should not be asked to do so again.

By default, new Razor Pages applications are configured to run over HTTPS, whether you use the Visual Studio new project wizard to create them or the `dotnet new webapp` command. You have to explicitly opt out of HTTPS configuration by passing `---no-https` to the CLI command or unchecking the Configure for HTTPS option in the Visual Studio new project wizard, although that isn't recommended. It is not even possible to opt out of HTTPS if you want to include authorization within your application when you first create it. An application configured to use HTTPS differs from a non-HTTPS application in the following three ways:

- It has HTTPS URLs configured in the launchSettings.json file for IIS Express and Kestrel.
- It includes HTTPS redirection middleware.
- It conditionally includes HSTS middleware.

The HTTPS redirection middleware is enabled by default and forces all requests to use the HTTPS protocol. If you attempt to browse the site using the configured HTTP port, the middleware constructs a new URL, using the HTTPS port, and sends that back in the location header of the response along with a 307 status code, which tells the user agent (browser) it should retain the original HTTP method. You may have noticed when running the CityBreaks application that it always ran under HTTPS. This was the result of the HTTPS redirection middleware in action. If this has escaped your notice, try it now.

Open a command prompt or terminal/Powershell window, navigate to the folder containing the CityBreaks.proj file, and execute the `dotnet run` command. The logger (Serilog, in my case) should confirm the application is running under two URLs: one HTTPS and the other HTTP. The actual port numbers may well differ from mine:

```
[08:17:56 INF] Microsoft.Hosting.Lifetime
Now listening on: https://localhost:7236
[08:17:56 INF] Microsoft.Hosting.Lifetime
Now listening on: http://localhost:5236
```

Open a browser and its developer tools (press F12 in most browsers), and ensure the Network tab is open. Then copy the HTTP URL into the browser address bar, and press Enter. You should see that the request results in a 307 error, leading to a new request (figure 13.3).

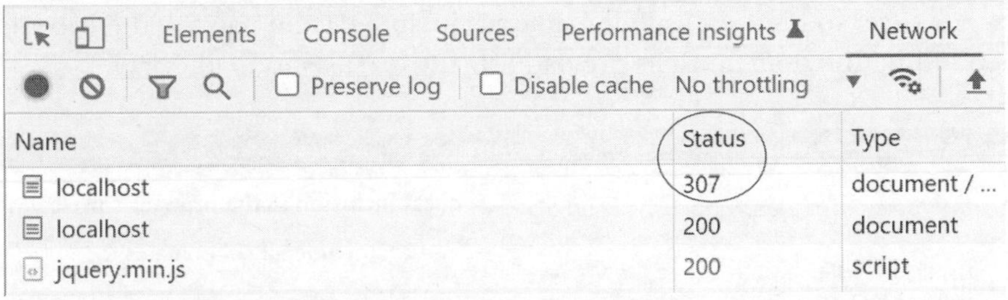

Name	Status	Type
localhost	307	document / ...
localhost	200	document
jquery.min.js	200	script

Figure 13.3 HTTPS redirection middleware generates a 307 status code if the request is not made over HTTPS.

HTTPS redirection middleware is positioned very early in the request pipeline, before the static files middleware:

```
app.UseHttpsRedirection();
app.UseStaticFiles();
```

This placement ensures all static files within your application are served over HTTPS, preventing *mixed content* issues, which occur when some elements of the page are served over HTTP, while the host page is served over HTTPS. Browsers actively block some content served in this way, such as JavaScript and CSS files, potentially rendering your application unusable.

HTTPS redirection middleware does not prevent users from requesting content over HTTP. It just redirects such requests when they happen. That first request is still insecure. You can minimize this vulnerability by adding an HTTP `Strict-Transport-Security` (HSTS) header to your responses, which tells the browser that your website should only ever be accessed over HTTPS. That is what HSTS middleware does.

13.1.3 Including HSTS in production

The HSTS header tells the browser it should only ever request resources for the domain in question over HTTPS. The HSTS header includes a `max-age` directive and a directive that specifies whether subdomains should be included. It also includes a `preload` directive that tells the browser you would like to add your domain to its preload list, ensuring the first request cannot be made over HTTP on subsequent visits.

NOTE The HSTS header is ignored by browsers when the request is made over HTTP because it is possible for a hacker to intercept the request and modify the header's `max-age`, for example. So you must include HTTPS redirection in your application to ensure requests are redirected to HTTPS. Once that redirection has taken place and the connection is secured via HTTPS, the browser will honor the directives within the HSTS header for all future requests. From then on the browser will replace HTTP with HTTPS when making any requests for the specified domain.

You configure HSTS middleware via the service container. In the following listing, the `max-age` is set to one year, subdomains are included, and you ask the browser to consider adding the domain to its preload list (https://hstspreload.org/).

Listing 13.1 Configuring HSTS middleware

```
builder.Services.AddHsts(options =>
{
    options.Preload = true;
    options.IncludeSubDomains = true;
    options.MaxAge = TimeSpan.FromDays(365);
});
```

Request inclusion in the browser's preload list.

Include all subdomains.

Set an expiry of one year from now. This is a sliding expiry, which is updated each time the browser accesses the website.

When configured to use HTTPS, the default project template only includes HSTS middleware when your application is not running in Development mode. I recommend you do not enable HSTS while in development in case you need to run the application without HTTPS at some stage.

Listing 13.2 Configuring HSTS middleware when not in Development mode

```
if (!app.Environment.IsDevelopment())
{
    app.UseExceptionHandler("/Error");
    app.UseHsts();
}
```

Checks to establish the mode the application is running in

Includes HSTS middleware if it is not development

Having configured your application for HTTPS, you have ensured communication is private and removed the prospect of *man-in-the-middle attacks*, when a bad actor intercepts web traffic and steals data or modifies content. The rest of this chapter will explore other common threats, as defined by the OWASP. You will understand the nature of vulnerabilities and how attacks can be performed. Once you appreciate the mechanics of a particular threat, you will learn how to mitigate it. You'll begin by looking at the area where the most common threats were found, according to the current 2021 OWASP Top Ten (https://owasp.org/www-project-top-ten/), which are grouped in a common category of broken access control.

13.2 Broken access control

An application's access control policies should be designed to restrict the operations a user is able to perform and the data they are able to access. This is known as the *least privilege principle*. The most common risk of broken access control is unauthorized access to, modification of, destruction of, or theft of data. In this section, we will look at some of the ways access control can become broken and how to prevent it. We will examine some best practices for applying and managing security policies first. Then we will look at the dangers cross-site forgery requests present and the mechanism Razor Pages provides to help protect against such attacks.

13.2.1 Incorrect security policies

Incorrect security policies is a broad category that covers missing, out-of-date, or incorrectly applied attempts to restrict access to unauthorized users (see chapter 10 for a review of the mechanics of authorization). There isn't a specific framework-based solution to this group of vulnerabilities, but there are some best practices you should try to apply as part of application development.

The first piece of guidance is to always implement your authorization policies on the server. As discussed a number of times previously, any client-side code is vulnerable to being amended or bypassed by any user who has minimal HTML or JavaScript knowledge.

At the time of writing, there is a recent case in which a news reporter discovered that the Social Security numbers of teachers were included in the HTML source code of web pages published by a particular state education department (http://mng.bz/p6EK). It is unclear why they were included or how—perhaps as HTML comments, because their exposure doesn't appear to be deliberate. Without wanting to prejudice any potential legal proceedings, this should serve as a reminder that comments in HTML source code are not private, despite the fact that browsers do not display them. If you are ever tempted to include information that is not intended for display in a Razor file, use Razor comments (`@* ... *@`) to prevent it from being rendered. The best practice is not to include anything confidential within content that might be exposed to users at all.

When we covered authorization, we looked at authorizing resources (section 10.5) as well as endpoints. Resource-based authorization is a best practice. It enforces record ownership rather than accepting that users can perform read, update, and delete on any record. It also mitigates against URL tampering, which might expose records the user is not entitled to access.

We also looked at using the `Authorize` attribute to apply authorization policies on a page-by-page basis. I recommended centralizing your policies, so they are easier to review and manage. This chapter provides a good opportunity to reinforce that advice. If you find access control review a time-consuming chore, you are less likely to do it as often as you should, which is more likely result in broken authorization.

13.2.2 Cross-site request forgery

Cross-site request forgery, or CSRF, exploits a vulnerability that causes an authenticated user to make an involuntary request to a website. The request could result in a command being processed by the website in question that the user did not intend, such as changing a password or transferring money.

To illustrate this, imagine you visit your banking website at mysavings.com. You log in, and the banking site adds an authentication cookie to your browser. The cookie remains valid for whatever term the banking site specified. While the cookie is valid, you visit another site, spoofsite.com, perhaps as a result of clicking an interesting looking link in a phishing email. The page you visit includes code that generates a post request to mysavings.com that results in some action being performed on your account. Landing on the page in spoofsite.com triggers the code, and the request is sent. This is the *cross-site* request. The banking site processes the request because it is accompanied by your authentication cookie, which tells your bank site you are currently logged in (figure 13.4).

The target site—mysavings.com—is vulnerable to CSRF in this example because it does not verify the source of the HTTP request. The recommended protection against CSRF is a pattern known as *double submit cookies*. This is what Razor Pages uses by default, and this is how it works: A random value is generated by the server and sent to the browser in a cookie. The cookie has its `SameSite` attribute set to `Strict`, ensuring it can be sent by the browser only if the request originates from the site that issued the cookie. The value, the *request verification token*, is also included as a request parameter in a hidden form field. When a form is submitted, the framework checks the value in the hidden field against that of the cookie. If they are both present and match, the request is verified as having originated from the original website and not a third party. Using this technique, it is impossible for spoofsite.com to send the request verification cookie to mysavings.com.

As you learned in chapter 6, the hidden form field containing the request verification token is generated automatically by the form tag helper whenever you set the method of a form element to `post`. You also learned how to generate the token directly, using the `IAntiforgery` service, or as a hidden form field, using the `Html.AntiForgeryToken`

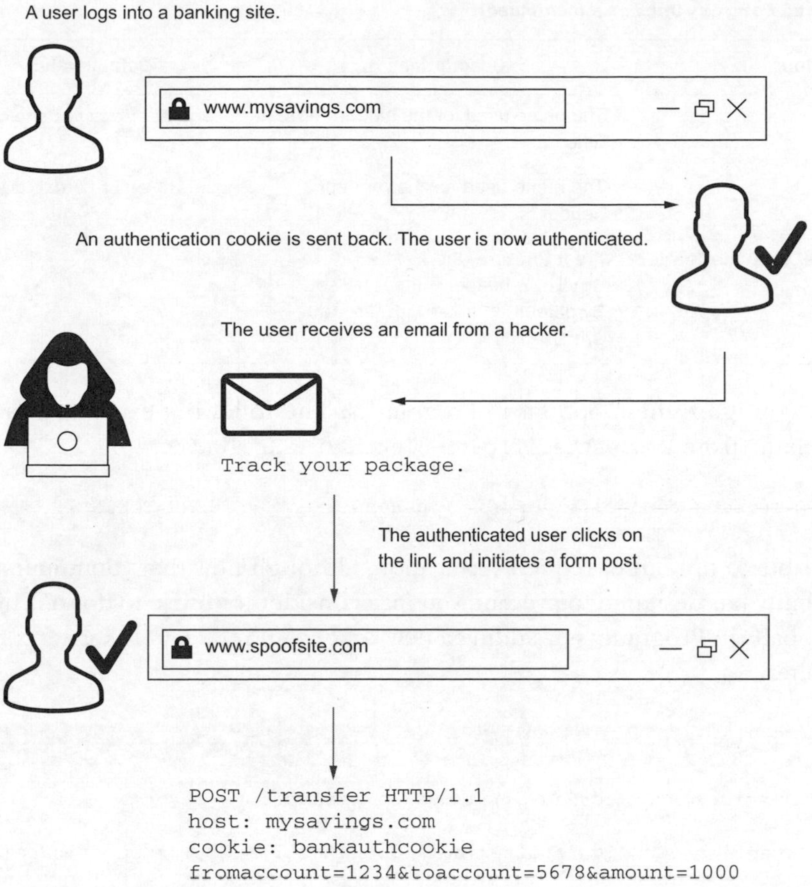

Figure 13.4 Cross-site request forgery takes advantage of your authenticated status on the target site.

helper, in the event you aren't using a form, in chapter 11, when we looked at working with client-side code.

CONFIGURING ANTIFORGERY OPTIONS

Various options relating to the antiforgery feature are configurable via the `AntiforgeryOptions` class, as shown in table 13.1.

Table 13.1 The `AntiforgeryOptions`

Option	Description	Default value
`Cookie`	Provides access to configuring aspects of the cookie.	If a value for the cookie name is not specified, a unique value will be generated prefixed with `.AspNetCore.Antiforgery`.

Table 13.1 The `AntiforgeryOptions` *(continued)*

Option	Description	Default value
`FormFieldName`	The name used for the hidden form field.	`__RequestVerificationToken.`
`HeaderName`	The name used for the request header.	`RequestVerificationToken.`
`SuppressXFrameOptionsHeader`	If set to `true`, the `X-Frame-Options` header will not be set. By default, it is set with the value `SAMEORIGIN`.	`'false'.`

You can configure these options in Program.cs. The following example changes the header name from `RequestVerificationToken` to `CSRF-TOKEN`:

```
builder.Services.AddAntiforgery(o => o.HeaderName = "CSRF-TOKEN");
```

It is possible to opt out of request verification, although now that you understand the vulnerability it is designed to prevent, you may consider it unwise to do so. This can be done globally in Program.cs by adding a new `IgnoreAntiforgeryTokenAttribute` as a global filter.

Listing 13.3 Disabling request verification globally

```
builder.Services.AddRazorPages().AddRazorPagesOptions(o =>
{
    o.Conventions.ConfigureFilter(new IgnoreAntiforgeryTokenAttribute());
});
```

Alternatively, you can selectively disable the check on a page-by-page basis by adding the `IgnoreAntiforgeryTokenAttribute` to the relevant `PageModel` class (not a handler method).

Listing 13.4 Disabling request verification selectively

```
[IgnoreAntiforgeryToken(Order = 1001)]
public class IndexModel : PageModel
{
}
```

The `ValidateAntiForgeryToken` attribute applied by default has an order of 1,000; therefore, the `IgnoreAntiforgeryToken` attribute needs a higher-order number to be activated. Alternatively, you can turn off request verification globally, as in listing 13.5, and then selectively apply it on a case-by-case basis by decorating the appropriate `PageModel` class with the `ValidateAntiForgeryToken` attribute (applying the same logic to the `Order` value as previously).

Listing 13.5 Enabling request verification selectively

```
[ValidateAntiForgeryToken(Order = 1001)]
public class IndexModel : PageModel
{
}
```

The built-in request verification feature is only invoked for *unsafe* HTTP methods—those methods that result in state being changed on the server. It is not invoked for GET requests, which should be used only for reading data. Consequently, it is important that you do not use GET for operations that result in changes to data.

13.3 Cryptographic failures

When we first looked at the ASP.NET Core Identity library in chapter 9, I warned against implementing your own authentication framework because it is so easy to get things wrong and introduce vulnerabilities into your application. Cryptography, the underpinning of a secure authentication framework, is a highly specialized area of work that is best left to experts. Cryptographic failures result in sensitive data being leaked and are the second most common types of vulnerabilities found in applications, according to the OWASP. In this section, we will look at a few specific examples of cryptographic failures and how to avoid them.

We will look at the dangers involved in storing user passwords and other sensitive data in plain text. You will then learn the differences between encryption and hashing and how the Identity library protects your data by hashing it where necessary. We will also walk through a demonstration showing how to use a core component of Identity, the PasswordHasher, to protect data, even if you have no intention of leveraging Identity-based storage or UI. Another item that comes under the heading of cryptographic failures is failure to enforce TLS for data transfer, which we've already explored in the first section of the chapter.

13.3.1 Plain-text passwords

Rule number one in the web security handbook (if there is such a thing) is never store user passwords in plain text. People are creatures of habit. Many of them will use the same password on your site that they use for every other site they have an account with. In the event of a data breach, you could be giving crooks the keys to all other websites your users access. The website Have I Been Pwned (https://haveibeenpwned.com/) lists over 500 websites that have suffered data breaches, many of them familiar names and a significant number of them yielding up passwords in plain text.

So how should you store users' passwords and other sensitive data? Some developers are tempted to encrypt passwords, so they can be decrypted for comparison with the password submitted in a login form. Because encryption is designed to be reversed, it is not secure should someone get access to the means for decrypting the data. The Identity framework secures user passwords by *hashing* them. Hashing is a one-way process that should always produce the same output for a given input. For a hashing algorithm to be considered cryptographically secure, it should be infeasible to reverse a hash through brute-force computation, based on the resources (equipment and time) required to do the job. The reality is that processing reduces in cost and increases in power all the time, which has resulted in older hashing algorithms, such as MD5, to become *broken.*

ASP.NET Core Identity uses the PBKDF2 hashing algorithm (which is one of the options recommended by the OWASP). The number of times the actual hashing function is iterated (the *work factor*) determines the difficulty of breaking PBKDF2 hashes. The recommended number of iterations increases all the time as hardware gets faster. In 2010, the number of iterations hardcoded into ASP.NET was 1,000. Currently, the default number of iterations is 10,000, which was the recommended minimum in 2017. The best advice is to increase this number to the largest that the authenticating server's resources will tolerate. The OWASP currently recommends a minimum of 310,000 iterations to conform to the US Federal Information Processing Standards (FIPS). The more iterations that the hashing function is called, the more resources it takes to generate the resulting value. There is a trade-off to be had between generating hashes that are as secure as possible and overloading your web server with too much work to generate the final hashed value. Users are not going to wait for 10 minutes to log in, while you hash their password twenty million times on underpowered hardware.

Password hashing in Identity is performed by the `PasswordHasher` class. You can configure the number of iterations of the hashing function through the `PasswordHasherOptions` class. The following listing demonstrates how to increase the number of iterations to the number recommended to conform to FIPS.

Listing 13.6 Increasing the `PasswordHasher` PBKDF2 iteration count to 310,000

```
builder.Services.Configure<PasswordHasherOptions>(options =>
{
    options.IterationCount = 310000;
});
```

When the `PasswordHasher` processes a password for storage, it uses a salt—a cryptographically generated random value that is added to the password before it is hashed. This prevents passwords from being cracked through the use of *rainbow tables*—collections of hashes of common passwords. The salt is stored along with the hashed password, the number of iterations that were applied to the hashing function, and the hashing function that was used (SHA256, by default). When a user logs in, the salt and the iteration count are retrieved and then used to hash the submitted password. The result is compared with the stored hash to validate the user.

If the user is validated and the iteration count configured via `PasswordHasherOptions` is higher than the iteration count stored with the password, the password is rehashed using the higher iteration count and updated in the database. This enables you to increase the iteration count over time to keep ahead of technical advances.

This operation is not reversible. If you reduce the iteration count, all passwords saved with the higher iteration count will continue to be subject to that higher count when they are verified.

All of this protection provided by Identity is great, but what if you don't want to use the Identity database schema or UI? Well the good news is that you can still leverage the expert technology within the `PasswordHasher` class itself to ensure you can store and verify passwords securely.

13.3.2 Using the PasswordHasher without Identity UI

In this section, we will take a look at the simple steps required to incorporate the `PasswordHasher` into your application without depending on EF Core–based storage of user data or the UI package we explored in chapter 9. You will create a simple form that captures a username and password; the password will be hashed using the `PasswordHasher`, and the resulting hash will be stored in a hidden field in the same form. When the form is resubmitted, the user will have to enter the password again. This time it will be verified against the previously generated hash, and the result of that operation will be displayed to the browser.

This exercise has been created in a brand-new web application project with HTTPS enabled. I have named my application PasswordHasherDemo. The first thing that needs to be done is include the ASP.NET Core Identity package. If you recall from chapter 9, you installed the `Microsoft.AspNetCore.Identity.EntityFrameworkCore` package because you wanted to leverage EF Core–based data access for storing user data. This time, you don't need that capability, so you only install the basic Identity library, which is in a package called `Microsoft.AspNetCore.Identity`. Next, you need to create a `User` class based on `IdentityUser`, just as you did in chapter 9. Add a new folder named Models, and then add the class in the following listing to it.

Listing 13.7 The `User` class

```
using Microsoft.AspNetCore.Identity;
namespace PasswordHasherDemo.Models;

public class User : IdentityUser        <-- Your user class derives from IdentityUser.
{
}
```

Having done that, you need to register the `PasswordHasher` as a service, which you do in Program.cs. The `PasswordHasher` class depends on the `IPasswordHasher` interface and takes a generic type argument representing the user class. The following listing shows the first few lines of Program.cs modified to add the registration.

Listing 13.8 Adding the `PasswordHasher` as a service

```
using Microsoft.AspNetCore.Identity;     | You will need these
using PasswordHasherDemo.Models;         | using directives.
```

```
var builder = WebApplication.CreateBuilder(args);

builder.Services.AddRazorPages();
builder.Services.AddSingleton<IPasswordHasher<User>, PasswordHasher<User>>();
var app = builder.Build();
```

Register the IPasswordHasher as a service.

Next you will make some changes to Index.cshtml.cs, as shown in listing 13.9. You remove the `ILogger` from the constructor and replace it with `IPasswordHasher` along with a backing field. You also add some properties to the `PageModel`, most of which having the `BindProperty` attribute and some data annotations to control validation and display.

Listing 13.9 The modified `IndexModel` class

```
using Microsoft.AspNetCore.Identity;
using Microsoft.AspNetCore.Mvc;
using Microsoft.AspNetCore.Mvc.RazorPages;
using PasswordHasherDemo.Models;
using System.ComponentModel.DataAnnotations;

namespace PasswordHasherDemo.Pages;

public class IndexModel : PageModel
{
    private readonly IPasswordHasher<User> _passwordHasher;
    Public IndexModel(IpasswordHasher<User> passwordHasher)
    {
        _passwordHasher = passwordHasher;
    }

    [BindProperty,Required,DataType(DataType.Password)]
    public string Password { get; set; }
    [BindProperty,Required,Display(Name ="User Name")]
    public string UserName { get; set; }
    [BindProperty,HiddenInput]
    public string HashedPassword { get; set; }
    public string Result { get; set; }
}
```

Inject the IPasswordHasher instead of a logger.

Add some properties for a login form.

Add a property for storing the hashed password in a hidden input.

Also add a property to capture the result of the validation operation.

Next you add a login form to the Index.cshtml file to capture the username and password and store the hashed password (listing 13.10). When the form is first submitted, the user is shown a message, confirming the password was hashed and they can sign in. When the user attempts to sign in, the password they enter is validated against the value in the hidden field, and the validation result is displayed.

Listing 13.10 The login form

```
@page
@model IndexModel
@{
    ViewData["Title"] = "Home page";
```

```
}
@if (Model.Result != null)
{
    <div class="alert alert-@(Model.Result == "Failed" ?
    ➥ "danger" : "success") col-4">@Model.Result</div>
}
<form method="post" class="col-4">
    <input asp-for="HashedPassword" value="@Model.HashedPassword" />
    <div class="form-group">
        <label asp-for="UserName"></label>
        <input asp-for="UserName" class="form-control" />
        <span asp-validation-for="UserName"></span>
    </div>
    <div class="form-group">
        <label asp-for="Password"></label>
        <input asp-for="Password" class="form-control" />
        <span asp-validation-for="Password"></span>
    </div>
    <div class="form-group mt-3">
        <button class="btn btn-sm btn-success">Submit</button>
    </div>
</form>
```

Inspect the Result property, and if its value is Success, display a message using the Bootstrap success color scheme; otherwise, use the danger color scheme.

Store the hashed password here. You need to explicitly assign the value; otherwise, it will be populated from ModelState, where it is null.

The final part of the jigsaw is an `OnPost` method, where you use the `PasswordHasher` to generate a hash or to compare the submitted password to the previously generated hash. This needs to be added to the `IndexModel`.

Listing 13.11 `OnPost` method where the `PasswordHasher` is used

```
public void OnPost()
{
    if (ModelState.IsValid)
    {
        var user = new User { UserName = UserName };
        if (string.IsNullOrEmpty(HashedPassword))
        {
            HashedPassword = _passwordHasher.HashPassword(user, Password);
            Result = "Password has been hashed. Please sign in.";
        }
        else
        {
            Result = _passwordHasher.VerifyHashedPassword(
            ➥ user, HashedPassword, Password).ToString();
        }
    }
}
```

If this hidden field is empty, this is the first time the form has been submitted. Hash the password.

Otherwise, you compare the submitted password to the one you created previously.

Run the application, and enter a username and password. Submit the form, and once it is displayed again, enter either the same password or a different one to observe the result. If you enter the same password, you should see the word Success above the form in green. Otherwise, you should see Failed. These are two of the three values in the `PasswordVerificationResult` enum returned by the `VerifyHashedPassword` method. The third value, `SuccessRehashNeeded`, says that verification was successful, but the password needs rehashing because it was originally hashed using a deprecated algorithm. This would be the case if you were to increase the number of iterations at some stage, which you may well do to ensure your application keeps up with the latest recommendations.

This contrived example serves purely to demonstrate usage of the `PasswordHasher` independent of the Identity UI and default storage. In a real-world application, you would store the hashed password in a permanent store and then retrieve it for verification. You don't actually need to take a dependency on the Identity package at all because you can use the Key Derivation APIs directly: http://mng.bz/O6Aw.

That takes care of protecting your users' passwords, but what about other types of passwords, such as those required in database connection strings or mail server credentials? Your existing connection string doesn't include a password, but it is commonly required for databases that support user logins. In addition, your application may need to store client secrets for connecting to third-party services. Storing those in plain text within application code presents a security risk.

ASP.NET Core supports the storage of application settings as environment variables for production applications and includes a feature called User Secrets for the safe storage of secret application settings during production. We will look at both of these options in the final chapter when we explore configuration.

13.4 Injection attacks

For a web application to be interactive, it must accept and process user input. Users can take advantage of this fact by injecting input, which, when processed under certain conditions, can affect the behavior of the application in ways the developers did not intend. In this section, we will take a detailed look at the two most common injection attacks: SQL injection and cross-site scripting. The side effects of both of these types of vulnerabilities can be catastrophic for users individually and your web application as a whole, so it is very important to understand how they arise and how you can protect yourself against them.

SQL injection attacks target your data access layer, while XSS attacks take advantage of your need to generate HTML dynamically. Given the potentially serious nature of the consequences that can arise from injection attacks, it should come as no surprise that the default behavior of well-designed frameworks is to protect you against them. In the case of SQL injection, EF Core provides great protection, as you will learn, and the Razor view engine mitigates XSS injection by default. There will be occasions in which the safety net provided by these tools is not available to you, so we will look at how to protect your application when that happens.

13.4.1 SQL injection

SQL injection is a vulnerability that allows an attacker to alter an SQL command the application executes, changing the expected behavior of the application. This can result in sensitive data exposure, data theft, data destruction, and even a compromised server. SQL injection vulnerabilities are introduced whenever you take user input and incorporate it into an SQL statement that is executed by the application. An attacker with knowledge of SQL can include text that alters the way the SQL is executed and the results it returns.

So far you haven't written any SQL statements directly, but it is not unusual to do so in a real-world application, even when using an ORM like Entity Framework. You may need to write your own SQL statements when the SQL generated by the ORM is not suitable from a performance point of view, for example; this can happen for some complex queries. Or you might choose to use a micro-ORM, like Dapper (https://github.com/DapperLib/Dapper), which requires you to write your own SQL throughout. Whatever the reason, let's assume you are using SQL to retrieve the city details in the City.cshtml.cs page. Remember that the filter value used to query the database is extracted for the URL. This is considered user input because the user can access and modify it. Think back to the section on binding sources in chapter 5 in which we looked at model binding. All of those binding sources—query string, form, route values, headers, and even cookies are potential sources of user input.

On the City page, your SQL statement might look something like the following, where you incorporate the value of the binding target, the `Name` property, into your query:

```
select * from cities where name = '" + Name + "';
```

If the value passed in the URL is `paris`, the resulting SQL statement will be

```
select * from cities where name = 'paris';
```

Now if the URL was altered so that the route value becomes `paris';drop table aspnetusers;--`, the resulting SQL will be

```
select * from cities where name = 'paris';drop table aspnetusers;--';
```

This is a perfectly valid SQL statement that will result in the city named Paris being retrieved from the database, followed by the user table being deleted in any database system that accepts bulk statements—which is most of them. Chances are you will notice this pretty quickly because the application will crash, and hopefully you will be able to restore from a backup, but you will likely lose data. But how about the following example, which results in all prices being set to 30% of their original value? How long will it take you to notice that users have been busy booking ultra-cheap vacations?

```
select * from cities where name = 'paris';
➥ update properties set price = price * 0.3;--';
```

This vulnerability occurs because there is no sanitizing of the user input undertaken. It is incorporated into the dynamically generated SQL statement as is. The solution for preventing SQL injection is to ensure nothing can creep into the SQL that might change the SQL itself. The best way to achieve this is to only use parameterized SQL, where placeholders are used to represent dynamic elements of the SQL statement, and the database engine replaces them with user input in a safe way.

The good news is that most ORMs like EF Core always generate parameterized SQL. Listing 13.12 shows the SQL generated when you follow an Edit link in the property manager for a specific property. It contains a parameter named `@__id_0`, which is replaced by the value passed to the `id` parameter in the URL: `property-manager/details?id=1`.

Listing 13.12 The parameterized SQL generated by EF Core

```
SELECT "p"."Id", "p"."Address", "p"."AvailableFrom",
➥ "p"."CityId", "p"."CreatorId",
 "p"."DayRate", "p"."Deleted", "p"."MaxNumberOfGuests", "p"."Name",
 "p"."SmokingPermitted", "c"."Id", "c"."CountryId", "c"."Name", "c"."Image"
     FROM "Properties" AS "p"
     INNER JOIN "Cities" AS "c" ON "p"."CityId" = "c"."Id"
     WHERE "p"."Id" = @__id_0    <-- The parameter is named @__id_0.
     LIMIT 1
```

When strings are passed to parameters, they are treated literally and cannot become part of the resulting SQL statement, which mitigates SQL injection as a vulnerability. If you are writing your own SQL, you must always use parameters to represent user input:

```
select * from cities where name = @name
```

How you go about executing this example will depend on the tool you are using. Dapper accepts the parameters as anonymous objects. The code in the next listing shows an example of the Dapper `QuerySingleAsync` method that takes the SQL statement followed by the parameter values.

Listing 13.13 Passing parameters to an SQL statement using Dapper

```
var sql = "select * from cities where name = @name";
var city = conn.QuerySingleAsync(sql, new {name = Name});
```

EF Core supports executing raw SQL queries via the `FromSqlRaw` method, which takes a `params` object that represents the parameter values. The EF Core equivalent to the parameterized Dapper command is shown in the following listing.

Listing 13.14 Passing parameters to an SQL statement using EF Core

```
var p1 = new SqliteParameter("@name", Name);
var sql = "select * from cities where name = @name";
var city = _context.Cities.FromSqlRaw(sql, p1).FirstOrDefault();
```

EF Core also supports passing format strings with parameter values in placeholders. When you use format strings with EF Core, the placeholders are converted to parameters at runtime:

```
var sql = "select * from cities where name = {name}";
var city = _context.Cities.FromSqlRaw(sql, Name).FirstOrDefault();
```

I tend to avoid this approach because the conversion of format string placeholders to parameters is not widely supported by other ORMs, and if you are not careful, you can inadvertently introduce an SQL injection vulnerability when swapping between one ORM and another.

13.4.2 Cross-site scripting

XSS is a type of injection attack, whereby the malicious user injects client-side script into the pages of a vulnerable website. Once the script is included in a page, it executes with the same privileges as the user, which, depending on the nature of the site, can have a serious impact. The injected code could be designed to capture keystrokes and transmit them via AJAX to a remote server, potentially exposing account numbers, usernames, passwords, and so on. It can also alter the DOM, changing the content of the page, so links take the user to an alternative site that may still look like the original site, for example.

So how does the client-side script find its way into a vulnerable site? The two most common routes are via a URL (reflected XSS) or a posted form, the contents of which are stored for later retrieval and rendering to the browser (stored XSS). Reflected XSS takes place when a bad actor creates a URL that includes a script:

```
https://vulnerable-domain.com/city?name=<script>...bad stuff..</script>
```

The victim won't necessarily see the script in the URL when they follow the link, which could be embedded in an HTML email, for example, but if the target website renders the value of the name query parameter as is, the contents of the script block will be executed. Stored XSS happens when the bad actor uses a form to submit a script that is displayed on a page. This might happen in a community forum, for example, where user comments are stored and retrieved from a database. Anyone who visits the page subsequently will cause the malicious script to execute.

In previous versions of ASP.NET, the default mitigation against XSS attacks was a feature known as *request validation,* which screened user input for potentially dangerous characters, like the angle brackets used to delimit HTML script tags: < and >. If the query string or a form field included blacklisted characters, an `HttpRequestValidationException` was raised, and the application crashed. As a developer, you had to opt out of this feature if you wanted to be able to accept angle brackets and so on from users. This feature was not included in ASP.NET Core on the basis that the ASP.NET team felt that it should be up to the developer of an application to decide what is valid and what isn't. Nowadays, the default mitigation against XSS is to have Razor automatically encode all output as HTML, as discussed in section 3.1.5.

There will be occasions in which the application relies on HTML being posted, stored in a database, and later retrieved for inclusion within the markup of a rendered page, using the `Html.Raw` method. Typically, you will use a rich text editor library, such as TinyMCE (https://www.tiny.cloud) or CKEditor (https://ckeditor.com/), to generate the markup. You should check their documentation for instructions on how to create a whitelist of permissible HTML tags, but bear in mind that this validation will take place on the client and cannot be relied on. You should also validate the submitted input on the server.

So how do you validate the input to prevent, for example, script tags from being included in posted submissions? You could use simple string methods like `IndexOf` or `Contains` to check for the presence of the dangerous string or possibly even regular expressions. My preference is to use AngleSharp (https://github.com/AngleSharp/AngleSharp), a great open source project that enables you to parse fragments of HTML and query it using CSS-like selectors to easily determine whether disallowed tags have been included in the posted fragment. To illustrate this, assume the `City` class has a `Description` property, where the user can provide some information about the city in question, and they can do this with HTML. In this case, you add a public property to the `CreateModel` class in the CityManager folder and decorate it with the `BindProperty` attribute:

```
[BindProperty]
public string Description { get; set; }
```

Then you add a label, text area, and validation tag helper to the Create form bound to the property via the `asp-for` attribute.

Listing 13.15 Adding a label and text area for the `Description` property

```
<div class="form-group">
    <label asp-for="Description" class="control-label"></label>
    <textarea asp-for="Description" class="form-control"></textarea>
    <span asp-validation-for="Description" class="text-danger"></span>
</div>
```

You install the AngleSharp library using your preferred package management approach. It is simply called AngleSharp, so the command is easy to intuit: `install-package AngleSharp` or `dotnet add package Anglesharp`. Then you add a using directive in the `CreateModel` class to bring the library into scope:

```
using AngleSharp;
```

Finally, you modify the `OnPostAsync` method to use AngleSharp. The first two lines of the newly added code are boilerplate code that prepares AngleSharp for consuming

HTML, while the third line parses the `Description` property and returns an `IDocument`, which serves as an entry point into the parsed HTML. The `IDocument` adheres to the W3C DOM API, so methods like `QuerySelectorAll` are supported. In this example, you use it to query the HTML fragment for script elements. If there are any, you reject the submission, adding an entry to the `ModelState` errors collection.

Listing 13.16 Using AngleSharp to validate posted HTML before saving it

```
public async Task<IActionResult> OnPostAsync()
{
    var config = Configuration.Default.WithDefaultLoader();
    var context = BrowsingContext.New(config);
    var document = await context.OpenAsync(req =>
    ➥ req.Content(Description));
    if (document.QuerySelectorAll("script")
    ➥ .Any())
    {
        ModelState.AddModelError("Description",
    ➥ "You must not include script tags");
    }
    if (ModelState.IsValid)
    {
        TempData["Name"] = Name;
        Photo = $"{Name.ToLower().Replace(
        ➥ " ", "-")}{Path.GetExtension(Upload.FileName)}";
        var filePath = Path.Combine(_environment.WebRootPath,
        ➥ "images", "cities", Photo);
        using var stream = System.IO.File.Create(filePath);
        await Upload.CopyToAsync(stream);
        return RedirectToPage("/CityManager/Index");
    }
    return Page();
}
```

This is standard boilerplate code for configuring an AngleSharp BrowsingContext.

Use the configured context to parse the incoming Description and assign it to an IDocument.

Use the DOM QuerySelectorAll method to locate all script elements within the fragment, and if any exist, add an entry to the ModelState error collection.

Run the application, sign in, navigate to /city-manager/create, and enter `<script src="something"><script>` into the text area along with valid data for the name and image fields. When you submit the form, you should see the error message appear next to the text area.

That wraps up our look at securing your application against hostile acts. We have only covered the most common vulnerabilities in this chapter, which include how ASP.NET and other libraries, such as Identity and EF Core, protect against these common vulnerabilities as well as what you need to do to maintain security if you bypass the built-in protection offered by these frameworks. If you would like to learn more about web security as it relates specifically to ASP.NET Core development, I recommend *ASP.NET Core Security* by Christian Wenz (https://www.manning.com/books/asp-net-core-security).

In the final chapter, now that your application is secure, you will prepare the application for deployment and publish it as a live website.

Summary

- All public websites are subject to attacks, many of them automated.
- The Open Web Application Security Project maintains a list of the most common vulnerabilities.
- The first step toward protecting your website and its users is using HTTPS.
- HTTPS requires a certificate from a trusted certificate authority.
- Domain validation certificates validate who controls a domain. These are the most common certificates in use and can be obtained at no charge from some issuers.
- Broken access control is the source of the most common application vulnerabilities.
- You should continuously review your application's access control policies to ensure they are kept up to date with changes in the application.
- CSRF tricks an authenticated user into issuing commands they do not intend.
- CSRF is prevented in Razor Pages by default by double submit cookies.
- You should hash user passwords to ensure they are properly secured.
- You can use the ASP.NET Identity `PasswordHasher` to hash passwords, using algorithms written by experts.
- SQL injection vulnerabilities expose your database to hackers, who can steal data and take control of your server.
- You should always use parameterized queries to prevent SQL injection attacks.
- Most ORMs use parameterized queries by default.
- XSS attacks exploit the fact that interactive websites have to process user input and may display it in the browser.
- Razor encodes all output by default, preventing XSS attacks from being successful.
- If you must display user input that contains HTML, you can use tools such as AngleSharp to screen out harmful content.

14 Configuring and publishing your application

This chapter covers

- Understanding and managing environments
- Managing application configuration with app settings
- Improving performance with caching
- Publishing your application

We got there! Well, almost. You've written your application and made sure it is secured against external threats. It's virtually ready to go live, but there are one or two things you need to attend to first, and this final chapter will wrap those up before walking through the publishing process.

The source of most issues that arise after an application has been deployed to a production web server is the difference between the development environment and the hosting environment. Various configurations, such as database connection strings or mail server settings, will often differ between the two environments. We will explore how ASP.NET Core helps you manage the differences between these environments seamlessly, using the *environments* concept I have referred to a few times throughout this book. In addition, you will take a much closer look at the primary means for storing application configuration data—the appSettings.json file—and learn several ways you can read its contents at runtime.

Just before you move your application into production, you will consider its performance. You want an application that is responsive to users—one that doesn't see them shut their browser down while waiting forever to display a page as the server processes the request. The most common processing bottleneck in a dynamic web application exists where the application communicates with the database. You will learn how to use caching to prevent unnecessary database operations when working with data that doesn't change very often. You will also look at using the cache tag helper to prevent unnecessary regeneration of sections of dynamic UI.

Finally, you will put your application into production. You will review some of the hosting options available to you and learn how to configure publishing your application to target some of those different options. Then you will focus on the steps required to deploy to Internet Information Services (IIS), Microsoft's primary web server in a Windows environment.

14.1 Working with environments

In chapter 9, you created a working implementation of the `EmailSender` interface, so you can test sending email confirmations to users when they register an account with your application. If you recall, the implementation that you developed writes emails to a folder on disk. This is very useful during the development phase because it enables you to easily access and read the emails you generate without having to rely on network connectivity. As you can imagine, this implementation is of limited use for an application when it is live. You will need another implementation that connects to a mail server and sends email properly. Once you have that, you need to be able to switch between the two implementations, depending on whether you are running the application in production or developing it further. The solution to this problem is a feature called *environments*. You have encountered this feature on a number of occasions previously. Now you will take a closer look at what it is and how you can use it.

14.1.1 Understanding and managing environments

ASP.NET Core specifies three values to indicate the runtime environment of your application: `Production`, `Staging`, and `Development`. The framework reads an environment variable named `ASPNETCORE_ENVIRONMENT` to determine which value to apply to a running application. If the environment variable has not been set on the host machine, the value defaults to `Production`. This obviously works well on a hosting server, where you may not have access to set environment variables. In addition to the three built-in environments, ASP.NET Core allows you to use any string to represent an alternative environment name (e.g., *QA*).

When you run your application on your local machine using Visual Studio or the `dotnet run` command, the environment is set to `Development`. The application is launched using the first profile in the launchSettings.json file (in the Properties folder), which is considered the default profile. The following listing shows the first profile in my launchSettings.json file. Yours should look similar, although the port numbers in the `applicationUrl` node will probably differ. In any event, the `environmentVariables` section will be the same, setting `ASPNETCORE_ENVIRONMENT` to `Development`.

Listing 14.1 The first profile in launchSettings.json

```
"CityBreaks": {
  "commandName": "Project",
  "dotnetRunMessages": true,
  "launchBrowser": true,
  "applicationUrl": "https://localhost:7236;http://localhost:5236",
  "environmentVariables": {
    "ASPNETCORE_ENVIRONMENT": "Development"    <-- This is where the environment
  }                                                is set for this specific profile.
}
```

When you run the application, using Visual Studio or the `dotnet run` command, you can choose another profile with a different environment. Let's create a new one and try it out.

14.1.2 Setting the environment

In this section, you will control the environment the application runs within by creating a new launch profile for the application and setting the environment profile accordingly. After that, you will look at other ways to set the environment. To start, copy the existing CityBreaks profile, and paste the copy just before the existing final profile. Change the name of the profile to CityBreaksStaging, increment both port numbers by one, and set the `ASPNETCORE_ENVIRONMENT` to `Staging`.

Listing 14.2 Adding a new launch profile to the launchSettings.json file

```
"CityBreaksStaging": {    <-- Name the profile CityBreaksStaging.
  "commandName": "Project",
  "dotnetRunMessages": true,                       Increment the port numbers by one.
  "launchBrowser": true,
  "applicationUrl": "https://localhost:7237;http://localhost:5237",    <--
  "environmentVariables": {
    "ASPNETCORE_ENVIRONMENT": "Staging"    <-- Set the environment to Staging.
  }
},
```

If you are using Visual Studio, your new profile is added to the options in the launch dropdown shown in figure 14.1.

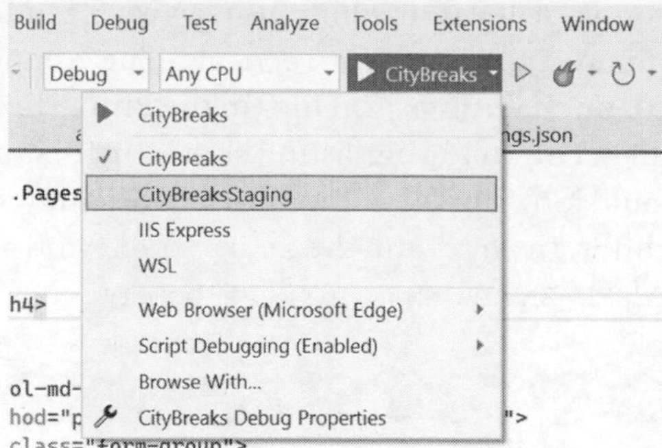

Figure 14.1 The new profile appears in the launch menu.

You can select the staging profile and press Ctrl-F5 or the green triangle to launch the application using the new profile. If you are using `dotnet run`, add a `--launch-profile` switch with the name of the new profile in quotes to the command:

```
dotnet run --launch-profile "CityBreaksStaging"
```

Either way, when you look at the log output from the application (replicated in the next listing), you can see the environment has been set to `Staging`.

Listing 14.3 Log output for CityBreaksStaging profile

```
[07:49:27 INF]
Starting up
[07:49:27 INF] Microsoft.Hosting.Lifetime
Now listening on: https://localhost:7237
[07:49:27 INF] Microsoft.Hosting.Lifetime
Now listening on: http://localhost:5237
[07:49:27 INF] Microsoft.Hosting.Lifetime
Application started. Press Ctrl+C to shut down.
[07:49:27 INF] Microsoft.Hosting.Lifetime
Hosting environment: Staging                    <-- Hosting is confirmed as staging.
[07:49:27 INF] Microsoft.Hosting.Lifetime
Content root path: C:\Repos\CityBreaks\CityBreaks\
```

As an alternative, you can also set the environment in code using the `WebApplicationOptions` object. This is passed to the `WebApplication.CreateBuilder` method in Program.cs. The following listing shows the environment being set to `Staging` using this approach.

Listing 14.4 Setting the environment via `WebApplicationOptions`

```
var builder = WebApplication.CreateBuilder(new WebApplicationOptions
{
    EnvironmentName = "Staging"
});
```

Now that you have set the environment, you can use it to conditionally add middleware and services. The default project template already includes an example of conditionally adding the `ExceptionHandler` and `Hsts` middleware when the `WebApplication`'s environment is not `Development`:

```
if (!app.Environment.IsDevelopment())
{
    app.UseExceptionHandler("/Error");
    app.UseHsts();
}
```

You will use the same approach to conditionally register services based on the `WebApplicationBuilder`'s environment.

14.1.3 Registering services conditionally for each environment

In this section, you will create an alternative implementation of the Identity UI `IEmailSender` interface that will represent a production-ready version that should send email rather than create files to be stored on disk. In fact, your version won't generate or send email messages; it will simply log an informational message. Once you have created the implementation, you will use extension methods on the `WebApplicationBuilder` type to determine which version to register with the application's service container, based on the current runtime environment. You will start by adding a class to the Services folder named `ProductionEmailService`, using the code shown in the following listing.

Listing 14.5 The `Production` version of `IEmailSender`

```
using Microsoft.AspNetCore.Identity.UI.Services;

namespace CityBreaks.Services
{
    public class ProductionEmailService : IEmailSender
    {
        private readonly ILogger<ProductionEmailService> _logger;
        public ProductionEmailService(ILogger<ProductionEmailService> logger)
        {
            _logger = logger;
        }

        public Task SendEmailAsync(string email,
        ➥ string subject, string htmlMessage)
        {
            _logger.LogInformation("Production email service used");
            return Task.CompletedTask;
        }
    }
}
```

Implement IEmailSender.

Inject a logger into the constructor and assign it to a private field.

Use the logger to confirm which version of the IEmailSender is being used.

Within Program.cs, amend the existing registration of the `IEmailSender` interface, so the `EmailService` is only registered if the environment is `Development`, and the new `ProductionEmailService` is used for all other environments, as in the following listing.

Listing 14.6 Conditionally registering implementations based on environment

```
if (builder.Environment.IsDevelopment())
{
    builder.Services.AddTransient<IEmailSender, EmailService>();
}
else
{
    builder.Services.AddTransient<IEmailSender, ProductionEmailService>();
}
```

Use the IsDevelopment extension method to determine if the environment is Development.

The `IHostEnvironment` type, exposed by the `Environment` property of both the `WebApplicationBuilder` and the `WebApplication` types, has extension methods for all the built-in environments. In addition to `IsDevelopment`, there are `IsStaging` and `IsProduction` methods. If you are using a custom environment name, you can check the value of the `Environment.EnvironmentName` to perform the same test:

```
if (builder.Environment.EnvironmentName == "QA")
```

That takes care of building pipelines and registering services conditionally based on the current environment, but what about other situations? Suppose you only want to log informational messages in development or you want to fetch external resources from a content delivery network (CDN) only in production. Depending on the situation, you can access the `IHostEnvironment` service to establish the current environment, or you can use the environment tag helper in Razor pages.

14.1.4 The IHostEnvironment service

The `IHostEnvironment` service provides information about the application's hosting environment. You have already encountered this type on a couple of occasions previously. As you have just seen, it is made available via the `WebApplication` and the `WebApplicationBuilder` `Environment` property. You used it within your original `EmailService` in chapter 9 too, when you used its `ContentRootPath` property to build a path to the email pickup folder. The `ContentRootPath` is the absolute path to the application's root directory. There is also a very similar `IWebHostEnvironment` service. This implements `IHostEnvironment`, providing access to `Environment` and `ContentRootPath`, but also exposes `WebRootPath`, which enables you to get or set the path to the content or static files—wwwroot by default.

Returning to the scenario in which you only want to log informational messages in development, you only need access to the `Environment`, so you will use `IHostEnvironment` to get this information. You'll alter the existing `IndexModel` to inject the `IHostEnvironment` services as a dependency and assign `IHostEnvironment` to a private field, and then use it to wrap the current logger call in a condition that uses the `IsDevelopment` extension method. The revised `IndexModel` class is shown in the next listing.

Listing 14.7 The revised `IndexModel` logging only in development

```
public class IndexModel : PageModel
{
    private readonly ICityService _cityService;
    private readonly ILogger<IndexModel> _logger;
    private readonly IHostEnvironment _environment;
    public IndexModel(ILogger<IndexModel> logger,
    ➥ ICityService cityService, IHostEnvironment environment)
    {
        _logger = logger;
        _cityService = cityService;
        _environment = environment;
    }

    public List<City> Cities { get; set; }
    public async Task OnGetAsync()
    {

        Cities = await _cityService.GetAllAsync();
        if (_environment.IsDevelopment())
        {
            _logger.LogInformation("{count} Cities retrieved", Cities.Count);
        }
    }
}
```

Inject the IHostEnvironment service, and assign it to a private field.

Use the IsDevelopment extension method to ensure logging takes place only when the environment is Development.

If you run the application normally and then use a launch profile or the `WebApplicationOptions` to change the environment, you should see that the log is only generated when the environment is `Development`.

> **NOTE** The use of the `IHostEnvironment` extension methods to control logging based on environments is not recommended. Later, you will see how to use the appSettings.json file to control application configuration, including logging, across different environments.

14.1.5 The environment tag helper

The environment tag helper supports rendering different content dependent on the current environment. You might use this tag helper to load different versions of script and CSS files, depending on whether the application is running in production or development. For example, it is common to include the full local version of a JavaScript or CSS file when you are developing because it makes debugging easier. When the application is in production, you aim to minimize the number and size of HTTP requests, so you use a tool to *minify* and bundle your external resources, or you might rely on a CDN-hosted version if it is a popular library, such as Bootstrap or jQuery.

The environment tag helper has three attributes, two of which behave identically. They are described in table 14.1. The example in listing 14.8 shows how to use the environment tag helper to load the local version of Bootstrap during development and a CDN-hosted version for all other environments, using the `include` and `exclude` attributes. If an environment name is part of an exclude list, the content will not be rendered under any circumstances for that environment. Inclusion in the exclude list overrides inclusion in the include list or the names list.

Table 14.1 The environment tag helper attributes

Attribute	Description
`names`	The name(s) of the environment(s) for which the content should be rendered
`include`	The name(s) of the environment(s) for which the content should be rendered
`exclude`	The name(s) of the environment(s) for which the content should not be rendered

Listing 14.8 Loading different resources based on the environment

```
<environment include="Development">
<link rel="stylesheet" href="~/lib/bootstrap/dist/css/bootstrap.min.css" />
</environment>
<environment exclude="Development">
<link href="https://cdn.jsdelivr.net/npm/bootstrap@5.0.2/dist/css/
            ➥ bootstrap.min.css"
    rel="stylesheet"
    integrity="sha384-
     EVSTQN3/azprG1Anm3QDgpJLIm9Nao0Yz1ztcQTwFspd3yD65VohhpuuCOmLASjC"
    crossorigin="anonymous">
</environment>
```

You have looked at how to set the runtime environment and use it to conditionally build a pipeline, register services, and include content. There is one final place where it is useful to be able to switch between environments: when you want to work with general application configuration settings. In the next section, you will look at the primary storage location, the appSettings.json file, in more detail and understand how it is designed to work with environments too.

14.2 Application configuration

ASP.NET Core includes an API for managing configuration settings needed by the application that includes a number of providers for retrieving data in a variety of different formats. Configuration is set up as part of the `WebApplication.CreateBuilder` method called in Program.cs. Various key-value stores are added to configuration by default:

- The appSettings.json file
- User secrets (if the environment is `Development`)
- Environment variables
- Command-line arguments

You can add other stores, such as XML files, .ini files, and so on, if required. Configuration is added to the dependency injection system and is accessible throughout the application via the `IConfiguration` service.

14.2.1 appSettings.json

The vast majority of applications are likely to only ever use an appSettings.json file for their configuration needs. Each configuration setting is stored in its own section. As you learned in the previous chapter, the default appSettings.json file includes a section that configures logging for the application along with an `AllowedHosts` property.

Listing 14.9 Default appSettings.json file

```
{
  "Logging": {
    "LogLevel": {
      "Default": "Information",
      "Microsoft.AspNetCore": "Warning"
    }
  },
  "AllowedHosts": "*"
}
```

`Logging` and `AllowedHosts` are referred to as *well-known* configuration settings, along with `ConnectionStrings` (which you have used in your application to connect to the database) and `Kestrel` (for configuring the Kestrel web server); all of which enjoy IntelliSense support in Visual Studio and VS Code. In addition to these well-known settings, you can add your own custom settings to extend application configuration.

WORKING WITH CUSTOM SETTINGS

Custom settings provide the easiest way to extend the application configuration. Using JSON as a storage format enables you to store complex information easily. This makes appSettings the perfect place to store mail server configuration information, for example. To illustrate this, you will extend the `ProductionEmailService`, so it uses MailKit to send mail. To do this, MailKit needs to know which mail server to connect to and on which port. It also needs to pass any credentials if the server requires authentication. You could include this configuration information within the `SendEmailAsync` method, but if you need to make changes to use a different server or credentials, for example, you must recompile the application. So you will store this information in a custom section within appSettings.json. Then if you need to make changes at a later date, you simply redeploy the updated version of the appSettings.json file.

Listing 14.10 shows the full version of your modified appSettings.json file. It contains a new section named `SmtpSettings`, which has a number of properties that represent the various values needed for configuring the mail server.

Listing 14.10 A custom appSettings.json section for mail server configuration

```
{
  "AllowedHosts": "*",
  "ConnectionStrings": {
    "CityBreaksContext": "Data source=Data/CityBreaks.db"
  },
  "SmtpSettings": {      <-- The top level section is named SmtpSettings.
    "Host": "smtp.myprovider.com",
    "Port": "587",
    "StartTls": "true",
    "Credentials": {
      "UserName": "mike",
      "Password": "Shh!-s3cret#"
    }
  }
}
```

The SmtpSettings section has four properties.

One of the properties, Credentials, also has properties.

Now that you have the configuration information stored in the appSettings.json file, you need to access specific config values. In the next couple of sections, you will look at some ways to achieve that. The first method shows how to reference values using string-based keys. Afterward, you will take a strongly typed approach instead, which reduces the potential for typing errors.

14.2.2 Accessing configuration settings programmatically by key

As mentioned previously, configuration data is accessible via the `IConfiguration` service, which is one of the default services registered with the DI system at application startup. You will make the `IConfiguration` service available to the `ProductionEmailService` class by injecting it into the constructor. Then you will use it to access individual settings using the section and property names as keys. The section is specified as the first part of the key, and subsequent properties are referenced by separating them with colons (:). For example, the `Host` property of the `SmtpSettings` section is referenced using the key `SmtpSettings:Host`. Listing 14.11 shows the fully modified `ProductionEmailService`.

> **NOTE** Because the colon is essentially a reserved character, you cannot include it in configuration keys. This precludes the use of fully qualified URLs as configuration keys, for example.

Listing 14.11 The modified service relying on external configuration

```
public class ProductionEmailService : IEmailSender
{
    private readonly ILogger<ProductionEmailService> _logger;
```

```
    private readonly IConfiguration _config;

    public ProductionEmailService(ILogger<ProductionEmailService>
    ➥ logger, IConfiguration config)
    {
        _logger = logger;
        _config = config;
    }
    public async Task SendEmailAsync(string email, string subject, string
    ➥ htmlMessage)
    {
        var message = new MimeMessage();
        message.From.Add(MailboxAddress.Parse("test@test.com"));
        message.To.Add(MailboxAddress.Parse(email));
        message.Subject = subject;

        message.Body = new TextPart("html")
        {
            Text = htmlMessage
        };
        var host = _config["SmtpSettings:Host"];
        var port = Convert.ToInt32(_config["SmtpSettings:Port"]);
        var startTls = Boolean.Parse(_config["SmtpSettings:StartTls"]);
        var userName = _config["SmtpSettings:Credentials:UserName"];
        var password = _config["SmtpSettings:Credentials:Password"];
        using var smtp = new SmtpClient();
        await smtp.ConnectAsync(host, port, startTls);
        await smtp.AuthenticateAsync(userName, password);
        await smtp.SendAsync(message);
        await smtp.DisconnectAsync(true);
        _logger.LogInformation("Production email service used");
    }
}
```

The IConfiguration service is injected and assigned to a field.

The configuration values are retrieved using string-based indexes.

This approach works, but as with all APIs that rely on strings, it is error prone. You are a typing mistake away from a `NullReferenceException` at run time. In the next section, you will create a class to represent the SMTP settings and leverage the binding system that is included as part of configuration to hydrate an instance, using the appSettings .json as the source for the data.

14.2.3 Strongly typed app settings

The configuration system's built-in capability to bind settings to a C# object is extremely useful because it enables you to work with configuration settings in a strongly typed manner. For binding to work, your class must not be abstract, and it must have a default empty constructor. The following listing shows a C# representation of the `SmtpSettings` section from your appSettings.json file that meets these criteria.

Listing 14.12 The `SmtpSettings` and `Credentials` classes

```
public class SmtpSettings
{
```

```
    public string Host { get; init; }
    public int Port { get; init; }
    public bool StartTls { get; init; }
    public Credentials Credentials { get; init; }
}

public class Credentials
{
    public string UserName { get; init; }
    public string Password { get; init; }
}
```

You can use the `IConfiguration.Get<T>` method to attempt to bind a specific configuration section to the type specified by the `T` parameter. You create a field in the `ProductionEmailService` class to hold an instance of `SmtpSettings`, and then within the constructor, you bind the `SmtpSettings` section contents to it.

Listing 14.13 Binding sections with the `IConfiguration.Get<T>` method

```
private readonly ILogger<ProductionEmailService> _logger;
private readonly IConfiguration _config;
private readonly SmtpSettings _settings;     <---- Create a field for the SmtpSettings.

public ProductionEmailService(ILogger<ProductionEmailService>
➥ logger, IConfiguration config)
{
    _logger = logger;
    _config = config;
    _settings = _config.GetSection(nameof(SmtpSettings))
    ➥ .Get<SmtpSettings>();
}
```

Access the SmtpSettings section, and attempt to bind to an instance of the SmtpSettings class.

Within the `SendEmailAsync` method, you use the instance of `SmtpSettings` to provide the values required to configure the `SmtpClient` in a type-safe and cleaner way than was demonstrated using the string-based keys.

Listing 14.14 Strongly typed configuration

```
using var smtp = new SmtpClient();
await smtp.ConnectAsync(_settings.Host,_settings.Port, _settings.StartTls);
await smtp.AuthenticateAsync(_settings.Credentials.UserName,
➥ _settings.Credentials.Password);
```

This is not the only way to enjoy strong typing with configuration. We will take a look at binding directly to plain old CLR objects (POCOs) soon, but before that, we will look at another approach that is not dependent on `IConfiguration`, known as the *options pattern*.

14.2.4 Using the options pattern

The options pattern works in a way similar to the previous approach in that it enables working with strongly typed configuration values and relies on the configuration system's built-in capability to bind settings to C# objects. The options pattern is intended to be used to group related configuration values together in individual classes. Rather than relying on `IConfiguration`, you inject `IOptions<TOptions>` into your service class constructor and access its `Value` property, which should return an instance of `TOptions`. Before that, you need to register the `SmtpSettings` configuration section with the service container, using the `Configure<TService>` method.

Listing 14.15 Binding settings using the `Configure` method

```
builder.Services.Configure<SmtpSettings>(
    builder.Configuration.GetSection(nameof(SmtpSettings)));
```

Now the configuration can be injected into constructors using the `IOptions<TOptions>` interface. You will need to add a using directive for `Microsoft.Extensions.Options` to the `ProductionEmailService` class; the only other change will be replacing the injected `IConfiguration` with an `IOptions<SmtpSettings>` and then assigning its `Value` property to the `SmtpSettings` field.

Listing 14.16 Using `IOptions<TOptions>` instead of `IConfiguration`

```
public class ProductionEmailService : IEmailSender
{
    private readonly ILogger<ProductionEmailService> _logger;
    private readonly SmtpSettings _settings;

    public ProductionEmailService(ILogger<ProductionEmailService>
    ➥ logger, IOptions<SmtpSettings> options)     ◁ Replace IConguration with IOptions<SmtpSettings>.
    {
        _logger = logger;
        _settings = options.Value;     ◁ Assign the Value property to the SmtpSettings field.
    }
    ....
```

14.2.5 Binding directly to POCOs

Finally, we will look at binding a configuration section directly to a POCO, using the `IConfiguration Bind` method. The hydrated POCO is then registered as a singleton with the DI container and can be injected into any service that requires it. This is possibly the cleanest way to manage strongly typed configuration in that it doesn't depend on `IConfiguration` or `IOptions`.

Listing 14.17 shows the code you use to bind the configuration section directly to an instance of `SmtpSettings`. This replaces the registration of the `SmtpSettings` configuration section you added to Program.cs in listing 14.15.

Listing 14.17 Binding the configuration to a POCO

```
var smtpSettings = new SmtpSettings();
builder.Configuration.GetSection(nameof(SmtpSettings)).Bind(smtpSettings);
builder.Services.AddSingleton(smtpSettings);
```

Within the `ProductionEmailService`, you change the constructor and inject `SmtpSettings` directly, relieving you of having to extract the configuration from `IOptions.Value`:

```
public ProductionEmailService(ILogger<ProductionEmailService> logger,
➥ SmtpSettings settings)
{
    _logger = logger;
    _settings = settings;
}
```

Having explored a number of ways to access configuration information programmatically from the appSettings file, we'll now circle back to where this chapter started: environments. You will see how different versions of appSettings.json can coexist to help you manage different configurations for different environments.

14.2.6 Environments

You should have noticed that the default project template includes two app settings files. One, which you have been working with, is simply named appSettings.json. The second, which is nested with the first in Visual Studio's Solution Explorer, is named appSettings.Development.json. This naming convention is used to enable you to specify different configuration values for different environments. The default configuration is held in the app settings file that does not include an environment within its filename. Any sections that appear in an environment-specific version of app settings take precedence over the content of the default file. So if you have a different SMTP server configuration for your development environment, you can add an SmtpSettings section to the appSettings.Development.json file, and the settings there will override the defaults when the environment is `Development`. Listing 14.18 shows an example of an alternative configuration that points to a local server that needs no authentication.

There's one important thing to note here: the `Credentials` properties are set to empty strings, so that the default values are overridden. If you were to declare the `Credentials` as an empty object or omit them altogether, the default values would be used.

Listing 14.18 Development-specific SMTP server configuration

```
"SmtpSettings": {
  "Host": "localhost",
  "Port": "25",
  "StartTls": "false",
  "Credentials": {
```

```
        "UserName": "",
        "Password": ""
    }
}
```

Configuration is a huge topic and probably deserves a chapter of its own. You've mainly looked at the appSettings.json file here, which is the first place most devs look to store application configuration data. However, you need to consider security when your application configuration includes sensitive information, such as passwords and third-party API secrets.

> **TIP** I recommend reviewing the official guidance, which explains how to use environment variables and user secrets to manage security, depending on the environment you are working with: http://mng.bz/G12D.

Before you move on to publishing your application, we will consider its performance. We will look specifically at how to use server-side caching to minimize unnecessary processing and, hopefully, deliver your pages to users more quickly.

14.3 Improving performance with caching

Deployed applications are subject to restrictions on their performance. It might be that your web-hosting company limits the resources available to your application, so they can cram as many other applications on the same server as possible. Or you may have compromised on processing power when selecting your cloud-based hosting server. For data-driven web applications, the most significant performance bottleneck is likely to involve the database. Each query or command results in a round trip to an external process, putting demands on system memory, processing, and networking. If you can minimize unnecessary database calls, you are less likely to suffer from performance issues.

Server-side caching is primarily used to improve performance in applications. This type of caching involves the storage of data or content on the server, particularly data or content that incurs a processing overhead, so it can be reused without incurring the cost of generation every time. In-memory storage is most likely to be used in applications hosted on a single server. Applications deployed to the cloud or on web farms are advised to use a distributed cache system—one that is separate from the application, so each instance of the application can access the same cached data. In this section, we will cover in-memory storage.

> **TIP** The official documentation provides guidance on distributed cache strategies, including the use of two popular solutions, Redis and NCache, along with one designed to work with SQL Server (http://mng.bz/z5g1).

The best candidate for caching is data that doesn't change very often. Lookup data, tag clouds, and menu-driven navigation are all classic examples that can benefit from caching. Remember your custom route constraint from chapter 4, where you validated the route data against an array of cities? We discussed doing this against the database, rather than a hardcoded list. In this section, you will cache the city data from the database, refreshing it when it changes, so the custom route constraint is always up to date without becoming a burden on the database.

Razor Pages offers two main ways you can manage the caching of pieces of content. One is using a cache provider's API, such as that offered by the `IMemoryCache` service. You will leverage this soon enough for the use case just discussed. Before that, you will take a quick look at the other option: the cache tag helper, which is designed to be used within a Razor page itself.

14.3.1 The cache tag helper

The cache tag helper enables you to cache regions of a Razor page in memory on the server. Typical uses for this helper are for view components or partial views that require relatively expensive database or web service calls, but where the content doesn't change very often. Unlike most other tag helpers, the cache tag helper doesn't target a standard HTML element. It targets the `<cache>` tag, which is not rendered to the browser and doesn't appear in the HTML source either.

The cache tag helper uses an in-memory-based store for content. This is volatile and can be cleared unexpectedly for any number of reasons, including app pool recycling, server restarts, low-memory pressure, and so on. The cache tag helper is not intended to be used for reliable long-term storage.

To demonstrate the value of the cache tag helper properly, you will create a view component that will produce the data-driven content currently being produced by the home page. If you recall from chapter 3, view components are similar to partials in that they are designed to encapsulate regions of pages, but they differ in that they are designed to work with services and generate their own data. View components are classes that derive from `ViewComponent` and implement an `Invoke` method that returns an `IViewComponentResult` or an asynchronous version that returns a `Task<IViewComponentResult>`. They must also have `ViewComponent` as a suffix to their name or be decorated with the `[ViewComponent]` attribute. Listing 14.19 shows a class named `CitiesViewComponent` (placed in a folder named ViewComponents) that follows these rules. It takes the `ICityService` as a dependency via its constructor and uses it to create a model consisting of a list of cities, which is then passed to its `View` method. It also logs an informational message when the database call is completed.

Listing 14.19 The `CitiesViewComponent` class

```
using CityBreaks.Services;
using Microsoft.AspNetCore.Mvc;

namespace CityBreaks.ViewComponents
{
    public class CitiesViewComponent : ViewComponent
    {
```

Name the class with ViewComponent as a suffix, which derives from ViewComponent.

```
        private readonly ICityService _cityService;
        private readonly ILogger<CitiesViewComponent> _logger;

        public CitiesViewComponent(ICityService cityService,
        ➥ ILogger<CitiesViewComponent> logger)
        {
            _cityService = cityService;
            _logger = logger;
        }

        public async Task<IViewComponentResult> InvokeAsync()
        {
            var cities = await _cityService.GetAllAsync();
            _logger.LogInformation("Cities
            ➥ retrieved from the view component");
            return View(cities);
        }
    }
}
```

Inject ICityService and a logger via the constructor as a dependency.

Obtain a list of cities, log a message, and pass data as a model to the View method.

The next task is to produce the view part of the component. By default, the view name is `default`, and it is expected to be found at \Pages\Shared\Components\[View Component Name]\default. So you create a folder named Components in \Pages\Shared and then add a folder to that named Cities. Within that folder, add a new .cshtml file—not a Razor page, just an empty file with the name default.cshtml. The file content is shown in the next listing. It features an `@model` directive, and the rest of the content is lifted directly from the \Pages\Index.cshtml file.

Listing 14.20 The view for the `CitiesViewComponent`

```
@model List<City>
@foreach (var city in Model)
{
    <div class="col-4 p-3" style="text-shadow: rgb(0, 0, 0) 1px 1px 1px">
        <div class="card p-3 shadow"
        ➥ style="background:url(/images/cities/@city.Photo) no-repeat
        ➥ center center;background-size: cover;height:240px;">
            <h3>
                <a class="text-white text-decoration-none" asp-page="/City"
                ➥ asp-route-name="@city.Name">@city.Name</a>
                <img src="/images/flags/@(city.Country.CountryCode).png"
                 ➥ aria-label="@($"{city.Name},
                 ➥ {city.Country.CountryName}")">
            </h3>
            <h6 class="text-white">@city.Properties.Count() properties</h6>
        </div>
    </div>
}
```

The view component tag helper targets the <vc> tag, with the name of the view component supplied using kebab-case after a colon. Next add the bold-font line in listing 14.21 to the ViewImports file, which activates the view component tag helper.

Listing 14.21 Activating the view component tag helper

```
@using CityBreaks
@using CityBreaks.Models
@namespace CityBreaks.Pages
@addTagHelper *, Microsoft.AspNetCore.Mvc.TagHelpers
@addTagHelper *, CityBreaks
```

Now that all the pieces are in place, you can replace the content in the home page with the view component using the view component tag helper, again shown in bold font in the following listing.

Listing 14.22 Using the view component tag helper

```
@page
@model IndexModel
@{
    ViewData["Title"] = "Home page";
}

<h1>City Breaks</h1>
<div class="container">
    <div class="row">
        <vc:cities />
    </div>
</div>
```

The final step is to comment out the OnGetAsync method in the existing \Pages\Index.cshtml.cs file and then run the application. You should see no visible difference, except this time the content is being generated by the view component, not the page itself. This should be confirmed by the logging output. Each time you refresh the page, the message should be logged again.

Now that you have a view component, you can test the use of the cache tag helper. Modify the code around the view component tag helper, so it is the same as the following listing. You simply wrap the view component in a cache tag helper.

Listing 14.23 The cache tag helper

```
<h1>City Breaks</h1>
<div class="container">
    <div class="row">
        <cache>
            <vc:cities />
        </cache>
    </div>
</div>
```

The cache tag helper wraps the content to be cached.

When you first run the application, the view component is invoked, the data is retrieved from the database, and the message is logged. The rendered content is stored in the cache. When you refresh the page, no further messages should be logged because the view component is never invoked. The content within the cache tag helper is retrieved from the cache instead of being regenerated by the view component.

That leaves the following question: how will you refresh the content if another property or city is added? The `cache` attribute has several attributes that enable you to manage cache expiration:

- `expires-after`—A `TimeSpan` representing the period of time after which the cached item should expire
- `expires-on`—A `DateTimeOffset` representing the absolute time at which the cached entry should expire
- `expires-sliding`—A `TimeSpan` representing the period of time after the last access that the item should expire

The following example uses the `expires-after` attribute to remove the cache item after 1 hour:

```
<cache expires-after="TimeSpan.FromHours(1)">...</cache>
```

It would be ideal to simply refresh the cache any time the content is changed; working directly with the `IMemoryCache` API enables you to do just that, as you will see next.

14.3.2 In-memory caching with IMemoryCache

Remember back in chapter 4 when you created a custom route constraint? It compares route values with the contents of a hardcoded list to determine whether a route matches. I mentioned at the time that this should perform a lookup against the contents of the database rather than a hardcoded list, which would potentially need constant updating. Implementing this as a constraint is problematic in that constraints are synchronous; any calls to asynchronous services must be made synchronously. You could move this task to middleware instead, or you could move the task to the actual page that uses the lookup: the City page. In this section, that's what you'll do, and you'll use the `IMemoryCache` service to cache the names of the cities, so the database lookup is only performed when necessary.

The `IMemoryCache` service is enabled as part of Razor Pages. The interface defines three methods for managing cache entries: `CreateEntry`, `Remove`, and `TryGetValue`. However, for getting and setting cache entries, you are more likely to use one of a number of extension methods instead, which have been designed to be simple to use. These are detailed in table 14.2.

Table 14.2 `IMemoryCache` extension methods

Method	Return type	Notes
`Get`	`object`	Gets the item with the specified key.
`Get<TItem>`	`TItem`	Gets the item with the specified key and attempts to cast it to the specified type.

Table 14.2 `IMemoryCache` extension methods *(continued)*

Method	Return type	Notes
`GetOrCreate<TItem>`	`TItem`	If the item doesn't exist in the cache, this method will add it.
`Task<TItem> GetOrCreateAsync`	`Task<TItem>`	Async version of above.
`Set<TItem>`	`TItem`	Also has four overloads that allow various options to be set.
`TryGetValue<TItem>`	`bool`	Generic version of the interface method.

To demonstrate the `IMemoryCache`, you are going to add a new method to the `ICityService` that returns a list of strings, representing all the city names in the database. The method implementation will check the memory cache first, and if the data exists there, it will be retrieved. Otherwise, the memory cache will be populated from the database before being returned from the method. Then, after ensuring the existing `CityRouteConstraint` has been applied to the City page's route template, you will use the service within the constraint to check whether the route value passed to the `name` parameter is valid.

Begin by injecting both the `IMemoryCache` service and a logger into the `CityService` class. To do this, you need to add a using directive for `Microsoft.Extensions.Caching.Memory`. The altered fields and constructor of the `CityService` are shown in the following listing.

Listing 14.24 Modified fields and constructor of the `CityService`

```
private readonly CityBreaksContext _context;
private readonly IMemoryCache _cache;
private readonly ILogger<CityService> _logger;

public CityService(CityBreaksContext context, IMemoryCache cache,
➥ ILogger<CityService> logger)
{
    _context = context;
    _cache = cache;
    _logger = logger;
}
```

Add the following new method to the `ICityService` interface, which returns a list of type string:

```
Task<List<string>> GetCityNamesAsync();
```

After adding a stub to the existing `SimpleCityService` (if you haven't removed it already), add an implementation to the `CityService`, which checks the cache and populates it from the database if it is empty (listing 14.25). So you can see what's going on, log different messages based on whether or not the data comes from the cache.

Use the `TryGetValue<TItem>` extension method to retrieve an item with the key specified by the first parameter. Also use the `nameof` operator and pass in the name of the enclosing method instead of using a simple string. This removes the likelihood of getting key names wrong as a result of a typographical error. If the method returns `true`, return the `out` parameter value. Otherwise, retrieve the data from the database and populate the cache using the `Set` method. Convert the city names to lowercase, and perform a comparison in lowercase to prevent casing issues.

Listing 14.25 The GetCityNamesAsync method using caching

```
public async Task<List<string>> GetCityNamesAsync()
{
    if(_cache.TryGetValue<List<string>>(
    ➥ nameof(GetCityNamesAsync), out var cityNames))
    {
        _logger.LogInformation(
        ➥ "Cities retrieved from memory cache");
        return cityNames;
    }
    _cache.Set(nameof(GetCityNamesAsync),
    ➥ await _context.Cities.Select(c =>
    ➥ c.Name.ToLowerInvariant()).ToListAsync());
    _logger.LogInformation("Cache empty.
    ➥ Storing cities in memory cache");
    return _cache.Get<List<string>>(
    ➥ nameof(GetCityNamesAsync));
}
```

Use the TryGetValue method to see if a cache entry exists.

If it exists, log a message and return the out parameter.

Otherwise, populate the cache from the database, log a different message, and then return the cache contents.

The `Set` method has a number of overloads that enable you to set an expiry on the item, similar to the expiry options available to use with the cache tag helper. Don't use any of these because you will manually expire the cache whenever you add a new city or update an existing one. To achieve that, simply add the following line to both the `CreateAsync` and `UpdateAsync` methods within the `CityService`, just before their return statements:

```
_cache.Remove(nameof(GetCityNamesAsync));
```

Now you can use this new method within the City page. You will replace the existing code in the `OnGetAsync` method, so it can perform a lookup against the data returned by the new method. If the city name passed in the route exists, fetch its details from the database. If not, return a `NotFoundResult`. The replacement code for the `OnGetAsync` method is shown in the following listing.

Listing 14.26 The CityCheckMiddleware class

```
public async Task<IActionResult> OnGetAsync()
{
    var cities = await _cityService.GetCityNamesAsync();
    if (cities.Contains(Name.ToLowerInvariant().Replace("-", " ")))
    {
        City = await _cityService.GetByNameAsync(Name);
        return Page();
    }
    else
    {
        return NotFound();
    }
}
```

- Get the list of city names from the CityService.
- Check the list of cities to see if it includes the one bound to the City property. If it exists, get the details from the database.
- Otherwise, set the status code to 404, Not Found.

Then run the application, and visit a City page. You should see an initial log message confirming the cache is empty and the cities are being stored there. Then revisit the home page and follow a link to any other City page. See from the logs that the cache is being used now, saving unnecessary database processing.

Finally, you are ready to present your application to the world. In the final section of this book, you will look at how to prepare your application for deployment in a process known as *publishing*.

14.4 Publishing your application

Whenever you run your application, either using the `dotnet run` command or Ctrl-F5 in Visual Studio, the first thing that happens is a build, which results in the source code being compiled into executables and placed in the Bin folder. The compiled output is not, however, something you can simply deploy to another environment, such as a web server. Another step is required to prepare your application for deployment. You need to *publish* it. This is achieved using the `dotnet publish` command or the publishing tooling within Visual Studio. In this section, we will explore the various configuration options available and then explore the published output. We will also consider some troubleshooting tips that will help resolve some of the most common issues that arise when the published application is finally deployed to a production server.

14.4.1 Self-contained and framework-dependent

The first configuration decision you need to make is choosing between publishing a *self-contained* application or a *framework-dependent* one. Both options result in your application code being built into .dll files, but the self-contained version includes the .NET Core runtime files as well. You will use this option if you are not sure whether the necessary .NET Core runtime is installed on the target machine. This option results in a relatively large published output. Your CityBreaks application, when published as a self-contained application, weighs in at just over 400 separate files (not including the wwwroot folder contents), occupying around 125 MB of space.

It is possible to use trimming to reduce the overall published output of a self-contained deployment. Trimming scans your code and removes any runtime assemblies that are not called into. You activate trimming by adding the following entry to your project file, just below the `TargetFramework` node:

```
<PublishTrimmed>true</PublishTrimmed>
```

Your CityBreaks application loses more than 60 libraries when trimmed and about 40 MB in space. Examples of libraries that are trimmed out include `System.Globalization.Calendars` and `System.IO.Compression.Zipfile`. None of your code requires these dependencies.

The framework-dependent option includes only the application files and any external packages the application requires. This option depends on a compatible .NET runtime being available on the target machine. For most web application deployments, this is the option you are more likely to adopt. You are unlikely to obtain hosting services without having ensured the requisite runtime is installed on the target machine or that you have sufficient access to the hosting server to install it yourself.

14.4.2 Publishing using the CLI

Now we will move on to the actual publishing process. We'll take a look at using the `dotnet` CLI to produce the published output, starting with the main options available to the `publish` command shown in table 14.3.

Table 14.3 The main `publish` command options

Option	Description
`-o, --output <OUTPUT_DIR>`	Output directory in which to place the published artifacts. The default is \bin\Debug\[target framework]\publish.
`-c, --configuration <CONFIGURATION>`	Configuration to use for building the project. The default for web app projects is `Debug`.
`-f, --framework <FRAMEWORK>`	Target framework to publish for. The target framework has to be specified in the project file.
`-r, --runtime <RUNTIME_IDENTIFIER>`	Publish the project for a given runtime. The default is to publish a framework-dependent app targeting the current operating system.
`--self-contained`	Publish the .NET Core runtime with your application, so the runtime doesn't need to be installed on the target machine. It defaults to `true` if a runtime identifier is specified.

Further options can be viewed using the help option (`--help` or `-h`) or in the official documentation (http://mng.bz/095J). If you execute `dotnet publish` from within the folder containing the project file, the published output will be generated at \bin\Debug\net6.0\publish in `debug` mode as a framework-dependent deployment targeting the runtime specified in the project file. `Debug` mode is not optimal for deployment, so at the very least, you should specify the configuration as `Release` when using the `dotnet publish` command, using the following option:

```
dotnet publish -c Release
```

Publishing to a local folder is the only option provided by the CLI commands. Most often, you will then use FTP or a similar tool to transfer the published output to the hosting location. Visual Studio, on the other hand, enables publishing to other targets as well as a local folder, which we will look at next.

14.4.3 Publishing using Visual Studio

The `publish` command within Visual Studio is available from the Build menu. You can also access it by right-clicking the web application project in Solution Explorer, where it will appear in the resulting context menu. Either way, you will be presented with the same interface for managing the publishing process. The first time you use this feature for your project, you will be prompted to create a *publish profile*. You begin this process by specifying your publishing target, or where you would like to publish to. The preconfigured options include a Docker container, an FTP server, to an IIS server using Web Deploy, or to a local folder. You are also provided with the option to import an external *publish settings* profile, which is what the publish wizard creates.

Once you have selected your publishing target, the wizard prompts you to configure the publish profile accordingly. For example, if you choose to publish to an FTP server, the wizard asks for the server address, the file path on the remote server for the deployed application, and any credentials required by the FTP server. We will look at publishing to a local folder in more detail here, so you can examine the published output.

> **TIP** Most of the other publishing options are supported by documentation (http://mng.bz/K0RX).

You'll start by selecting the Folder option and then either noting the default location (bin\Release\net6.0\publish) or changing it to one that is more accessible. Next click the Finish button. Note that the default configuration is `Release` (compared to `Debug` when using the CLI). You have the option to delete all existing files each time the application is published to ensure only the latest versions are deployed. You can also configure the target runtime, which, by default, is set to Portable, which enables the application to be deployed to any platform where a runtime is installed.

You can edit the configuration by clicking the pencil icon next to each setting or by clicking the link to Show all settings, which gives you access to the settings. Take a look at the contents of the target runtime selector. As well as Portable, it includes a variety of operating system and architecture configurations. If you leave the selection as Portable, architecture-specific files are included for all platforms in a folder named Runtimes as part of the published output, increasing the size of the deployment. Ideally, you should select the target runtime if you know what it is. For example, if you are deploying your application to a server that runs IIS, you should select `win-x64`.

When you save your configuration, it is saved to a publish settings file—one with a .pubxml extension in a folder named PublishProfiles, which, in turn, is placed in the Properties folder. This is the kind of file the Import Profile option expects if you are to choose that option from the initial dialog. Given the content is XML, it is easy to modify in a text-based editor if you wish. You can create as many publish profiles as you want. Once you have created your profile, ensure it is selected and click the Publish button. Once the process has completed, you can click the link next to the Target Location setting to access the output location and see the published output.

THE PUBLISHED OUTPUT

Figure 14.2 shows the published output that results from publishing a web application that consists purely of the project template files. It has no third-party dependencies and gives you a clear picture of the published artifacts without any interference from the various dependencies your CityBreaks application has acquired along its journey.

Name	Type	Size
wwwroot	File folder	
appsettings.Development.json	JSON File	1 KB
appsettings.json	JSON File	1 KB
web.config	XML Configuratio...	1 KB
WebApplication1.deps.json	JSON File	1 KB
WebApplication1.dll	Application extens...	51 KB
WebApplication1.exe	Application	145 KB
WebApplication1.pdb	Program Debug D...	34 KB
WebApplication1.runtimeconfig.json	JSON File	1 KB

Figure 14.2 The artifacts generated by the publishing process

The contents of the wwwroot folder are copied directly from the original application, as are the app settings files. A web.config file is generated, which is used by IIS to configure the application as a website.

The .exe file is the host for the application and is specific to a particular operating system and architecture. It is not cross-platform and will target the current platform by default, unless you specify an alternative using the Target Runtime option in Visual Studio or the `--runtime` or `-r` option when publishing with the CLI. The actual application is compiled to a .dll file that is named after the project by default. A .pdb file is also generated. This contains information about debug symbols in the application and is only useful if you need to attach a debugger to the application when it is on the live server. If not, you don't need to include the .pdb file when you deploy the application. You can suppress their generation by navigating to the project properties (at the bottom of the Project menu in Visual Studio); go to Build > General, and then select No Symbols Are Emitted from the Debug Symbols option (figure 14.3).

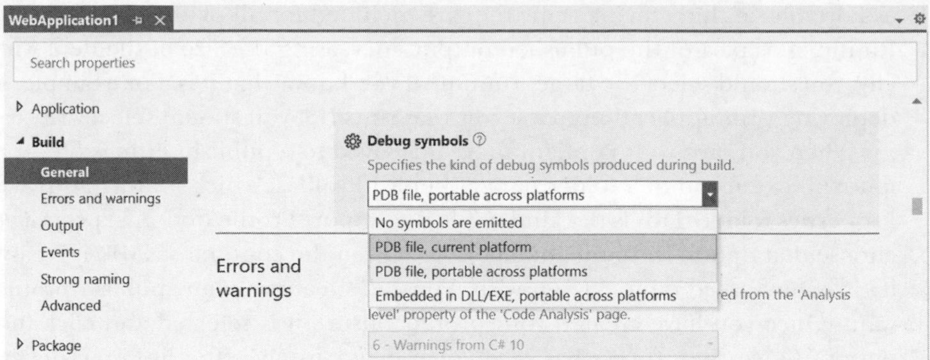

Figure 14.3 Suppress generation of the .pdb file when publishing.

Two .json files are generated. One contains information about runtime configuration (*.runtimeconfig.json), and the other contains data about all of the dependencies the application relies on (*.deps.json). This can grow quite large because it includes not only details of the NuGet packages you have included but also all of their dependencies.

The only thing that remains to be done is transferring the application to the target server. How you go about that task is dependent on what the target supports and is not covered in this book. You should check the documentation of your hosting provider, or if you are configuring the server yourself, you should refer to your provider's support material. Before this book ends, however, there are a few common things to watch for when publishing and deploying your application.

LOCKED ASSEMBLIES AND APP_OFFLINE FILES

When the site is running on IIS, the application's .dll file is loaded by the host process and is locked. If you use FTP to upload the published content, you will need to stop the process to release the .dll files, so they can be overwritten.

There are a number of ways to accomplish this. If you have access to the web server, you can stop the site's application pool and then restart it when the new files have been uploaded. However, this won't provide the visitor with a particularly good experience. A cleaner alternative is to use an app_offline.htm file. When placed in the root folder of the site (that is, the location returned by the `IWebHostEnvironment.ContentRootPath` property), the presence of a filename app_offline.htm results in the graceful shutdown of your website and any further request to the application being served with the content of the file. Therefore this file is most commonly used to display a message explaining the site is currently undergoing maintenance.

The name of the file is important, although case insensitive. The easiest way of switching this feature on and off is using an FTP client to rename the file to something else when the site should be live (e.g., by adding the letter *l* to the extension) and then altering it back when the site should be offline. Because requests for other files will be ignored, you should not link to local resources such as stylesheets, JavaScript, and images in your app_offline.htm file. You should embed these in the file itself. Images can be embedded as Base64-encoded strings.

Prior to ASP.NET Core, this issue was managed by the framework, which used shadow copying to enable the seamless replacement of application assemblies. This has been introduced as an experimental feature in .NET 6 and is enabled by adding the following `handlerSettings` section to the `aspNetCore` section in the web.config file.

Listing 14.27 Enabling experimental shadow copy

```
<aspNetCore processPath=".\WebApplication1.exe" stdoutLogEnabled="false"
  stdoutLogFile=".\logs\stdout" hostingModel="inprocess">
  <handlerSettings>
    <handlerSetting name="experimentalEnableShadowCopy"
      ➥ value="true" />
    <handlerSetting name="shadowCopyDirectory"
      ➥ value="../ShadowCopyDirectory/" />
  </handlerSettings>
</aspNetCore>
```

The handlerSettings section enables experimental shadow copying.

Note that shadow copying is experimental in .NET 6, and the recommendation remains to use the app_offline.htm file to manage this situation.

SUPPRESSING LANGUAGE FOLDERS

You may see a collection of folders named Ccs, Dde, Ees, and so on within the published output. These folders contain localized resources (translated error messages, warnings, and so on) for a variety of libraries and are not intended to be deployed with your application. They typically result from including design tool libraries within your application. You have included two in the CityBreaks application: `Microsoft.EntityFrameworkCore.Tools` and `Microsoft.VisualStudio.Web.CodeGeneration.Design`. The second of these was actually included for you by the page scaffolder. To suppress generation of the localized resources, just add `PrivateAssets="All"` to the relevant package reference within the project file:

```
<PackageReference Include="Microsoft.EntityFrameworkCore.Tools"
➥ Version="6.0.0" PrivateAssets="All" />
```

ENABLE STDOUT LOGGING

If you haven't already incorporated logging within the application, enabling basic logging provides an easy way to get full details of startup errors within the deployed application. In listing 14.27, you can see within the `aspNetCore` section that `stdoutLogEnabled` is set to `false` by default. Set this to `true`, and text-based log files will be generated to a folder named logs in the root of the application. The folder will be created if one doesn't exist already:

```
<aspNetCore processPath=".\WebApplication1.exe" stdoutLogEnabled="true"
➥ stdoutLogFile=".\logs\stdout" hostingModel="InProcess" />
```

You should disable stdout logging once any errors have been resolved. It should not be used for routine logging; you should instead use a third-party library that incorporates log file management.

FIXING THE SDK VERSION USED FOR PUBLISHING

The <TargetFramework> node in your application's .csproj file specifies the version of the .NET Framework that your application targets. However, this does not prevent your application being built or published against a newer version of the framework. The dotnet commands build and publish will be executed by the latest version of the .NET Core SDK installed on the machine. This can result in a published application referencing dependencies that don't exist on a hosting server.

To prevent accidentally building and publishing your application against a newer version of the .NET Core SDK than is supported by your host, you can fix the version your application targets. You do this by adding a global.json file to the directory structure of the project. This can be placed in either the folder containing the .csproj file or any of its parent folders.

The global.json file has an sdk node that is used to specify the version of the .NET Core SDK to use when executing commands against the project (including publishing). The example in the following listing fixes the version at 6.0.101.

Listing 14.28 Fixing the SDK version in global.json

```
{
  "sdk": {
    "version": "6.0.101"
  }
}
```

You can use the dotnet CLI to generate a global.json file. Navigate to the folder in which you want to create the file, and run the following command, which specifies the sdk version via the sdk-version option:

```
dotnet new globaljson --sdk-version 6.0.101
```

Summary

- Environments enable you to adjust the configuration of your application based on where it is running.
- The environment setting is taken from an environment variable, and if none exists, it defaults to Production.
- Launch profiles configure your application to run in Development.
- You can use the environment tag helper to manage different environment-based configurations within your pages.
- The primary source of application configuration information is the appSettings .json file.

- You can use a string-based indexer to access configuration information via the `IConfiguration` service.
- You can also bind configuration sections to your own objects in a strongly typed manner.
- Alternatively, you can use the options pattern to bind configuration sections to business objects.
- App settings files can be customized to a particular environment by including the environment name within the filename.
- Caching can improve performance by reducing the number of calls to external processes, such as databases.
- Default caching is saved to memory and is cleared when the application restarts.
- The cache tag helper can be used to store generated sections of HTML.
- The `IMemoryCache` service can be injected into classes that need it.
- You can set absolute or sliding expiry on cached items.
- Publishing is the process that prepares an application for deployment.
- You can generate a deployment that targets a specific framework or includes its own runtime.
- You can use the Visual Studio publishing dialog or the `dotnet publish` command to generate files for deployment to a target machine.

index

Symbols

A

B

C

N

O

P

Q

R

S

T

U

V

W

X